Land Tenure Reform in Asia and Africa

Land Tenure Reform in Asia and Africa

Assessing Impacts on Poverty and Natural Resource Management

Edited by

Stein T. Holden
Norwegian University of Life Sciences, Ås, Norway

Keijiro Otsuka
National Graduate Institute for Policy Studies, Tokyo, Japan

and

Klaus Deininger
Development Economics Research Group, World Bank, Washington, DC, USA

palgrave
macmillan

First published 2013 by
PALGRAVE MACMILLAN

Palgrave Macmillan in the UK is an imprint of Macmillan Publishers Limited, registered in England, company number 785998, of Houndmills, Basingstoke, Hampshire RG21 6XS.

Palgrave Macmillan in the US is a division of St Martin's Press LLC, 175 Fifth Avenue, New York, NY 10010.

Palgrave Macmillan is the global academic imprint of the above companies and has companies and representatives throughout the world.

Palgrave® and Macmillan® are registered trademarks in the United States, the United Kingdom, Europe and other countries

ISBN 978-1-349-46586-6 ISBN 978-1-137-34381-9 (eBook)
DOI 10.1057/9781137343819

This book is printed on paper suitable for recycling and made from fully managed and sustained forest sources. Logging, pulping and manufacturing processes are expected to conform to the environmental regulations of the country of origin.

A catalogue record for this book is available from the British Library.

A catalog record for this book is available from the Library of Congress.

Contents

List of Boxes, Figures and Map

Boxes

Figures

Map

List of Tables

Preface

Land and land tenure issues have been and will continue to be high on the policy agenda in a large number of countries, including those in Africa and Asia. The highly political and contested nature of land policy issues makes it highly relevant to provide in-depth analyses of such issues in diverse contexts. While attempts have been made to develop 'silver bullet' solutions in this area, we advocate humility in the causal analysis of past reforms due to the contextual complexity and limited data quality as well as in the prescription for future land tenure reforms. Pilot testing before scaling up based on empirical evidence seems like an approach with higher probability of success as compared to some of the large-scale failed interventions of the past.

One of the motivations for this book has been to address land tenure policies from an international perspective. Soon after we (Holden and Otsuka) published the edited book, *The Emergence of Land Markets in Africa: Assessing the Impacts on Poverty, Equity, and Efficiency* (2009), we realized that in order to address land tenure policy issues deeply, we should undertake another book project with stronger and clearer focus on policy issues in a number of countries. This multi-country approach is badly needed, as there are both commonalities and differences in land tenure reform issues. Fortunately, Klaus Deininger, who has been actively working on land tenure issues in diverse settings, agreed to join this new project.

Another motivation was to involve young scientists from the countries that have been studied as a contribution to building national capacity. In the process of creating the book, these young scientists were exposed to many senior scientists and scientists coming from countries with a very different history of land tenure policies. We see this building of capacity and exchange of experiences as a complementary public beneficial outcome of this project. We hope the book can also serve as a valuable input for national and international teaching programs focusing on land tenure reform issues.

While the book has primarily been written by economists who have used sophisticated statistical methods in the analysis of large datasets, we have attempted to keep the book non-technical to make it accessible to the broader public interested in land tenure policy issues. Many of the interpretations and conclusions are tentative, with the intention of creating constructive and open-minded debate. Such debates are fundamental for the development of evidence-based land tenure policies conducive to efficiency, equity, and sustainability of farm and forest land management in the future.

Acknowledgments

First of all, we would like to thank all the authors for committing their valuable time to this project through participation in three workshops and preparation of the chapters, which required responses to countless requests for revisions to accommodate them within the book's format and to ensure its quality. The book is the outcome of tireless commitment and international collective action by both junior and senior researchers on policy and research issues of increasing importance for the world.

We thank the Environment for Development (EfD) network, with its main center at Göteborg University, which is supported by Swedish SIDA. EfD funded and hosted the first two workshops, at Peking University in Beijing and in Debre Zeit in Ethiopia. Special thanks go to Gunnar Köhlin, Jintao Xu and Alemu Mekonnen for facilitating these invaluable workshops as meeting places in the process of the development of the book. Thanks also go to the Centre of Land Tenure Studies (CLTS) at the Norwegian University of Life Sciences for funding and hosting the third and last workshop at Jevnaker in Norway. Thanks go to Lars Mørk for the arrangements relating to this workshop. CLTS has, together with National Graduate Institute for Policy Studies (GRIPS), Tokyo, contributed to the final editing of the book. We would also like to thank Kazuko Yamamura and Eirik Schmidt Holst for their valuable secretarial services in the final stages of editing.

Notes on Contributors

Jeetendra P. Aryal is a researcher at the International Maize and Wheat Improvement Center, Delhi, India.

Derek Byerlee is an independent scholar based in Washington, DC, USA.

Ashokankur Datta is an assistant professor at the Shiv Nadar University, New Delhi, India.

Klaus Deininger is a lead economist in the Development Economics Research Group in the World Bank, Washington, DC, USA.

Nobuhiko Fuwa is a professor at the Graduate School of Asia-Pacific Studies, Waseda University, Tokyo, Japan.

Hosaena Ghebru is a post-doc researcher at International Food Policy Research Institute, Washington, DC, USA

Stein T. Holden is a professor at the School of Economics and Business and Centre for Land Tenure Studies (CLTS), Norwegian University of Life Sciences, Ås, Norway.

Xuemei Jiang is a lecturer at the College of Economic Management, Beijing Forestry University, Beijing, China.

Songqing Jin is an associate professor at the Department of Agricultural, Food and Resource Economics, Michigan State University, Michigan, USA.

Menale Kassie is a researcher at the International Maize and Wheat Improvement Center, Nairobi, Kenya.

Luu Duc Khai is a deputy director of the Research Department on Rural Economic Development Policies at the Central Institute for Economic Management (CIEM), Hanoi, Vietnam.

Gunnar Köhlin is an associate professor at the School of Business, Economics and Law, University of Gothenburg, Gothenburg, Sweden.

Julius Mangisoni is an associate professor in the Department of Agricultural Economics, Lilongwe University, Lilongwe, Malawi.

Thomas Markussen is an associate professor at the Development Economics Research Group (DERG), Department of Economics, University of Copenhagen, Denmark.

Simon McCoy is an economist at the Department for International Development (DfID), Edinburgh, UK.

Alemu Mekonnen is an associate professor at Department of Economics, Addis Ababa University, Addis Ababa, Ethiopia.

Mariapia Mendola is an assistant professor at the Department of Economics, University of Milano-Bicocca, Milan, Italy.

Wilfred Nyangena is a senior lecturer at the School of Economics, University of Nairobi, Nairobi, Kenya.

Clement Nyirongo is an agricultural economist retired from the Malawi Civil Service and currently working as a freelance consultant. He is based in Lilongwe, Malawi.

Maurice Juma Ogada is an environmental and resource economist, currently working with the International Livestock Research Institute (ILRI) in Nairobi. He is also a PhD (Economics) candidate at Kenyatta University, Nairobi, Kenya, and a research associate with the Environment for Development Initiative in Kenya (EfD-Kenya).

Henning Øien is a doctoral candidate at the Department of Health Management and Health Economics, University of Oslo, Norway.

Keijiro Otsuka is a professor at the National Graduate Institute for Policy Studies, Tokyo, Japan.

Narayan Raj Poudel is a doctoral candidate at the Graduate School of Asia-Pacific Studies, Waseda University, Tokyo, Japan.

Geophrey Sikei is an agricultural and resource economist, currently working with the Environment for Development Initiative in Kenya (EfD-Kenya).

Franklin Simtowe is a policy officer responsible for Markets and Trade at the Alliance for Green Revolution in Africa (AGRA), Nairobi, Kenya.

Finn Tarp is a director at the World Institute for Development Economics Research (WIDER), Helsinki, Finland, and a professor at the Development Economics Research Group (DERG), Department of Economics, University of Copenhagen, Denmark.

Alex Tatwangire is an independent scholar in Kampala, Uganda.

Hardwick Tchale is a senior agricultural economist at the World Bank based in Freetown, Sierra Leone.

Henrik Wiig is a senior researcher in the Department for International Studies at the Norwegian Institute of Urban and Regional Research, Oslo, Norway.

Jintao Xu is a professor at the National School of Development, Peking University, Beijing, China.

Vandana Yadav is a professor at Michigan State University, Michigan, USA.

Yuanyuan Yi is a doctoral candidate at the School of Business, Economics and Law, University of Gothenburg, Gothenburg, Sweden.

1

Land Tenure Reforms, Poverty and Natural Resource Management: Conceptual Framework

Stein T. Holden, Keijiro Otsuka and Klaus Deininger

1.1 Introduction

Land reforms have played a central role in the political economy of many countries in the world and have been subject to massive disagreements between different political interest groups and ideologies. The 20th century included many of the largest social land reform experiments in history, as in the erstwhile Soviet Union and in Eastern Europe, China, Vietnam and Ethiopia. Many of these reforms have since been partly reversed. In other countries with a colonial history, there have been tensions between the property rights established during the colonial period and traditional (customary) land rights; the ways to adapt these to changing conditions have become critical issues. Some countries have had very skewed land distributions rooted in ethnic, colonial and other historical circumstances, and this skew has created demands for land redistribution, both to reduce discrimination and poverty, and to stimulate economic development.

Several factors have created a new interest in land reforms around the world:

- The Millennium Development Goals sharpened the international focus on poverty reduction and legal empowerment of the poor as seen by the establishment of the Commission for Legal Empowerment of the Poor (CLEP).
- Population growth, population concentration and land degradation have created land scarcity and the emergence of land markets

in densely populated countries in Africa, and this has created a new interest in land reforms, stimulating more efficient and sustainable land management.

- Excessive regulation of land transactions in some countries in Asia (for example, India, Nepal and the Philippines) has created both inefficiency in land use and inequity in operational land distribution.
- Economic growth in Asia has led to changes in eating habits towards more land-demanding foods (meat and milk), and to a growing shortage of usable land and water.
- Increasing demand for land for food and energy production have spurred a new land race to ensure national food security in countries with increasing food deficits. This has triggered sharp increases in demands for land in relatively land-abundant countries where the property rights and other institutional arrangements have not been developed adequately to handle these new demands or to protect the land rights of traditional land users and facilitate sustainable investments.
- Deforestation is one of the main causes of climate change, and the increasing international concern about this issue, and the support for the stopping and reversing of deforestation, have stimulated new thinking on how property rights and land reforms can play a part in reducing deforestation and forest degradation, and stimulate tree planting and better forest management.

New land reforms have been promoted by international institutions, such as the World Bank and UN organizations, donor countries, new governments and pressure groups within countries. Such reforms have typically aimed at stimulating economic growth by enhancing land use efficiency and investment, reducing poverty and promoting more sustainable land management. However, many of these reforms have not had the intended effects, or there have been disagreements about what the effects of the reforms have been. Given the complexity of the relationships, the problems in assessing the intended and possible unintended effects of said reforms may be related to both the design of the land tenure reforms and the measurement problems due to poor data. The problem of the disagreements about the effects of the reformshas also been caused by insufficient attention to the need for careful impact assessments and the data collection required to facilitate such assessments.

The renewed interest in land reforms has also spurred a new requirement to carefully monitor and measure their impacts. New standards are being established as to how to carry out program evaluation, not only through rigorous internal validation but also by giving more emphasis to external validation (Ravallion, 2009). Development economics research has moved in the direction of randomized social experiments as a preferred way of identifying unbiased estimates of program impacts; but so far it has been rather difficult to implement randomized social land tenure reform experiments.

New reforms in several countries have involved elements of randomized control trials related to the design of reforms, and these can provide valuable future lessons; however, for our purpose of evaluating past and recent ongoing reforms we have not, unfortunately, been able to draw on such experiments for this book. On the other hand, there may be clever ways of identifying natural experiments in relation to land tenure reform programs, and these may help to identify impacts whenever random social experiments are found, for whatever reason, to be unfeasible. This book tries to utilize such natural experiments as one source of evidence of the performance of past tenure reforms.

This book aims to identify the impacts and draw lessons from land tenure reforms in a number of countries in Africa and Asia, and to discuss the internal and external validity of the findings. The nature of the data and the complexity of the issues make it necessary to be cautious about the conclusions and their robustness. Good knowledge of the historical context and process of implementation of the specific land tenure reforms is essential for careful interpretation of evidence from past reform. In addition, the book draws heavily on recent rural household surveys as a basis for assessment of reform impacts. The authors combine historical, process and recent statistical evidence to infer causal implications about impacts of land tenure reforms. Subjective judgment is a necessary part of such analyses, as is any historical analysis based on limited evidence.

The book focuses on five major land tenure reform issues:

a) Land to the Tiller reforms (Nepal and India);
b) Market-assisted Land Redistribution reforms (Malawi and South Africa);
c) Land tenure security-enhancing reforms (Ethiopia, Vietnam and Uganda);
d) Forest tenure reforms (China, India, Nepal, Ethiopia and Kenya); and
e) The need for new land tenure reforms in Africa with the expanding demand for land.

We present a brief literature review related to these five areas in boxes that also provide the basis for our conceptual framework. We start by providing a discussion and review of literature on why land tenure security is so important for enhancing economic and social development.

1.2 Why securing land rights is important

Development economists have long highlighted the central role of institutions, that is, the socially imposed constraints on human interaction that structure incentives in any exchange, and in shaping growth and the distribution of its gains among the population (Greif, 1993; North, 1971). Property rights are social conventions, backed by the enforcement power of the state (at various levels) or of the community, allowing individuals or groups to lay 'a claim to a benefit or income stream that the state will agree to protect through the assignment of duty to others who may covet, or somehow interfere with, the benefit stream' (Sjaastad and Bromley, 2000).

Since in most contexts, land and associated real estate is one of households' most important assets, societies have from the earliest days of recorded history developed customs and laws on how to define land rights, and many societies have set up registries to make public the assignment of rights and their transfer among private parties (Powelson, 1988). The creation and maintenance of such a property rights system is an important public good that reduces the need for landholders to expend resources (for example, hiring private armies) to protect their rights. Key avenues through which property rights systems affect economic outcomes are increased investment incentives (or a reduction of the need to spend resources on defensive measures) through reduced risk of land loss and the facilitation of market transactions (Besley and Ghatak, 2010). In light of such long-term effects, they will also be of relevance for political power.

Investment incentives: Secure property rights affect economic outcomes most immediately by reducing the risk of land loss, increasing investment incentives and reducing the need for individuals to spend resources on protecting their rights. In fact, historically, land rights emerge at the transition from the hunter–gatherer stage when investment in land becomes important (Binswanger et al., 1995). The prospect of being able to enjoy the fruits of their labor encourages owners to make long-term land-related investments, and manage land sustainably (Besley, 1995). Positive impacts of land tenure security on investment in rural areas have been documented in China (Jacoby et al., 2002), Thailand (Feder et al., 1988), Latin America (Bandiera, 2007), Eastern Europe (Rozelle and Swinnen, 2004), and Africa (Holden et al., 2009; Fenske, 2011; Goldstein and Udry, 2008).

If there is widespread insecurity of property rights, clarification of such rights through systematic adjudication and registration of land rights can be a cost-effective way to increase tenure security. The magnitude and distribution of the associated benefits will depend on the reduction in enforcement effort afforded by formal recognition, the increment in security afforded by the intervention (which will depend on the legitimacy and legality of existing arrangements and the level of disputes), and the availability of investment opportunities. The benefits will be greater if the increment in tenure security is large – for instance, if land tenure had previously been insecure or conflict-ridden while the new arrangements enjoy wide legitimacy – and if payoffs from land-related investment are high.

Land transfers and financial markets: Economic development normally involves specialization and a move of part of the labor force out of the agricultural sector. Such movement creates heterogeneity in the population, increasing the scope for efficiency-enhancing land transfers. Institutions allowing such transactions at low cost, and without those who transfer use rights having to fear that they may lose their land, can increase productivity of land use. As land rental allows labor to move from agriculture to non-agriculture without forgoing the benefits – for example in terms of a social safety-net function – associated with land ownership, in most cases such transfers will be through rental rather than sale. Initially they are likely to involve community members. High transaction costs, which can also arise because rights are unclear or because of institutional inefficiencies, can reduce the number of such transactions or drive them into informality, with potentially negative impacts on long-term economic development (Libecap and Lueck, 2011).

Asymmetric information and risk have long been shown to lead to credit rationing in equilibrium and the use of collateral as one way of reducing such credit rationing (Stiglitz and Weiss, 1981). The immobility and relative indestructibility of land make it the ideal collateral. However, banks will use it for this purpose on a large scale only if they have access to a low-cost means of making reliable inferences on ownership, and the absence of other encumbrances, for any given plot of land. Such information is normally provided by land registries; if it is reliable and comprehensive, it can eliminate the need for physical inspection of the land in question, or enquiry with neighbors, thus reducing the transaction cost of exchanging land in impersonal markets and creating the preconditions for using it as collateral to secure loans. While this provides the conceptual foundation for credit impacts from land titling or registration, such effects may be expected only if there is already a latent and unsatisfied demand for credit (that is, a portfolio of viable projects), if foreclosure is possible, if registry information is comprehensive and remains up to date over time, and if third parties, such as mortgage lenders, can access reliable registry information at low cost on a routine basis.

Compared to the overwhelming empirical support for investment impacts, evidence of credit impacts from land titling, although not entirely absent (Feder et al., 1988), is very limited. These credit impactsmay accrue only to wealthy producers (Carter and Olinto, 2003); and in a number of cases where there were expectations for property rights reform to improve credit access (de Soto, 2000), these failed to materialize (Field and Torero, 2006). One reason is that better access to information on land ownership will affect credit supply only if other impediments are absent, that is, if agents have been credit-constrained beforehand, and are endowed with sufficient levels of illiquid wealth that can be foreclosed on at reasonable cost (Besley and Ghatak, 2010). Lack of investment opportunities, risk aversion, and political, social or economic restrictions on land market liquidity that make foreclosure difficult are key reasons identified by the literature as underlying causes that contribute to the limited attractiveness of rain-fed agricultural land to lenders.

Power relations: The limited overall availability of land implies that, especially in settings where land is the main asset, the way in which access to and use of land is organized becomes highly political (Boone, 2007). While this has long been documented qualitatively (Binswanger et al., 1995), a growing number of studies now provide quantitative evidence of long-term impacts of land institutions on outcomes such as provision of public goods and attainment of education in India (Banerjee and Iyer, 2005; Iyer, 2010), human capital formation and democratic development in Central America (Nugent and Robinson, 2010), transparency and governance in Brazil (Naritomi et al., 2009) and financial sector development across US counties (Rajan and Ramcharan, 2011). Land institutions and changes in these have thus sustained impacts on economic outcomes through a large number of channels.

1.3 Conceptual framework

1.3.1 Basic models

Property rights to land, being a social construct, may be seen along a continuum or as a bundle of rights, where the government in most cases plays a role. The rights belong to agents that may be groups or individuals, and these rights may be more or less secure, depending on their social recognition, competition, and enforcement. We approach property rights to land from a social welfare perspective, where an important question is how land tenure rights should be designed to ensure efficient and sustainable land use by land rights holders.

Our starting point is the relationship between tenure (in-)security and the bundle of land rights that land users have. Tenure security refers to the extent of protection and duration of one's land rights. The bundle of land rights is divided into three main categories; use rights, mortgaging rights and transfer rights. Owners with publicly registered full private property rights have all these three rights categories, while in more restricted property regimes one or two of these may be restricted or missing. Each of these rights categories needs further specification and can be embedded in customary law or statutory law. The rights may be allocated to individuals or groups, may be time-limited or extend into perpetuity, and may be conditional (implying certain obligations) or unconditional. Mortgage rights, for which land can serve as collateral, are also conditional on transfer rights, but do not necessarily follow from transfer rights.

While the state has a key role to secure tenure and make information on it publicly available, state action has often also contributed to tenure insecurity or has undermined clarity in the assignment of property rights to land. Sources of tenure insecurity can therefore include the both state itself and private sources. The state may limit individual or group property rights and expropriate land for public purposes such as infrastructure development, urban expansion, and conservation of natural resources, or for redistribution to other groups. Unclear laws and overlapping or contradictory laws, unreliable enforcement of laws, and violation of laws by government officials due to ignorance or corruption are other reasons for state-related tenure insecurity. Furthermore, interstate conflicts and wars can cause additional state-related tenure insecurity.

Private sources of risk include powerful agents that try to gain access to land claimed by others, neighbors competing over land where there

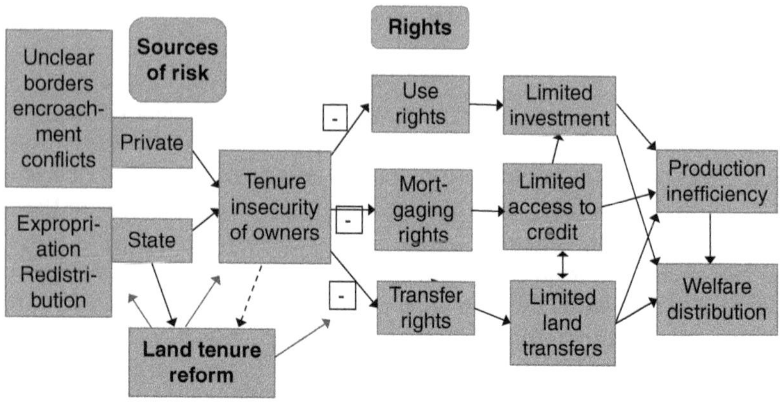

Figure 1.1 Basic model illustrating the links between land reforms, tenure insecurity, land rights and production incentives

are unclear border demarcations, theft and damage to property, and violation of land rights-related contracts causing multiple types of land conflicts. In relation to land reforms, there may be strategic agents that try to take advantage of the law reform in ways that lead to unintended outcomes, or in other cases powerful private groups are able to enforce law reforms to their own benefit but at the expense of others.

Figure 1.1 illustrates our basic conceptual framework, which captures the three categories of land rights and the two main sources of risk that cause tenure insecurity. It also captures the links from tenure insecurity to categories of land rights, and on to investment and productivity impacts. We see that tenure insecurity can have negative effects on all the three main categories of land rights (illustrated by the small boxes with negative signs) and can therefore have negative effects on investments and productivity.

We expect that these sources of risk contribute to a varying degree to tenure insecurity, and various types of land tenure reforms may address this tenure insecurity directly or indirectly, or may in other cases contribute to aggravated tenure insecurity for certain groups in a society. Land tenure reforms typically aim to strengthen the rights of some groups or individuals in a society, and this may or may not be at the expense of other individuals or groups in the society at that point in time. With increasing competition over land, and with unequal land distribution, the strengthening of the rights of some groups or individuals is likely to negatively affect the rights of other groups or individuals;

land tenure reforms are not likely to take place until a certain level of competition for, and scarcity of, land has been reached such that there is a demand for such a reform (whether democratic or not), taking its expected benefits and costs into consideration.

The issue of demand for land tenure reform vs. its social optimality is complex as illustrated by the following stylized examples. We can think of three cases of inefficient outcomes:

a) There is demand from certain broad groups, and the reform is perceived as socially optimal but is nevertheless blocked by powerful groups (*laissez faire* outcome: no reform where it is needed);
b) A powerful group implements a reform for its own benefit that has large negative impacts on others and is not socially optimal (bad reform where it was not needed);
c) A well-intended land tenure reform that was perceived to be socially optimal yields unwanted and sub-optimal outcomes (bad reform due to incompetence in design and/or implementation, or 'elite capture').

Figure 1.1 shows that land reforms implemented by the state may affect the underlying causes of tenure insecurity as well as tenure insecurity itself and the bundle of land rights and their distribution. It is also possible that tenure insecurity is a reason for the implementation of land reforms, as shown by the dotted arrow. However, in order to identifythe more specific causal relationships and possible impacts on a range of outcome measures, it is necessary to have more specific information about the nature of each specific type of land tenure reform, together with the setting within which it has been or is being implemented. We use variants of this simple model to illustrate some of these more specific land reforms with more specific expected outcomes in what follows.

We use this simple conceptual model as a starting point to discuss the effects of the various land tenure reforms. First, we distinguish between countries with unegalitarian and egalitarian land distributions. It is particularly in countries with unegalitarian land distribution that landlessness may be an important cause of poverty; and where land redistribution has been identified as a policy instrument to obtain a more just distribution, that also can lead to poverty reduction. However, the tolerance of inequitable land distributions also depends on the non-farm employment opportunities, the cultural and political norms and the power structure in the society. Basically, we are interested in the fundamental issue of what the determinants of the

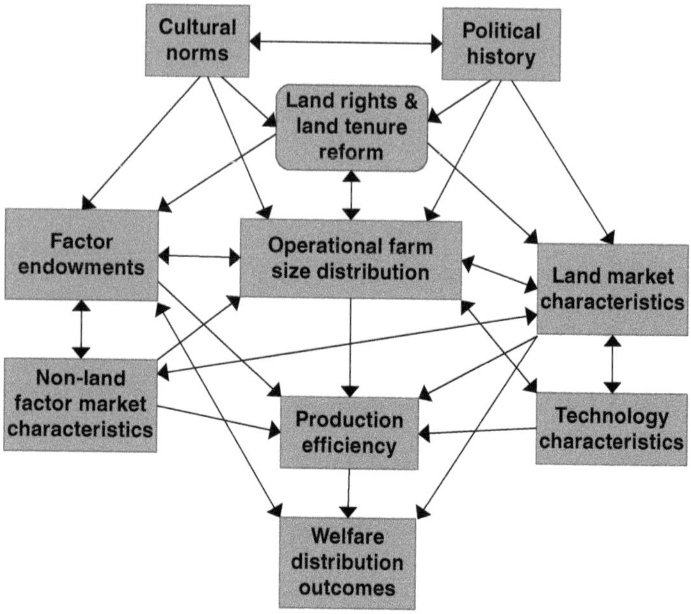

Figure 1.2 Determinants of the farm size distribution with effects on production efficiency and the distribution of welfare

actual farm size distribution are, to what extent land tenure reforms and land policies affect this farm size distribution, and how this affects both the efficiency of utilization of the land resources and the welfare distribution effects of these. This is illustrated graphically in Figure 1.2 which expands from Figure 1.1 by including more detail about the most important inter-relationships between land tenure reforms put in a political and cultural context that determines the extent, or even non-existence, of land markets, the distribution of other endowments and how these interact and create an operational farm size distribution with a related distribution of output and welfare outcomes. The many arrows indicate important dynamic effects that include causal effects as well as the trade-offs and synergies which form part of the dynamic equilibrium. The welfare effects of a land tenure reform therefore depend on the initial distribution of land and non-land resource endowments, its direct production effects on land users, the land access and market participation effects of the reform, and the ability of land users and owners to take advantage of the tenure reform.

We see from Figure 1.2 that the political history, factor endowments and cultural norms (that are interrelated) determine the distribution of land rights, including the farm size distribution. Non-land factor market characteristics and the distribution of land and non-land factors of production are important determinants of incentives for redistribution of land through land sales and land rental markets (Holden et al., 2008). In particular, imperfections in non-land factor markets caused by pervasive transaction costs and imperfect information in the production relations are basic determinants of production relations in tropical agriculture (Binswanger and Rosenzweig, 1986). The spatial dispersion of production, the immobility of land, seasonality and covariate risk, moral hazard and fragility of resources and products, all play important roles. The outcome is pervasive imperfections in markets for land, labor, traction power, other inputs, credit and insurance. Over time, market forces and agricultural technology adoption influence what are operational farm sizes and whether these are optimal farm sizes for enhancement of production efficiency. Land tenure reforms affect land market characteristics that will influence the extent of redistribution of land resources towards more optimal farm sizes from an efficiency point of view. Political forces also affect land tenure reforms and may restrict the extent of land redistribution through the market or through administrative redistribution – and this again will have production efficiency as well as welfare distribution implications. Over time, there will be complex interactions between the elements in this dynamic equilibrium. The equilibrium may respond to various types of exogenous shocks such as changing world food prices, new technologies, population growth etc.

1.3.2 Specific models

We will now discuss more specific types of land tenure reforms. It is well known that while conventional land titling has not been a success in Africa (Migot-Adholla et al., 1994; Platteau, 1996; Jacoby and Minten, 2007; Benjaminsen et al., 2009), it has been more successful in some Asian countries, such as Thailand (Feder et al., 1988). The combination of titling on demand and high costs of titling have, however, tended to favor the wealthy and well-connected, and have contributed to increased tenure insecurity and alienation of the poor who could not afford land titling. While land titling on demand is still practised in many countries, this is not a major focus of this book. We refer to the general literature existing on the topic, and we focus on other types of reforms where important knowledge gaps still exist.

Our basic hypothesis is that tenure insecurity is caused by private as well as state actions, and that this tenure insecurity negatively affects the various types of rights – and this, again, affects investment, production efficiency and welfare in a society. Thus, tenure reforms that have aggravated tenure insecurity (intentionally or otherwise) of landowners have resulted in inefficient land use and have not contributed to any substantial reduction of poverty. Conversely, tenure reforms that have enhanced the tenure security of landowners have also enhanced efficiency, investment, sustainability, land transfers and land access for the poor.

We first look at the Land to the Tiller reforms, which aim to redistribute land ownership rights from land owners to tenants, in Nepal (Chapter 2) and India (Chapter 3); these reforms were intended to improve the land access and welfare of land-poor households. Our specific hypothesis is that this type of reform has, however, had the unintended effect of aggravating tenure insecurity, causing increased Marshallian inefficiency on sharecropped land, in turn reducing the extent of land rental and making access to land more difficult for the land-poor. The basic linkages are illustrated in Figure 1.3.

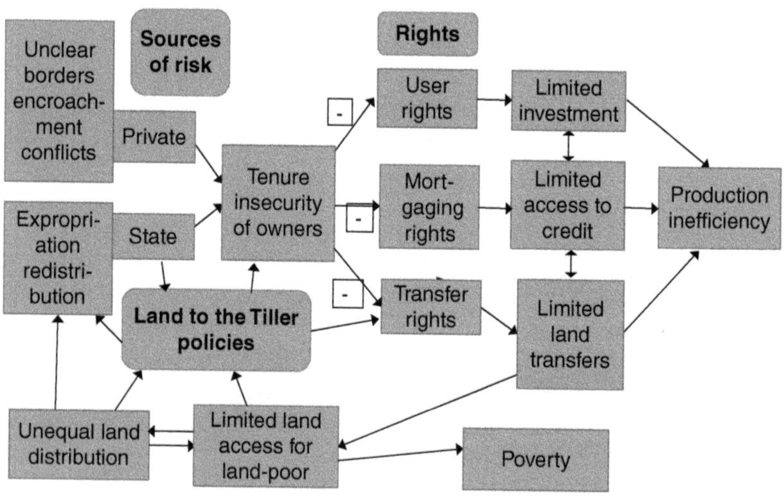

Figure 1.3 Effects of land to the Tiller policies on tenure insecurity, transfer rights and access to land for the land-poor

Box 1.1 Land to the Tiller policies

Traditionally, one of the major policy means of eradicating rural poverty in Asia has been land tenure reforms, defined here as Land to the Tiller and Tenancy Reform programs. The Land to the Tiller program, which is nothing more than a program from large landlords owning more than a certain threshold level to their tenants, was enthusiastically implemented in South Asia during the 1950s and 1960s (Khusro, 1973; Warriner, 1969; Ladejinsky, 1977; Herring, 1983) and in the Philippines in the 1970s (Prosterman and Riedinger, 1987; Hayami et al., 1990). Since the Land to the Tiller program applied to tenant-cultivated land, whereas land under 'personal cultivation' was in most cases exempted from the land transfer program, incentives were created for landlords to evict tenants and then to resume personal cultivation with employment of hired labor, so far as compensation for the landlords was lower than the market value of land. According to Bhalla (1976), Dantwala and Shah (1971), and Bardhan (1989), many landlords actually evicted tenants in India. Yet, at the All India level the percentage of farm area under tenancy declined from 20 percent in the pre-reform period of the mid-1950s to about 12 percent in the mid-1960s, at least partly because of the implementation of the Land to the Tiller program (Narian and Joshi, 1969). A similar program was also implemented effectively in favorable rice-growing areas in the Philippines (Otsuka, 1991). Variants of such tenancy reform often rule out the practice of share tenancy, and regulate leasehold rent to a low level, or reduce output sharing rate in favor of share tenants, as in the cases of West Bengal and Sri Lanka.

The major thrust of the reforms was to free tenants from the exploitation of the landed classes. No less important were presumptions that share tenancy is inefficient because of the disincentive effect of output sharing on tenants' work effort (that is, Marshallian inefficiency), and that small farms are more efficient than large ones. Thus, the traditional land reform programs had dual objectives of alleviating rural poverty and improving production efficiency (Lipton, 2009).

The limitation of the Land to the Tiller program (as well as the Tenancy Reform program), is that it redistributes wealth from the landed class to tenants – but not to the landless agricultural laborers who belong to the poorest segment of the poor rural society. Furthermore, in order to 'protect' or preserve the status of land reform beneficiaries, those beneficiaries were given usufruct rights, but not the right to lease or sublease. So under these programs, the first rung of the agricultural ladder for the landless agricultural laborers to become tenants tends to be out of reach (Otsuka, 2010).

An alternative reform to the Land to the Tiller reform to improve access of land-poor households in countries with unegalitarian land distribution is to allow voluntary transfers, possibly facilitated by a cash grant to eligible beneficiaries, a policy commonly referred to as Market-assisted Land Redistribution reform. We look at case studies in Malawi (Chapter 5) and South Africa (Chapter 4) to assess the impacts of this type of reform. We hypothesize that although this

Box 1.2 Market-assisted Land Redistribution reforms

These reforms were intended to modify the distribution of land ownership in settings with very skewed land distributions considered unfair and not conducive to broad-based economic growth. Market-assisted Land Redistribution reforms have been implemented in the Philippines, Malawi, South Africa, Zimbabwe, Brazil, and Guatemala. The mode of land acquisition in such reforms remains, however, controversial. The principle of 'willing seller and willing buyer' was introduced with the aim of reducing the opposition and the conflicts related to land redistribution. But land redistribution reforms have not always followed this principle – and even when the principle has been followed, this has not prevented conflict. The choice of appropriate beneficiaries or willing buyers in terms of emphasis on ability, motivation, access rights or need, and the need for and extent of direct and indirect support to facilitate efficient agricultural production and rural development, are important and politically sensitive issues; they have important implications for the efficiency and equity and consequent poverty-reduction effects of the reforms (Binswanger et al., 2009). Meanwhile, Lipton (2009) argues that conventional land redistribution remains an important policy option in cases where massive unemployment exists in combination with highly inequitable land distributions. However, this type of reform has also been controversial, and not very successful in creating more equitable land distribution due to political opposition, for instance in south Asian and Latin American countries (de Janvry and Sadoulet, 1989; Gauster and Isakson, 2007).

The funding of such reforms remains a challenge as well. Recent research findings revealing negative long-term impacts on economic growth of very skewed land distributions have triggered new thinking about a further need for land redistribution in some countries that have not been successful in reducing rural poverty, such as Brazil, Colombia, Guatemala, and South Africa (Deininger, 2003; Acemoglu et al., 2001, 2002). There have been few rigorous impact studies of Market-assisted Land Redistributive reforms, while such studies may hold the potential to resolve some of the controversies regarding the design of the reforms (Binswanger et al., 2009).

type of reform has the potential to improve land access for the poor, the reform is sensitive to the design of the reform and context. As long as the land contribution is voluntary and compensated, it is less likely to be resisted by political elites. It is more likely to be successful if the settlers have access to complementary inputs and social services including farmer skills, credit and market access. We also believe that it is more likely to succeed if the settlers are granted secure individual rights rather than group tenure rights and the farm sizes are tailored to the farming capacity of the settlers. With farm size and land transfer restrictions, we expect to observe production inefficiencies and to observe an inverse farm size–productivity relationship, in which land-abundant households cultivate the land less intensively than do labor-rich and more land-poor households. We have illustrated the expected impacts in Figure 1.4.

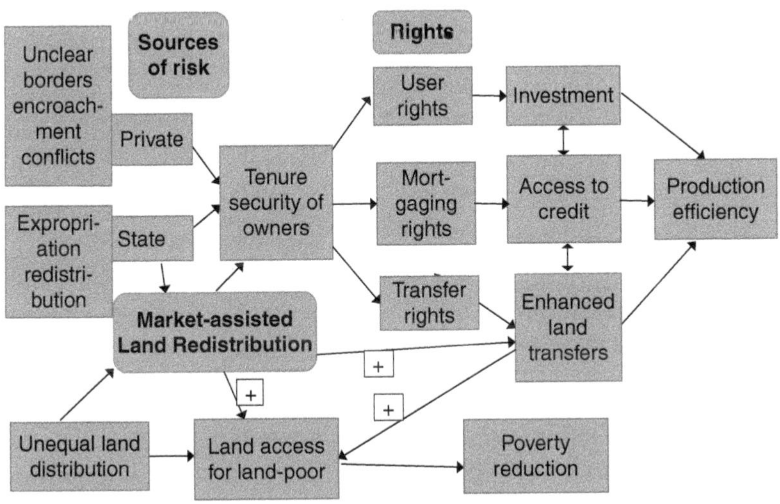

Figure 1.4 Impacts of Market-assisted Land Redistribution on land access for the poor

Box 1.3 Low-cost land registration and certification

Ethiopia is renowned for its low-cost approach to land registration and certification involving rapid, broad-based and large-scale registration and certification of rural land of agricultural households (Deininger et al., 2008, 2011a; Holden et al., 2009, 2011a, b; Toulmin, 2009). More than 20 million parcels of land were registered within a period of five years at a cost of about US$1 per parcel, implying a cost of about US$3 per household; compare this to the cost of US$150 per farm in a standard titling on demand in Madagascar (Deininger et al., 2008; Jacoby and Minten, 2007). The tenure security-enhancing effects of the reform have been documented by Holden et al. (2011b) and Deininger et al. (2011a), while Holden et al. (2011a) record a significant reduction in border disputes after the reform. Significant investment and land productivity effects from the low-cost tenure reform have been documented (Holden et al., 2009; Deininger et al., 2011). Furthermore, land rental activity has increased as landlords (often female-headed households) have become more tenure-secure and more willing to rent out their land (Holden et al., 2011b; Bezabih et al., 2012).

Vietnam passed a new land law in 1993 that provided the basis for land registration and certification. The law provided time-limited Land Use Right Certificates that could be sold, leased or mortgaged, and were renewable. Both mass-issuing and individual issuing of such certificates were common, and costs were fairly low. Administrative costs were only US$0.64–3.18 per certificate – but the surveying costs could be about US$19 per 1000m^2 (Smith et al., 2007). Ravallion and van de Walle (2008) have carried out a comprehensive assessment of the tenure security-enhancing low-cost reform in Vietnam.

The next type of reform we assess focuses on countries that have had radical land redistribution reforms in the past (Ethiopia, Vietnam and China). In these countries, this reform was successful in achieving an egalitarian land distribution – but it also had negative effects in terms of high tenure insecurity, weak individual land rights, limited investment in land, and production inefficiencies. Low-cost land registration and certification was therefore introduced to strengthen tenure security and enhance individual tenure rights, including use rights and transfer rights. We posit that this reform has been successful in enhancing investment, land productivity and land rental activity, and that these effects have also contributed to improved social welfare of the recipients of land certificates. Figure 1.5 illustrates the basic impacts we expect to find for this type of reform. Chapters 6 and 7 assess the reforms in

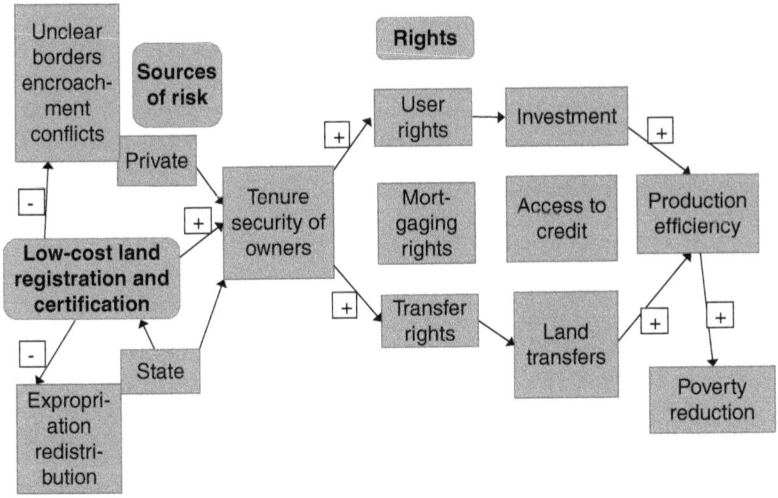

Figure 1.5 Impacts of low-cost land certification on tenure security, production efficiency and welfare

Ethiopia and Vietnam which experienced radical land reforms in the past. We have also included a study in Uganda, in Chapter 8, where recent land tenure reforms have similarly strengthened tenure security and transfer rights to land in areas with a range of initial tenure regimes established during the colonial period. The chapter assesses the functioning of land markets after the recent reform in freehold, *mailo*, leasehold and customary tenure regimes. Chapter 11, on forest tenure reform in China, also focuses on the effects of strengthened individual land rights through the provision of forestland certificates to individual households in recognition of tenure security and investments in forest land.

Chapters 2–8 have only looked at land tenure reforms regarding agricultural land. Chapters 9–13 focus on forest land and forest tenure reforms, where we have studies: in China (Chapter 11), Ethiopia (Chapter 13), India (Chapter 10), Kenya (Chapter 12) and Nepal (Chapter 9).

Box 1.4 Forest tenure reforms

There is little consensus on the optimal property rights regime for forest land and how various factors affect the choice of property regime for forest land. There does seem to be a consensus, however, that state ownership and management of forest land has failed in many cases, and has resulted in *de facto* open access deforestation and forest degradation. Many countries have therefore started reforms that devolve forest land rights and management to local communities, assuming that those communities have the capacity to implement collective action leading to better management of such forest land and positive welfare effects for local people, including the poor (Ostrom, 1990). However, some more recent studies show that there are examples of success and failure for all broad types of ownership regimes (government property, communal property and private property) (Gibson et al., 2005). Meanwhile, Ostrom et al. (2007) have argued for moving beyond panaceas, referring to a blueprint for a single type of land governance system to handle complex socio-ecological systems. Instead, there is a need for deep diagnostic assessments as a basis for design of land tenure reforms. There could also be potential conflicts between short-term needs of people and the long-term sustainability objectives for forest land, as a substantial time may elapse between the point when an investment in forest conservation is made and the time when the benefits from it can be derived. This means that both the long-term dimensions and the collective action requirements can be challenging for communal organizations; their success will depend on a number of characteristics that have been outlined by Ostrom (1990). These include the resource characteristics, the group characteristics, the institutional arrangements, and the external environment; each of these affects the individual and group incentives which again affect institutional reforms.

Some countries have observed problems with communal collective management of forests and have started to further distribute forest land to individual households. We look at China as a case where a transition from community forestry to more individual forestland management has expanded in recent years by providing individual households forestland certificates for 30–70 years for forestland plots.

In India and Nepal, the roles of community organizations are assessed in relation to the management of communal forests with a varying degree of state involvement and influence. With increasing population pressure, local communal forests may no longer be able to supply all the forest products needed by the local population; the more degraded the forests and the more restrictive the harvesting regimes implemented to rehabilitate such forest lands, the more likely this is to be the case. Such restrictive harvesting regimes (exclusion) are likely to create incentives for private farm tree planting to meet the needs for building materials as well as firewood. We assess the relationships between forestland degradation and access, and forestland protection reforms and incentives to plant trees on individual farms, in Ethiopia and Kenya. In Kenya, the factors associated with participation in Community Forestry Groups and how these affect tree planting on individual farms are explored. In Ethiopia, there are also restrictions on tree planting on individual farmland intended for food crop production, while land certification on household land may have stimulated longer-term investments on the land, including tree investments – but such investment incentives may also be affected by access to community forests that have been protected as area enclosures. The basic relationships investigated in these forestland chapters are illustrated broadly in Figure 1.6.

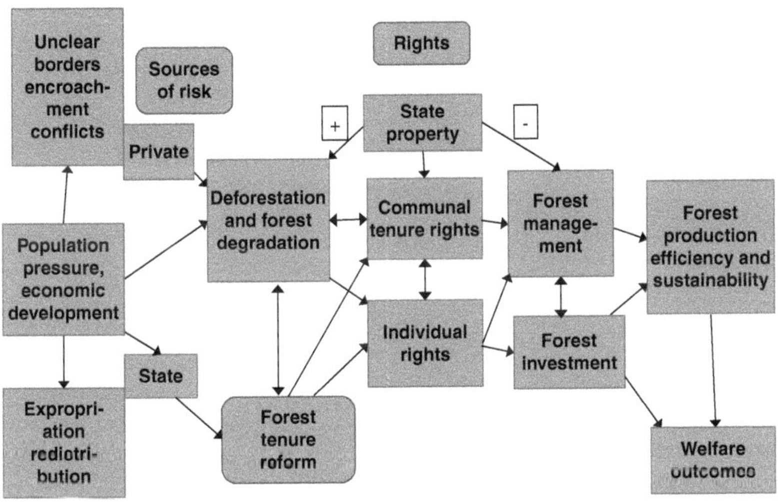

Figure 1.6 Forest land rights and forest tenure reforms for enhanced forest protection and utilization

Box 1.5 Large scale land acquisitions ('land grab')

The world first became aware of a renewed trend towards large scale land acquisition and the challenges it poses in 2008, when evidence of a Korean firm obtaining more than 1 million ha in Madagascar 'for free', that is with virtually no compensation to local people, was widely circulated in the global press. The resulting controversy contributed to the collapse of the country's government and the withdrawal of the investment. But three factors contributed to the surge in the demand for land, especially in Africa:

(i) expectation of continued strong growth of demand for foods and their increased price volatility in agricultural commodities;
(ii) increased use of what might traditionally have been considered as 'marginal' lands for the production of environmental services; and
(iii) the fact that in the current macro-economic environment, many actors in the financial sector consider land as an asset with highly desirable properties.

Even though agricultural investment in developing countries is much needed and there are examples demonstrating that it can help improve access to technology, markets, and finance for smallholders, the sudden nature and enormous magnitude of such demand (Anseeuw et al., 2012) put enormous strains onto existing institutional capacity. Even though interest in acquiring land did not always translate into actual deals (Schoneveld, 2011), many of the resulting land transfers are unlikely ever to generate local benefits (Deininger et al., 2011b) and some have already been abandoned. As experts expect commodity prices to remain at higher levels for the foreseeable future, improvements in land governance will be important to create an institutional basis that will allow such demands to be dealt with successfully. Four critical areas are

(i) the recognition of existing rights;
(ii) the identification of state land;
(iii) the establishment of mechanisms for decentralized land transfers; and
(iv) local infrastructure.

Much land in Africa, even if it has been occupied by local communities for a long time, is legally considered 'state land' that can be transferred to investors without first going through a process of ascertaining or compensating existing use rights. Failure to go through such a process has often led to conflict. Recent examples show, however, that if legal provisions are in place, rights to large areas of land can be adjudicated quickly, cost-effectively and in a way that includes land use planning, thus identifying areas that could be made available to outsiders.

In many countries, legal provisions require that land intended to be transferred to investors be first expropriated or converted into state land. But in many countries the acquisition and divestiture of state land are a key area of corruption and bad governance. Moreover, with such provisions, even communities that are interested in transferring land to an investor or establishing joint ventures either will be unable to do so or will not benefit from it directly. So legislation that requires expropriation as a precondition for transfers to investors or that gives wide latitude to expropriation for transfer to private interests should be amended, first to give a clear rationale (for example, in terms of environmental externalities) for declaring areas as state land, and then to follow this up with an inventory that unambiguously demarcates such lands on the ground. Importantly, there should be transparent mechanisms for the divestiture of land that does *not* meet these criteria, with preference given to actual users.

To provide investment incentives and facilitate the conversion of land to its best use, it is critical that current and comprehensive information on property rights is broadly and cost-effectively accessible. This should allow low-cost registration of any transfers among private parties and include relevant contractual details. High levels of fees which in many instances act as a strong disincentive to the transfer of land to better uses – or indeed better users – should be lowered and replaced with a regime of land taxation (which would provide incentives to bring land into use) or taxation of profits with no loopholes.

The fact that demand for land, at least in Africa, has somewhat receded from its peak (Arezki et al., 2011) provides an opportunity for governments to undertake reforms in these areas. Countries with large amounts of land that might be of interest to investors may need to combine these with ways to promote investment in line with the country's comparative advantages and its envisaged long-term development path. Key areas of concern relate to

(i) clustering, to piggy-back onto existing infrastructure and attain synergy from a focused approach to technology and markets;
(ii) transparent screening of investment proposals, to reduce the risk of irreversible damage being inflicted by deals that are non-viable from a technical point of view;
(iii) agile mechanisms for dispute resolution and arbitration, to adjust knowledge and institutional arrangements to emerging needs; and
(iv) options for investors to signal compliance with standards, to attract capital at low cost and set in motion a race to the top.

International organizations have reacted to these new large land acquisitions – the 'land grab' – by implementing studies of the phenomenon and offering training and build-up of national capacity to reform laws and national and local institutions in ways that can better protect local interests.

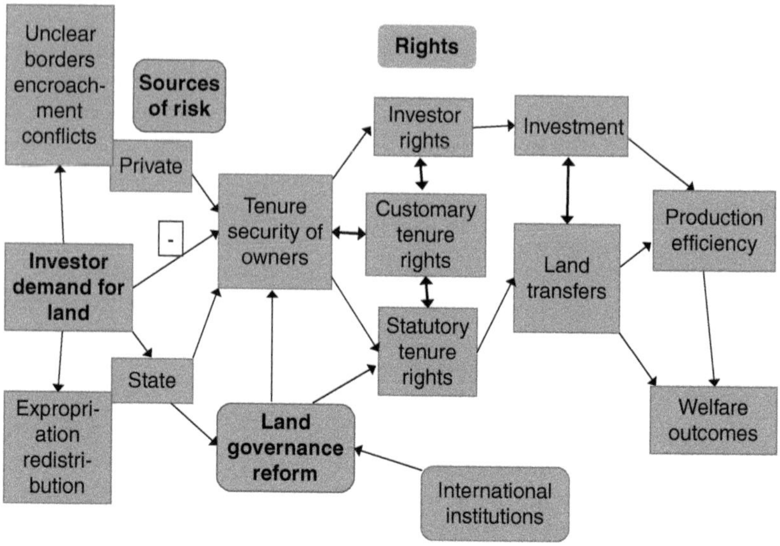

Figure 1.7 New investor demand for land and the need for improved land governance reform

Such reforms need to be tailor-made to each country by building on existing institutions, agro-ecological and market characteristics. We therefore end the book with a discussion of the future land governance challenges; some of the main issues are illustrated in Figure 1.7. In particular, the relationship between statutory law, customary land rights and investor rights have to be clarified, otherwise new investor demand for land can create tenure insecurity and cause alienation of traditional land users unless land governance systems can be established that can ensure that their rights are protected and that they are included in the growth process.

Our basic proposition is that the new demand for land in countries with weak land rights creates not just more tenure insecurity and risk of loss of customary land rights for indigenous populations, but also political instability, which increases the risk for investors as well. We suggest that new land tenure reforms are essential to establish sustainable benefits that can lead to broad economic growth in these countries. Failure to implement such reforms can lead to very skewed land rights distributions, which are bad for economic development and the scope for poverty reduction in the short, medium and long term.

Super-large farms do not provide economic benefits to society beyond that which is already provided by medium-size and small farms. The hasty establishment of such large farms that are not recognized by the local people can easily lead to conflicts between the investors and the local people and lock development into an inappropriate development pathway.

The challenges posed not only by the land rush examined in Chapter 14 but also by continued urban expansion have led to a recognition of the need for capacity building and improvements in land governance by the international community. That need has been articulated in a number of policy statements, such as the Voluntary Guidelines supported by FAO (Food and Agricultural Organization of the UN, 2012) and the UN Economic Commission for Africa's Land Policy Initiative and African Union's Declaration on Land Policies and Challenges in Africa (African Union, 2009). These documents are likely to greatly advance the debate in the sector, especially if they can be translated into broad-based dialogue that results in consensus on priorities and action at country level.

In Chapter 15, we review the land governance assessment framework (LGAF) which has been developed to address this challenge. Experience suggests that by facilitating dialogue among land sector stakeholders who often fail to communicate with each other, the LGAF can help identify priority policy actions that can feed into the policy dialogue at higher level, including passage of legislation and institutional reform. This can prepare the way for the piloting of innovative approaches to the various factors underlying tenure insecurity and weak land governance. We end the book by drawing our conclusions in Chapter 16.

References

Acemoglu, D., Johnson, S. and Robinson, J.A. (2001) 'The Colonial Origins of Comparative Development: An Empirical Investigation', *American Economic Review*, 91(5), 1369–401.

Acemoglu, D., Johnson, S. and Robinson, J.A. (2002) 'Reversal of Fortune: Geography and Institutions in the Making of Modern World Income Distribution', *Quarterly Journal of Economics*, 117(4), 659–94.

African Union (2009) 'Land Policy in Africa: A Framework to Strengthen Land Rights, Enhance Productivity and Secure Livelihoods', African Union and Economic Commission for Africa, Addis Ababa.

Anseeuw, W., Bache, W., Bru, T., Giger, M., Lay, J., Messerli, P. and Nolte, K. (2012) 'Transnational Land Deals for Agriculture in the Global South: Analytical Report Based on the Land Matrix Database', CDE/CIRAD/GIGA, Bern/Montpellier/Hamburg.

Arezki, R., Deininger, K. and Selod, H. (2011) 'What Drives the Global Land Rush', *IMF Working Paper* WP/11/251, International Monetary Fund, Washington D.C.

Bandiera, O. (2007) 'Land Tenure, Investment Incentives, and the Choice of Techniques: Evidence from Nicaragua', *World Bank Economic Review*, 21(3), 487–508.

Banerjee, A. and Iyer, L. (2005) 'History, Institutions, and Economic Performance: The Legacy of Colonial Land Tenure Systems in India', *American Economic Review*, 95(4), 1190–213.

Bardhan, P.K. (1989) 'Poverty, Growth, and Rural Labor Markets in India', *Economic and Political Weekly*, 24, A21–38.

Benjaminsen, T.A., Holden, S.T., Lund, C. and Sjaastad, E. (2009) 'Formalisation of Land Rights: Some Empirical Evidence from Mali, Niger and South Africa', *Land Use Policy*, 26, 28–35.

Besley, T. (1995) 'Property Rights and Investment Incentives: Theory and Evidence from Ghana', *Journal of Political Economy*, 103(5), 903–37.

Besley, T. and Ghatak, M. (2010) 'Property Rights and Economic Development', in M.R. Rosenzweig and D. Rodrik (eds), *Handbook of Economic Development*, Vol. 5 (Oxford and Amsterdam: Elsevier).

Bezabih, M., Holden, S.T. and Mannberg, A. (2012) 'The Role of Land Certification in Reducing Gender Gaps in Productivity in Rural Ethiopia', *CLTS Working Paper* No 9/2012, Centre for Land Tenure Studies, Norwegian University of Life Sciences, Ås, Norway.

Bhalla, S. (1976) 'New Relations of Production in Haryana Agriculture', *Economic and Political Weekly*, 11(13), 23–30.

Binswanger, H.P., Deininger, K. and Feder, G. (1995) 'Power, Distortions, Revolt and Reform in Agricultural Land Relations', *Handbook of Development Economics*, 3B, 2659–772.

Binswanger, H.P. and Rosenzweig, M.R. (1986) 'Behavioural and Material Determinants of Production Relations in Agriculture', *Journal of Development Studies*, 22, 503–39.

Binswanger- Mkhize, H P., Bourguignon, C. and van den Brink, R. (eds) (2009) *Agricultural Land Redistribution: Towards Greater Consensus* (Washington D.C.: The World Bank).

Boone, C. (2007) 'Property and Constitutional Order: Land Tenure Reform and the Future of the African State', *African Affairs*, 106(425), 557–86.

Carter, M.R. and Olinto, P. (2003) 'Getting Institutions "Right" for Whom? Credit Constraints and the Impact of Property Rights on the Quantity and Composition of Investment', *American Journal of Agricultural Economics*, 85(1), 173–86.

Dantwala, M.L. and Shah, C.H. (1971) *Evaluation of Land Reforms*, Vol. 1 (Bombay: University of Bombay Press).

de Janvry, A. and Sadoulet, E. (1989) 'A Study of Resistance to Institutional Change: The Lost Game of Latin American Land Reform', *World Development*, 17(9), 1397–407.

de Soto, H. (2000) *The Mystery of Capital: Why Capitalism Triumphs in the West and Fails Everywhere else* (New York: Basic Books).

Deininger, K. (2003) *Land Policies for Growth and Poverty Reduction* (Washington D.C.: World Bank).

Deininger, K., Ali, D. and Alemu, T. (2011a) 'Impacts of Land Certification on Tenure Security, Investment, and Land Market Participation: Evidence from Ethiopia', *Land Economics*, 87(2), 312–34.

Deininger, K., Ali, D., Holden, S.T. and Zevenbergen, J. (2008) 'Rural Land Certification in Ethiopia: Process, Initial Impact, and Implications for the Other African Countries', *World Development*, 36(10), 1786–812.

Deininger, K., Byerlee, D., Lindsay, J., Norton, A., Selod, H. and Stickler, M. (2011b) *Rising Global Interest in Farmland: Can It Yield Sustainable and Equitable Benefits?* (Washington, D.C.: World Bank).

Feder, G., Chalamwong, Y., Onchan, T. and Hongladarom, C. (1988) *Land Policies and Farm Productivity in Thailand* (Baltimore and London: Johns Hopkins University Press).

Fenske, J. (2011) 'Land Tenure and Investment Incentives: Evidence from West Africa', *Journal of Development Economics*, 95(1), 137–56.
Field, E. and Torero, M. (2006) 'Do Property Titles Increase Credit Access among the Urban Poor? Evidence from Peru', Mimeo, Harvard University, March.
Food and Agricultural Organization of the UN (2012) *Voluntary Guidelines on the Responsible Governance of Tenure of Land, Fisheries and Forests in the Context of National Food Security* (Rome: FAO).
Gauster, S. and Isakson, R. (2007) 'Eliminating Market Distortions, Perpetuating Rural Inequity: An Evaluation of Market-assisted Land Reform in Guatemala', *Third World Quarterly*, 28(8), 1519–36.
Gibson, C.C., Williams, J.T. and Ostrom, E. (2005) 'Local Enforcement and Better Forests', *World Development*, 33(2), 273–84.
Goldstein, M. and Udry, C. (2008) 'The Profits of Power: Land Rights and Agricultural Investment in Ghana', *Journal of Political Economy*, 116(6), 980–1022.
Greif, A. (1993) 'Contract Enforceability and Economic Institutions in Early Trade: The Maghribi Traders' Coalition', *American Economic Review*, 83(3), 525–48.
Hayami, Y., Quisumbing, M.A. and Adriano, L.S. (1990) *Toward an Alternative Land Reform Paradigm: A Philippine Perspective* (Quezon City: Ateneo de Manila University Press).
Herring, R.J. (1983) *Land to the Tiller: The Political Economy of Agrarian Reforms in South Asia* (New Haven, CT: Yale University Press).
Holden, S.T., Deininger, K. and Ghebru, H. (2009) 'Impacts of Low-Cost Land Certification on Investment and Productivity', *American Journal of Agricultural Economics*, 91(2), 359–73.
Holden, S.T., Deininger, K. and Ghebru, H. (2011a) 'Does Land Registration and Certification Reduce Land Border Disputes?' *CLTS Working Paper* No. 5. Centre for Land Tenure Studies, Norwegian University of Life Sciences, Ås, Norway.
Holden, S.T., Deininger, K. and Ghebru, H. (2011b) 'Tenure Insecurity, Gender, Low-cost Land Certification and Land Rental Market Participation', *Journal of Development Studies*, 47(1), 31–47.
Holden, S.T., Otsuka, K. and Place, F. (eds) (2008) *The Emergence of Land Markets in Africa: Impacts on Poverty, Equity and Efficiency* (Washington D.C.: Resources For the Future Press).
Iyer, L. (2010) 'Direct Versus Indirect Colonial Rule in India: Long-Term Consequences', *Review of Economics and Statistics*, 92(4), 693–713.
Jacoby, H.G. and Minten, B. (2007) 'Is Land Titling in Sub-Saharan Africa Cost-Effective? Evidence from Madagascar', *The World Bank Economic Review*, 21(3), 461–85.
Jacoby, H.G., Li, G. and Rozelle, S. (2002) 'Hazards of Expropriation: Tenure Insecurity and Investment in Rural China', *American Economic Review*, 92(5), 1420–47.
Khusro, A.M. (1973) *The Economics of Land Reform and Farm Size in India* (Bombay: Macmillan Press).
Ladejinsky, W. (1977) *Agrarian Reform as Unfinished Business: The Selected Papers of Wolf Ladejinsky*, edited by L.J. Walinsky (Oxford: Oxford University Press).
Libecap, G.D. and Lueck, D. (2011) 'The Demarcation of Land and the Role of Coordinating Property Institutions', *Journal of Political Economy*, 119(3), 426–67.
Lipton, M. (2009) *Land Reform in Developing Countries: Property Rights and Property Wrongs* (Abingdon: Routledge).
Migot-Adholla, S.E., Place, F. and Oluoch-Kosura, W. (1994) 'Security of Tenure and Land Productivity in Kenya', In J.W. Bruce and S.E. Migot-Adholla (eds), *Searching for Land Tenure Security in Africa* (IA: Kendall Hunt Publ.).

Narian, D. and Joshi, P.C. (1969) 'Magnitude of Agricultural Tenancy', *Economic and Political Weekly*, 4, A139–42.

Naritomi, J., Soares, R.R. and Assuncão, J.J. (2009) 'Institutional Development and Colonial Heritage within Brazil', *IZA Discussion Paper* No. 4276, Institute for the Study of Labor, Leibniz Information Centre for Economics, Bonn.

North, D.C. (1971) *Structure and Change in Economic History* (New York: W.W. Norton).

Nugent, J.B. and Robinson, J.A. (2010) 'Are Factor Endowments Fate?' *Revista de Historia Economica*, 28(1), 45–82.

Ostrom, E. (1990) *Governing the Commons: The Evolution of Institutions for Collective Action* (New York: Cambridge University Press).

Ostrom, E., Janssen, M.A. and Anderies, J.M. (2007) 'Going Beyond Panaceas', *PNAS*, 104(39), 15176–8.

Otsuka, K. (1991) 'Determinants and Consequences of Land Reform Implementation in the Philippines', *Journal of Development Economics*, 35(2), 339–55.

Otsuka, K. (2010) 'Efficiency and Equity Effects of Land Markets', in R.E. Evenson and P. Pingali (eds), *Handbook of Agricultural Economics*, Vol. IV (Amsterdam: Elsevier).

Platteau, J-P. (1996) 'The Evolutionary Theory of Land Rights as Applied to Sub-Saharan Africa: A Critical Assessment', *Development and Change*, 27, 29–86.

Powelson, J.P. (1988) *The Story of Land: A World History of Land Tenure and Agrarian Reform* (MA: Lincoln Institute of Land Cambridge).

Prosterman, R.L. and Riedinger, J.M. (1987) *Land Reform and Democratic Development* (Baltimore, MD: Johns Hopkins University Press).

Rajan, R. and Ramcharan, R. (2011) 'Land and Credit: A Study of the Political Economy of Banking in the United States in the Early 20th Century', *The Journal of Finance*, 66(6), 1895–931.

Ravallion, M. (2009) 'Evaluation in the Practice of Development', *The World Bank Research Observer*, 24(1), 29–53.

Ravallion, M. and van de Walle, D. (2008) *Land in Transition. Reform and Poverty in Rural Vietnam* (New York and Washington D.C.: Palgrave Macmillan and the World Bank).

Rozelle, S. and Swinnen, J.F.M. (2004) 'Success and Failure of Reform: Insights from the Transition of Agriculture', *Journal of Economic Literature*, 42(2), 404–56.

Schoneveld, G.C. (2011) 'The Anatomy of Large-scale Farmland Acquisitions in Sub-Saharan Africa', *Working Paper* No. 85, Center for International Forestry Research, Bogor.

Sjaastad, E. and Bromley, D. (2000) 'The Prejudices of Property Rights: On Individualism, Specificity, and Security in Property Regimes', *Development Policy Review*, 18(4), 365–89.

Smith, W., Williamson, I., Burns, A., Chung, T.K., Ha, N.T.V. and Quyen, H.X. (2007) 'The Impact of Land Market Processes on the Poor in Rural Vietnam', *Survey Review*, 39(303), 3–20.

Stiglitz, J.E. and Weiss, A. (1981) 'Credit Rationing in Markets with Imperfect Information', *American Economic Review*, 71(3), 393–410.

Toulmin, C. (2009) 'Securing Land and Property Rights in Sub Saharan Africa. The Role of Local Institutions', *Land Use Policy*, 26(1), 10–19.

Valsecchi, M. (2010) 'Land Certification and International Migration: Evidence from Mexico', *Working Papers in Economics* No. 440, University of Gothenburg, Gothenburg.

Warriner, D. (1969) *Land Reform in Principle and Practice* (London: Oxford University Press).

Part I

Land Redistribution Reforms

2
Land Reforms, Caste Discrimination and Land Market Performance in Nepal

Jeetendra P. Aryal and Stein T. Holden

2.1 Introduction

The caste system is an inherent part of Nepal's institutional structure, as are class formation, political instability and conflict. The group the caste system discriminates against the most forcefully is the Dalit, the so-called 'untouchables'. Dalits have for many centuries faced religious, occupational and even territorial discrimination; they were traditionally excluded from receiving education and using public resources, and had no rights to own land (Dahal, 1995; CHRGJ, 2005; Haug et al., 2009). The situation of the Dalits in Nepal, especially before 1951, can best be explained by a patron–client dependency in which landed patrons (high-caste households) provided the Dalits with access to small pieces of land and other basic requirements for subsistence living – and in return for that, they were bound to provide their services to their patron; in essence, a feudal system. Although caste discrimination is outlawed now, it still has impacts on their lives, because it restricts their access to economic resources; as a result, nearly 75 per cent of Dalits in Nepal are functionally landless (Wily et al., 2008). Traditional religious justification combined with poverty and landlessness contribute substantially to the social ostracism of the Dalits (Banerjee and Knight, 1985).

The Dalits started to raise their voices against caste-based discrimination in the 1940s, but until 1990 the Dalit movement remained subsumed within the larger struggle for democracy (DFID and World Bank, 2006). With the establishment of democracy in 1990, however, the Dalit movement gained momentum; the Dalit organizations demanded land reform, with the shares of land to be in proportion to the population size (UNDP, 2008). Yet even so, except for a small proportion of the hill region Dalits who have improved their livelihood by participating in paid activities, the majority of the Dalits remain below the poverty line (Hatlebakk, 2008).

Despite being a democratic state after 1990, Nepal failed to establish an inclusive polity because the caste-based norms and networks persisted throughout all its institutions. This provided a launchpad for the radical movement launched by the Maoists. Among other factors, the Dalit grievances were one of the powerful factors leading to the success of the Maoist war in Nepal (Murshed and Gates, 2005); the Maoists were able to recruit many Dalits in their army because the Maoist demands such as ending caste discrimination, and radical land reforms were closely related to the Dalit grievances. In addition, the Maoists also campaigned against caste discrimination by punishing non-Dalits who practised caste-based discrimination, such as preventing Dalits from entering temples or fetching water from public wells, or indeed any kind of humiliation (CHRGJ, 2005).

The Maoist war ended in 2007, and the Interim Constitution of Nepal 2007 guaranteed to remove all caste-based discrimination. However, in the case of Dalits the constitutional provision alone was, and still is, not enough, as they had previously been deprived of access to economic resources such as land, education and regular employment; the consequent inequality in land ownership continues to hold even today, because in Nepal inheritance remains the major form of land transfer from one generation to the other in Nepal. The legal practice until now has been to divide the parental property (both land and non-land) equally among the male heirs. In addition, although participation in the land market is possible, the purchase of land is beyond the capacity of poor Dalits, as the credit market is highly imperfect. These two factors mean that land tenure reform should be a major area of concern.

Previous land reform measures (see Section 2 for details) did not take into account the disadvantaged position of Dalits with regard to land ownership (Hatlebakk, 2008). Furthermore, many of the beneficiaries of past land redistributions turned out to be other than the poor and unprivileged (Pandey, 1993). The past land tenure reform measures were focused on the Land to the Tiller policy, but without proper attention being paid to any consequences that might arise from it (Yadav, 1999). The Land to the Tiller policy set up a provision that a formal tenant can claim the ownership rights on part of the rented land (Yadav, 1999; Bhandari, 2006), and as a result, formal tenancy transactions decreased, as landlords feared participating in land tenancy transactions (Yadav,

1999). This provision also resulted in dual ownership of rented land, which in turn discouraged investment in land for quality improvements. Overall, these past land policies have distorted the functioning of the land rental market in Nepal.

The failures of the past land reforms in redistributing land might be one of the reasons why the Maoists acquired stronger support from Dalits and landless people (Hatlebakk, 2008). Inequality in land distribution, along with poverty, provided a basis for the rural support for the Maoists. As a result, under the leadership of the Maoists, landless people took land belonging to others not only during the war but also after the Peace Agreement (Tiejun and Kinchi, 2008; Jolly, 2009). The Maoists have issued repeated threats to the landowners to not sell or use the land, stating that it will be distributed to landless people, and this has created frequent political and social unrest in Nepal.

So it was failures of the past land reform measures that contributed to the Maoist insurgency, because the war began with land reform as one of the major political demands (Wily et al., 2008). Overall in south Asia, the caste system and land tenure reform legislation have between them hindered access to the agricultural ladder whereby landless households could become tenants and later owner-operators (Otsuka et al., 1992).

Unremitting social discrimination in Nepal – and indeed anywhere – primarily contributes to social unrest and conflict, and may accelerate political unrest. A peaceful development will require policies that facilitate a more just distribution of resources and it calls for a renewed interest in land redistribution. At the same time, it is important to draw lessons from the failures of the past attempts at land tenure reform; an understanding of the implications of the past Land to the Tiller policies, and their unintended consequences, would provide a basis for designing appropriate land tenure policies in Nepal.

In an agrarian nation like Nepal, access to land is a critical issue, because it is strongly associated with welfare and poverty. Land tenure reform measures are essential not only for the social equity that minimizes political conflict and unrest, but also for enhancing agricultural productivity and thus promoting welfare and food security. A recent study (Aryal and Holden, 2009) in the western part of Nepal indicated that Dalits are land-poor – but they are more productive farmers than non-Dalits. Therefore, land redistribution towards Dalits is not only important for reducing a possible Dalit uprising, as in India, but also for enhancing land productivity. Land redistribution, therefore, is linked with several important issues, such as equity in distribution, efficiency of production, and a minimizing of the possibility of political and social unrest.

Against this backdrop, this chapter focuses particularly on the implications of caste discrimination and past land reforms on the land rental market performance, land productivity and land use intensity. We analyzed these issues using data from western Nepal. For the purpose of analysis, we classified all sample households into two broad categories: high-caste (which, for the purposes of this analysis, means all castes/ethnic groups except Dalits) and low-caste (Dalits only). This classification is appropriate because, due to the caste system, none of the other groups faces social exclusion as do the Dalits. For most of the analyses, this chapter draws from the recent studies by the authors in Nepal.

The rest of the chapter is structured as follows. Section 2 contains a brief review of past land reform measures in Nepal and their failure, followed by the testable hypotheses in Section 3. Section 4 provides the analysis of caste discrimination, and its implications for land rental market performance and land productivity. The last section presents the conclusions and recommendations.

2.2 Past land tenure reform measures and its failures

The first reform measure taken in the land tenure system in Nepal was the provision of private property rights in the interim constitution of Nepal, in 1951. This provision made the *Birta*[1] and *Jagir*[2] landholders become the permanent owner of the land, by securing private property rights. Although its primary intention was to strengthen private property rights, it in fact resulted in an even worse inequality in the distribution of land, as it institutionalized the hierarchical relationship between landed élites and peasants (Regmi, 1976; Joshi and Mason, 2008). This ensued because the people who had already acquired Birta and Jagir land were the government officials, military officers, Brahmins and members of the ruling classes (Joshi and Mason, 2008). Land tenure security in such a context resulted in the highly unequal distribution of land ownership, and thereby intensified the need, as some people saw it, for agrarian reform in Nepal.

In 1951, the government also enacted the Tenancy Rights Acquisition Act. This Act had a provision that tenants would be provided with title to the land on which they paid land tax. However, this provision did not serve its original purpose, because the land tax, although collected from tenants, was registered officially in the name of landlords. As a result, it had precisely the opposite effect to that apparently intended, giving permanent legal title of land ownership to those landlords who managed to pay the land tax (Regmi, 1976). In such circumstances, the land tenancy reform measures that had been implemented thus far remained largely ineffective (Yadav, 1999; Joshi and Mason, 2008; Wily et al., 2008).

Another reform measure taken in the land tenure system in Nepal was the abolition of Birta tenancy in 1957 which converted all Birta land into *Raikar.*[3] This provision was implemented when the first democratically elected government of Nepal, the Nepali Congress Government, came into power in 1959. However, this could still not make any substantial change in the inequality of land distribution, as most of the Birta land owners, who belonged to ruling élites, were successful in transferring the Birta land into their private land.

The Land Act of 1964 was the most comprehensive of all the measures taken in the land sector, and even today this occupies the central place in land reforms in Nepal (Wily et al., 2008). Initially, the Act was implemented over three consecutive years, starting from 1964, and was revised several times. The main objectives of this were to achieve more equitable land distribution and poverty reduction by redistributing land to small farmers, tenants and agricultural workers. The main components of the Land Act 1964 were:

(i) Abolishing land tax collection by intermediaries (*Zamindari Pratha* in Nepali).
(ii) Imposing fixed ceilings on ownership landholdings, whereby a family could hold an area of 16.93 ha in the Terai[4] area, 4.07 ha in the Hills and Mountains area, and 2.54 ha in the Kathmandu Valley.
(iii) Fixing land rent as half of the output of the main crop.
(iv) Implementing a compulsory saving program to provide an alternative source of credit to farmers.
(v) Imposing measures to improve farming practices.
(vi) Imposing a ceiling on tenancy holdings of land, whereby a family could hold an area of 2.67 ha in the Terai, 1.51 ha in the Hills and Mountains, and 1.02 ha in the Kathmandu Valley.

The abolition of intermediaries was used as an instrument to reduce the feudal and semi-feudal tenure system. There was also provision to distribute the land acquired as a result of landlords possessing land above the ceiling fixed by the Act. In addition, several supporting laws were enacted to improve the registration of land and tenants.

But the Land Act 1964 was only partially implemented... as its implementation took several years, many large landowners were able to circumvent the land ceiling fixed by the act – either by selling their surplus land or by distributing it among close relatives (Yadav, 1999). As a result, the government was unable to acquire the amount of land that could have been expected when the program was initiated. Yadav (1999) reported that by implementing the new ceilings on land, as defined in the Land Act 1964, a mere 31,800 ha of land were acquired, of which only 29,100 ha were distributed among the landless and small landholders. The total land acquired for distribution was therefore less than 2 per cent of the total agricultural land in the country (Yadav, 1999; Bhandari, 2006). Worse, not all the redistributed land was received by the intended beneficiaries due to inefficient land administration and the strong alliance between the landed class and bureaucracy (Regmi, 1976; Bhandari, 2006). So, assessed in terms of actual land acquired and redistributed, the land reforms program of 1964 did not seem to be effective. However, the program was at least successful in abolishing the local intermediary (*Zamindar*) system for collecting land tax, and as a result cultivators were no longer subjugated to this particular form of overlordship (Kuhnen, 1971).

Another major area where the land reform program of 1964 had a strong influence was the tenants' and tenancy regulations. The Nepali government initiated a program to identify the real tenants and grant them formal tenancy certificates – but as it turned out, of the 600,000 tenants, less than half were able register as formal tenants due to the lack of a proper registration system (IDS, 1986). After the implementation of the Land Act 1964, both the number of recorded tenants and the total area under tenancy declined (more about this below). Table 2.1 shows the proportion of tenant households as a portion of the total farm households and area under tenancy as a portion of the total area under cultivation.

As mentioned above, in the first two decades after 1964, the percentage of formal tenant households substantially declined, from 40.4 to 9.5 per cent. Then from 1981 it increased slightly from that very low level. The decrease was largely attributable to the provision of dual ownership of

Table 2.1 Proportion of tenants and area under tenancy (%)

	Year				
Description	**1961**	**1971**	**1981**	**1991**	**2001**
Tenant households	40.4	19.0	9.5	15.9	12.2
Area under tenancy	25.5	15.9	6.2	8.5	8.7

Source: Ministry of Land Reform and Management (2006).

rented land by both landlord and tenant when a formal tenancy was adopted. Furthermore, this provision was later interpreted to mean that the tenant would receive half the tenanted land. The land reform law not only prohibited the eviction of tenants but also restricted the land-owner from selling the land under tenancy because it would be under shared ownership of the landlord and tenant. In consequence, landlords attempted to circumvent the implementation of the Land to the Tiller program – and the share tenancy contracts of poor tenants then became even more insecure than before. This gave rise to informal tenancy, as landlords would make personal agreements through oral contracts with their tenants, for them not to claim tenancy rights (Acharya and Ekelund, 1998). Another reason for the decline in formal tenancy was that most of the tenants were illiterate and were unable to register as a formal tenant within the time limit set by the government; about 560,000 tenants failed to register as formal tenants and so lost any claim to their tenancy rights (Land Watch Asia, 2009).

The provision of sharing the rented land between landlord and tenant increased landlords' tenure insecurity and resulted in them not being amenable to entering into formal tenancy contracts. This encouraged landlords to rely on short-term, informal (mostly verbal) contracts, due to a fear that the tenants might claim tenancy rights. This fear even caused the landlords to keep their land fallow or only partially cultivated, and also increased landlord–tenant disputes. Although the figures are contested, it is estimated that nearly 25 per cent of cultivable land is reported to have been left fallow due to land ownership disputes (Land Watch Asia, 2009).

Although there are no exact records on how much land is under informal tenancy in Nepal (Yadav, 1999), recent studies have claimed that the number of informal tenants surpasses the number of formal tenants (CSRC, 2007; Wily et al., 2008). This has discouraged both landlords and tenants from investing in land improvements. Studies (Pandey, 1993; Yadav, 1999; Wily et al., 2008) show that the land reform in 1964 was largely ineffective in achieving its stated objectives. In essence, there was no significant improvement in land distribution and the land tenure system before 1990, as the country was under an absolute monarchy in which the king was above the law; his close relatives and ardent supporters were often the feudal landlords.

After the political upheavals of 1990, Nepal adopted a multi-party democracy system with a constitutional monarchy, and thus the power of the king was substantially reduced. This political transformation created an opportunity to readdress land reform, and in 1995 a High

Level Land Reform Commission (HLRC) was formed. This commission set up new provisions for tenancy reform, with the target of abolishing tenancy by handing over a share of the rented land to tenants, resulting in a more equitable distribution of land (Wily et al., 2008). Some of the major recommendations made by the commission in relation to land tenure were:

(i) If both landlord and registered tenants are farmers, the land under tenancy will be equally divided between them.
(ii) If the landlord does not farm the entire land, all the land under tenancy will be handed over to the tenant. In this case, the landlord will receive the market value of 50 per cent of the land rented out. If the tenant is unable to purchase the landlord's share of the rented land, it will be sold elsewhere.
(iii) The ceiling of maximum size of ownership landholding should be reduced, so that a family can possess up to 3 ha in Terai, 2 ha in Hills, 4 ha in Mountain, 1 ha in the Kathmandu Valley (but only 0.5 ha in the urban areas of Kathmandu Valley), and 1 ha in all other urban areas.
(iv) The subdivision of land below a minimum farm size should not be allowed, and this would apply even when transferring land to tenants.
(v) Tenancy rights, including the right to receive 50 per cent of rented land, would be given to any farmer who had tilled the land for three consecutive years.
(vi) Tenancy rights would be inheritable.
(vii) Tenancy rights would mostly be granted to marginal farmers.

For the first time ever, the HLRC (1995) also addressed the problem of land fragmentation. The Agriculture Perspective Plan of Nepal, initiated in 1996, also recognized agricultural land fragmentation as one of the major constraints on agricultural development, and recommended taking action toward consolidating land. Although several reforms had been initiated, the governments from 1996 to 2007 were not able to implement most of the policies, as the country was engulfed in the Maoist war.

Since the end of the war, however, land tenure reform has again become a major item on the agenda. The interim constitution of Nepal 2007 has clearly stated that the country will implement a scientific land reform. The difficult question now facing Nepal is: what truly constitutes a scientific land reform?

In the interim, several non-governmental organizations, such as the Community Self-Reliance Centre (CSRC) and Land Watch Asia, have been working on this issue. It is surprising to see that most of them advocate the Land to the Tiller policy as a basic objective, and consider tenancy transactions as inefficient and feudal. However, recent studies in India (Deininger et al., 2008, 2009) and China (Kung, 2002; Deininger and Jin, 2005; Jin and Deininger, 2009) showed the importance of rural land rental markets and claimed that restrictions in the land rental market negatively affect productivity and equity by reducing the scope for rental transactions that improve efficiency. Deininger and Jin (2005) showed that rural land rental markets are more effective in reallocating land than is administrative reallocation, and so improving land rental markets increases productivity.

Land reform needs to be viewed from the broad perspective of agrarian reform rather than just a Land to the Tiller program. For a farmer, land reform may mean precisely that – but for a country, land reform should refer to a fundamental institution-building instrument to strengthen the overall national economy. The success of land reform in East Asia shows that land reform is not in fact a part of any political philosophy; despite this, most of the left-wing parties in Nepal still believe that land reform could be successful only under a strong communist regime (Tiejun and Kinchi, 2008). The formation of appropriate land policies to improve the efficiency of markets, enhance agricultural investment and increase productivity necessitates a critical understanding of the specific rural market imperfections, their effects on access to land, and the way they interact with tenure security (Holden et al., 2008).

The studies on the land reform are often biased against the landlord. It should be clear, however, that not all landlords are feudal. For example, if a household owns land with an area under the limit set by the existing land laws and uses the land rental market rather than directly cultivating its land, is the household a feudal landlord? – or a participant in the land rental market? And if a household head emigrates in order to earn a decent wage (now common in most of the villages in Nepal) and due to the consequent lack of family labor the family rents out its land for some time rather than cultivating it, is that household a feudal landlord? These cases are increasing in rural Nepal and so improving the land rental market could be a better solution than relying primarily on land redistribution policies. The role of land rental market should not be undermined, because a better functioning land rental market provides a poor farmer with the opportunity to climb the agricultural ladder.

2.3 Testable hypotheses

Caste discrimination against Dalits throughout the history of Nepal has created inequality in access to and distribution of economic resources. In the past, the state itself institutionalized caste-based discrimination. Although such discrimination is now outlawed, it still has impacts on the distribution of economic resources such as land. Inequality in asset-holding along with labor market discrimination, especially in regular off-farm employment, may have efficiency implications, given that market imperfections are a feature common to rural areas of Nepal – as indeed in other developing countries. Based on this, we propose the following testable hypotheses:

H1: Low-caste households have a lower land endowment and poor access to skilled off-farm employment, and so are more likely both to rent additional land and to work as agricultural laborers.

H2: Land productivity is higher on the land operated by low-caste households as compared to that of high-caste households (due to discrimination causing high transaction costs and low opportunity cost of labor in the labor market).

H3: Low-caste households are rationed in the land rental market, restricting their access to land.

H4: There is an inverse relationship between land productivity and farm size (IR), caused by caste discrimination (so low-caste households must face high transaction costs in labor and land rental markets).

H5: Low-caste households are too poor to invest in their land, vs. implies that H5 and H6 are opposing hypotheses.

H6: Low-caste households depend more on agricultural production on limited land, and so invest more per unit of land to increase their productivity, and have higher-intensity production.

In order to test these hypotheses, we used the primary data collected in 2003 from 500 households in the Mardi watershed area, situated in the western hills of Nepal. The household survey was carried out in three Village Development Committees[5] (VDCs), namely Lwang-Ghalel, Rivan and Lahachok. The data was collected both at household level and at farm plot level. Therefore, in the case of household level analysis our sample size is 489 households (we dropped 11 households due to certain inconsistency in the data); and for the farm plot level analysis we have 1131 plots. We have collected a wide range of household information as well as biophysical information on farm plots. Table 2.2 presents the total households and their caste distribution, and the sample size of this study.

Table 2.2 Population and sample selection for the study

	Total households		**Caste distribution**		**Sample size**	
VDC	**Number**	**%**	**High (%)**	**Low (%)**	**Number**	**%**
Lahachok	721	36.2	77.8	22.2	177	35.4
Rivan	334	16.8	85.5	14.5	83	16.6
Lwang-Ghalel	935	47.0	77.0	23.0	240	48.0
Total	1990	100	80.1	19.9	500	100

Source: VDC office and field study (2003).

Notes: We have divided all households into high caste and low caste for the analysis. High-caste households include Brahmins, Chhetries, and ethnic groups (Gurung and Magar), whereas low-caste households include all Dalits (Damai, Sarki, Gandharva and Kami).

We made a complete list of all households in the study area using the information obtained from the Village Development Committee office. Then, the 25 per cent of the total households were selected randomly as sample households for this study. Data was collected using a structured questionnaire, which was pre-tested in a study village. After an intensive training during the pre-testing of the questionnaire, local school teachers were deployed as enumerators. For details, we refer to the study by Aryal (2011).

2.4 Caste discrimination, and its implications for land market performance and land productivity

In our study villages of western Nepal, the caste status of the household was found to have been associated with several factors: land ownership, land rental market participation, labor market access and participation, investment behaviour on land conservation, intensity of cropping, and land productivity. Table 2.3 presents some of the major household characteristics variables by caste.

From Table 2.3, it is clear that the average ownership land holding is 0.64 ha in the case of high-caste households, while it is only 0.17 ha in low-caste households. But by participating in the land rental market, low-caste households are able to increase their operational holding to 0.35 ha. In general, low-caste households have a lower land endowment and poor access to skilled off-farm employment, and so are more likely to rent in additional land, and work as agricultural laborers. Table 2.4 shows the land rental and agricultural labor market participation of the sample households by caste.

Table 2.3 Major household characteristics variables by caste

Variables	High caste	Low caste	All sample	Test
Number of households	382	107	489	–
Ownership land holding (in ha)	0.64	0.17	0.53	8.83***
Operational land holding (in ha)	0.63	0.35	0.56	5.86***
Male head dummy (in %)	20	65	30	82.72***
Literate head (in %)	35	19	31	10.40***
Farm income (in Rs.)	32035	15312	28376	5.57***
Remittance income (in Rs.)	20127	3449	16478	4.41***
Total income (in Rs.)	72360	30928	63294	8.02***
Value of asset (in Rs.)	38581	15173	33459	8.29***
Agricultural wage employment (unskilled) (in %)	12.3	69.8	24.94	7.16***
Non-agricultural wage employment (unskilled) (in %)	34.2	25.6	32.31	3.78***
Regular salary jobs (at least one member) (in %)	41.3	9.2	26.58	5.71***
At least one member earning pension (in %)	26.7	5.6	22.09	3.96***

Source: Authors' survey data.

Notes: Test shows the difference between high-caste and low-caste households; t-test is used for continuous variables and chi-square test for categorical variables. In all employment variables, we refer to households that have participated in a particular employment type. Regular salary jobs include the jobs both in and outside the country. Significance levels: *** $p<0.01$, ** $p<0.05$, * $p<0.1$.

Table 2.4 Land rental and agricultural labor market participation of sample households

	Land rental market											
	High-caste households						Low-caste households					
	Landlord		Non-participant		Tenant		Landlord		Non-participant		Tenant	
Agricultural labor market	No.	%	No.	%	No.	%	No.	%	No.	%	No.	%
Net seller	0	0	21	5.5	22	5.7	4	3.7	37	34.6	48	44.9
Non-participant	48	12.6	50	13.1	13	3.4	2	1.9	8	7.5	5	4.7
Net buyer	28	7.3	171	44.8	29	7.6	0	0	3	2.8	0	0
Total	76	19.9	242	63.4	64	16.8	6	5.7	48	44.9	53	49.5

Source: Authors' survey data.

From Table 2.4, we can see that nearly 50 per cent of the low-caste households are tenants, while about 83 per cent hire their members out as agricultural labor. Typically, the agricultural labor market still exhibits the caste-based hierarchy: it is low-caste household members that largely work as agricultural laborers. The results in Tables 2.3 and 2.4 support hypothesis H1 above.

Against this backdrop, we assessed how caste-related differences in land productivity are associated with caste-related differences in endowments and market access (Aryal and Holden, 2011b). In order to examine this, we compared the land productivity:

(i) on the owner-operated land of low-caste households vs. owner-operated land of high-caste households and
(ii) on the owner-operated land of high-caste households vs. rented-in land of low-caste households.

The results showed that in both cases low-caste households have higher land productivity than high-caste households, and thus hypothesis H2 cannot be rejected. Low-caste households, meanwhile, are found to have significantly higher land productivity on their owner-operated (28 per cent higher) and sharecropped-in (21 per cent higher) land than the owner-operated land of the high-caste households. Table 2.5 presents the results.

Table 2.5 Land productivity difference by caste

Variable	Kernel matching	Variable	Kernel matching
Land productivity		**Land productivity**	
Owner-operated plots – low caste	81834.46	Rented-in plots – low caste	77139.9
Owner-operated plots – high caste	63783.15	Owner-operated plots – high caste	63783.2
Difference	18051.31	Difference	13410.7
Standard error	6601.92	Standard error	4966.3
t-statistic	2.73***	t-statistic	2.71***
Number of observations		**Number of observations**	
Owner-operated plots – low caste	99	Rented-in plots – low caste	94
Owner-operated plots – high caste	639	Owner-operated plots – high caste	646

Note: Significance levels: *** $p<0.01$, ** $p<0.05$, * $p<0.1$.

In addition, we did not find significant Marshallian inefficiency (measured as the land productivity difference between owner-operated and rented-in land of the same household) in the case of low-caste tenants (the result of the propensity score-matching method is reported in Table 2.6 below).

In order to gain a deeper understanding of the phenomena, we jointly assessed the association between Marshallian inefficiency, allocative inefficiency of the land rental market, and IR; then we attempted to examine how caste discrimination could influence these phenomena (Aryal and Holden, 2010). For this analysis, we have been inspired by the research gap identified by Otsuka (2007) in his review of the empirical literatures on share tenancy, allocative inefficiency of land rental markets, the IR and land-related investment. His review revealed that most studies have focused independently on only one of these issues, although they are closely related, and a joint study of these would lead to a deeper understanding.

Table 2.6 presents the results of the assessment of Marshallian inefficiency. From Table 2.6, it is clear that Marshallian inefficiency was significant only in the case of high-caste tenants.

We got similar findings from a fixed-effects model even after controlling for plot quality differences and plot selection bias. The results are presented in Table 2.7.

We tested the IR after controlling for the influences of the Marshallian disincentives for owner–tenants (for details on the methods to achieve this, see Aryal and Holden, 2011b). The results are presented in Table 2.8.

Table 2.6 Assessment of Marshallian inefficiency (kernel matching)

Land productivity	**All households**	**Low caste**	**High caste**
Rented-in plots	56936.9	67456.6	53700.6
Owner-operated plots	65207.1	69920.8	62823.2
Difference	–8270.2	–2464.2	–9122.6
Bootstrapped std. error	4164.2	9277.1	3455.5
t-statistic	–1.98**	–0.27	–2.64***
Number of observations			
Owner-operated plots	56	20	36
Rented-in plots	136	32	104

Notes: Number of observations reduced as we included only owner–tenant households. Significance levels: *** $p<0.01$, ** $p<0.05$, * $p<0.1$.

Table 2.7 Assessment of Marshallian inefficiency (household fixed-effects models)

	All households		**Low caste**		**High caste**	
Total value product/ha	**w/o IMR**	**IMR**	**w/o IMR**	**IMR**	**w/o IMR**	**IMR**
Tenure dummy (rent in = 1)	–0.180**	–0.182**	–0.045	–0.036	–0.233**	–0.209*
IMR (plot)		–0.018		–0.592		0.132
Joint test for plot quality variables	15.65***	7.40***	22.65***	16.58***	78.35***	334.60***
Constant	11.43***	11.44***	11.43***	11.30***	11.41***	11.30***
Number of observations	217	217	52	52	165	165

Notes: Significance levels: *** $p<0.01$, ** $p<0.05$, * $p<0.1$. All continuous variables are in logarithms. IMR refers to inverse mills ratio and we report bootstrapped standard errors for models with IMR. We resampled households (bootstrapped with replications 500) in order to get corrected standard errors. F-test results are used in fixed-effects models (without IMR) while chi-square are used in the bootstrapped models (with IMR). The number of households in this analysis was reduced due to the exclusion of pure tenant households; out of 117 tenant households, this left 71 available for analysis.

Table 2.8 shows that the IR remains and is strongly associated with caste discrimination even after controlling for Marshallian inefficiency; thus hypothesis H4 cannot be rejected. This indicates that caste discrimination and high transaction costs in land and labor markets, rather than Marshallian inefficiency, are likely to be the most important explanations for the IR. Table 2.8 also shows that participation in the labor market did not eliminate the IR, demonstrating that participants in the labor market also faced adjustment costs (non-linear transaction costs) in this market. This also indicates that members of low-caste groups may face higher transaction costs in off-farm labor markets and are thus compelled to work on their farm or work as an agricultural laborer in the village.

We analyzed the land rental market participation of the households using double hurdle (Cragg) models. The results are shown in Table 2.9. A smooth adjustment in the land rental market implies that, in the truncated models, the coefficient on owned land should be close to -1 in the case of tenants, while it should be close to +1 for landlords. From Table 2.9, we see that the coefficient on own land for tenant households

Table 2.8 Analysis of the relationship between fixed-effects error component, farm size, caste dummy and labor market participation

Fixed-effect error component	Model 1	Model 2	Model 3	Model 4	Model 5	Model 6
Farm size	−0.535**	−0.341	−0.549**	−0.320	−0.585**	−0.276
Low-caste dummy (1)		0.319***		0.345***		0.348***
Labor market participation (1= seller)			−0.046	0.047	−0.045	0.072
Labor market participation (1= buyer)			−0.119	0.046	−0.177	0.065
Labor buyer dummy*farm size					−0.009	−0.095
Labor seller dummy*farm size					0.236	−0.070
Constant	0.132**	0.005	0.185**	−0.033	0.194**	−0.046
Number of observations	217	217	217	217	217	217
Number of groups	70	70	70	70	70	70
Chi² statistic	5.92**	34.97***	9.10**	35.03***	10.35**	36.12***

Notes: Significance levels: *** $p<0.01$, ** $p<0.05$, * $p<0.1$. Standard errors corrected for clustering at household level.

in the truncated model is -0.126 – well away from -1 – while for land rented out, the coefficient is 0.765 – also significantly smaller than +1. This indicates that there are significant transaction costs limiting adjustment on both sides of the land rental market, but stronger on the tenant side of the market; thus, hypothesis H3 cannot be rejected. On including an interaction variable for caste and farm size, this variable became highly significant and positive, showing that landless or very land-poor, low-caste households face even higher transaction costs in the land rental market and can access even less land. This is probably related to a stronger fear that such households can claim the land they rent in, in the spirit of the Land to the Tiller policies.

Returning to the farm size-productivity relationship, we show in Figure 2.1 the differences in productivity by caste and farm size. While in the low-caste households there was no significant difference in productivity between the owner-operated and rented-in plots, in the high-caste households the rented-in plots had significantly lower land productivity than the owner-operated ones.

This leads to a query: why do many high-caste households still rent out land to other high-caste households, even though low-caste tenants

Table 2.9 Assessment of the allocative efficiency of the land rental market

	Land rented in (Yes = 1)				Land rented out (Yes =1)	
	Probit models		**Truncated models**		**Probit model**	**Truncated model**
Owned land (ha)	–1.752***	–1.918***	–0.126**	–0.207***	1.213***	0.765***
Male head dummy (1)	0.219	0.240	0.105*	0.123**	–0.234	–0.112
Literate head dummy (1)	0.089	0.089	–0.085	–0.073	–0.077	–0.122*
Number of adult males	0.215	0.238	0.191***	0.201***	0.139	–0.055
Oxen holding	0.581***	0.580***	0.082***	0.084***	–0.663***	–0.137***
Low-caste dummy (1)	0.724***	0.467	–0.154**	–0.247***	–0.397	0.369**
Village dummy (1= Lahachok)	–0.375*	–0.352	0.064	0.077	–0.874***	0.256***
Village dummy (1= Rivan)	–0.071	–0.038	–0.042	–0.015	–0.495**	0.308***
Share of irrigated land	0.458**	0.539**	0.059	0.076*	–0.219***	0.006
Caste *farm size		1.421		0.717***		
Number of observations	407	407	117	117	372	82
Chi^2 statistic	245.7***	247.1***	73.1***	84.5***	102.5***	98.8***
Log likelihood of double hurdles	–81.35				–111.7	

Notes: Significance levels: *** $p<0.01$, ** $p<0.05$, * $p<0.1$. All continuous variables are in logarithms. Censored Tobit models for each side of the land rental market were estimated and tested against double hurdle models, and the likelihood ratio tests favored the double hurdle models.
The results of the censored Tobit model can be obtained from the authors upon request. We did not report (but included in our estimation) the coefficients for variables like number of adult females and average distance to plot, as these are not significant in all models.
To reduce the size of the table, we did not report all insignificant coefficients.

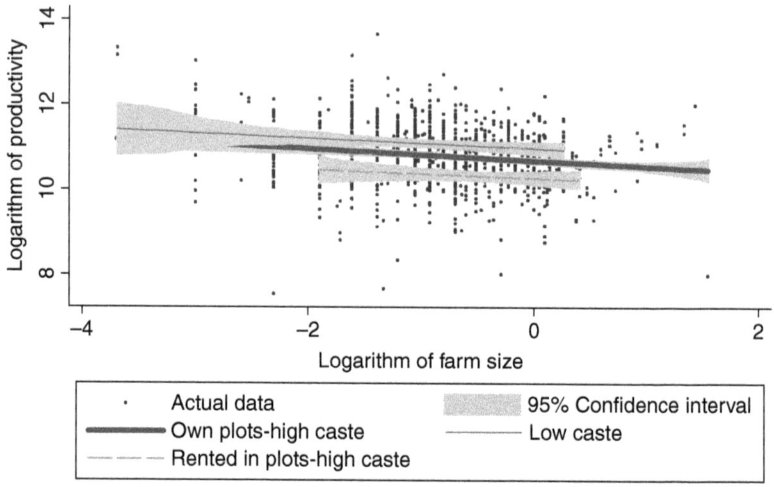

Figure 2.1 Analysis of the farm size–productivity relationship using local polynomial regression

are more productive? The most plausible reason might be the fear of land loss due to the past Land to the Tiller policy, aggravated by the Maoist penchant for the same policy. Therefore, landlords want to minimize the risk of losing land by renting out to the households on the lower social scale (Bhandari, 2007).

Low-caste owner–tenant households had higher land productivity than high-caste owner–tenant households – even after controlling for farm size and other household and farm characteristics and adjustment for labor and land rental market participation. A strong and significant IR was found for high-caste households, whereas low-caste households are land-poor; they apply more labor per unit of land, and thus achieve higher land productivity on rented-in land as well, due to their poorer access to off-farm employment and the transaction costs faced in the land rental market. So policies that can reduce the transaction costs in land and labor markets may reduce the level of caste discrimination and lead to more efficient resource allocation. In order to improve the efficiency of the land rental market, there is a need to remove the Land to the Tiller policy, especially the provision that a tenant can claim ownership rights on a certain percentage of rented land. This will reduce tenure insecurity among landlords, and thus increase tenants' access to land through the land rental market.

It will also reduce conflicts between landlords and tenants. However, there is a need to redistribute land from the less efficient to the more efficient farmers, and this can be done peacefully by imposing a progressive land tax by means of which to induce land sales by large land owners. Furthermore, the government should establish a land bank where a poor farmer can receive a loan to purchase land at a subsidized rate.

The findings that both Marshallian inefficiency and the IR are stronger for high-caste households, while low-caste households are found to have higher land productivity in general, might be due to the lower opportunity cost of labor. These findings thus raised the question: How are these differences between low-caste and high-caste households related to the differences in investment and the intensity of production?

In order to answer this question, we assessed the impact of caste discrimination in resource and market access on investment and intensity of production (Aryal and Holden, 2011a). In Nepal, resource poverty is one of the consequences of caste discrimination. Low-caste households are therefore land-poor, and this can have direct effects on their willingness and ability to invest in their land. However, caste discrimination in the labor market and in the education system may also affect the opportunity cost of labor as well as the ability to invest in human capital. Then, higher land scarcity combined with lower opportunity cost of time due to labor market discrimination may cause low-caste households to concentrate more of their investments on their limited land resources – unless, that is, they are too poor to invest. As we linked the caste issue with poverty, the major research question is whether or not low-caste households invest more than high-caste households. We therefore studied how the investment and intensity of production differ between high-caste and low-caste households by analyzing the differences in short-term investments (in terms of fertilizer and manure) and longer-term investments (in terms of terrace maintenance expenses and intensity of cropping). Table 2.10 summarizes the major results of the empirical analysis.

Table 2.10 showed that low-caste households are more likely to apply manure to land. The likelihoods of using fertilizer and adopting conservation investment were not significantly different between low-caste and high-caste households. However, the amount of fertilizer used was significantly lower among the low-caste households; intensity of fertilizer use was positively associated with farm size, indicating that land-rich households invest in labor-saving inputs like fertilizer

Table 2.10 Determinants of the probabilities and level of fertilizer, manure and conservation investment

	Fertilizer		Manure		Conservation	
	Probability	Level	Probability	Level	Probability	Level
Low-caste dummy (1)	–0.253	–0.212**	0.519**	0.028	–0.032	–0.049
Plot size	0.033	–0.455***	0.100	–0.707***	0.368***	–0.701***
Farm size	0.069	0.155**	0.111	–0.064	0.086	–0.043
Male head dummy (1)	–0.108	0.020	0.093	0.561***	0.177	0.565***
Male labor per ha	–0.041	0.104**	0.061	0.205***	0.214**	0.105**
Female labor per ha	0.152	–0.047	0.045	0.212***	–0.195**	–0.027
Distance to plot	0.107**	0.027	–0.411***	–0.246***	–0.140***	–0.033
Livestock owned	–0.135***	–0.052***	0.249***	0.089***	0.094***	0.027
Off-farm access dummy (1)	0.051	–0.085	0.004	0.062	–0.275***	0.069
Labor market dummy (buyer)	0.304***	0.064	–0.024	0.047	–0.219**	–0.022
Labor market dummy(seller)	0.089	–0.093	–0.037	–0.028	–0.010	0.008
JCT (land quality variables)	152.1***	24.8***	19.1**	15.9**	98.5***	34.5***
Number of observations	990	563	990	716	990	544
Number of groups	489	369	489	424	489	377
Chi^2 statistic	205.1***	227.8***	88.9***	614.7***	144.5***	693.7***

Notes: Significance levels: *** $p<0.01$, ** $p<0.05$, * $p<0.1$. DH refers to double hurdle model. JCT refers to joint chi-square test of all land quality variables including slope dummies, soil type, soil depth, and irrigation status of the plot. To reduce the size of the table, not all the non-significant coefficients in the models are shown.

whereas low-caste households, with relatively low opportunity cost of labor, invest more in labor-intensive inputs such as manure. Hypothesis H5, that low-caste households are too poor to invest in their land, cannot be rejected in the case of fertilizer use, while it is rejected in the case of manure use. Households with access to off-farm employment were less likely to invest in land conservation. In addition, male-headed households, and households with more male labor endowment relative to ownership land holding, were found to invest more in land conservation. Low-caste households were found to have higher cropping intensity than high-caste households, indicating that land-poor but labor-rich households intensify their production by growing more crops per year (Aryal and Holden, 2011a). The figures also indicate that land-poor households rely primarily on intensification when it is difficult to expand agricultural land, and thus hypothesis H6 cannot be partly rejected.

The major limitation of our study was that we were unable to explicitly analyze the effects of the Maoist war on tenure insecurity; because our survey took place during the Maoist war there was high degree of risk involved, and a consequent inability to ask questions on this topic.

2.5 Conclusion and recommendations

Low-caste households remain poorer than high-caste households in terms of income as well as holding of other economic assets such as land and livestock. Furthermore, due to a lack of education, family networks and the presence of caste-based discrimination, low-caste households participate less in regular off-farm employment. The initial distribution of land is not only inequitable but also biased against the low-caste households. Moreover, the effect of caste on the land productivity differential is explained by historical, socio-economic and political structure that shaped the differences in access to land and regular off-farm employment. Limited opportunities outside the farming sector have forced low-caste households to concentrate their labor on farming on their own small plots or the limited land that they are able to rent in.

The productivity differential between high-caste and low-caste households remains significant even after the participation of households in the land rental market. An IR is observed; high transactions costs in the land rental market and caste discrimination are the main causes of the IR identified in the study area. This result suggests that the land rental market needs to be improved, and caste-based discrimination reduced, in order to enhance land productivity. In addition, this result calls for land redistribution to enhance land productivity.

Many high-caste landlords are found to have rented out land to other high-caste households despite the fact that low-caste tenants farm more efficiently. This indicates that the inefficiency of share tenancy is more likely to be a consequence of the tenure insecurity created by the Maoist war and the Land to the Tiller policy that they advocate rather than any inherent difficulty in enforcing contractual terms under share tenancy.

Based on this, three major recommendations are made:

i. *Market-assisted Land Redistribution:* Our findings on the IR validate a need for land redistribution. This is necessary because improving the land rental market alone cannot rectify the fundamental inequity arising from the unequal distribution of land throughout history. The following changes are recommended for successful land redistribution in Nepal:

(a) change the ceilings of ownership holding;
(b) progressive land tax;
(c) establish a land bank;
(d) improve land administration system; and
(e) facilitate market-assisted land distribution through the above measures.

ii. *Improving the land rental market:* The change in household labor force and participation in off/farm activities, especially in remittance earning activities can change a household's ability to operate land and create a need for rental transactions. Under such a situation, restricting the land rental market leads to more fallowing or less intensive use of agricultural land. Therefore, setting clear rules for land tenancy transactions improves the efficiency of land use rather than abolishing land tenancy transactions. Nepal should learn from recent experiences in China and Vietnam, where the removal of land tenancy restrictions contributed in transferring land to more productive and land-poor farmers in a more effective way than could otherwise be achieved with administrative redistribution of land or the Land to the Tiller policies (World Bank, 2003).

   1. To improve the land rental market, the following changes are necessary in present land laws in Nepal:

(a) Removal of the dual ownership of land which was introduced in the Land Act of 1964;
(b) Remove the provision that a tenant can claim ownership rights on rented land; and
(c) Remove the restrictions on the amount of land involved in tenancy transactions.

2. Together, these reforms should increase tenure security and improve land access for land-poor and more efficient producers.

iii. *Reduce caste-based discrimination:* There is a need to address the sources of caste discrimination. The constitution has already formally abolished caste discrimination, therefore, awareness in society should be intensified by providing free education to the poor, and especially to low-caste people. Access to education and training programs can improve their long-term income and hence enable them to buy more land. In addition, special land reforms targeting Dalits can be carried out as they are among the very poor and landless. As Dalits have become more aware of their rights recently, there is a very real possibility of a Dalit uprising, as in India. Therefore, it is better to investigate feasible options for land reform, as was done in the case of the *Kamaiya* (bonded labor) system in Nepal (Hatlebakk, 2007).

Overall, land reforms need to be integrated with the overriding objective of poverty alleviation and increasing productivity rather than radicalizing it. Structure of the society including caste discrimination, access to land and other markets, and caste-related social exclusion need to be analyzed carefully to design a policy that can address the problems associated with the land tenure system in Nepal.

Notes

1. Land granted by the state to individuals, usually on an inheritance basis. Such land was tax-exempt.
2. State land assigned to government employees in lieu of salaries.
3. Land owned by the state.
4. The low-lying plains south of the Himalayan foothills, bordering India.
5. A Village Development Committee (VDC) is the administrative unit at the village level. Each VDC consists of nine wards.

References

Acharya, R.N. and Ekelund, J.R.B. (1998) 'Mixed and Pure Sharecropping in Nepal: Empirical Evidence Supporting the Traditional Hypothesis', *Applied Economics*, 30, 37–50

Aryal, J.P. (2011) 'Caste Discrimination, Land Tenure, and Natural Resource Management in Nepal', Department of Economics and Resource Management. Norwegian University of Life Sciences, Ås.

Aryal, J.P. and Holden, S.T. (2009) 'Caste and Land Productivity in Rural Nepal', Nordic Conference in Development Economics, 18–19 June 2009, Oscarberg, Norway.

Aryal, J.P. and Holden, S.T. (2010) 'Caste, Marshallian Inefficiency, and the Farm Size-Productivity Relationship', Department of Economics and Resource Management. Norwegian University of Life Sciences, Ås.

Aryal, J.P. and Holden, S.T. (2011a) 'Caste, Investment and Intensity of Production', 18th Annual Conference of the European Association of Environmental and Resource Economists (EAERE), 29 June–2 July 2011, Rome, Italy.

Aryal, J.P. and Holden, S.T. (2011b) 'Caste, Land and Labor Market Imperfections, and Land Productivity in Rural Nepal', Department of Economics and Resource Management, Norwegian University of Life Sciences, Ås, Norway.

Banerjee, B. and Knight, J.B. (1985) 'Caste discrimination in the Indian Urban Labour Market', *Journal of Development Economics*, 17(3), 277–307.

Bhandari, R. (2006) 'Searching for a Weapon of Mass Production: The Case of Market-Assisted Land Reforms in Nepal', International Conference on 'Land, Poverty, Social Justice and Development', 9–14 January 2006. Institute of Social Studies (ISS), The Hague, The Netherlands.

Bhandari, R. (2007) 'The Role of Social Distance in Sharecropping Efficiency: The Case of Two Rice-Growing Villages in Nepal', *Journal of Economic Studies*, 34(4), 290–310.

CHRGJ (2005) 'The Missing Piece of Puzzle: Caste Discrimination and the Conflict of Nepal', Center for Human Rights and Global Justice.

CSRC (2007) 'Reflections: Land Rights Movements in Nepal', Community Self-Reliance Centre (CSRC), Kathmandu.

Dahal, D.R. (1995) 'Ethnic Couldron, Demography and Minority Politics: The Case of Nepal', in D. Kumar (ed.), *States, Leadership and Politics of Nepal* (Centre for Nepal and Asian Studies (CNAS), Kathmandu).

Deininger, K. and Jin, S. (2005) 'The Potential of Land Rental Markets in the Process of Economic Development: Evidence from China', *Journal of Development Economics*, 78, 241–70.

Deininger, K., Jin, S. and Nagarajan, H.K. (2008) 'Efficiency and Equity Impacts of Rural Land Rental Restrictions: Evidence from India', *European Economic Review*, 52, 892–918.

Deininger, K., Jin, S. and Nagarajan, H.K. (2009) 'Determinants and Consequences of Land Sales Market Participation: Panel Evidence from India', *World Development*, 37(2), 410–21.

DFID, World Bank (2006) 'Unequal Citizens: Gender, Caste and Ethnic Exclusion in Nepal', Department for International Development (DFID) and The World Bank (WB), Kathmandu.

Hatlebakk, M. (2007) 'Economic and Social Structures That May Explain the Recent Conflicts in the Terai of Nepal', CMI, Bergen, Norway.

Hatlebakk, M. (2008) 'Inclusive Growth in Nepal', CMI, Bergen, Norway.

Haug, M., Aasland, A. and Dahal, D.R. (2009) 'Patterns of Socio-Political Participation in Nepal and Implications for Social Inclusion', *The Nordic Journal of Development Research*, 36(1), 105–36.

Holden, S.T., Otsuka, K. and Place, F.M. (eds) (2008) *The Emergence of Land Markets in Africa: Assessing the Impacts on Poverty, Equity, and Efficiency* (Washington D.C.: Resources for the Future (RFF)).
IDS (1986) 'Study on Land Tenure System of Nepal', Integrated Development Systems (IDS), Kathmandu.
Jin, S. and Deininger, K. (2009) 'Land Rental Markets in the Process of Rural Structural Transformation: Productivity and Equity Impacts from China', *Journal of Comparative Economics*, 37(4), 629–46.
Jolly, J. (2009) 'Growing Fragility of Nepal's Peace Process', BBC News. British Broadcasting Corporation (BBC), News, Kathmandu.
Joshi, M. and Mason, T.D. (2008) 'Between Democracy and Revolution: Peasant Support or Insurgency versus Democracy in Nepal', *Journal of Peace Research*, 45(6), 765–82.
Kuhnen, F. (1971) 'Land Tenure and Agrarian Reform in Asia: A Re-appraisal of Priorities in Agrarian Re-organization for Rural Development', Asian Regional Seminar on the Contribution of Rural Institutions to Rural Development, Particularly Employment, 3–16 November 1971. International Labor Organization, New Delhi, pp. 162–182.
Kung, J.K.S. (2002) 'Off-farm Labor Markets and the Emergence of Land Rental Markets in Rural China', *Journal of Comparative Economics*, 30(2), 395–414.
Land Watch Asia (2009) 'Asserting Freedom from Central Control: Nepal Country Paper', Land Watch Asia.
Murshed, S.M. and Gates, S. (2005) 'Spatial-Horizontal Inequality and the Maoist Insurgency in Nepal', *Review of Development Economics*, 9, 121–34.
Otsuka, K. (2007) 'Efficiency and Equity Effects of Land Markets', in R. Evenson and P. Pingali (eds), *Handbook of Agricultural Economics* (Amsterdam: Elsevier).
Otsuka, K., Chuma, H. and Hayami, Y. (1992) 'Land and Labor Contracts in Agrarian Economies: Theories and Facts', *Journal of Economic Literature*, 30(4), 1965–2018.
Pandey, T.R. (1993) 'The Failure of Confidence Mechanism: Reflections on the 1990's Social Change Movement in the Light of Policy Measures Affecting Farming System in Nepal', *Occasional Papers in Sociology and Anthropology*, 3, 96–127.
Regmi, M.C. (1976) *Landownership in Nepal* (Berkeley: University of California Press).
Tiejun, W. and Kinchi, L. (2008) 'Land Reform and National Development in Nepal', Land Research Action Network.
UNDP (2008) 'The Dalits of Nepal and a New Constitution. A Resource on the Situation of Dalits in Nepal, Their Demands and the Implications for a New Constitution', United Nations Development Programme, Kathmandu.
Wily, L.A., Chapagain, D. and Sharma, S. (2008) 'Land Reform in Nepal: Where Is It Coming from and Where Is It Going?' DFID Nepal.
World Bank (2003) 'Land Policies for Growth and Poverty Reduction', A World Bank Policy Research Report. The World Bank and Oxford University Press.
Yadav, R.P. (1999) 'Land Tenure Situation in Nepal', HMG Ministry of Agriculture/ Winrock International Kathmandu, Nepal.

3

Does Sharecropping Affect Long-term Investment? Evidence from West Bengal's Tenancy Reforms

Klaus Deininger, Songqing Jin and Vandana Yadav

3.1 Introduction

In India, land reform has been high on the political agenda since independence in 1947, and early efforts at abolishing intermediaries are widely credited with having brought about significant social benefits. The most prominent type is tenancy reform. As it does not extinguish landlords' ownership rights, tenants – who may have benefited from rent ceilings and cannot be evicted – still have to pay annual share rent. This weakness of rights may fail to create the incentives for effort supply and long-term investment that have underpinned the success of land reforms elsewhere, effectively adding a dynamic inefficiency to the disincentives created by the Marshallian inefficiency of sharecropping. This could imply that despite the high political price of implementing land reform in India, the schemes so far have failed to reach their productivity and poverty reduction potential.

To explore this issue empirically, we used a 2008/9 survey of more than 9,000 parcels in 200 villages from 10 West Bengal districts. These are owned by some 2000 owner-cum-tenants who had benefited from tenancy reforms which the state had implemented during the late 1970s and early 1980s. The production data relating to plots allowed us to explore the extent to which productivity from land reform plots differs from that of owned plots within the same household. We also assessed whether, beyond the traditional effects of share tenancy, limits on tenants' ownership rights – in particular the fact that part of the return from any investment will be transferred to the landlord as a higher share rent – reduce incentives for investment in soil conservation and irrigation. A complete listing of all 90,000 households in the survey villages allowed us to put the findings in perspective and provides the necessary context.

In line with results from earlier studies of sharecropping in India, we find that levels of non-contractible input use as well as output are significantly lower on tenanted as compared to owned plots in the same household. The size of this inefficiency ranges between 14 and 16 percentage points for gross and net revenue, respectively. Beyond this, holding land under tenancy rather than full ownership reduces investment incentives; tenanted plots are 26 percent less likely to have received labor-intensive investment in land improvements during the last eight years, and 7 percent less likely to have private irrigation investment attached to them. A lower bound estimate for the total output loss due to tenancy is thus close to 20 percent. Even if it were to involve paying an amount equivalent to current levels of share rent forever to the landlord, a transfer of full land ownership to current users could thus generate significant social benefits and might be implementable without large public subsidies.

Our findings are related to and contribute to two strands of literature. First, our study suggests that notwithstanding the enormous social advances permitted by West Bengal's tenancy reform, it falls short of its potential by a significant margin, consistent with a drop in agricultural growth following the spurt of the 1980s and early 1990s. Second, while a number of recent studies found little evidence of a Marshallian inefficiency, in West Bengal the reform-induced imposition of sharecropping as the only legal form of land leasing leads to a static as well as a dynamic inefficiency. This could be because effective enforcement of anti-eviction laws deprives landlords of the possibility of using eviction threats as an incentive device, while incomplete property rights by tenants limit incentives for investment. Although restrictions on beneficiaries' rights in West Bengal may be more far-reaching than in other contexts, many land reforms provided only incomplete property rights. Our results suggest that by affecting beneficiaries' ability to put the assets they received to productive use, such restrictions will affect not only recipients' welfare but also reduce the effectiveness with which a key productive resource is used by society. Even if the provision of restricted rights might have been necessary to make redistributive land reforms feasible politically, the removal of such restrictions may be an easy way to improve the productivity and welfare of some of the most disadvantaged groups.

This chapter is organized as follows. Section 3.2 sets the stage by highlighting the economic motivation for land reform as a means to eliminate obstacles to investment, describing cases where such a policy was implemented with some success, and reviewing land reform policies and evidence of their impact in India and West Bengal. Section 3.3 lays out the econometric approach and descriptive evidence from the listing and the detailed household survey that forms the basis for our analysis. Section 3.4 provides econometric results on the productivity and investment effects of sharecropping for owner-cum-tenants, and Section 3.5 concludes by drawing out implications for policy and research.

3.2 Background and relation to the literature

Land reform can be justified socially if it increases investment by allowing access to credit markets in situations where credit market imperfections are combined with the need for lumpy investments. Alternatively, land reforms can break privileged access to political institutions. A number of examples illustrate the scope for swift implementation of land reforms measures to generate positive long-term impacts in ways that capitalize on market forces. In India, land reforms have been meaningfully implemented in only a few states, including West Bengal. Impact studies largely use aggregate data and focus on the change brought about by reform instead of the extent to which it lived up to its potential and stimulated investment.

3.2.1 Land reform: economic justification and empirical evidence

Recent years have seen a significant increase in attention paid to the initial distribution of resources and political power role as key determinants of institutional development, with far-reaching impacts on socio-economic and human development (Acemoglu and Johnson, 2005; Nunn, 2009). In India, differences in historical institutions led to very different policy choices, so that the areas where landlords had the proprietary rights to the land were characterized by vastly lower agricultural productivity and growth – as well as lower investments in health and education growth – than those areas where such rights continued to be held by their cultivators (Banerjee and Iyer, 2005; Iyer, 2010).

Credit market constraints in the presence of indivisible investments, for example in education or for starting up a business, can be a key reason for persistence of inefficient outcomes (Banerjee and Newman, 1993; Galor and Zeira, 1993; Vollrath, 2009). With such constraints, the wealth distribution at any one time determines the shares of individuals who can access credit and thus invest in lumpy inputs. This may in turn affect equilibrium returns to different types of occupations and, through intergenerational transfers, the distribution of wealth in future generations, creating the possibility of multiple steady-state distributions and path dependence (Ghatak and Jiang, 2002).

Inequality of land ownership may contribute to destructive tensions and social strife that can directly and indirectly undermine the basis of economic growth (Conning and Robinson, 2007) or increase the cost of distributional conflict (Hidalgo et al., 2010). If this is correct, land reform could have significant long-term benefits in terms of accumulation of physical and human capital in an economy (Gersbach and Siemers, 2010). This could be through a one-time redistribution of assets, or more broadly through an increase in bargaining power (Mookherjee and Ray, 2002), for example via institutional changes that increase the ability of hitherto excluded groups to make their voice heard politically. In practice, a number of land reforms have been credited with not only redistributing land but also setting in motion a self-reinforcing virtuous cycle of higher productivity and investment that can have significant direct and indirect benefits for the poor (Lipton, 2009).

The impact of rapid and decisively implemented land reform on the facilitation of subsequent industrial growth in Taiwan (King, 1977), Korea (Jeon and Kim, 2000), and Japan (Kawagoe, 1999) is well established. In some cases with less favorable circumstances, significant impacts are reported as well. For example in the Philippines, contemporaneous improvements in technology allowed former tenants to gain enormous benefits by adopting green revolution technology, driving a wedge between the value of land and designated land rent or amortization fees (Otsuka, 1991). There was also the case of Chile, where the 1958 introduction of a secret ballot precipitated far-reaching changes in voting behavior that helped the reform of land relations (Baland and Robinson, 2008). Localities with strong patron–client relationships had more support for traditional right-wing parties before the reform than after it.

Even where land reform has led to very positive outcomes in the short term, longer-term impacts depend on efforts being sustained and beneficiaries receiving rights that are sufficient both to provide incentives for investment and to allow them access to the credit market. An inability to sustain efforts has compromised some of the initial benefits from land reform, in cases such as Kenya and Guatemala. A number of studies also make the point that restrictions on the type of rights they received will affect beneficiaries' ability to use the land and thus productivity; for example, the fact that early reforms in Zimbabwe provided use-only rights limited the investment incentives (Deininger et al., 2004). In Latin American countries, the fact that peasants received land under restricted tenure rather than full ownership has been interpreted as a way of favoring élites (Diaz, 2000), and it greatly reduced positive reform impacts in the long term (World Bank, 2002). In the Philippines, having banks subject to strict land ceilings made it impossible for them to foreclose, thereby creating negative externalities beyond reform beneficiaries by limiting credit supply to the entire agricultural sector (Fabella, 2003). India also restricts land reform beneficiaries' rights, and rigorous study of associated welfare and productivity implications is desirable.

3.2.2 Land reform in India

To overcome land inequality and economic stratification inherited from the colonial masters, land reform was high on the agenda from the earliest days of India's post-independence government. Three areas were identified, namely

(i) abolition of intermediaries (*zamindars*);
(ii) ceiling laws to expropriate land by any given owner above a state-specific ceiling for redistribution to the poor; and
(iii) tenancy laws to increase tenure security by sitting tenants through registration, in most cases combined with rent ceilings and restrictions on the scope for new rental transactions.

While the abolition of intermediaries was put in place swiftly and fairly successfully, ceilings and tenancy reforms remained controversial and were difficult to implement, partly because landlords took action to reduce their exposure to reforms, generally by evicting tenants before the legislation to protect tenancies became effective, or by exploiting loopholes (Appu, 1997). As implementation responsibility was with each state, the scale and the scope of the reform efforts varied widely.

In light of state responsibility for reform implementation, a number of studies used cross-state differences in land reform implementation to explore the impact of such measures. The number of land reform *laws* is found to have had a positive effect on poverty reduction but not on productivity, possibly due to general equilibrium wage effects (Besley and Burgess, 2000), a result somewhat sensitive to specification (Ghatak and Roy, 2007).[1] Household data, together with state-level information on actual implementation by type of reform, point towards positive reform effects on income, consumption, and accumulation of human and physical capital that are more pronounced for the poor (Deininger et al., 2009).

West Bengal is one of the few states that moved decisively on implementing land reforms once the Left Front had been elected in 1978 (Lieten,

1996). In fact, the state's land reform efforts are widely credited with having contributed to uninterrupted rule by the Communist Party in the 1978 to 2011 period.[2] Once in power, the Left Front passed legislation to

(i) prohibit fixed (cash) rental and impose ceilings on the share rent a tenant can be charged – 25 percent or 50 percent, depending on whether the landlord supplies inputs;
(ii) protect registered tenants (bargadars) from eviction as long as they pay their rent; and
(iii) make share tenancies (bargas) inheritable, but abolish their transfer to third parties via subleasing.

In contrast to other states, many of which have similar laws on the books, this was complemented by a massive drive for systematic tenant registration (Operation Barga) and identification of ceiling surplus land. Built on some progress made before 1978, more than 1.6 million sharecroppers registered, and about a million acres of vested land were distributed to 2.5 million poor *pattadar* households within a short period of time (Bandyopadhyay, 2003). Between local governments, it was electoral competition and re-election concerns rather than local government control by the Left Front that were the key factors for the effectiveness with which reforms were implemented (Bardhan and Mookherjee, 2010). Observers agree that even though official statistics might have been biased, these achievements were impressive from an operational point of view, and ushered in a period of rapid productivity growth (Rawal, 2001).

Given the size of this effort, scholars have long been interested to ascertain the determinants and quantify the impact of West Bengal's land reforms. District-level data comparing the state with neighboring Bangladesh suggest a gain of between 51 and 63 percent (28 percent of post-reform agricultural productivity growth), a result similar to that obtained from pipeline comparison based on inter-district variation in program implementation within the state (Banerjee et al., 2002). A study using village-level data estimates the effect of tenancy registration on rice yields to be of similar magnitude, although it is noted that impacts from other interventions undertaken contemporaneously at village level need to be accounted for. Data at household level suggest that once endogenous program implementation and the link to other efficiency-enhancing local government programs have been controlled for, general equilibrium effects (that is, via better access to credit or technology) on non-tenant farms outweigh the direct impact of land reform on registered tenants (Bardhan and Mookherjee, 2008). While the results still point towards a positive impact of tenancy reform (*barga*), in contrast to no impact of the distribution of small plots of vested land,[3] the estimated productivity impact of tenancy reform is smaller than that found in other studies. There are also indications of Marshallian inefficiency for High Yielding Variety (HYV) rice, but not for other crops. As a limited sample size may have biased the results towards zero, a study of these issues with different data would be warranted.

3.3 Data and descriptive evidence

We used data from a 2008/9 survey in 10 West Bengal districts to explore the impact of land reform on productivity and investment. We focused on identifying impacts through within-household regressions for owner-cum-tenants, who account for a modest but increasing share of rural West Bengal, for two reasons; first, more than 30 years after the reform effort started, it is still difficult to establish a credible historical counterfactual; second, even if political realities in 1978 required limits on the rights given to beneficiaries, it will be critical, in light of the recent stagnation of productivity in West Bengal's rural sector, to explore the potential obstacles standing in the way of full realization of the reforms' productivity potential. Descriptive data points towards limited mobility over time, while suggesting that for this group the levels of output, input use and investment are all lower on tenanted plots compared to owned ones.

3.3.1 Hypotheses and estimation strategy

The package of tenancy reform applied in West Bengal will affect outcomes through two channels. First, the rent ceilings paid will increase in tenants' net wealth and their bargaining power *vis-à-vis* the landlord, and thus may reduce the level of Marshallian inefficiency.[4] Second, making tenancies permanent and inheritable will deprive landlords of the ability to use eviction as a threat in order to get their tenants to increase the level of effort or investment they supply (Banerjee and Ghatak, 2004). Also, by outlawing subleasing and requiring a specific format for all tenancy contracts, reform is likely to affect the incentives for landlords to lease out in a way that is likely to reduce land-leasing activity. But this could then restrict market transactions to sales which are less flexible and more affected by credit market imperfections.[5] Given the data challenges and methodological difficulties involved in establishing a historical counterfactual, we focus on the static and dynamic inefficiencies of tenancy compared to ownership.

Specifically, we expect *barga* tenure to affect productivity and investment. For productivity, Marshallian inefficiency is likely to arise, as tenants are not residual claimants to profit. Although rents are capped by legislative fiat, the fact that the limit is set as a share of output rather than a fixed amount implies that the tenant's return from any investment will be similarly reduced by the need to transfer a share of the incremental output generated from such investment to the landlord. To quantify the effect of *barga* tenure on revenues from agricultural production and the probability of making long-term land-attached investments, we follow the literature (Bell, 1977; Shaban, 1987) and use plot-level data on production and investment from our sample of owner-cum-tenants to estimate

$$Y_{ij} = \alpha_i + \beta R_{ij} + \gamma X_{ij} + \varepsilon_{ij} \tag{1}$$

where Y_{ij} is the outcome – either the value of gross or net revenue excluding family labor and level of input use per acre, or an indicator of investment having been made in the past – on plot j by cultivator I; α_i captures unobserved determinants of productivity by I, including farming skills, access to technology and credit etc; R_{ij} is an indicator variable for *barga* plots; and X_{ij} is a vector of observable plot characteristics including size, soil type or quality, access to irrigation and drainage, and distance from the operator's homestead.[6] To implement this empirically, issues of identification and truncation need to be considered.

Regarding identification we note that, as α_i will be correlated with R_{ij} (or $E(\alpha_i|R_{ij} = 1) \neq 0$), the ordinary least squares (OLS) estimation of β will be biased. To deal with this, we limit our sample to owner-cum-tenants, so that β can be identified from within household variation as applied in other studies relying on plot-level data (Jacoby and Mansuri, 2009; Shaban, 1987).[7] A second source of bias is that $E(\varepsilon_{ij}|R_{ij} = 1) \neq 0$; in fact sharecropped plots are often assumed to be of lower quality than owned ones.

There are two factors that mitigate against such concerns in our estimates. First, we are able to control for a wide range of observable plot attributes. Moreover, after 1978, the acquisition of new barga plots came essentially to a standstill. Differences in unobserved soil quality attributes (such as capillarity and texture) are likely to have been affected by actions undertaken in the 30 years since then, and thus be attributable to tenure-related underinvestment rather than pre-existing differences. If there were still some unobserved quality attributes, they would bias our estimates of the Marshallian inefficiency upwards, because of failure to adjust for unobserved land quality. Assuming that payoffs from investment are negatively related to current land quality, the estimate of tenancy-induced investment effects will be biased downwards.

We also note that, for investments and some inputs, the data will include a large amount of zeros. To account for these, we adopt the semi-parametric trimmed LAD approach (Honoré, 1992) to estimate a fixed-effect Tobit to complement the linear probability model to ascertain the probability of any investment being made. If investment incentives are systematically lower when sharecropped than on owned land, the total effect of barga tenure will be the sum of Marshallian inefficiency and investment effects. For observable investments (such as irrigation) that enter the production function, we can approximate the total productivity impact by multiplying coefficients.

3.3.2 Evidence from listing data

Our data is from a 2008/9 survey, conducted jointly by the World Bank and the FAO, in 200 randomly selected villages from 10 West Bengal districts.[8] Sampling was in two stages. A complete listing first provided basic information on the approximately 96,000 households in our universe. Information included the current household structure, current and historical endowments of basic assets, and the extent and nature to which they were affected by land reform.[9] A second stage consists of an in-depth follow-up of some 1800 owner-cum-tenants with the goal of comparing productivity, intensity of input use, and investment between owned plots and those whose inheritable barga rights were received due to the 1978 reform.

Table 3.1 reports key initial household characteristics based on recall, overall and for the landless, pure owners, owner-cum tenants, bargadars and pattadars in 1978. We note marked differences in socio-economic status between the groups for example in educational status, with 70 percent of households overall having an illiterate head, a share that reaches some 85 percent for both types of land reform beneficiaries, 76 percent for the landless, and 67 percent for owner-cum-tenants. This is mirrored by the head's formal education, which ranges from some four years for owners to less than two years for reform beneficiaries and the landless, who are more likely to live in houses with thatch or a plastic roof and bamboo or mud walls. As reform beneficiaries also own little or no land and are more likely to come from scheduled castes or tribes, our data is in line with evidence from other studies suggesting that in villages where reform was implemented, it targeted the less fortunate (Bardhan, 1999). Although listing data provides only a very broad indication, it does not point towards a level of improvement in the situation of the beneficiaries of land reform beyond general trends.

The transition matrices for the total sample and households formed before and after 1978, respectively, are reported in Table 3.2. They suggest a slight decline in the number of the landless (54 to 49 percent of the sample), and in the share of owners (from 37.6 to 34.7 percent); and a slight increase in the number of bargadars (2.6 to 3.4 percent) and owner-cum-tenants (2.3 to 3.4 percent). It was the number of pattadars that increased greatly (3.4 to 9.1 percent).

For the 15,399 households (16.5 percent of the sample) that had been in existence since 1978, the numbers of bargadars, pure owners, owner-cum-tenants, and pattadars all increased (by 241, 322, 502, and 1205, respectively) together with a considerable decrease in the share of the landless, from 49 to 34 percent, suggesting some upward movement. Of the dynasties that have split since then (84 percent of the sample or 80,527 households), the number of landless, owner-cum-tenants, and bargadars have increased slightly (by 2,665, 1,013, and 777) and the number of pattadars have more than doubled (2,584 to 6,817) while the number of pure owners dropped correspondingly. Movement in the 30 years since the land reform seems limited compared to what has been observed in other settings such as Taiwan or Korea over a comparable period. While some of the transitions from bargadar to landlord or owner-cum-tenant may be based on the mutually agreed transfer of ownership rights to tenants reported in the literature (Hanstad and Nielsen, 2004), the total number of such transfers seems limited due to credit market and coordination failures.

Table 3.3 illustrates key attributes for the entire population as well as subgroups defined by current land ownership status, that is, pure owners (34.7 percent), landless (49 percent), pure bargadars who cultivate barga land only (3.4 percent), and owner-cum-tenants (3.8 percent). 19 percent of household heads among pure bargadars, or 16 percent in the owner-cum-tenants group, took non-farm jobs as their major occupation (including both off-farm wage and off-farm self-employment) compared to 27 percent of pure owner and 53 percent landless, whose major occupation is in the off farm sector. Among beneficiaries, owner-cum tenants rely more on agriculture than do those in the pure bargadar category, most likely due to their higher land endowment compared to that of pure tenants (2.35 vs. 1.41 acres: approx 1 vs. 0.6 ha).

Beneficiaries from tenancy reform had considerably lower incomes than non-beneficiary households (Rs 4352 per capita for pure tenants and Rs 4665 for owner-cum-tenants, vs. Rs 5914 for pure owners and

Table 3.1 Key household characteristics in 1978 and changes therein by initial tenure status

Variable	Total	Pure owners	Pure bargadars	Owner-cum-tenants	Pattadars	Landless
Household characteristics in 1978						
Household size	6.21	6.74	6.17	6.66	5.86	5.75
Head's age	31.17	32.21	31.01	32.49	31.91	30.04
Head's educ (years)	2.83	3.96	1.57	3.19	1.18	1.90
Illiterate head	0.70	0.62	0.85	0.67	0.84	0.76
SC/ST	0.45	0.39	0.58	0.42	0.70	0.49
Bad roof (thatch/plastic/mud)	0.72	0.71	0.86	0.78	0.84	0.71
Bad wall (mud/bamboo)	0.70	0.70	0.89	0.88	0.74	0.68
Owns livestock	0.46	0.66	0.60	0.73	0.47	0.29
Owns bicycle	0.12	0.18	0.11	0.15	0.10	0.07
Owns motorcycle	0.00	0.00	0.00	0.00	0.00	0.00
Occupation & land ownership 1978						
Wage work main occ.	0.36	0.14	0.33	0.11	0.50	0.54
Farming main occ.	0.40	0.71	0.60	0.83	0.40	0.13
Off-farm wage main occ.	0.10	0.11	0.03	0.03	0.03	0.10
Off-farm work main occ.	0.12	0.12	0.04	0.04	0.04	0.12
Own rain-fed land (acres)	0.81	1.91	0.00	1.58	0.00	0.00
Own irr. land (acres)	0.32	0.77	0.00	0.40	0.00	0.00
Barga land	0.08	0.00	1.87	1.45	0.11	0.00
Patta land	0.03	0.01	0.00	0.04	0.75	0.00

Change between the two periods						
Household size	–1.45	–1.82	–1.34	–1.63	–1.16	–1.14
Illiterate head	–0.16	–0.21	–0.22	–0.24	–0.18	–0.11
Bad roof (thatch/plastic/mud)	–0.40	–0.46	–0.36	–0.44	–0.34	–0.35
Bad wall (mud/bamboo)	–0.15	–0.21	–0.11	–0.15	–0.07	–0.12
Owns livestock	0.01	–0.06	–0.04	–0.08	0.07	0.07
Owns bicycle	0.51	0.56	0.47	0.57	0.52	0.47
Ag. wage work main occ.	–0.07	0.03	0.00	0.07	–0.05	–0.15
Farming main occ.	–0.11	–0.22	–0.20	–0.26	–0.09	–0.02
Off-farm wage main occ.	0.06	0.05	0.05	0.07	0.04	0.06
Off-farm work main occ.	0.10	0.10	0.09	0.11	0.08	0.10
Own rain-fed land	–0.50	–1.33	0.09	–0.91	0.15	0.10
Own irr. land	–0.07	–0.26	0.06	–0.06	0.04	0.08
Barga land	0.05	0.05	–1.28	–0.90	0.12	0.14
Patta land	0.04	0.04	0.04	0.02	–0.39	0.05
No. of observations	95,666	38,682	2,236	2,161	2,687	49,900

Source: Own computation from 20/9 West Bengal listing survey.

Table 3.2 Transition matrices between tenure types, overall and for households formed before and after 1978

	In 1978	Pure owner	Bargadar	Owner-cum tenant	Pattadar	Landless	No of obs.
In 2008				**Entire sample**			
	Pure owner	72.99	8.33	19.34	7.12	11.69	33,261
	Bargadar	0.00	51.88	5.32	2.43	3.48	3,295
	Owner-cum-tenant	0.00	9.01	55.34	2.03	4.21	3,675
	Pattadar	5.01	5.64	3.79	64.88	8.77	8,695
	Landless	22.00	25.14	16.20	23.55	71.86	47,000
	No of obs.	36,075	2,498	2,161	3,257	51,935	95,926
In 2008				**Households established before 1978 only**			
	Pure Owner	86.32	8.08	15.23	2.67	14.07	6,603
	Bargadar	0.00	67.88	3.81	3.27	4.80	736
	Owner-cum-tenant	0.00	11.92	76.14	3.57	6.79	896
	Pattadar	5.94	4.85	3.30	85.74	11.79	1,878
	Landless	7.74	7.27	1.52	4.75	62.55	5,286
	No of obs.	6,281	495	394	673	7,556	15,399
In 2008				**Households established after 1978 only**			
	Pure Owner	70.18	8.39	20.26	8.28	11.28	26,657
	Bargadar	0.00	47.93	5.66	2.21	3.25	2,559
	Owner-cum-tenant	0.00	8.29	50.71	1.63	3.78	2,780
	Pattadar	4.81	5.84	3.90	59.44	8.25	6,817
	Landless	25.01	29.56	19.47	28.44	73.44	41,714
	No of obs.	29,794	2,003	1,767	2,584	44,379	80,527

Source: Own computation from 2008/9 West Bengal listing survey.

Rs 5469 landless). We also noted severe imbalances in land rental markets. Compared to almost two thirds (63 percent) of sample households who want to rent in (78 percent of pure bargadars and pattadars), only 1 percent indicate having rented out land and only 3 percent are interested in leasing out. Beyond potential Marshallian inefficiency,

Table 3.3 Household characteristics in 2008, overall and by tenure type

Variable	Total	Pure owners	Pure bargadars	Owner-cum-tenants	Pattadars	Landless
Household characteristics						
Household size	4.75	5.08	4.99	5.57	4.75	4.41
Members <14 years old	1.50	1.43	1.55	1.52	1.42	1.56
Members 14 to 60 years old	2.99	3.32	3.21	3.63	3.03	2.66
Members > 60 years old	0.26	0.32	0.24	0.42	0.30	0.19
Head's age	44.57	47.60	46.46	49.51	46.94	41.15
Head's educ (years)	3.11	4.48	1.82	3.65	1.45	2.27
Share of heads illiterate	0.54	0.42	0.70	0.47	0.74	0.62
Area of own land (ac.)	0.57	1.37	0.00	1.10	0.00	0.00
Area of barga land	0.13	0.00	1.41	1.07	0.66	0.00
Area of patta land	0.06	0.08	0.00	0.18	0.41	0.00
Barga under 25/75 sharing rule	–	–	0.48	0.44	–	–
Barga under 50/50 sharing rule	–	–	0.52	0.56	–	–
Head's occupation and income sources						
Wage work main occupation	0.31	0.14	0.33	0.14	0.47	0.44
Farming main occ.	0.30	0.58	0.48	0.70	0.30	0.03
Off-farm wage main occ.	0.27	0.18	0.14	0.11	0.17	0.38
Off-farm work main occ.	0.12	0.09	0.05	0.05	0.06	0.15
Income per capita (Rs)	5504.66	5913.92	4351.95	4665.49	4192.01	5469.39
.. share from wage & salaried work	0.65	0.43	0.58	0.38	0.72	0.77
.. share from crop prod	0.15	0.38	0.32	0.47	0.15	0.01
..share from self-employment	0.13	0.12	0.07	0.09	0.07	0.15
.. share from livestock prod	0.02	0.03	0.01	0.03	0.02	0.01
.. share from other sources	0.05	0.05	0.03	0.03	0.04	0.06
Agricultural market participation						
Ever rented out land	0.01	0.03	0.00	0.01	0.01	0.00
Would like to rent in land	0.64	0.64	0.78	0.70	0.78	0.62
Would like to rent out land	0.03	0.04	0.04	0.03	0.04	0.01
No. of observations	95926	36053	2740	3094	6457	46609

Source: 2008/9 West Bengal listing survey.

reform-induced restrictions on land rental may thus reduce the scope for rural productivity growth. Detailed analysis of this issue is, however, beyond the scope of this chapter.

3.3.3 Descriptive evidence at plot level

The plot-level data in Table 3.4 overall and by type of tenure suggest that while plot characteristics for owned and barga plots are virtually indistinguishable, the intensity of input use, productivity and investment are much lower on the latter. Plots measure 0.4 acres (0.16 ha) on average (0.36 vs. 0.46 acres: 0.15 vs. 0.19 ha) for owned and barga, respectively) with barga plots about 170 m (185 yards) more distant from the home. Differences between owned and barga plots in soil color, type, and condition are insignificant throughout, with the exception of salinity and drainage, where barga plots are slightly less productive.[10] As these plots were obtained some 30 years ago, this could be a legacy of past neglect. Productivity per acre on land reform plots is significantly lower than owned plots, by some 24 percent for gross and net revenue excluding family labor (Rs 16,693 vs. Rs 22,062, and Rs 11,051 vs. Rs 14,565, respectively). This difference in net revenues is not due to higher levels of input use on barga plots; on the contrary, intensity of fertilizer, pesticide, seed, draught power and family labor use on these are all significantly lower than on owned plots. Econometric analysis can help assess if this is due to unobserved household fixed effects or tenure.

Data on investment points towards a correlation between tenure type and incentives for land-attached investment, which is much lower on barga than on owned plots. We find a 10 percentage point difference in access to private irrigation, largely boreholes, which benefits 54 percent of owned, but only 44 percent of barga, plots. Access to public irrigation, by comparison, is no different between owned and barga plots.[11] This is only a stock and thus a coarse measure. Evidence regarding the flow of less observable investments to maintain or improve land quality points, however, in the same direction, suggesting that, over the last eight years, such investment was undertaken on 39 percent of owned but only on 12 percent of barga plots by the same household. In addition, the amount of capital and family labor spent on such investment in 2007 is between three and four times larger on the former (Rs 203 vs. 51 and 6.8 vs. 1.8 days, respectively).

Table 3.4 Plot-level data on output and input use as well as investment for owner-cum-tenants[a]

	All	Own land	Barga land	Difference
Plot characteristics				
Land area (acres)	0.40	0.36	0.46	*
Distance to homestead (meters)	878.8	810.9	979.1	***
Grey soil	0.853	0.854	0.853	
Sandy soil	0.145	0.148	0.142	*
Loam soil	0.111	0.111	0.110	
Light clay soil	0.457	0.458	0.455	
Heavy clay soil	0.259	0.257	0.261	
No salinity	0.460	0.466	0.452	***
Moderate salinity	0.512	0.506	0.520	***
Easy to drain	0.350	0.354	0.340	**
Moderately easy to drain	0.504	0.505	0.503	***
Difficult to drain	0.146	0.141	0.152	
Input use & productivity				
Used any fertilizer	0.970	0.969	0.972	
Used any manure	0.596	0.632	0.544	***
Used any pesticides	0.866	0.885	0.837	***
Used any seeds	0.984	0.978	0.992	***
Used any draught power/transport	0.311	0.328	0.300	***
Used any casual labor	0.672	0.660	0.681	
Used any family labor	0.928	0.920	0.941	***
Fertilizer & manure (Rs/acre)	1942.06	2195.05	1569.15	***
Pesticides (Rs/acre)	605.61	666.13	516.40	***
Seeds (Rs/acre)	1256.45	1428.47	1002.88	***
Draught power/transport (Rs/acre)	1010.87	1087.02	898.62	***
Casual labor cost (Rs/acre)	886.98	942.67	804.90	***
Family labor use (Days/acre)	70.07	74.74	63.17	***
Gross production value (Rs/acre)	19,892.1	22,062.2	16,693.3	***
Net production value (Rs/acre)	13,145.3	14,565.9	11,051.3	***
Land-related investment				
Invested in soil & water conservation (y/n)	0.28	0.39	0.12	***
... if yes, cost (Rs)	141.48	203.08	50.67	***
No. of family days invested in 2007	4.78	6.78	1.83	***
Access to private irrigation (y/n)b	0.50	0.54	0.44	***
Access to public irrigation (y/n)	0.17	0.17	0.18	
Number of plots	9285	5532	3753	

Source: Household questionnaire from the 2008/9 West Bengal survey.

[a] Significance levels: *** $p<0.01$, ** $p<0.05$, * $p<0.1$ (based on simple *t*-test for the mean difference between own land and barga land).

[b] Private irrigation includes ponds, wells and boreholes.

3.4 Econometric results

Controlling for unobserved household characteristics allows us to better quantify impacts and compare them to the literature. With a 16 percent difference in net revenue between owned and sharecropped plots, the estimated size of the Marshallian inefficiency is in line with comparable studies. Input use is significantly lower on barga plots as well, though the size of the effect varies. Most surprising is evidence of a negative investment effect, the estimated magnitude of which ranges between 26 percent for soil conservation and 7 percent for private irrigation.

3.4.1 Effects on productivity and input use

Table 3.5 reports results from the household fixed-effect regressions for gross or net revenue from crop production on a given plot. As household fixed effects are included, the set of explanatory variables is limited to plot size and distance, irrigation status and soil quality indicators, in addition to the barga dummy of interest. The coefficient on the latter is significant throughout, and suggests that net and gross revenues on barga plots are 16 and 14 points lower than on owner-cultivated ones in the same household. This is comparable to estimates of the Marshallian inefficiency in India by Shaban (1987), and at 22 percent in West Bengal by Bardhan et al. (2009b). Although it is much larger than the result by Jacoby and Mansuri (2009) for Pakistan, it is comparable to their estimate of 18 percent for plots that are not subject to landlord supervision. This suggests that although a rent ceiling should have increased their bargaining power, West Bengal's land reform legislation did little to reduce the static efficiency losses traditionally associated with sharecropping.

Table 3.5 Household level fixed-effect estimates for impact of land tenure on plot-level gross and net output[a]

	Gross value		Net value	
Barga land (y/n)	−0.145***	−0.145***	−0.156***	−0.156***
Plot size (ac.)	−0.014	−0.013	0.005	0.006
Dist. to homestead (km)	−0.073***	−0.068***	−0.094***	−0.091***
Irrigation access (y/n)	0.629***	0.626***	0.494***	0.496***
Soil/plot chars incl.	**No**	**Yes**	**No**	**Yes**
Observations (plots)	9215	9165	9215	9165
Number of HHs	1777	1777	1777	1777
R2	0.87	0.87	0.88	0.87

Notes: [a] Dependent variable is log of gross or net value of output as explained in the text. Significance levels: *** $p<0.01$, ** $p<0.05$, * $p<0.1$.

Adding plot and soil characteristics in Columns 2 and 4 (coefficients not reported) leaves the main result virtually unaffected. Irrigation and distance to the homestead affect output separately; having irrigation on a plot is estimated to increase gross revenue by 63 percent and net revenue by 50 percent, in line with more intensive input use on irrigated plots. The coefficient on the distance to the homestead is negative as expected, suggesting that gross or net revenue for plots owned by the same household that are located 1 km further away is lower by 7 and 9 percent respectively. Plot size is estimated to have no appreciable impact on output.

Regarding input use, results from the fixed-effect Tobit estimation in the lower panel of Table 3.6 suggest that for all input except seeds and casual labor, which are easily observed, the amount of input applied on

Table 3.6 Household level fixed-effect estimates for impact of land tenure on use and intensity of different inputs[a]

	Fertilizer	Pesticide	Seeds	Bullock	Casual labor	Family labor
	Use of input (fixed-effects linear probability model)					
Barga land (y/n)	−0.123***	−0.023***	0.006**	−0.002	−0.010	0.008**
Plot size (ac.)	0.029***	0.022***	0.008**	−0.044***	0.163***	0.005
Dist. to homestead (km)	−0.004	0.004	0.018***	−0.016**	0.012**	0.006
Irrigation access (y/n)	0.170***	0.174***	0.014	−0.040***	0.018	0.027***
R2	0.09	0.07	0.02	0.04	0.16	0.02
	Value of input used (fixed-effect Tobit model)					
Barga land (y/n)	−528.548***	−106.816***	−222.134	−98.519**	−47.223	−6.229***
Plot size (ac.)	−927.094***	−308.147***	−319.127	−172.194***	16.897	−61.421***
Dist. to homestead (km)	−0.061	−0.017**	−0.025	−0.020	0.015	−0.004
Irrigation access (y/n)	3533.12***	805.285***	3418.473	835.439***	741.564***	38.715***
No. of obs.	9219	9219	9219	9219	9219	9219

Notes: [a] Soil and plot characteristics are included throughout. Significance levels: *** $p<0.01$, ** $p<0.05$, * $p<0.1$.

tenanted plots is significantly below that on owned ones, as predicted by theory.[12] Comparing these coefficients with the mean levels of application suggests that the difference ranges from 8 percent for family labor and draught power (bullocks or tractors) to 16 percent for pesticide and 24 percent for fertilizer.

3.4.2 Investment effects

While a large literature discusses how share tenancy may affect investment incentives at the conceptual level (Ray, 2005; Ray and Singh, 2001), few studies have explored this relationship empirically. Evidence from a linear probability model for investment in soil fertility in columns 1 and 2 of Table 3.7 suggests that incentives for private investment are much lower on tenanted than on owned plots, contrary to the goal of land reform to enhance investment. For the sample of owner-cum-cultivators, the probability of the average barga plot having received any investment to maintain or improve land quality during the last eight years is 26 percentage points below that of a plot owned by the same household. Unsurprisingly, as family labor is the most important component of such investment, the probability of having used family labor to improve soil quality is 22 percentage points lower on barga than on owned plots in the same household. In both cases, public irrigation increases incentives for land-improving investment by some 10 points, presumably because it increases the associated payoff and reduces its variance.

Compared to soil fertility improvements, investment in private irrigation is more capital intensive and, due to indivisibilities of the equipment, may generate external effects.[13] Indeed, the coefficient on access to private irrigation is much smaller than that on land maintenance. Barga plots are estimated to be 7 percent less likely to have private irrigation installed on them. The coefficient on public irrigation is insignificant, as one would expect, allaying fears that other unobserved factors are driving our results. We also note that private irrigation is significantly less likely on plots located further from the homestead and connected to public irrigation; the former is marginally significant and negative (that is, with the 'wrong' sign) for public irrigation infrastructure. While other studies have explored commitment problems that might lead to underprovision of non-contractible investment in rural Pakistan (Jacoby and Mansuri, 2008), the nature of investment considered (manuring) and the size of the estimated impact are well below what is found here. The fixed-effect Tobit model for actual cash and labor days spent during the last eight years or 12 months in the last two columns of Table 3.7 are negative and significant at 1 percent. Coefficients suggest that the

Table 3.7 Household level fixed-effect estimates for impact of land tenure on investment [a]

	Fixed-effect linear probability model				Fixed-effect Tobit model	
	Any land improvement past 8 years	Family labor used in 2008	Access to private irrigation	Access to public irrigation	Exp. on land improvement in past 8 years	No. of days to improve land in 2008
Barga land (y/n)	–0.263***	–0.216***	–0.069***	–0.004	–959.081***	–21.068***
Plot size (ac)	0.002	0.002	0.003	0.001	516.436	17.508***
Dist. to homestead (km)	–0.006	–0.005	–0.066***	0.011*	–81.310	0.294
Public irrigation (y/n)	0.108***	0.092***	–0.211***		266.075	8.599**
No. of obs. (plots)	9166	9166	9166	9166	9166	9101
No of households	1777	1777	1777	1777	1777	1777
R2	0.17	0.14	0.06	0.01		

Notes: [a] Observable soil and plot characteristics are included throughout. Significance levels: *** $p<0.01$, ** $p<0.05$, * $p<0.1$.

amount of family labor days for soil improvements is 21 days lower, and the amount of cash is Rs 959 (Rs 120/year) on barga plots.

Assuming that barga tenure will affect only private irrigation investment (that is, neglecting any impacts from soil improvement), the investment-related impact of tenure on output would amount to 3.4 and 4.4 percentage points for gross or net revenue.[14] Adding this to the Marshallian inefficiency estimate obtained earlier would imply a total efficiency loss from barga tenure of close to 20 percent. At least for owner-cum-tenants, providing secure ownership rights to such land would thus appear like a promising strategy, and has indeed been debated in policy circles. Our results not only support the underlying intuition, but also suggest that there will be viable options to finance a buyout of landlords' residual interests – equivalent, say, to their rental share at current output levels – that would be socially optimal and could potentially attract private finance.

Our main empirical results are that productivity, input use intensity, and incidence and level of long-term investment are all much lower on barga plots than on own plots cultivated by the same households. Validity of these results relies on the assumption that barga plots and owner-cultivated plots are not affected by unobserved factors differently after the observed factors and household fixed-effects have been controlled for. While we cannot directly test this hypothesis, we can check whether the size difference between barga and owner-cultivated land drives this as a robustness check. To do so, we interact the barga land dummy with five land size dummies (each dummy variable for each quintile of land size); the results for the relevant regressions are available upon request. All coefficients on interaction terms are negative and statistically significant, suggesting that the inefficiency is robust across all land size categories, leading us to conclude that our results were not driven by the land size between barga land and own land in any significant way.

3.5 Conclusion and policy implications

Students of India's land reforms have long been concerned that in a setting where sharecropping is the only permissible way of land leasing, increases in tenure security brought about by eliminating the threat of eviction may fail to eliminate Marshallian inefficiency but may also, in light of weak ownership rights, undermine investment incentives. Our analysis suggests that such concerns are justified and that in West Bengal their combined effect reduces output by at least 20 percent. The associated disincentives to labor-intensive investment, an area where land reform beneficiaries should have a strong comparative advantage, suggest that these arrangements may not be optimal from a policy perspective either.

Enhancing the ability of beneficiaries to invest in physical and human capital is a key long-term objective of land reform. While land reforms have had an undisputed impact on transforming social relations, our analysis shows that they fell short of the potential in terms of enhancing beneficiaries' incentives and ability to invest and increase agricultural productivity. This strengthens the case for 'completing' land reforms in West Bengal, by giving beneficiaries full ownership rights rather than permanent and inheritable usufruct. Doing so will be more important as, with the passage of time, the effects of tenure-induced underinvestment accumulate up to the point where they could outweigh the original gains from reform-induced asset transfers. In light of rising concern about productivity growth in West Bengal's agriculture having stalled (Bandyopadhyay, 2008), the scope for such productivity gains is important and opens up options to make the award of full ownership to land reform land financially viable, without undermining either party's property rights. Reports about cases of spontaneous transfer of residual land rights suggest that this could be attractive to private parties and may, in addition, help to realize additional efficiency gains by removing reform-induced restrictions on the operation of land lease markets. By allowing reallocation of land through means other than land sales, this could facilitate significant increases in productivity beyond the limited number of reform beneficiaries, benefit those with low levels of agricultural skills, and encourage broader structural transformation of West Bengal's rural economy.

Acknowledgement

The data for this study has collected by EIT, Calcutta under the FAO-World Bank Cooperative Program. We thank D. Gustafson and P. Munro-Faure for their support; T. Hanstad, T. Haque, H.K. Nagarajan, Gershon Feder, Michael Carter and participants at the AAEA Annual Meetings for insightful comments and discussions; and A.K. Roy and D. Mazumdar for outstanding efforts in data collection and processing. Financial support from the Global Land Tools Network is gratefully acknowledged. The views expressed in this chapter are those of the authors and do not necessarily reflect those of the World Bank, its executive directors, or the countries they represent.

Notes

1. If an output measure that excludes livestock yields a positive though insignificant impact of tenancy reform and a negative and significant impact of land ceiling and consolidation laws (Ghatak and Roy, 2007).
2. The lasting political success of the Left was due partly to a clientelist relationship and partly to the gratitude of poor voters for the broad-based changes that had been introduced (Bardhan et al., 2009a). It is somewhat ironic that the botched acquisition of 1000 acres (400 ha) of land for industrial development in the same state seems to have been one of the key reasons for the regime to lose power (Ghatak and Gosh, 2011).
3. Vesting of land under patta was found to have failed to yield positive productivity impacts as it focused on low-quality land and contributed to uneconomically small holding sizes that could not be transferred.
4. From the data reported in Banerjee et al. (2002); the main change appears to have been in the proportion of contracts with a landlord share of 0.5, which declined from around 80 percent to about 60 percent.
5. Limitations on land leases imposed by prohibition on subleasing of barga land and the de facto elimination of rental contracts other than those in compliance with stipulations of the reform legislation may discourage land rental (Deininger et al., 2008). With credit market constraints, this drives a wedge between the distribution of skills and of operational landholdings, as documented for Brazil (Assunçao, 2008) While our data points towards disequilibria in tenancy markets, analytically rigorous treatment of this topic is beyond the scope of this chapter.
6. In the private irrigation regression, only public irrigation is included; and all irrigation dummies are excluded in the public irrigation regression.
7. Although an assessment of overall welfare effects would require information on the cost of supervision, landlord monitoring can limit the efficiency loss associated with share tenancy. In a Pakistani sample, the Marshallian inefficiency, estimated to be about 18 percent – very close to the 17 percent obtained by Shaban's study – is virtually eliminated for tightly monitored share tenants, (Jacoby and Mansuri, 2009).
8. The survey was implemented by EIT, a Kolkata-based firm, Villages were selected randomly with probability of selection proportional to the number of beneficiaries in the 1978 land reforms, based on official lists obtained from the State Institute of Panchayats & Rural Development (Chakraborti et al., 2003). The data is thus representative of the universe of West Bengal's land reform beneficiaries.
9. The listing contains information on demographics, the head's occupation, and income from different economic activities, land ownership, land market history, and land quality.
10. 46.6 percent (50.6 percent) of owner-cultivated, compared to 45.2 percent (52 percent) of barga plots, have no (moderate) salinity problems. Similarly, 35.4 percent (14.1 percent) of owner-cultivated plots are reported to be 'easy (difficult) to drain' compared to 34 percent (15.2 percent) barga plots.
11. This can be consistent with the finding that tenancy reforms, institutional credit and public support through distribution of minikits fostered irrigation

investment and drops in water prices that benefited all farmers and drove the 1980s and 90s green revolution (Bardhan et al., 2009b).

12. As most bargadars obtain land from just one landlord, lack of within-household variation in input sharing makes it difficult to assess whether or by how much landlord monitoring or provision of inputs might help to attenuate the Marshallian inefficiency. Including an interaction between share tenancy and a dummy for 75/25 (or 50/50) sharing rule is insignificant throughout, a finding that could also be due to the fact that the choice of sharing role is an endogenous response to transaction partners' endowment and their preference profile but has little systematic impact on observed outcomes.
13. In fact, increased supply of irrigation water by land reform beneficiaries to their neighbors and the associated price drop has been identified as a key channel for indirect effects from land reform to materialize (Bardhan et al., 2009).
14. The estimate is obtained by multiplying coefficients from the revenue function (0.63 and 0.50) with that from the investment equation (0.069).

References

Acemoglu, D. and Johnson, S. (2005) 'Unbundling Institutions', *Journal of Political Economy,* 113(5), 949–95.

Appu, P.S. (1997) *Land Reforms in India: A Survey of Policy, Legislation and Implementation* (New Delhi: Vikas Publishing House).

Assunçao, J. J. (2008) 'Rural Organization and Land Reform in Brazil: The Role of Nonagricultural Benefits of Landholding', *Economic Development and Cultural Change,* 56(4), 851–70.

Baland, J.M. and Robinson, J.A. (2008) 'Land and Power: Theory and Evidence from Chile', *American Economic Review,* 98(5), 1737–65.

Bandyopadhyay, D. (2003) 'Land Reforms and Agriculture: The West Bengal Experience', *Economic and Political Weekly,* 38(9), 879–84.

Bandyopadhyay, D. (2008) 'Does Land Still Matter?' *Economic and Political Weekly,* 43(10), 56–65.

Banerjee, A.V. and Ghatak, M. (2004) 'Eviction Threats and Investment Incentives', *Journal of Development Economics,* 74(2), 469–88.

Banerjee, A. and Iyer, L. (2005) 'History, Institutions, and Economic Performance: The Legacy of Colonial Land Tenure Systems in India', *American Economic Review,* 95(4), 1190–213.

Banerjee, A.V., Gertler P.J. and Ghatak, M. (2002) 'Empowerment and Efficiency: Tenancy Reform in West Bengal', *Journal of Political Economy,* 110(2), 239–80.

Banerjee, A.V. and Newman, A.F. (1993) 'Occupational Choice and the Process of Development', *Journal of Political Economy,* 101(2), 274–98.

Bardhan, P. (1999) 'Institutions, Governance and Political Economy of Development: Some Reflections', *Journal of African Economies,* 8, 149–67.

Bardhan, P., Mitra S., Mookherjee, D. and Sarkar, A. (2009a) 'Local Democracy and Clientelism: Implications for Political Stability in Rural West Bengal', *Economic and Political Weekly,* 44(9), 46–58.

Bardhan, P., Mookherjee, D. and Kumar, N. (2009b) 'State-led or Market-led Green Revolution? Role of Private Irrigation Investment vis-a-vis Local Government Programs in West Bengal's Farm Productivity Growth', Working Paper No. 184 (Boston, MA: Department of Economics).

Bardhan, P.K. and Mookherjee, D. (2008) 'Productivity Effects of Land Reform: A Study of Disaggregated Farm Data in West Bengal', BREAD Working Paper No. 184 (Cambridge, MA: Bureau for Research and Economics Analysis of Development).

Bardhan, P.K. and Mookherjee, D. (2010) 'Determinants of Redistributive Politics: An Empirical Analysis of Land Reforms in West Bengal, India', *American Economic Review,* 100(4), 1572–600.

Bell, C. (1977) 'Alternative Theories of Sharecropping: Some Tests Using Evidence from Northeast India', *Journal of Development Studies*, 13(4), 317–46.

Besley, T. and Burgess, R. (2000) 'Land Reform, Poverty Reduction, and Growth: Evidence from India', *Quarterly Journal of Economics*, 115(2), 389–430.

Chakraborti, A.K., Mukhodpadhyay, A.K. and Roy, D. (2003) 'Beneficiaries of Land Reforms: The West Bengal Scenario' (Spandan, Kolkata: State Institute of Panchayats & Rural Development).

Conning, J.H. and Robinson, J.A. (2007) 'Property Rights and the Political Organization of Agriculture', *Journal of Development Economics*, 82(2), 416–47.

Deininger, K., Hoogeveen, H. and Kinsey, B.H. (2004) 'Economic Benefits and Costs of Land Redistribution in Zimbabwe in the Early 1980s', *World Development*, 32(10), 1697–709.

Deininger, K., Jin, S. and Nagarajan, H.K. (2008) 'Efficiency and Equity impacts of Rural Land Market Restrictions: Evidence from India', *European Economic Review*, 52(5), 892–918.

Deininger, K., Jin, S. and Nagarajan, H.K. (2009) 'Land Reforms, Poverty Reduction, and Economic Growth: Evidence from India', *Journal of Development Studies*, 45(4), 496–521.

Diaz, A. (2000) 'On the Political Economy of Latin American Land Reforms', *Review of Economic Dynamics*, 3(3), 551–71.

Fabella, R.V. (2003) 'The Comprehensive Agrarian Reform Program and Coase Theorem', *Philippine Review of Economics*, 40(1), 109–14.

Galor, O. and Zeira, J. (1993) 'Income Distribution and Macroeconomics', *Review of Economic Studies*, 60(1), 35–52.

Gersbach, H. and Siemers, L.H.R. (2010) 'Land Reforms and Economic Development', *Macroeconomic Dynamics*, 14(4), 527–47.

Ghatak, M. and Gosh, P. (2011) 'The Land Acquisition Bill: A Critique and a Proposal', *Economic and Political Weekly*, 46(41), 65–72.

Ghatak, M. and Jiang, N.N.-H. (2002) 'A Simple Model of Inequality, Occupational Choice, and Development', *Journal of Development Economics*, 69(1), 205–26.

Ghatak, M. and Roy, S. (2007) 'Land Reform and Agricultural Productivity in India: A Review of the Evidence', *Oxford Review of Economic Policy*, 23(2), 251–69.

Hanstad, T. and Nielsen, R. (2004) 'West Bengal's Bargadars and Landownership', *Economic and Political Weekly*, 39(8), 853–5.

Hidalgo, F.D., Naidu, S., Nichter, S. and Richardson, N. (2010) 'Economic Determinants of Land Invasions', *Review of Economics and Statistics*, 92(3), 505–23.

Honoré, B.E. (1992) 'Trimmed Lad and Least-Squares Estimation of Truncated and Censored Regression-Models with Fixed Effects', *Econometrica*, 60(3), 533–65.

Iyer, L. (2010) 'Direct Versus Indirect Colonial Rule in India: Long-Term Consequences', *Review of Economics and Statistics*, 92(4), 693–713.

Jacoby, H.G. and Mansuri, G. (2008) 'Land Tenancy and Non-contractible Investment in Rural Pakistan', *Review of Economic Studies*, 75(3), 763–88.

Jacoby, H.G. and Mansuri, G. (2009) 'Incentives, Supervision, and Sharecropper Productivity', *Journal of Development Economics*, 88(2), 232–41.

Jeon, Y.D. and Kim, Y.Y. (2000) 'Land Reform, Income Redistribution, and Agricultural Production in Korea', *Economic Development and Cultural Change*, 48(2), 253–68.

Kawagoe, T. (1999) 'Agricultural Land Reform in Postwar Japan: Experiences and Issues', Policy Research Working Paper No. 2111 (Washington DC: World Bank).

King, R. (1977) *Land Reform: A World Survey* (London: G. Bell and Sons).

Lieten, G.K. (1996) 'Land Reforms at Centre Stage: The Evidence on West Bengal', *Development and Change*, 27(1), 111–30.

Lipton, M. (2009) *Land Reform in Developing Countries: Property Rights and property Wrongs* (New York: Routledge or Taylor and Francis).

Mookherjee, D. and Ray, D. (2002) 'Contractual Structure and Wealth Accumulation', *American Economic Review*, 92(4), 818–49.

Nunn, N. (2009) 'The Importance of History for Economic Development', *Annual Review of Economics*, 1(1), 65–92.

Otsuka, K. (1991) 'Determinants and Consequences of Land Reform Implementation in the Philippines', *Journal of Development Economics*, 35(2), 339–55.

Rawal, V. (2001) 'Agrarian Reform and Land Markets: A Study of Land Transactions in Two Villages of West Bengal, 1977–1995', *Economic Development and Cultural Change*, 49(3), 611–29.

Ray, T. (2005) 'Sharecropping, Land Exploitation and Land-Improving Investments', *Japanese Economic Review*, 56(2), 127–43.

Ray, T. and Singh, N. (2001) 'Limited Liability, Contractual Choice, and the Tenancy Ladder', *Journal of Development Economics*, 66(1), 289–303.

Shaban, R.A. (1987) 'Testing between Competing Models of Sharecropping', *Journal of Political Economy*, 95(5), 893–920.

Vollrath, D. (2009) 'The Dual Economy in Long-run Development', *Journal of Economic Growth*, 14(4), 287–312.

World Bank (2002) 'Mexico – Land Policy: A Decade after the Ejido Reforms' (Washington, DC: The World Bank, Rural Development and Natural Resources Sector Unit).

4
Would Small be More Beautiful in the South African Land Reform?

Henrik Wiig and Henning Øien

4.1 Introduction

It was white people who, under Apartheid, were the owners and entrepreneurs of South African agriculture, while blacks were reduced to the status of serfs or were pushed into traditional farming on unproductive land in the black homelands. When the Apartheid regime was overthrown in 1994, the new government launched the ambitious plan of redistributing 30 percent of the agricultural land to black farmers. However, hindering this plan was the fact that hardly any black people had the agricultural experience, management capacity, or capital to run the large-scale farms – part of the price of 80 years of systematic discrimination that no political intervention can undo in the short run.

Apart from addressing historical injustices, the main goals of the land reform in South Africa are rural poverty alleviation, economic growth, and redistribution of income (DLA, 1997). But the reform has made little progress, in terms of both the amount of land redistributed and the success of those who have received land through the reform; the redistributed farms are to a large degree unproductive or have failed completely (Hall, 2008; Lahiff, 2008). Nevertheless, despite its lack of success, politicians still seem to be committed to reaching the redistribution target, and there is a call to speed up the process through radicalization of the reform (Lahiff, 2007b).

Land redistribution should lead to greater equality but is also more importantly expected to increase agricultural productivity and employment. The Inverse Relationship (IR) between farm size and productivity is considered a stylized fact in development economics (Banerjee, 2005). Large farms, both privately and collectively run units, face the moral hazard of hired labor, while smaller farms tend to be worked by families, who work harder and invest more as they retain the full return of their inputs.

Apartheid favored large, mechanized farms and restricted subdivision, creating an agricultural sector dominated by a white élite (van Zyl et al., 1995). Restrictions on subdivision are still in place on the land reform farms, due to perceived economy of scale (Hall, 2008; Lahiff, 2007a) – however, the beneficiaries have neither the resources nor the skills to run mechanized commercial farms, and beneficiaries in collectively owned farms find it hard to collaborate with one another (Lahiff, 2007b). Hence, splitting farms into family-size units might increase production, employment, and investments, potentially reducing the high rural poverty rate.

We tested the IR hypothesis on farms controlled by land reform beneficiaries using the Quality of Life Survey (QoL) from 2005. The estimated elasticity of value of crop production per land unit with respect to cultivable area, controlling for land value, irrigation, fallow land, and organizational form, is significant and negative – ranging in [–0.87, –0.49]. The results are supported and further interpreted by applying qualitative information from personal visits to 31 land reform farms in 2009. Our quantitative study supports critical reports based on case studies (du Toit, 2004; Lahiff, 2008), but of greater concern is the fact that our field visits show an even more negative effect over time. Several recorded large farm 'successes' in the QoL dataset from 2005 had in fact by 2009 ceased to produce due to internal conflicts of interest and mismanagement. Therefore, an updated dataset could give an even stronger IR effect. However, small farms are a conditional success, as they apply traditional technology and do not satisfy the South Africans politicians' own perception of efficient production.

4.2 Land reform policy in South Africa

4.2.1 Correcting historic injustice

In 1994, the first democratically elected government of South Africa inherited one of the most unequal land and income distributions in the world; a white minority, 10.9 percent of the population, controlled 86 percent of total agricultural land, while the African majority was confined to just 13 percent of the territory, known as the homelands (Lahiff, 2007b). The agricultural sector was, and still is, separated by means of production, as a highly mechanized commercial sector coexists with black small-scale subsistence-oriented farmers. The emergence of large-scale white farms was made possible by artificially depressing the wages of black workers, the creation of marketing monopolies, direct transfers and output subsidies (Christiansen and van den Brink, 1995; Binswanger and Deininger, 1993; Bundy, 1988). In fact, during the nineteenth century the African tenant and owner-operated farms had been outcompeting large-scale farms operated by European settlers and dependent on hired labor (Christiansen and van den Brink, 1995; Binswanger and Deininger, 1993; Bundy, 1988). The main reason for the comparative advantage of the African farmer was the simple technology and the large amount of labor used in production (Christiansen and van den Brink, 1995). So the white large-scale farm owners argued that labor shortages made it impossible to compete, and lobbied for policies to curb competition from black farmers (Christiansen and van den Brink, 1995). As a result, the restrictions on farms owned by black Africans became more pronounced. Tenancy emerged as a response, and by the end of the nineteenth century 50 percent of African farmers were tenants on white-owned land (Christiansen and van den Brink, 1995). Concerns that the success of the African tenant farmers would make them difficult to govern, and the sharp increase in demand for labor from the emerging mining sector, led to an act that had a profound impact on South African history (Christiansen and van den Brink, 1995).

In 1913, the parliament of the then three-year-old Union of South Africa passed the Natives Land Act. The act formalized by law the borders of the African reserves, and declared that natives, defined as members of an aboriginal race or tribe of Africa, only had rights to conduct agricultural activities within these reserves (Feinberg, 1993). Two-thirds of the population would hence be obliged to farm on only 7.8 percent of the available agricultural land, which soon led to land degradation (Christiansen and van der Brink, 1995). The Africans could not own, rent, or lease land outside the homelands, which later became known as the Bantustans (Feinberg, 1993). Independent farmers had to give up, and become cheap labor in the mining industry or employees for white farmers. The black rural population lost their agricultural capital, farming skills and information base that had been accumulated over generations (Christiansen and van der Brink, 1995). In this way, the rural sector became dominated by highly mechanized white farms, despite the historical comparative advantage of labor-intensive production (Deininger and May, 2000).

At the end of Apartheid in 1994, a white paper of the new government introduced three concepts in the land reform program (DLA, 1997). *Restitution* implied that people that had been wrongfully evicted after the Natives Land Act (NLA) in 1913 (or their descendents) would get their land back or a monetary compensation (Hall, 2008). *Tenure* aimed to secure property rights by issuing formal land titles to individuals as well as communities. *Redistribution* aimed to provide land for landless labor tenants and farm workers, as well as new entrants to agriculture. Redistribution is the most important component of the land reform, as it is expected to make the most substantial contribution and benefit the greatest number of people (Lahiff, 2007b). The redistribution is based on the principle of willing seller – willing buyer. This means that the seller and buyer engage in voluntary negotiations, and the role of the state is to provide grants to eligible beneficiaries to buy land on the market (Deininger, 1999). Until the year 2000, a one-time grant of maximum R1600 was made available for households earning less than R1500 per month (Lahiff, 2007b). Restrictions on subdivision, as discussed below, and the relatively large holdings available on the market as a consequence of the policies described above, forced beneficiaries to pool their resources to be able to buy land under the Settlement Land Acquisition Grant (SLAG) program and then farm collectively (Hall, 2008). The lack of success of the land reform projects led to restructuring of the grant system to make it more focused on targeting emerging black commercial farmers and smaller groups, under the new Land Redistribution for Agricultural Development Grant (LRAD) program in year 2000. The income ceiling was abandoned, and own contributions from the beneficiaries were (and still are) required either in cash or in kind. The grants are given on a sliding scale, depending on the size of the contribution made by the beneficiaries. This has raised the concern that the land reform is leaving the poor behind; as the grant system depends on the beneficiaries' own contribution, it will target people with a previously strong asset base (Hall, 2008).

4.2.2 Restrictions on subdivision

The lack of small farms on the market is a consequence of the Subdivision of Agricultural Land Act (SALA) of 1970 that restricted the fragmentation of agricultural land (Hall, 2008). The land reform projects are formally exempted from the act; however, a market for small parcels consisting only of potential land reform beneficiaries is too small to be profitable for large landowners to bear the cost of subdividing their land and selling it in multiple parcels (Lahiff, 2007b). In this way, the act indirectly restricts the opportunities for beneficiaries to buy small and medium-sized farms. This is a crucial obstacle, since small-scale farms are the ones most sought after by the rural poor and landless (Lahiff, 2007b). The reasons for restricting the subdivision of agricultural land were to prevent the rise of black small-scale farmers and secure a minimum income level for white farmers (van Zyl et al., 1995); SALA was repealed in 1998, but the repeal has still not been signed into law by the President – it has never yet officially been brought into effect (Hall, 2008).

Furthermore, institutional and ideological obstacles have prevented subdivision of land reform projects after they have been acquired in the market (Hall, 2008). The major obstacle is the general skepticism among officials in central positions towards restructuring the agricultural sector. Land reform projects that propose subdividing existing farm units or applying for grants to start small-scale production stand little chance of being accepted, even though the largest demand is for small-scale production (Lahiff, 2007b). Our own qualitative interviews also demonstrate that beneficiaries fear governmental revenge in one form or another if they subdivide. This skepticism is based on the belief that productive farming can only be conducted on large-scale farms, and this stems from the fact that a large part of the rural population has never seen a successful and productive small farm because of the distortions imposed under apartheid (Deininger, 1999). As argued by Lahiff (2007b), beneficiaries have numerous problems accessing credit markets, and lack of credit makes many of these land reform projects unworkable.

The large-scale commercial agricultural sector is highly mechanized and a substantial employer, while the current small-scale sector is relatively unproductive. The wish to keep the large-scale commercial sector intact is therefore understandable. However, as discussed above, decades of discrimination against the black rural population has led to the loss of agricultural skills and capital, and it may therefore be over-optimistic to expect that beneficiaries can turn into commercial farmers overnight. Small-scale and medium-scale production may be a more efficient and productive approach, at least in the short run. Van den Brink et al. (1995) point out that it would be unfair to compare the productivity of the commercial sector with the traditional sector because of the discriminatory policies against the latter. It has also been impossible to do so due to the general lack of data on the traditional sector. However, the authors referred to some case studies where black small-scale producers were not facing severe discrimination, and these studies concluded that small-scale farms were more efficient. Van Zyl et al. (1995) analyze the relationship between farm size and total factor productivity within each of the sectors, instead of analyzing between sectors; they find that smaller farms in the commercial sector are generally more efficient, and that they use a relatively more labor-intensive production technique. However, they find that farms in the former homelands seems to be scale-inefficient, although the results should be treated with caution because all those farms are relatively small. This result is not surprising, as part of the Apartheid system was to make small-scale farmers in the homelands unable to be self-sufficient so that they were forced to seek outside work (Deininger and May, 2000). Recognizing the problem of the relatively unproductive small-scale sector has led to a shift of focus to emerging commercial black farmers and businessmen, perhaps moving the land reform away from its goal of rural poverty reduction (Hall, 2008). The continuation of the focus on large-scale farming is likely to benefit a small, privileged group and may not be labor-absorbing, which is crucial for combating rural poverty.

4.3 Theory and literature

The IR between farm size and yield became a stylized fact in development economics after numerous studies had found a negative relationship between farm size and the value of output per land unit. Berry and Cline (1979) was one of the first studies to analyze the IR econometrically; they found a significant negative relationship in two land-abundant Latin American countries and four land-scarce countries in Asia. (See also Bhalla, 1979; Carter, 1984 and Cornia, 1985 for similar studies and results.) Consequently, this empirical observation became a major argument for efficiency of land redistribution reforms.

The theoretical explanations of the IR focus on the labor, capital and land market imperfections that lead factor prices to be dependent on farm size, causing input use per land unit, and hence yield, to be different on large and small farms. This is because there is widespread evidence on constant return to scale (CRS) technology in agricultural production (Berry and Cline, 1979; Bhalla, 1979; Heltberg, 1998; van Zyl et al., 1995).[1] Given CRS technology, input ratios and yield should be constant across farm scale, but if factor prices depend on farm size, the input ratios will be distorted and this would lead to a relationship between yield and farm size. Large farms face higher labor costs, due to higher supervision cost of hired labor. Family labor is the residual claimant of the farm's output and will thus have an incentive to apply an optimal level of effort. Hired labor, on the other hand, who do not receive even the marginal value of their effort, have an incentive to shirk, leading to high costs for low productivity, and, further, supervision costs arise on larger farms. Ceteris paribus, the small-scale farms will have higher output per land unit than large-scale farms because they employ more people due to lower labor costs (Bhalla, 1979;

Binswanger and Rosenzweig, 1986). This effect on productivity might be offset by lower capital costs for large-scale farmers who have access to cheaper credit. The total effect will depend on the output per land unit compared to small farms. This depends on the relative decrease of land and capital prices as farm size increases, the substitution between capital and land, and the substitution between capital and labor (Berry and Cline, 1979). There can also be economy of scale in marketing, control of product quality, and the introduction of innovative technologies, irrigation etc.

The presence of an IR remains highly controversial and contested. The main objection is the failure to control for unobservable factors that are correlated with farm size and yield. For instance, Benjamin (1995) asserts that the empirical results are biased when land quality is unobservable. To control for land quality, Bhalla and Roy (1988) use data from India with detailed information on soil fertility; Heltberg (1998) uses village and household fixed effects; and Benjamin (1995) instruments farm size, using data from Java with various measures of population density. The two former studies find a smaller IR effect when taking land quality into account, and in the latter study, the IR disappears altogether when instrumenting for farm size. However, the instruments used are weak and the sample contains mostly small farms, as pointed out by Heltberg (1998).

4.4 Data and descriptive statistics

The cross-sectional Quality of Life (QoL) survey is described in May et al. (2009). Data was collected at the household and the project (defined as community) level. Our purpose is to analyze whether there is an inverse relationship between output per hectare and farm size on farms that are run by 2002 beneficiary households and their corresponding 207 land reform projects.[2] The sample selection probability for a project is proportional to its size, that is, households in larger projects have an equal probability of being surveyed to households in smaller projects. Twelve households were then randomly selected within each project (May et al. 2009).

There are four categories of land in the survey:

(i) private land outside the project;
(ii) individually farmed project land;
(iii) collectively farmed project land with individual output; and
(iv) collectively farmed land with collective output.

Beneficiaries receive part of the profit in the last category, while in the third category the participants actually split the physical production volume between them. We then introduce the concept 'farm' as our analytical unit by aggregating parcels within each category. We consider all parcels of private land in category (i) in the household survey for a given household as one farm, and equally for all parcels registered under category (ii). This implies that the same household might have two 'farms'; one close to their house and one individual farm on the project land. For collectively farmed land, we prefer to use information given in the project manager/leader questionnaire for the whole land reform project as a unit.[3] However, it is then impossible to split between (iii) and (iv), and hence we aggregate into a single farm all parcels reported to be collectively run in the project questionnaire. Missing information is a considerable problem in the QoL data base. We exclude the household if information on size and production of land 'mostly used' for farming is missing for one of its parcels, for example, dryland crops, gardens, or irrigated land. Reported zero production is regarded as valid information. We also regress the models excluding zero observations, and these results do not alter the conclusion.

The resulting dataset has 545 farm observations, of which 47 percent is private land, 46 percent is individually used land on land reform projects and 7 percent is collectively farmed land on land reform projects. There is some overlap in size between the three categories, but individual parcels tend to be small and collective farms large, as shown in the kernel densities of farm area for the three categories in Figure 4.1, below. Private farms are generally smaller than the project farms, which illustrates the restrictions on subdivision as discussed in Section 4.2. We introduce the variable 'organization form' in the empirical model to control for this effect, as it correlates with cultivable land size (which might still be lying fallow, even though it is cultivable).

The majority of the farms in our dataset are small, that is, 75 percent are smaller than 1 ha, 12 percent are between 1 and 10 ha, 6 percent are between 10 and 100 ha, 5 percent are between 100 and 1000 ha, and 1 percent of them are above 1000 ha. See Table 4.1.

The value of crop production (Y) is calculated by multiplying the crop production volume[4] by the median crop prices in each of the three regions.[5] The figure is reported in South African rands. Farm areas are denoted in hectares. Cultivable area (CL) only includes the relevant uses, that is, it excludes non-relevant uses like housing, grazing, etc.

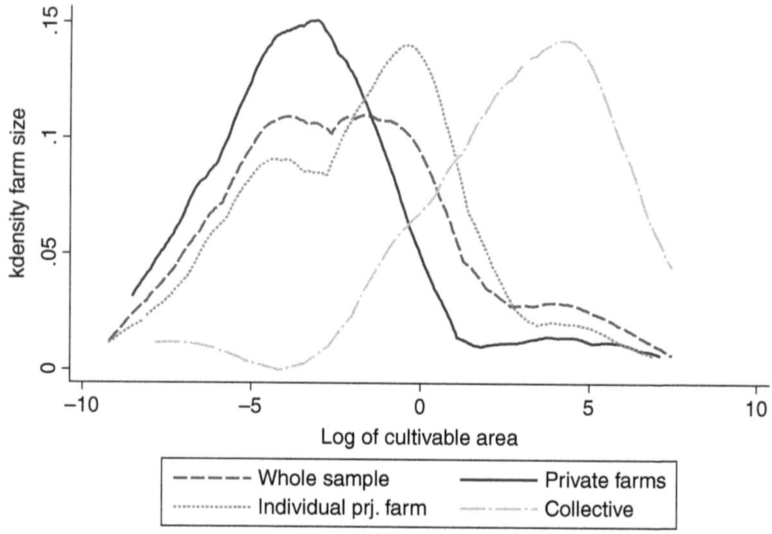

Figure 4.1 K-density function of the three farm categories: private, individual project, and collective farms

Source: Quality of Life dataset.

4.5 The farm size–productivity relationship in the South African land reform

4.5.1 Empirical specification

The conventional approach to empirically test the IR is to use ordinary least squares (OLS) estimation on the following econometric model (Bhalla and Roy, 1988; Carter, 1984; Heltberg, 1998):

$$ln\frac{Y_i}{FS_i} = \beta_0 + \beta_1 lnFS_i + \varepsilon_i \tag{1}$$

The main parameter of interest β_1 is equal to the elasticity of value of output per land unit (Y/FS) with respect to farm size (FS). The OLS estimators will be unbiased if the error term ε_i, representing all residual variation in the dependent variable, is uncorrelated with FS. The impact of farm size on yield is seen as an indirect test for the market imperfections explained above. If capital market imperfections dominate, we will have high capital/land ratios on large farms dominating over the labor market imperfections, and we should expect β_1 to be positive. If labor

Table 4.1 Summary of variables

	#Obs.	Unit	Mean	Std. dev.	Min.	Max.
Cultivable land						
Whole sample	545	HA	27.5	137.2	0.0001	1713
Individual private	251	HA	18.8	119.0	0.0002	1200
Individual project	249	HA	13.3	76.2	0.0001	1024
Collective	45	HA	154.9	318.4	0.0004	1713
Farms with pos. production	514	HA	25.6	131.9	0.0001	1713
Regions: Cape	129	HA	56.1	189.5	0.0002	1024
Inland	144	HA	26.7	151.3	0.0003	1713
Coast	178	HA	12.8	64.0	0.0001	684
Crop production						
Whole sample	545	Rand	70,200	594,616.9	0	8587592
Individual private	251	Rand	35771.6	390,509.2	0	6000.000
Individual project	249	Rand	44,613.2	509054.6	0	7743600
Collective	45	Rand	403814.8	1385661	0	8587592
Farms with pos. production	514	Rand	74433.9	612061.5	1.56	8587592
Regions: Cape	129	Rand	39315.9	1574221	0	1403666
Inland	144	Rand	49234.4	49234.4	0	6000000
Coast	178	Rand	121564.6	895147	0	8587592
Crop production per hectare						
Whole sample	545	Rand/HA	1.52e7	3.41e8	0	7.97e9
Individual private	251	Rand/HA	757,888.5	5274949	0	7.5e7
Individual project	249	Rand/HA	465735.7	2597077	0	2.81e7
Collective	40	Rand/HA	1.77e8	1.19e9	0	7.97e9
Farms with pos. production	514	Rand/HA	1.61e7	3.51e8	0.06	7.97e9
Regions: Cape	129	Rand/HA	222311.6	1574221	0	1.76e7
Inland	144	Rand/HA	609671.8	6251226	0	7.5e7
Coast	178	Rand/HA	4.56e7	5.97e8	0	7.97e9
Crop inputs per hectare:						
Whole sample	545	Rand/HA	31039.9	272112	0	4175000
If crop input is positive	231	Rand/HA	73232.8	414763.8	0.217	4175000
Land value per hectare (if >0)						
Whole sample	451	Rand/HA	120488	570320.6	60	7000000
Regions: Cape	129	Rand/HA	224615.2	809831	100	7000000
Inland	144	Rand/HA	66781.1	288505.4	60	2900000
Coast	178	Rand/HA	88473.3	523593.7	200	6000000
Irrigated farms	36		| Farms with	fruits trees		| 42

and land market imperfections are dominant, there will be a tendency towards labor-intensive small-scale farms. Such farms will use more of the available cultivable land and more labor on each hectare than will large-scale farms. In this case, we should expect β_1 to be negative, and we have an IR (Bhalla, 1979).

The main objection to Equation (1) is that farm size (FS) is correlated with the error term. That is, if there is a non-random relationship between farm size and other variables explaining the value of output per land unit, the results will be biased, and an observed IR could, at least in part, be attributed to an omitted variable. In an attempt to control for this endogeneity problem, we include variables that explain variation in value of output per land unit and that are potentially correlated with farm size.

Land unsuitable for cultivation

A concern is that the existence of large farms is due to the fact that they are situated in remote areas where there is no real basis for agricultural production.[6] One hypothesis is that areas with a high proportion of land that is unsuitable for agricultural production would experience low population growth and less pressure to subdivide land holdings (Carter, 1984). If the proportion of unusable land increases with farm size, then β_1 will have a downward bias. The best way to control for this potential bias would be to exclude from our analysis the share of the farm size that is non-arable. However, we do not have information on the share of farm that is actually non-arable; therefore, in Equation (1) we replace FS with land 'mostly used for' cultivation (CL).

Land quality

The main objection to Equation (1) is that larger farms are characterized by systematically lower land quality, because more productive land tends to be split into smaller units than less productive land. The best method to control for land quality would be to have information on soil type, color, and depth; variables that directly explain land quality. According to Berry and Cline (1979), the price of land is the principal indicator of land quality, and should reflect both inherent land quality differences and the location of the land. Our respondents assess the sales value of their land, and we use the value of cultivable area (FV) as a control for land quality.

But there are two problems with using land price as a proxy for land quality. First, the land price also reflects expected output based on previous realized yields; the land price will then depend on the expected yield, and this would lead to correlation between the error term and land price. Secondly, the land price as a quality term may be biased in favor of small farms;[7] if there are more potential buyers for small holdings, the land price per hectare will be higher for small farms than for large farms, creating an illusion of higher quality land on small farms. However, leaving out a control variable for land quality can bias the results. Therefore, we use the price per cultivable land unit as an indicator of productivity, with the implicit assumption that the assessed price mainly reflects land quality differences.

Another factor determining yield and soil quality is the availability of irrigation. Irrigation makes it possible to have higher cropping intensity and also to have production during the dry season, so an observed IR can be the result of a higher share of irrigated area on small farms if small farms have a higher proportion of irrigated land than large farms. Previous studies have used the proportion of arable land that is irrigated; however, we preferred to construct a dummy variable for the existence of irrigation (I). Only 7 percent have irrigation, but those actually irrigate most of the land.

To further control for differences in land quality, we divided the sample into geographical regions with more homogenous soil quality. Due to data scarcity, it is not possible to divide the sample into provinces, so we disaggregated the observations into Cape (Northern, Western and Eastern Cape); Inland (Limpopo, Mpumalanga, North West, Gauteng, and Free State); and Coast (KwaZulu–Natal).

Product mix

Another feature that may cause a downward bias in the relationship between yield value and farm size is if large farms systematically cultivate low-value crops that need more land and less of the relatively expensive labor per unit of output. One way to control for a supposed shift in product mix as farm size increases is to regress the above models within a crop sector, for example to analyze the models only for farms producing maize. The data used here is not suitable for separating farms into different sectors, as 67 percent of all households have reported producing more than two crops (May et al., 2009). Even if it were possible to separate farms into different sectors, this might not be the best approach since crop mix itself can be a response to the discussed market imperfections (Benjamin, 1995). Holding the product mix constant will neutralize the inefficiencies caused by large farms shifting to crops that need less labor and more land, which gives low values of output per land unit.

Berry and Cline (1979) argue that Equation (1) is a more accurate way to control for the shifting of product mix. The argument is that evaluating the output achieved relative to available land and controlling for land quality leaves no reason to believe that there should be a systematic difference in cropping patterns between large-scale and small-scale farms. Keeping unusable land and land quality constant will choose the product mix that maximizes the value of output per land unit independent of scale. If market imperfections make large farms shift to crops that are less intensive in the relatively more expensive inputs and give a low value of output per land unit, the land will not be used to its full potential. This is an inefficiency that should be captured in the model.

Organization

Restrictions on the subdivision of relatively large farms supplied on the market and the relatively small grants forced beneficiaries to form groups in order to be able to acquire farms as a result of the land reform. The indications from our farm visits are that these groups seemed to have major management problems and internal conflicts relating to investment decisions and division of workload. As larger farms are more expensive, there is a chance that a higher proportion of large farms will be organized as collectives, and this correlation can cause a bias on the estimated elasticity in the models presented above. Deininger (1995) argues that agricultural collectives are far less efficient than independent family farms, because members of collectives will not reap the full reward of their actions, leading to undersupply of effort and investment. If this is true, and a higher proportion of large farms in the sample are organized as collectives, then this could lead to downward-biased results in our models. On the other hand, Platteau (1995) claims that some forms of cooperative land management are superior to private farms in Sub-Saharan Africa. Communities perceived as indigenous and gaining property rights to land that is historically viewed as communal land may have well developed community institutions, organizational policies, and trust amongst community members. This may enable them to pool their resources, efficiently divide the workload, and have a greater scope of labor specialization. To control for organizational form, we have included dummies for individual project land and collective project land. The complete model estimated is therefore:

$$\ln\frac{Y_i}{CL_i}=\beta_0+\beta_1\ln CL_i+\frac{\beta_2\ln FV_i}{CL_i}+\beta_3 I_i+\beta_4 Dind_i+\beta_5 Dcoll_i+\varepsilon_i \qquad (2)$$

Where Y is the value of output for farm i. CL is the size of cultivable area. The parameter of interest, β_1, measures the elasticity of value of output per land unit with respect to cultivable area. FV/CL is equal to the value of cultivated land per hectare. I is a dummy for the existence of irrigation on farm i. *Dind* is the dummy variable for land that is individually farmed on the land reform project farms, and *Dcoll* is likewise for collectively farmed land on the same farms. The reference category is hence individual farmed land that is not on the land reform project, for example 'at home'. Equation (2) also gives a formal test of the claim given in Deininger (1995), that large farms, organized either privately or collectively, will face the same problems that lead to an inverse relationship, since β_1 now reflects the land elasticity with respect to operational area, keeping organizational form constant. The results of the econometric analysis are presented in the next section.

4.5.2 Results and discussion

The results are presented in Table 4.2 below. The estimated elasticity of value of crop production per hectare with respect to farm size is substantial, –0.867 in the simplest model – that is, a 1 percent increase in farm size is associated with a 0.867 percent reduction in the value of crops produced per hectare. The effects drop when we control for land quality, using land value as indicator, irrigation as production input, organizational form, and geographical region. The coefficient for the IR effect is still –0.486 in our preferred Model 5, in Table 4.2 below, and different from zero at a 1 percent significance level. However, we regard these results as partial correlations rather than causal relations, since simultaneity and omitted variable biases are potential problems in such cross-section estimations. The result, however, is quite clear; the larger the farm, the lower the gross income per hectare.

Land value as an indicator of land productivity is highly significant, while the positive effect of access to irrigation turns out to be insignificant. Introducing a control variable for land quality should, as explained above, control for shifts in product mix and a non-random relationship between farm size and land quality. The elasticity drops to –0.588, and the consequent shift in product mix and lower land quality can hence explain some of the observed IR effects in Model 1 in Table 4.2.

We further find that beneficiaries considered to be individual owners of their land had a significant higher productivity, as the dummy coefficient is 1.327, which is significantly higher than the reference category *Private non-LR farm land*. One possible explanation is that the latter suffers from soil mining. Another is the more secure property rights to *Private non-LR*

Table 4.2 Estimation of relationship between crop yield and cultivation area

	Model 1	Model 2	Model 3	Model 4	Model 5
	ln(Y/CL)	ln(Y/CL)	ln(Y/CL)	ln(Y/CL)	ln(Y/CL)
Cultivable area (lnCL)	−0.867***	−0.588**	−0.592***	−0.499***	−0.486***
Land value (ln(FV/CL))		0.357**	0.354**	0.453***	0.462***
Irrigation (Dummy)			0.142	0.571	0.684
Ind. project land (Dummy)				1.618***	1.327*
Collective land (Dummy)				−1.106	−1.220
Coast (Dummy)					0.464
Cape (Dummy)					−0.121 (0.768)
Constant	5.057***	1.841	1.853	0.352	0.260
R^2	0.194	0.192	0.192	0.209	0.211
Adj. R^2	0.192	0.189	0.187	0.201	0.198
#Obs.	545	451	451	451	451

Note: Dependent variable is the logarithmic value of production per hectare of cultivable land (lnY/CL). Significance levels: *** $p<0.01$, ** $p<0.05$, * $p<0.1$.

land, which will make the owners report unused land as well – as long as it belongs to them. Weak property rights on collective farms, however, imply that the farmers would only report the plots they actually farm individually. Our visits also showed that the remaining beneficiaries had grabbed the better part of failing collective run farms, leaving the less productive parts idle, that is, a 'tenderloin' effect. However, the QoL does not have any information on the share of cultivable land actually farmed, and hence we are not able to test this hypothesis quantitatively. The coefficient for *Collective land* is negative, although not significantly different from the *Private non-LR land* category. The significantly lower productivity compared to individual project land is an argument for allowing subdivision in the South African land reform.

Land productivity might be linked to regional differences within the enormous South African continent. The dummy coefficient for the *Cape* and *Coast* provinces compared to the reference category *Inland* are not significant, implying that our chosen regions show no differences in productivity levels (Models 6–11, Table 4.3). The

Table 4.3 Extending Model (5) with estimated crop inputs, Model (6) uses scale, Model (7) dummy for any crop input and (8) includes regional dummies

	Model 6	Model 7	Model 8	Model 9	Model 10	Model 11
Dep. Var.	**ln(Y/CL)**	**ln(Y/CL)**	**ln(Y/CL)**	**ln(Y/CL)**	**ln(Y/CL)**	**ln(Y/CL)**
Cultivable area (lnCL)	–0.531***	–0.472***	–0.568***	–0.542**	–0.576***	–0.203
Cultivable area squared	–0.017				–0.011	
Land value (ln(FV/CL))	0.470***	0.462***	0.369**	0.373**	0.378**	0.445***
Irrigation (I) (Dummy)	0.734	0.691	1.127	1.294	1.299	0.659
Ind. project land (Dummy)	1.332*	1.286*	1.275*	1.303*	1.312	1.216
Collective land (Dummy)	–0.932	–1.316	–1.557	–0.676	–0.601	–1.541
Cape (Dummy)	–0.079	–0.136	–0.429	–0.436	–0.404	–1.002
Coast (Dummy)	0.469	0.432	–0.122	–0.134	–0.128	–0.463
Crop input (per hectare)		0.075	0.067	0.069	–0.081	
Fruit trees (Dummy)			–3.819***	–3.801***	–3.768***	
Collective land* Cultivable area				–0.369	–0.319	
Ind. project land* Cultivable area				0.025	0.029	
Coast*CL						–0.399*
Cape*CL						–0.385*
Constant	0.419	0.306	1.749	1.783	1.805	1.247
R^2	0.212	0.212	0.233	0.235	0.236	0.218
Adj. R^2	0.198	0.197	0.217	0.216	0.215	0.203
#Obs.	451	451	451	451	451	451

Note: Significance levels: *** $p<0.01$, ** $p<0.05$, * $p<0.1$.

alternative specification, with interaction between region and cultivable land, shows a significantly stronger IR effect in the *Coast* and *Cape* than in the reference category *Inland*; the IR coefficient for the latter is now –0.203 and insignificant, while the interaction coefficient is negative and significant for *Cape* and *Coast* in Model 11 in Table 4.3. The regional differences in the IR effect are also apparent in separate regional regression Models 12–17 in Table 4.4; the IR effect is

Table 4.4 Model 3 and 5 run on regional sub-samples

Region	Coast		Inland		Cape	
	Model 12	Model 13	Model 14	Model 15	Model 16	Model 17
Dep. Var.	ln(Y/CL)	ln(Y/CL)	ln(Y/CL)	ln(Y/CL)	ln(Y/CL)	ln(Y/CL)
Cultivable area (lnCL)	–0.606***	–0.347	–0.151	–0.211	–0.902***	–0.635**
Land value (ln(FV/CL))	0.442*	0.779***	0.614**	0.597**	0.083	0.255
Irrigation (I) (Dummy)		-3.025		3.036		1.366
Ind. project land (Dummy)		3.078***		–0.217		0.239
Collective land (Dummy)		0.284		–0.269		-4.150*
Constant	1.633	–3.676	–0.241	–0.427	4.013	2.772
R^2	0.231	0.274	0.102	0.108	0.265	0.290
Adj. R^2	0.223	0.253	0.087	0.076	0.253	0.261
#Obs.	178	178	144	144	129	129

Note: Significance levels: *** $p<0.01$, ** $p<0.05$, * $p<0.1$.

strongest in the *Cape* provinces, and the effect is less significant in the *Coast* region, while there is no significant effect in the *Inland* region.

We include a dummy for the existence of fruit trees as productive capital; these tend to be more common on smaller farms and hence a potential source of estimation bias in the IR effect. However, the effect is significantly negative rather than, as expected, positive. Two potential explanations for this counterintuitive result appeared during the farm visits: fruit farms that had become unprofitable were sold as LR farms, and the new owners had problems finding buyers since product quality in fruit plays a more important role than it does for crops such as maize and vegetables. So some farms had started to cut down fruit and citrus trees to start arable farming. In Models 7–10 in Table 4.3, we find no significant effect for the value of inputs for crop production like fertilizers, pesticides, and seeds, as control variables.[8] This implies that the IR effect is mostly due to labor market imperfections and not capital/input market imperfections. Van Zyl et al. (1995) stress that total factor productivity (TFP) would be the relevant measure of efficiency, but such calculation is beyond the quality of our dataset.

Of the 545 farm observations included, 31 have zero production. We prefer to include those in the regression models by adding a small

Table 4.5 Corresponding to Models 1–5 without zero production observations

	Mode 11*	Mode 12*	Mode 13*	Mode 14*	Mode 15*
Dep. Var.	ln(Y/CL)	ln(Y/CL)	ln(Y/CL)	ln(Y/CL)	ln(Y/CL)
Cultivable area (lnCL)	–0.781***	–0.555***	–0.603***	–0.698***	–0.676***
Land value (ln(FV/CL))		0.286***	0.257***	0.228***	0.241***
Irrigation (Dummy)			1.805***	1.188**	1.394***
Ind. project land (Dummy)				0.433*	–0.126
Collective land (Dummy)				2.448***	2.247
Coast (Dummy)					0.949***
Cape (Dummy)					–0.091
Constant	6.620***	4.102***	4.214***	3.986***	3.785***
R^2	0.530	0.553	0.567	0.590	0.603
Adj. R^2	0.529	0.551	0.563	0.585	0.596
#Obs.	514	425	425	425	425

Note: Significance levels: *** $p<0.01$, ** $p<0.05$, * $p<0.1$.

number to all observations.[9] The IR effect is stronger when zero production farms are excluded in the core Models 1*–5*, given in Table 4.5. Large farms often produce something and are hence included, while smaller farms more often do not produce anything and are hence excluded.[10]

The summary statistics in Table 4.1 disclose that some outlying observations of production per hectare, as reported through the mean in summary statistics of Table 4.1, potentially drive our results. However, our log–log model will put less weight on these outliers. We re-estimate models in Table 4.2, leaving out 5 percent of the observations with the highest value of production per hectare. The elasticity of value of production per hectare with respect to cultivable area is still significantly negative for this alternative dataset, reported in Models 1**–5** in Table 4.6 – although it is also weaker, with an IR coefficient value of –0.353. The effect is in accordance with expectations, as some observations with unrealistically high yield figures appear on some collectively run farms due to reported small land size.

Table 4.6 Corresponding to Models 1–5 without 5 percent highest yield outliers

	Mode l1**	Mode l2**	Mode l3**	Mode l4**	Mode l5**
Dep. Var.	ln(Y/CL)	ln(Y/CL)	ln(Y/CL)	ln(Y/CL)	ln(Y/CL)
Cultivable area (lnCL)	−0.761***	−0.510***	−0.506***	−0.365**	−0.353**
Land value (ln(FV/CL))		0.324**	0.326**	0.432***	0.440***
Irrigation (Dummy)			−0.118	0.708	0.766
Ind. project land (Dummy)				−2.487*	−2.534*
Collective land (Dummy)				1.238*	1.245
Coast (Dummy)					−0.151
Cape (Dummy)					−0.297
Constant	4.977***	2.056	2.045	0.831	0.900
Adj. R^2	0.146	0.144	0.142	0.159	0.156
#Obs.	517	427	427	427	427

Note: Significance levels: *** $p<0.01$, ** $p<0.05$, * $p<0.1$.

4.5.3 Qualitative insights from farm visits

The IR effect in the QoL cross-section dataset was partly confirmed in our visit to 31 land reform farms all over the country in 2009. The informal prohibition of subdivision implied that most farms became collective property, while the transition from SLAG to LRAD programs did not imply a major change in the policy on the ground. Few black capitalists actually want to buy farms in spite of the subsidy. However, groups of people united in order to raise the necessary funds to buy the large farms: small businessmen, retrenched workers, or poor who paid their contribution in 'sweat equities'. The large numbers of beneficiaries gave rise to several problems: for example, sleeping partners who had never participated in farm work might actually make claims on the production of the active members; and beneficiaries with a short time horizon actually led several farms into non-sustainable strategies, such as selling off machinery, small animals, seeds, etc., and in order to maximize short-run payoffs sold whatever existed of capital and distributed financial support between them.

The land reform farms in general lacked machinery and crop inputs like fertilizers, seeds, etc. When investments took place, there was often a mismatch between type of machinery purchased and needs; the beneficiaries could have a biased perception of need, perhaps buying fancy tractors rather than seeds. Furthermore, they often felt forced to accept what turned out to be bad advice from consultants hired by the agricultural authorities, for fear of losing financial support.

The sustainability of the larger LRAD projects is also questionable when they were owned by a group of small-scale commercial interests. They were often split between people genuinely interested in farming and mere investors. If the former strived and became efficient farmers, for example through out-grower schemes for the national and international food industry (the government had set up a program forcing the food industry to buy a certain amount of input from black farmers), co-owners might still demand the sale of the farm when land prices had risen due to urban sprawl or tourism.[11] Such farms are recorded as productive in the QoL data, but the land is now lying fallow. This partial effect of increased probability of failure over time contradicts Keswell et al. (2010), who find a positive income effect over time on the LRAD subsample of the QoL dataset.

The normal presumption is that farms do better over time due to experience, while these examples show, in contrast, that the probability of infighting and hence project failure increases.

The few individual LRAD projects visited were normally involved in chicken production. The black entrepreneurs we visited were more or less bankrupt, in spite of huge transfers of governmental money; they lacked either the necessary experience and the birds died unproductively, or the long-term market connections needed to get a good price for their products.

Joint ventures between groups of black – normally former farm workers – and white consultants or farmers took place, mostly under the restitution program. But some of these large farms are now bankrupt; the black farmers could seldom put up their counterpart for new investments, and they would, furthermore, lose interest if dividends were not paid regularly (in addition to a normal salary for farm workers). Their main interest would actually be to construct individual housing to prevent dependency on the white farmers. The sustainability of these projects was also questionable due to lack of investment, tension and lack of trust between the partners.

None of the large-scale farms came close to their productivity potential. In some cases, highly efficient neighboring white farmers simply rented the land for a minor payment. Then if collective farming did not work out, subdivision would be the reasonable option to take.[12] Only some cases existed, however, as the politicians had signaled that such division would not be tolerated, and hence the beneficiaries were afraid of retaliation in the form of the ministry holding back funds designated for the project. Few beneficiaries would also risk investing money and labor in subdivided parcels, as they feared other beneficiaries would make claims on the harvest – a real risk, as many beneficiaries did indeed perceive the land reform as an act to build society rather than create individual benefits. Such perception is especially prevalent amongst the majority of older beneficiaries, making young people unwilling to invest labor and money.

However, subdivision did take place on some land reform farms. Constructing affordable housing in semi-urban areas could be the real motive, with fairly large, highly productive kitchen gardens around each house. In other cases, most beneficiaries had left the project and the remainder agreed to divide between them the most fertile land and vital inputs like irrigation water. They would normally practise traditional farming techniques, and then, if they had the money available, hire outsiders to plough. This resulted in fairly high productivity on the small part of the whole farm that was actually cultivated, leaving farmland with less potentially fallow land; for example just four families with outdated equipment could farm only a small part of the holding originally given to 80 beneficiaries.

The most successful farmers seemed to be small household units employing mostly their own members as laborers and designating their products for less demanding markets, for example, selling goats and milk to the poorer black townships close by. Geographical location can be crucial to success; beneficiaries mostly come from densely populated areas, and it is questionable if they would relocate to remote places to practise small-scale farming. So proximity to population centers might be just as vital a success factor of the land reform as the creation of the small farm size itself. Respondents indicated no need for more individual parcels, as they already had enough land for subsistence production in their home towns, and they did not intend to move their family to sparsely populated areas with few public services.

4.6 Conclusion and policy recommendations

We find a robustly significant and substantial inverse relationship between farm size and value of crop production per hectare using the QoL survey data. Taken at face value, the results indicate that small-scale beneficiaries are more productive than large-scale ones. This further indicates that it would be favorable for the land reform in South Africa to take a new direction and equalize land distribution. Possible explanations of the results are that the factors that can lead to external economies of scale in agricultural production – skill, access to credit, and markets – are to a certain degree absent in the population that the land reform is trying to target, and this makes small- and medium-scale farms more successful.

The qualitative results from the farm visits tend to confirm the empirical results. We observed that smaller land reform projects, which were controlled by small groups of beneficiaries, were relatively more successful – relatively successful in the sense that smaller land reform projects cultivate and harvest a larger proportion of the available land than do large-scale land reform projects; however, none of the farms we visited were producing at their full potential. Our interpretation of this observation is that the average beneficiary lacks agricultural management skills, has problems accessing markets, and lacks credit (because of bureaucratic problems and lack of trust in farmers), which implies they were not able to make the necessary (and correct) investments in machinery and infrastructure to run a large-scale commercial farm.

The empirical results should be treated with caution. Due to data quality, we were unable to isolate the causal effect between production scale and productivity. Nevertheless, the empirical results and the qualitative robustness check indicate the presence of an IR. Hence we repeat the pre-land reform policy recommendation given in Binswanger and Deininger (1993):

> By (the beneficiary group) having the freedom to choose their farms, internal management schemes, and subdivisions, they can select locations and farming systems most appropriate to the capital and skill endowments of their members.

Thus far, South Africa's land reform has been far from successful. Radicalizing the process to reach the target of redistributing 30 percent of white agricultural land without the ability of the redistributed projects to engage in production that is actually productive could be devastating for the rural economy and the economy as a whole. Recognizing the political and emotional importance of the redistribution of land in South Africa, as well as its economic importance for the rural poor, makes it important to evaluate the reform and identify criteria for success. Much can be done to improve the efficiency of the program itself and increase productivity on the land reform farms.

So, since cooperation enforced top-down by the financing system often fails, the most obvious step is to allow subdivision. Both our qualitative and quantitative data indicate that smaller farms do at least farm using traditional cultivation methods to achieve moderate yields. However, allowing subdivision alone is not a sufficient condition for success, due to low demand for such units in distant areas, where the income potential is low. Intermediate farm size, suited to traditional entrepreneurs serving informal markets in poor settlements in highly populated areas, is probably a more viable strategy to make land reform projects more successful. To speed up the process, the government could consider buying farms, splitting them into several sections, and drawing up land titles in accordance with the preferences and skills of the beneficiaries.

Notes

1. See especially van Zyl et al. (1995) for economies of scale in South African agricultural production.
2. The survey applies a quasi-experimental approach, interviewing both beneficiary and non-beneficiary households. However, we used the former, since our interest was to analyze whether there is an inverse relationship on farms that are run by households and communities that have received land through the land reform.
3. We regard information about the collective land in the household survey as less reliable, since the numbers differ between informants in the project.
4. There are 25 different crops cultivated by the beneficiaries. 67 percent of households report growing more than two crop types, and 20 percent grow more than four (May et al., 2009). The variable of interest here is the total value of crops harvested, so the composition of Y will not be of interest.
5. We chose median crop prices, since the mean would be heavily influenced by unrealistic outliers.
6. For example, a 258 ha land reform project interviewed on the field trip has only 4 ha of cultivable land.
7. Small farms may be a sign of land scarcity, due to higher population density which implies higher prices. Higher prices may also be associated with market access, but this should also be reflected in the prices. However, we do not possess data to correct for these possible effects.
8. Unreported regression models with crop inputs as dependent variables show that smaller farms are more likely to apply inputs per hectare of cultivable land. Collective farms tend to apply more fertilizers compared to larger collective farms. The same applies to collectively run farms compared to the individual categories, while significantly fewer farms in *Coast* and *Cape* spend money on crop inputs. The inclusion of crop inputs reduces the IR effect in Model 7 in Table 4.3 in spite of not being significant, while the change in our preferred Model 5, is much smaller.
9. We could not find a suitable instrument in a Heckman model, i.e. it only influences production decision and not production level. We further argue that the Cragg model requirement of independence of expected productivity from the residual is not satisfied.

10. We indirectly test whether the IR effect is due to moral hazard in labor and coordination problems, by running a regression on only farms larger than 12 ha, which we consider too big to be handled by a single family. The vanishing IR effect for this subsample gives some indicative evidence that this is the source. However, these results can also be due to smaller sample size.
11. The general rule was that LR beneficiaries had to wait 10 years before they were allowed to resell to the highest bidder, but for some reason it was easier for LRAD farms to circumvent this rule. We did not have the information to evaluate whether such sales were profitable in a strict economic sense, compared to continue farming. However, we noticed that people who wanted to sell put more emphasis on immediate payoffs than the committed farmers.
12. This has normally been the result on Latin American land reform farms. The radical military regime in Peru in the 1960s expropriated large farms and gave them to the farm workers. They were expected to proceed as cooperatives, as the government was afraid fragmentation would reduce productivity and represent a poverty trap in the long run. Hidden resistance, however, led to bankruptcy, and the government finally gave in and allowed subdivision to the individual farmers (Wiig et al., 2011). The Guatemala restitution farms for war combatants and refugees were similar. As cooperative efforts failed, they soon found fragmentation to be the only viable option, and they then managed to agree on an internal distribution which everyone respected (Borchgrevink et al., 2007).

References

Banerjee, A.V. (2005) 'Prospects and Strategies For Land Reform', in G.M. Meier and J.E. Rauch (eds), *Leading Issues in Economic Development* (New Yord: Oxford University Press).

Benjamin, D. (1995) 'Can Unobserved Land Quality Explain the Inverse Productivity Relationship?' *Journal of Development Economics*, 46, 51–84.

Berry, R.A. and Cline, W.R. (1979) *Agrarian Structure and Productivity in Developing Countries* (Baltimore and London: John Hopkins University Press).

Bhalla, S.S. (1979) 'Farm Size, Productivity and Technical Change in Indian Agriculture', in R.A. Berry and W.R. Cline (eds), *Agrarian Structure and Productivity in Developing Countries* (Baltimore and London: John Hopkins University Press).

Bhalla, S.S. and Roy, P. (1988) 'Mis-Specification in Farm Productivity Analysis: The Role of Land Quality', *Oxford Economics Papers*, 40, 55–73.

Binswanger, H.P. and Deininger, K. (1993) 'South African Land Policy: The Legacy of History and Current Options', *World Development*, 21(9), 1451–75.

Binswanger, H.P. and Rosenzweig, M.R. (1986) 'Behavioural and Material Determinants of Production Relations in Agriculture', *Journal of Development Studies*, 22(3), 503–39.

Borchgrevink, A., Acevedo, S., Braathen, E., Haslie, A., Haug, M., Holm-Hansen, J., López Rivera, J.F., Norato García, S.A., Solstad, M. and Wiig, H. (2007) 'Evaluation of the Development Cooperation through Norwegian NGOs in Guatemala: NORAD'.

Bundy, C. (1988) *The Rise and Fall of the South African Peasantry*, 2nd edition (Cape Town: David Phillip Publishers).

Carter, M.R. (1984) 'Identification of the Inverse Relationship between Farm Size and Productivity: An Empirical Analysis of the Peasant Agricultural Production', *Oxford Economic Papers*, 36, 131–45.

Christiansen, R.E. and van der Brink, R. (1995) 'South African Agriculture: Structure, Performance and Options for the Future', World Bank, Southern Africa department.

Cornia, G.A. (1985) 'Farm Size, Land Yields and the Agricultural Production Function: An Analysis for Fifteen Developing Countries', *World Development*, 13(4), 513–34.

Deininger, K. (1995) 'Collective Agricultural Production: A Solution for Transitional Economies?' *World Development*, 23(8), 1317–34.

Deininger, K. (1999) 'Making Negotiated Land Reform Work: Initial Experience from Colombia, Brazil and South Africa', *World Development*, 27(4), 651–72.

Deininger, K. and May, J. (2000) 'Can There be Growth with Equity? An Initial Assessment of Land Reform in South Africa', Policy research working paper, World Bank.

DLA. (1997) White paper on the South African land policy.

Du Toit, P. (2004) *The Great South African Land Scandal* (Centurion: Legacy Publications).

Feinberg, H.M. (1993) 'The 1913 Natives Land Act in South Africa. Policies, Race and Segregation in the Early 20th Century', *The International Journal of African Historical Studies*, 26, 65–109.

Hall, R. (2008) 'Land Reform for What? Land Use, Production and Livelihoods', in R. Hall (ed.), *Another Countryside? Policy Options for Land and Agrarian Reform in South Africa* (Cape Town: PLAAS).

Heltberg, R. (1998) 'Rural Market Imperfections and the Farm Size – Productivity Relationship: Evidence from Pakistan', *World Development*, 26(10), 1807–26.

Keswell, M., Carter, M.R. and Deininger, K. (2010) 'Poverty and Landownership: Quasi-Experimental Evidence from South Africa', *Economic Research Southern Africa*, No. 190.

Lahiff, E. (2007a) 'Business Models in Land Reform', Research report, PLAAS UWC.

Lahiff, E. (2007b) 'Willing Seller, Willing Buyer: South Africa's Failed Experiment in Market-Led Agrarian Reform', *Third World Quarterly*, 28(8), 1577–97.

Lahiff, E. (2008) 'Land Reform in South Africa – A Status Report 2008', Research report, PLAAS UWC, Cape Town.

May, J., Keswell, M., Bjåstad, E. and van den Brink, R. (2009) *Monitoring and Evaluating the Quality of Life of Land Reform Beneficiaries and the Impact of Land Transfers: 2005/2006*, Unpublished manuscript.

Platteau, J.-P. (1995) 'Land Reform and Structural Adjustments in Sub-Saharan Africa: Controversies and Guidelines', FAO Economic and Social Development Paper 107, FAO Economic and Social Policy Department, Rome.

Van den Brink, R., Thomas, G., Binswanger, H., Bruce, J. and Byamugisha, F. (1995) 'Consensus, Confusion and Controversy', World Bank Working Paper No. 71, World Bank, Washington, D.C.

Van Zyl, J., Binswanger, H.P. and Thirtle, C. (1995) 'The Relationship between Farm Size and Efficiency in South African Agriculture', Policy Research Working Paper, World Bank, Washington D.C.

Wiig, H., Bråten, R. and Fuentes, D.O. (2011) 'The Impact of Land on Women's Empowerment in Peruvian Communities', *Background paper for World Development Report 2012*, World Bank, Washington D.C..

5
The Economic Effects of Land Redistribution: The Case of a Community-Based Rural Land Development Project in Malawi

Franklin Simtowe, Mariapia Mendola, Julius Mangisoni, Hardwick Tchale and Clement Nyirongo

5.1 Introduction

Land reform in countries with high levels of land inequality is seen by most development experts as an effective means of reducing poverty, since land enriches the asset portfolio of poor households (HHs) and carries with it the potential for agricultural production and entrepreneurship. The objectives of land redistribution are largely classified into (i) social, (ii) economic (iii) political and (iv) environmental. As expressed by Binswanger et al. (2009), advocates of social land reform expect little overall economic gain from the reform, but see it as a way to provide some security and subsistence to a large unemployed rural labor force. To them, the main thrust of agricultural development is to come from large-scale farms and the supporting agro-industrial sectors. The advocates of economic land reform stress the productive superiority of family farms; and they expect the land reform to make a significant contribution not only to agricultural production, but also to rural employment, self-employment, and poverty reduction. The arguments in favor of economic land reform presented above are also consistent with the economic theory which states that a one-time egalitarian distribution of assets in an environment of imperfect markets is associated with permanent higher levels of growth (Deininger et al., 1999). Consistent with this notion, Aghion et al. (1999) express the fact that redistribution in an economy can be conducive to growth. Furthermore, cross-country regressions (Birdsall and Londono, 1998; World Bank, 2001) also provide evidence that greater inequality in the distribution of assets such as land is associated with lower subsequent growth.

Binswanger et al. (2009) also state that advocates of political land reform appreciate, for instance, the dissolution of feudal relationships of production and excessively concentrated and exploitative élite power structures. Specific objectives of political land reform include the creation of political stability and peace. Finally, the advocates of environmental land reform seek the environmentally sustainable management of land, forests and wildlife resources by turning over their ownership and management to defined communities.

Although access to land is not the only pathway out of poverty, most authors (e.g. de Janvry and Sadoulet, 2001) contend that there is ample evidence suggesting that it is effective in helping rural households to generate higher incomes. Increased access to land by the poor can contribute to reduction in food insecurity, poverty and inequality, as it enables the poor to participate in agricultural production.

In Malawi, the rapid expansion of estate agriculture, particularly for the production of tobacco from the 1960s to the 1980s, resulted in an unequal distribution of land in rural Malawi (Lele, 1989). Emphasizing the magnitude of land inequality, Chirwa and Chinsinga (2008) report that while 55 percent of smallholder farmers in Malawi cultivate less than a hectare, there are about 30,000 estates cultivating between 10 to 500 hectares. Furthermore, it is estimated that about 28 percent of the country's cultivable arable land (about 2.6 million ha), lies underutilized or unutilized in rural areas.[1] The existing land inequality, coupled with the underutilization of land in large estates, has been used as a justification for land redistribution in Malawi. Acknowledging the feasibility of land redistribution in Malawi, Chirwa (2004) expresses how there are several opportunities for land redistribution on a voluntary basis in Malawi, and yet the landless do not have information on the availability of land and the resources that would allow them to migrate to such areas.

However, as expressed by Robilliard et al. (2002), there is little agreement on how land reform can be best designed and implemented. The analyses and experience from other countries have shown that land redistribution is not nearly as straightforward as might be hoped. It can be costly in program resources; it can reduce productivity and be an instrument of political patronage. Substantial personnel and financial resources are necessary to assess and purchase (or expropriate) land, select beneficiaries, and supply training and credit.

In Malawi, changes in the policy environment, such as the liberalization of tobacco farming in the 1990s, created competition for tobacco estate owners, which, coupled with declining tobacco prices, reduced the profitability of their farms and led an increasing number of estate owners to sell off their land. In 2002, a new National Land Policy was adopted by the government of Malawi to correct some of the historical wrongs on land issues and land inequality. The positive land policy environment, along with the availability of land for sale by willing estate owners, provided an opportunity favorable to the introduction of a land redistribution program based on voluntary land transfers between landowners (willing sellers) and the land-poor (willing buyers).

In 2004, with financial assistance from the International Development Association (IDA) of the World Bank, the government of the Republic of Malawi, through its Ministry of Lands, Housing and Urban Development, started implementing a Community-Based Rural Land Development Project (CBRLDP). Through this project, 15,142 households were relocated and provided with land on which to live and cultivate; this represents about 0.5 percent of the rural households in Malawi who have received about 1 percent of the agricultural land through this redistribution.

The Project has been viewed by most experts as one of the most significant interventions ever implemented to address the highly unequal land ownership patterns in postcolonial Malawi. However, a full impact analysis had not been conducted.

This chapter investigates the impact of the CBRLDP on land availability, agricultural productivity, input use, income and expenditure of beneficiary households. The analysis is based on a four-year panel household survey data collected among 1194 households in six pilot districts (Mulanje, Thyolo, Mangochi, Machinga, Balaka and Ntcheu) in southern and central Malawi, from 2005 through to 2009. We apply a combination of matching and double difference methods to the panel data, while a cost–benefit analysis is also conducted to compute economic and financial benefits as well as to assess the project viability. Results show that the land redistribution project significantly increased land holdings, agricultural output and crop-specific land productivity for maize and tobacco of beneficiary households. Moreover, beneficiary households significantly improved their food security and agricultural income levels after joining the project. In general, these impacts are higher in the short term, while they decrease slightly over time. Overall, the findings suggest that there is scope for reducing poverty and inequality in developing countries by implementing a decentralized, community-based, voluntary, and market-assisted approach to land reform through the provision of land to landless and land-poor households.

The rest of the chapter is structured as follows: Section 5.2 presents the background of the CBRLDP, its components and implementation process. The methodological approach is discussed in Section 5.3. A discussion on the impact of the CBRLDP on land holding, agricultural productivity, livestock, farm inputs and incomes is presented in Section 5.4, and Section 5.5 concludes.

5.2 The CBRLD project, implementation process and its components

5.2.1 Brief history of land reform in Malawi

Land tenure issues in Malawi can be better understood from a description of the historical perspectives that date as far back as the nineteenth century. As expressed by Machira (2008), prior to the creation of the British protectorate of Nyasaland in 1891, European settlers, missionaries and companies had started acquiring land from African chiefs or headmen under a 'master–servant' kind of relationship. Under the African Orders in Council 1889 and 1892, the British government appointed a commissioner who was responsible for formalizing these agreements and making new land grants in the name of the Crown. European settlers were provided with 'certificates of claim'; they acquired some of the best land, most of it in the Shire Highlands located in the southern part of the country. Through this process, the Crown allocated to European settlers and companies about 15 percent of the total land in Malawi, or 27 percent of the total land suitable for cultivation. According to the Presidential Commission of Inquiry on Land Policy Reform (1998), this process led to the granting of about 73 percent of the granted land to a single entity, the British South Africa Company. When Malawi gained independence from Britain in 1964, the country inherited 'a rural settlement structure in which some of the most fertile and well-watered lands were reserved to white farmers' (Saidi, 1999 cited in Holden et al. (2006).

In 1996 a Presidential Commission of Inquiry on Land Policy Reform (PCILPR) was established to undertake a broad review of land problems throughout Malawi, and recommend the main principles of a new land policy which would foster a more economically efficient, environmentally sustainable and socially equitable land tenure system. The objective of the Commission was also to recommend a national land policy that would promote equitable access to land, security of title to land, and improved land administration. The findings by PCILPR led to the formulation of a New Land Policy which was approved by cabinet in 2002 (government of the Republic of Malawi, 2002).

5.2.2 The CBRLD project

In 2004, the government of the Republic of Malawi, through the Ministry of Lands, Housing and Urban Development, started implementing the Community-Based Rural Land Development Project (CBRLDP). This is a market-based model by which government and donor agencies provide finances and services to encourage communities to buy land themselves. The Community-Based Rural Land Development Project (CBRLDP) is one of the initiatives by the government of Malawi's Land Reform Programme (LRP) implemented with financial assistance in form of a grant from the International Development Association of the World Bank. The Project's development objective was to increase agricultural productivity and incomes of about 15,000 poor rural families by implementing a decentralized, community-based and voluntary approach to land reform in six pilot districts: Mulanje, Thyolo, Machinga, Mangochi, Balaka and Ntcheu, in southern Malawi.

The project was piloted in five districts of the southern region of Malawi, namely, Machinga, Mangochi, Mulanje, Thyolo and Balaka, and in Ntcheu district in central Malawi. According to a final report of the 2008 Malawi Population and Housing Census (Government of Malawi, 2008), the total population for Machinga, Mangochi, Mulanje and Thyolo was about 2.4 million in 2008, representing 18.4 percent of the national population. The total population for Balaka and Ntcheu districts was 623,847. The total population in the project areas was about 3.2 million (24.5 percent of the country's population). Based on the 2008 population statistics, Mulanje and Thyolo have one of the highest population densities in Malawi, estimated at 208 and 268 inhabitants per square kilometer, respectively. It is also reported that the two districts of Mulanje and Thyolo are, coincidentally, also the main tea-growing areas of the country. Most of the good arable land in the two districts is under tea estates, largely owned by foreign investors. In contrast, Machinga and Mangochi districts are said to have a much lower population density, averaging around 97 people per square kilometer.

Community-driven, the Project focused on rural areas and it had four components: (i) Land Acquisition and Farm Development, (ii) Land Administration, (iii) Capacity Building; and (iv) Project Management, Monitoring and Evaluation. The details of each of the project components are described in Simtowe et al. (2011). The Project did not have any provision for social amenities (infrastructure, water, school, health etc) for beneficiary households; after relocation, beneficiary communities were to apply to the Malawi Social Action Fund (MASAF) for the provision of community assets such as boreholes, access roads, schools and clinics, in line with MASAF principles and criteria of demand-driven development and community participation. But it was in only very few cases that MASAF provided schools and hammer mills to project beneficiaries and surrounding communities. Most beneficiary groups did not have ready access to education and health facilities, demonstrating weak and ineffective coordination among stakeholders in the implementation of the project.

The project was set up so as to provide conditional cash and land transfer to poor families to relocate, purchase, develop and register new (larger) plots of farm land. Each beneficiary household received approximately two hectares of land, a cash grant held in a group bank account, and title to the land through a group-level title deed. The total amount per household was $1,050, with 30 percent that could be spent on the purchase of land; 8 percent was given as a relocation allowance prior to resettlement, with the balance to be applied to farm development. The amounts given to each beneficiary were standard. Cash was released in tranches to the beneficiary groups (BGs) upon request.[2] The project ended in September 2011.

5.3 Methodology

5.3.1 Description of the data

The empirical analysis is based on a four rounds household panel dataset collected among 1194 households in six districts (Mulanje, Thyolo, Mangochi, Machinga, Balaka and Ntcheu) in Malawi between 2006 and 2009. The dataset was collected by ECI Africa (Pty) Ltd, an economic development consulting firm and Invest in Knowledge Initiative (IKI) over the time. The distribution of the households across districts and years is presented in Table 5.1.

As depicted in Table 5.2 below, the data consists of 391 beneficiary households, or 'treatment group', plus some 'indirectly treated households', that is, 190 households left behind in the vacated areas and 214 households in the receiving areas; households in the latter group are partially affected by the project as well (for example, by the changes in land availability, and labor demand or supply as a consequence of the departure or arrival of new households). Finally, the dataset contains information on 397 households in similar areas of the neighboring districts of Chiradzulu and Balaka, in order to get a totally unaffected control group. It is this group that is used as the counterfactual in our analyses.

Table 5.1 Distribution of households surveyed in the panel dataset

	Round number				
District	**Baseline**	**Yr 2**	**Yr 3**	**Yr 4**	**Total**
Balaka	205	205	205	205	820
Chiradzulu	192	192	192	192	766
Machinga	371	371	371	371	1483
Mangochi	345	345	345	345	1381
Mulanje	49	49	49	49	196
Thyolo	32	32	32	32	128
TOTAL	1194	1194	1194	1194	4776

Source: CBRLDP dataset.

Table 5.2 The distribution of households by treatment status

	Balaka	**Chiradzulu**	**Machinga**	**Mangochi**	**Mulanje**	**Thyolo**	**Total**
Treated			185	206			391
Control group	205	192					397
Indirectly affected group (surrounding area)			140	74			214
Indirectly affected group (vacated area)			46	65	49	32	190
Total	205	192	371	345	49	32	1194

Source: CBRLDP dataset.

Since these three groups (in vacated areas, in receiving areas, and the direct beneficiaries) are likely to be affected by the project, they have to be treated as 'treatment groups', although for some indicators they are unlikely to be affected by the moving of households, so they could also be treated as control groups. In order to get a totally unaffected control group, 397 households in similar areas of neighboring districts were selected as the long-term control group.

Baseline data collection was conducted after households' relocation in 2006. Subsequent rounds followed in 2007, 2008 and 2009, tracing the implementation process and schedules of prior rounds.

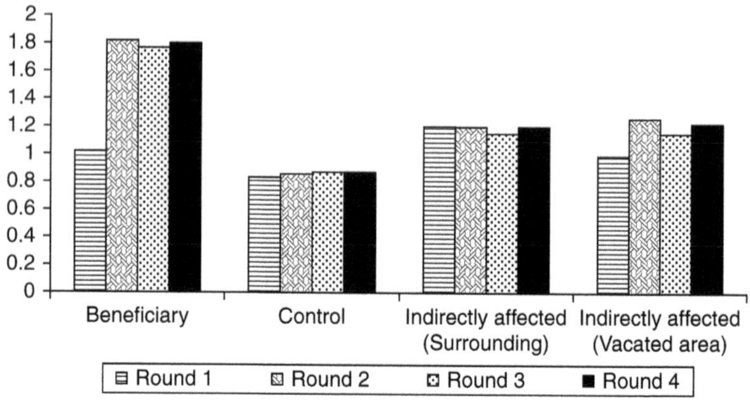

Figure 5.1 Average total owned land size (ha) by category of household

The analysis for this chapter makes use primarily of the first and second rounds (immediately after the program was implemented) in order to test short-run effects. However, we also test the medium-term impacts, using the last two rounds as well. Control group households located in neighboring districts share many of the same characteristics as beneficiary households. Yet, in order to be sure that groups are statistically comparable, a propensity score-matching technique is used to identify a control group from among the ineligible population that is similar to the beneficiaries at baseline.

Figure 5.1 reports the agricultural land (or garden) size owned, disaggregated by beneficiaries and different control groups (non-project areas, surrounding areas and vacated areas) over time. Results for households from control groups show a rather stable pattern (below 1.0 ha, on average). On the contrary, project households' land holding increases over time, starting from 1.0 ha in first survey round in 2006, reaching a peak of 1.8 ha in Round 4 (2009).

Table 5.3 displays the mean values of key agricultural outcome indicators across project and non-project households in the baseline (Period 1 or pre-treatment) and for subsequent survey rounds (Periods 2 to 4 or post-treatment). With the exception of total land size (agricultural and residential), all indicators generally moved in the expected direction over time, with a tendency to increase over the period in both project and non-project areas. During the first year, beneficiary households allocated 0.43 ha and 0.12 ha of this land to maize and tobacco, respectively. The land allocated to maize by beneficiary households rose to 0.75 ha

Table 5.3 Summary statistics: trends in cultivated land for maize and tobacco

Type of household	Time (round)	Maize area (ha)	Tobacco area (ha)
Beneficiary households (391 HHs)	1	0.43	0.12
	2	0.70	0.62
	3	0.65	0.44
	4	0.65	0.00
	Average	0.62	0.30
Control group households (397 HHs)[a]	1	0.51	0.06
	2	0.52	0.05
	3	0.53	0.07
	4	0.53	0.00
	Average	0.52	0.05

Note: [a] This is only for the non-project sites.

in the second year, but stabilized at 0.65 ha in subsequent years. On the other hand, the land allocated to maize by non-beneficiary households only increased modestly, from 0.51 ha in the first year to 0.53 ha in the fourth year. The findings, based on the descriptive analysis, suggest that beneficiary households cultivated more maize than did non-beneficiaries.

As for tobacco, beneficiaries increased the land allocated to tobacco, from 0.12 ha in the first year to 0.62 ha in the second year. This, however, declined sharply in subsequent years, a trend consistent with national trends. In general, the land allocated to tobacco has been on the decline nationwide due to declining producer prices. Table 5.4 displays the mean values of key agricultural outcome indicators across project and non-project households in the baseline (Period 1 or pre-treatment) and for subsequent survey rounds (Periods 2 to 4 or post-treatment). With the exception of total land size (agricultural and residential), all indicators generally moved in the expected direction over time, with a tendency to increase over the period in both project and non-project areas.

5.3.2 Econometric analysis

The impact evaluation was conducted using baseline data and the subsequent three years annual household surveys using an Average treatment effects framework. Using the four-year integrated panel data provided by the project, the Evaluation Team conducted an impact evaluation analysis on Key Performance Indicators (KPI) such as household landholding size, agricultural productivity, food security and household income. A full list of indicators is presented in Table 5.5.

Table 5.4 Summary statistics: agricultural outcome variables (mean)

	Time	Total land cultivated (hectares)	Quantity of maize (kg)	Quantity of tobacco (kg)	Maize land productivity (kg/ha)	Tobacco land productivity (kg/ha)
Beneficiary HHs (391)	1	1.02	688.24	53.66	1535.99	1153.03
		[0.93]	[806.41]	[203.74]	[1176.33]	[1273.50]
	2	1.81	1355.91	100.55	2476.14	954.53
		[0.68]	[1112.73]	[264.48]	[6543.21]	[1208.58]
	3	1.76	866.12	113.72	1446.14	746.90
		[0.69]	[793.22]	[220.50]	[1200.79]	[806.70]
	4	1.79	846.44	185.43	1464.63	875.83
		[0.72]	[744.84]	[388.54]	[1448.99]	[658.19]
	Average	1.6	939.18	113.34	1729.63	886.95
		[0.83]	[910.67]	[282.56]	[3472.63]	[932.69]
Non-project HHs (397)	1	0.88	579.55	9.40	1268.61	2722.77
		[0.62]	[550.08]	[87.72]	[955.25]	[2355.67]
	2	0.92	575.95	1.88	1308.61	783.83
		[0.64]	[468.49]	[20.12]	[1140.82]	[515.26]
	3	0.91	559.89	4.12	1205.90	1199.26
		[0.69]	[485.77]	[34.73]	[884.89]	[1147.23]
	4	0.95	662.86	5.78	1474.21	731.56
		[0.76]	[597.25]	[49.92]	[1519.80]	[615.49]
	Average	0.91	594.56	5.29	1314.53	1352.82
		[0.68]	[528.94]	[54.33]	[1155.65]	[1546.59]

Note: Standard deviations in square brackets.

Table 5.5 Key performance measures assessed

Name of indicators	Unit of measurement
Farm input use	
Receipt of subsidized inputs (coupons)	(1 = yes, 0 = otherwise)
Number of contacts with agricultural extension staff	Frequency per year
Use of inorganic fertilizer	(1 = yes, 0 = otherwise)
Use of compost manure	(1 = yes, 0 = otherwise)
Agricultural outcome variables	
Agricultural land	Ha
Quantity of maize produced	Kg
Quantity of tobacco produced	Kg
Maize yield	Kg/ha
Tobacco yield	Kg/ha
Total annual non-food expenditure	MK

The analysis entailed comparison of these KPIs before and after relocation of the treatment groups (beneficiaries), and between treatment and control groups (vacated, surrounding/ receiving and non-project). Yet, in this study an assessment of the impact of the project on selected indicators, by comparing the simple difference in mean outcomes of the treated and the control groups would not explicitly point to the 'causal effect' of the land redistribution program. Indeed, in order to assess the impact of a new program on KPIs, the researcher should be able to assess what the situation would be like if the 'treatment' had not been adopted, that is, the counterfactual situation. If not, that could lead to misleading policy implications, as at the household level many other factors may have changed along with the program. This is an important methodological concern if we want to evaluate the true causality of change. In order to tackle this apparently counterfactual problem the quasi-experimental design of the project was exploited, and impact evaluation methods were used to compare 'treated' and 'control' households. Thus the longitudinal framework of the project was exploited and *difference-in-difference estimator (DID)* was employed to compare treated and control groups, before and after the treatment (double differencing). However, the two groups may not be comparable. This is so because there is a general problem of 'self-selection' in that the households (partly) determine whether or not they receive the treatment, and their decision may be related to the KPIs.

Ideally, randomization can correct for the problem of 'causal inference', by randomly assigning households or groups to treatment and control groups. In this case, we would have the information on the counterfactual situation and would be able to calculate the difference in the outcome of interest between the treated and the control group, that is, the Average Treatment Effect (ATE) (Imbens and Angrist, 1994). This was not possible, however, in this study, since selection into the program was not random.

Most important, is the issue of the *unobserved heterogeneity in participation* or, in other words, the problem of missing data for the counterfactual (see for example, Blundell and Costa Dias, 2000; Wooldridge, 2001). The latter is related to the general problem of self-selection, and emanates from the fact that households (partly) determine whether they receive the treatment and so their decision may be related to the variables of outcome.

In order to tackle the above concern we employed difference-in-difference (DID) and propensity-score-matching (PSM) methods. DID estimation relies on comparison of treatment and control groups in terms of outcome changes before (baseline) and after the intervention. That is, given a two-period setting where t = 0 before the program and t = 1 after implementation of the program, letting Y_i^T and Y_i^C be the respective outcomes for a program beneficiary and non-treated units in time *t*, the DID method will estimate the average program impact as follows:

$$DID = E(Y_1^T - Y_0^T | T_1 = 1) - E(Y_1^C - Y_0^C | T_1 = 0) \tag{1}$$

The DID estimator allows for *unobserved heterogeneity* (the unobserved difference in mean counterfactual outcomes between treated and untreated units) that may lead to selection bias, by assuming that it is time invariant, so the bias cancels out through differencing.

Within a regression framework, the estimating equation would be specified as follows:

$$Y_i = \alpha + \beta T_{i1} t + \rho T_{i1} + \gamma t + \varepsilon_{it} \tag{2}$$

In Equation (3) the coefficient β on the interaction between the post-program treatment variable T_{i1} and time *t* gives the average DID effect of the program. In addition to the interaction term, the variables T_{i1} and *t* are included separately, to pick up any separate mean effects of time as well as the effect of being targeted versus not being targeted.

Yet the DID estimator requires that the error term be uncorrelated with the other variables in the equation, that is:

$$\begin{aligned} &Cov(\varepsilon_{it}, T_{i1}) = 0 \\ &Cov(\varepsilon_{it}, t) = 0 \\ &Cov(\varepsilon_{it}, T_{i1} t) = 0 \end{aligned} \tag{3}$$

The last assumption, also known as *parallel-trend* assumption, is critical, as it means that unobserved characteristics affecting program participation do not vary over time with treatment status. In order to tackle this issue and allow the possibility of time-variant selection bias due to initial observables, we use the predicted probability of participating in the program (the propensity score) to match the treatment units with observationally similar control units before estimating the weighted DID impact (where the weights are equal to 1 for treated units and to the frequency given to each matched observation for comparison units).

PSM constructs a statistical comparison group that is based on a model of the probability of participation in the treatment, using observed characteristics. Participants are then matched on the basis of this probability, or *propensity score,* to non-participants. The validity of PSM depends on two conditions: (a) conditional independence (namely that after controlling for observed characteristics, unobserved factors do not affect participation) and (b) sizable common support or overlap in propensity scores across the participants and non-participant sample. The latter condition ensures that treatment observations have comparison observations 'nearby' in the propensity score distribution (Heckman et al., 1999).

Hence, we combine PSM and DID so that the average treatment effect of the program is estimated by matching units in the common support, and calculating the weighted difference in the outcome variables between participants and controls before and after the intervention. Yet, even if comparability of control and project areas could be ensured before the program through PSM upon observables, the DID approach might falter if macroeconomic changes during the program affected the two groups differently.

5.3.3 Financial and economic analysis

A cost–benefit analysis technique was employed to assess the financial and economic viability of the project. A cost–benefit analysis measures return on investment over a given time period; the process involves discounting the cost–benefit flows to reflect the value of time. Net present value (NPV), cost–benefit ratio and internal rate of return (IRR) are the three key indicators to determine the viability of an investment in a given area.

In the financial analysis, we look at the current and potential income situation on an enterprise level and firm (farm) level, taking the analytical framework used at the project design and mid-term review for ease of results comparison. This type of analysis contributes to the identification of problems and opportunities in the project area by assessing the effect of the project (investment) on the community farms or firms. The financial analysis gives an answer to the question of whether the investment is attractive to a farmer or a group of farms; the financial analysis was not only limited to NPV, IRR and cost–benefit analysis, but also included preparation of budgets for land, labor and capital to adjust demand for and supply of those resources.

An economic analysis also gives an answer to the question of whether the project is attractive to the society as a whole. Thus some adjustments are made and distortions in the prices of inputs and outputs removed;

for instance, costs partly or completely borne by the government and not completely passed on to the entities involved in the project need to be included in the economic analysis. A positive NPV or an IRR higher than the cut-off point means that the project is acceptable to the society (from an efficiency point of view).

Representative farm household models were developed based on the farm characteristics and behavior of the survey households. We assumed that primary economic benefits of the project accrued from increased agricultural productivity due to the redistributed land and the use of improved crop varieties and agricultural inputs, as well as the distributional benefits gained from increasing the incomes of about 15,000 poor and land-poor rural families.

5.4 Results and discussion

5.4.1 Econometric impact assessment using DID results

Tables 5.6 and 5.7 present DID estimates of Equation (3) discussed above, assuming that there is no time-varying self-selection into treatment. Here in particular the analysis estimates mean impacts comparing beneficiary and non-beneficiary households' outcomes in the baseline and for subsequent survey rounds. Non-project households are used as a control group, to be compared with beneficiary households. The households in vacated and receiving (surrounding) areas are left out of this analysis because they are considered to be 'indirectly treated groups', in that they may be affected by the project via spillover effects.

Control variables included in the regression are household size, gender, age and level of schooling of the household heads, household's religion and ethnic group, inheritance tradition, and district fixed effects (that is, dummies at district level, which were eventually included in order to control for any observable and unobservable district characteristics that might affect both the project placement and households' outcomes). The size of working-age family members was different between the farms. Several empirical studies, for example, Rosenzweig and Binswanger (1993), reported about inverse relationships between farm size and productivity; this led us to test whether there was an inverse relationship between land productivity and labor intensity (*farm area per working-age member*). This test is necessary in order to guide in deciding whether or not to allow for farm size adjustment through land transactions carried out to enhance land productivity on redistributed land. The test was conducted by including the ratio of land to the number of working-age

Table 5.6 DID estimates on agricultural outcome variables[a]

	(1)	(2)	(3)	(4)	(5)	(6)	(7)
	Land (agr & residential)	**Land (agr)**	**Quantity of maize (kg)**	**Quantity of tobacco (kg)**	**Quantity of tot. crop (kg)**	**Maize land productivity**	**Tobacco land productivity (kg/ha)**
Panel A: baseline versus the following survey round (2006 and 2007)							
Post-program*Beneficiary	0.72***	0.53***	661.45***	52.26***	720.92***	879.09**	1,356.22
Controls	Yes	Yes	Yes	Yes	Yes	Yes	Yes
Observations	1,548	1,570	1,570	1,570	1,570	1,549	184
R-squared	0.274	0.163	0.177	0.078	0.199	0.036	0.153
Panel B: baseline versus the following 3 survey rounds (2007, 2008 and 2009)							
Post-program*Beneficiary	0.73***	0.59***	322.83***	81.10***	418.97***	244.27	1,122.37***
Controls	Yes	Yes	Yes	Yes	Yes	yes	yes
Observations	3,129	3,127	3,112	3,109	3,129	3,127	554
R-squared	0.295	0.181	0.108	0.107	0.144	0.023	0.099

Note: [a] Significance levels: *** $p<0.01$, ** $p<0.05$, * $p<0.1$.

Table 5.7 DID estimates on farm inputs use[a]

	(1)	(2)	(3)	(4)
Variables	**Gov. coupon (1 = yes, 0 = otherwise)**	**Exten. Service (1 = yes, 0 = otherwise)**	**Fertilizer (1 = yes, 0 = otherwise)**	**Compost (1 = yes, 0 = otherwise)**
Panel A: baseline versus the following survey round (2006 and 2007)				
Post-program* Beneficiary	–0.17***	0.18***	0.09***	0.01
Controls	Yes	Yes	Yes	Yes
Observations	1,563	1,556	1,548	1,546
Pseudo R-squared	0.15	0.028	0.11	0.11
Panel B: baseline versus the following 3 survey rounds (2007, 2008 and 2009)				
Post-program*Beneficiary	–0.09**	0.15***	–0.02	0.02
Controls	Yes	Yes	Yes	Yes
Observations	3,129	3,127	3,112	3,109
Pseudo R-squared	0.14	0.013	0.088	0.11

Notes: [a] The estimates are based on a non-linear model since all outcome variables are categorical. Significance levels: *** $p<0.01$, ** $p<0.05$, * $p<0.1$.

members (labor force) as an explanatory variable in Equation (3), in order to analyze if the different endowment of land relative to labor would affect productivity in the absence of land renting. The variable returned a positive but insignificant sign, rejecting the hypothesis of inverse relationship between labor force and productivity.

Results are always given for two time periods, namely 2006 to 2007 (Panel A) and 2006 to 2009 (Panel B), referred to as the short and medium term (this is also done in order to compare current results with those provided by former IEG impact evaluation analysis). Under the Evaluation assumptions these estimates reflect causal effects of the CBRLDP.

Table 5.6 presents DID estimates of causal effects on agricultural outcomes and results, both for short and medium term, show that – as expected given the project design – there is a statistically significant impact on land size (either agricultural or residential). There is also a positive impact on crop output, in particular on the quantity of maize and tobacco produced. Results on short-term maize yields (that is, *maize product* over *land devoted to maize*) are positive and significant, while tobacco yields (*tobacco product* over *land devoted to tobacco*) are not significantly affected, suggesting that participation in the program immediately increases maize land productivity. In the medium term, though, the impact on maize output per hectare is no longer significant, while tobacco yields turn out to be significant. This may reflect some crop-specific distinctive features of maize and tobacco production; the latter has been shown to be more labor-intensive than maize production in terms of both tasks and duration of work. Furthermore, tobacco requires more inputs such as seeds, fertilizer, manure and materials for barns and bales, so that it requires more working capital than maize. Entry barriers to tobacco production are high, and only farmers who can afford such high production costs can engage in tobacco growing (Takane, 2007). However, since both maize and tobacco production are sensitive to weather, these trends could be affected by seasonal variations in the onset of rainfall. However, we lack detailed data on rainfall distribution to validate this hypothesis.

Overall the longer-term gains from the project seem to be primarily in terms of land size and quantity of production, suggesting potential benefits in terms of food security. The fact that maize yield (kg/ha) declines may be due to the declining access to farm inputs such as fertilizer; but an alternative explanation for the long-run decline in productivity for maize could be the shortage of labor. Unfortunately there are no data in the survey on the degree to which sample households are able to access hired labor, but anecdotal evidence does point to labor market imperfections in the area under study (Takane, 2007).

Table 5.7 reports the impact of the project on the use of farm inputs. The results point to a significant decrease in the government input subsidy coupons received by beneficiary households after the project, while the use of extension services and fertilizers significantly increase after the project – the latter only in the short run, probably due to the exhaustion of the initial grant available for farm operations. Malawi has been implementing a comprehensive fertilizer and seed subsidy program to boost its agricultural production and to enhance food security in the country. The program aims to provide coupons for the purchase of subsidized fertilizer and seeds to targeted poor rural households. The decrease in fertilizer input over time may be attributed to the fact that beneficiaries receive free fertilizer in the first year of relocation, but none in subsequent years. Households in vacated and surrounding areas are likely to have higher social capital than relocated households; such social ties to non-beneficiaries may be used to obtain inputs through other sources such as subsidies and credit.

5.4.2 PSM combined with DID results

As mentioned above, conventional DID gives unbiased estimates based on the assumption that the selection bias is constant over time. However, if there is *self-selection* into treatment, as in our case, or in other words if there are *time varying factors* that influence treatment, then land acquisition is still correlated with the error term in the differenced equation. To allow for the possibility of time variant selection bias due to initial observables, we use the predicted probability of participating in the land redistribution project (the propensity score) to match the comparison households in the DID estimate. PSM is implemented using a logit that includes initial conditions that may affect subsequent land trajectories as explanatory variables. Our impact estimates are then constructed by comparing the before and after project change in outcome measures for the beneficiary households with those for the matched comparison group. We apply nearest-neighbor (NN) matching, which consists of considering each treated (control) unit and searching for the control (treated) unit with the closest propensity score, that is, the nearest neighbor. We further impose a tolerance level on the maximum propensity score distance among matched units (*caliper = 0.01*)[3] in order to increase the matching quality (treated that cannot find a matched control within the caliper are discarded). NN with caliper is the method that should achieve the highest reduction of the bias. However, its variance is expected to be higher than for other methods (Caliendo and Kopeinig, 2008); this is because if fewer matches can be performed, the variance of the estimates increases (because of reduced sample size). However, it is obvious that some of these matches can be fairly poor, because for some treated units the nearest neighbor may have a very different propensity score, yet it would nevertheless contribute to the estimation of the treatment effect independently of this difference.

The key assumption of PS-matched DID in this context is that the selection bias is conditional on the *observed* covariates in the baseline. The estimates will be biased if there are unobservable factors that affect both project placement and outcome changes. Since all project households were selected prior to the project start date based on initial *observable* conditions (that is, landless, poverty) as reflected in our baseline, we need not worry about latent factors that might influence changes in both treatment and outcomes over time. Anyway, in the logit model used to calculate the propensity scores, we control for an array of initial conditions that may subsequently affect changes in households' well-being. The results of the logit estimation of the propensity score are reported in Table 5.8, where we include a set of observable household-level characteristics.

The common support condition is imposed (namely the propensity score is bounded away from 0 and 1), and after considering a good set of covariates and some interaction terms, the balancing property is satisfied at 1 percent significance level.

The logit regression results for the final model where balancing was satisfied are presented in Table 5.9. As also shown in that table, treatment and matched controls do not differ significantly on any of the main household characteristics measured at baseline – with the exception of the age of the household head, whose remaining unbalance, though, is not huge (7 percent) and is indeed much lower than it was before matching (34 percent). Thus the propensity score model allows us to have almost all of the covariates well balanced (that is, percent ASB after matching below 5 percent). Furthermore, all variables included in the model are assumed not to have been affected by the treatment as they are pre-treatment characteristics. For example, the agricultural land size before participating in the project cannot have been influenced by the project. The process helped in identifying an appropriate counterfactual group for comparison. This also led to a reduction of the sample size, as unmatched households were dropped out.

Table 5.8 Estimation of the propensity score (logit specification)[a]

Variables	
Total agricultural land size in hectares	–0.25
HH head female	–0.03
Household size	0.11*
Household head age	0.01
Household head squared	–0.00
Household head attended primary schooling	–0.30
Household head age*primary school attendance	0.01
Muslim	0.24
Yao ethnic group	–0.41
Matrilineal inheritance	–0.32
Housing conditions (index)	0.51***
Housing condition squared	–0.11*
Value of assets	–0.00
Constant	0.28
Observations	

Notes: [a] Muslim (whose frequency is 50 percent of the sample) is a dummy variable equal to 1 if household's religion is Muslim, 0 otherwise. The latter includes Christian, which represents almost 49 percent of the pop., and Buddhism and traditional, which both represent less than 2 percent of the sample. Significance levels: *** $p<0.01$, ** $p<0.05$, * $p<0.1$.

Figure 5.2 provides a simple diagnostic on the data examined, plotting the histograms of the estimated propensity scores for treatment and control groups based on pre-treatment data. Here we discard six treated households for which good matches are not found (that is, we condition on the common support). As expected, the first intervals of diagram contain most of the remaining controls, but the number of comparison units in the other bins is approximately equal to the number of treated units.

We combined a DID with PSM, and the results were consistent with DID estimates, as shown in Tables 5.10 and 5.11.

Table 5.10 reports results on agricultural outcomes and consistently with the DID analysis above, the project displays a significant positive impact on land size (both agricultural and residential), maize, tobacco and total output. In particular, participant households' land size rises by 0.71 ha after joining the project (0.51 ha if considering agricultural land only), and total crop output rises by 763 Kg.

These figures only indicate changes in agricultural outcome variables that can be attributed to land redistribution. Thus although each household acquired 2.0 ha, the results suggest that after controlling for other pre-treatment factors (including land owned prior to relocation),

Table 5.9 Balancing tests for beneficiaries and matched controls

Variable	Sample	Mean			%reduct	t-test	
		Treated	Control	%bias	[bias]	t	p > |t|
Total agricultural land size in hectares	Unmatched	0.56848	0.69439	–21.5		–3.02	0.003
	Matched	0.57315	0.54973	4.0	81.4	0.67	0.506
HH head female	Unmatched	1.2379	1.2789	–9.4		–1.32	–0.188
	Matched	1.2338	1.2286	1.2	87.3	0.17	0.864
Household size	Unmatched	4.6061	4.2663	17.8		2.51	0.012
	Matched	4.5688	4.4987	3.7	79.4	0.53	0.594
Household head age	Unmatched	38.739	43.877	–34.3		–4.81	0
	Matched	38.834	37.725	7.4	78.4	1.15	0.249
HH head attended primary schooling	Unmatched	0.24808	0.24874	–0.2		–0.02	0.983
	Matched	0.25195	0.23896	3.0	–1862.1	0.42	0.676
Muslim	Unmatched	0.52685	0.47487	10.4 –		1.46	0.145
	Matched	0.52208	0.54545	4.7	55	–0.65	0.516
Yao ethnic group	Unmatched	0.5243	0.53015	–1.2		–0.16	0.869
	Matched	0.52468	0.53247	–1.6	–33.1	–0.22	0.829
Matrilinear inheritance	Unmatched	0.79284	0.85176	–15.4		–2.17	0.03
	Matched	0.8	0.81818	–4.8	69.1	–0.64	0.522
Housing conditions (index)	Unmatched	0.41464	–0.12733	51.5		7.23	0
	Matched	0.40056	0.37003	2.9	94.4	0.43	0.667
Value of assets	Unmatched	11619	17791	–21.8		–3.05	0.002
	Matched	11738	10835	3.2	85.4	0.62	0.537

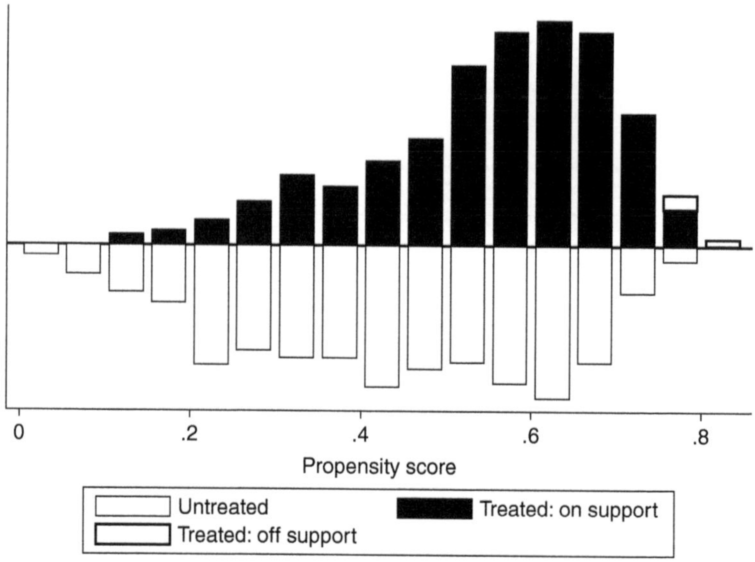

Figure 5.2 Estimated p-score for treated and control groups

on average the land size of a beneficiary increased by only 0.71 ha. Also, from the PSM–DID results, maize and tobacco productivity are both positive and significant, either in the short or in the long term, suggesting that when selecting the most appropriate comparison group of households via the matching technique, beneficiary households do report a positive impact in terms of maize and tobacco land productivity as compared to non-project households.

Table 5.11 reports results on agricultural input use: consistently with DID results, beneficiary households report a higher use of extension services and fertilizers after the project, even though the latter is no longer significant in the long term, probably due to the exhaustion of the initial grant available for farm operations as mentioned above.

5.4.3 Economic and financial impact

An economic and financial analysis of the project to quantify the project benefits was conducted. This was based on the assumption that primary economic benefits of the project accrue from increased agricultural productivity due to the redistributed land and the use of improved crop varieties and agricultural inputs, as well as the distributional benefits

Table 5.10 P-score-DID estimates on agricultural outcome variables[a]

	(1)	(2)	(3)	(4)	(5)	(6)	(7)
	Land (agr. & residential) (ha)	**Land (agr.) (ha)**	**Quantity of maize (kg)**	**Quantity of tobacco (kg)**	**Quantity of tot. crop (kg)**	**Maize land productivity (kg/ha)**	**Tobacco land productivity (kg/ha)**
Panel A: baseline versus the following survey round (2006 and 2007)							
Post-program*Beneficiary	0.71***	0.51***	713.30***	48.96***	762.76***	10004.21**	3524.24***
Controls	Yes	Yes	Yes	Yes	Yes	Yes	Yes
Observations	1,503	1,525	1,525	1,525	1,570	176	176
R-squared	0.330	0.263	0.234	0.083	0.277	0.042	0.206
Panel B: baseline versus the following 3 survey rounds (2007, 2008 and 2009)							
Post-program*Beneficiary	0.71***	0.54***	361.98***	76.87***	453.67***	354.33	2,723.45
Controls	Yes	Yes	Yes	Yes	Yes	Yes	Yes
Observations	3,035	3059	3057	3,059	3,059	3,036	539
R-squared	0.359	0.259	0.165	0.112	0.214	0.033	0.132

Notes: [a] Controls include household size, household head's gender, age and level of schooling, household's religion and ethnic group, inheritance, tradition, a dummy variable equal to 1 if the household was not interviewed in real time (recall variable) and district fixed effects. Significance levels: *** $p<0.01$, ** $p<0.05$, * $p<0.1$.

Table 5.11 P-score-DID estimates on farm inputs use[a]

Variables	(1) Gov. coupon (1= yes, 0 = otherwise)	(2) Exten. service (1 = yes, 0 = otherwise)	(3) Fertilizer (1 = yes, 0 = otherwise)	(4) Compost (1 = yes, 0 = otherwise)
Panel A: baseline versus the following survey round (2006 and 2007)				
Post-program* Beneficiary	−0.15***	0.12**	0.012**	0.00
Controls	Yes	Yes	Yes	Yes
Observations	1513	1518	1501	1499
Pseudo R-squared	0.12	0.029	0.13	0.13
Panel B: baseline versus the following 3 survey rounds (2007, 2008 and 2009)				
Post-program*Beneficiary	−0.08**	0.08**	−0.03	−0.00
Controls	Yes	Yes	Yes	Yes
Observations	3037	3050	3024	3021
Pseudo R-squared	0.120	0.018	0.096	0.15

Notes: [a] Controls include household size, household head's gender, age and level of schooling, household's religion and ethnic group, inheritance, tradition, a dummy variable equal to 1 if the household was not interviewed in real time (recall variable) and district fixed effects. Significance levels: *** $p<0.01$, ** $p<0.05$, * $p<0.1$.

gained from increasing the incomes of about 15,000 poor and land-poor rural families (government of Malawi and the World Bank, 2007).

This analysis is only a partial analysis, because two important benefits have not been included: (i) the relieving of the negative externalities associated with tensions around the land issue, and (ii) the value in piloting new approaches to land redistribution, in particular, market-assisted transactions, and community-driven approaches. These were left out because there were minimal tensions around the land issues hence fewer externalities from potential tensions. The market-assisted approach was effective in preventing tensions.

The analysis was based on two representative farm models: subsistence farmers (80 percent) and semi-commercial farmers (20 percent), based on agro-climatic zones within the six pilot districts. The internal rate of return for each of these farm models is calculated by taking into account all financial and economic costs and benefits. The change in household income, due to own-consumption and cash sales of crop surplus, are examined. The analysis aggregates from the individual farm models to determine project benefits, based on a project benefit build-up as beneficiary households enter the project. The project costs are based on the cost estimates that result from the detailed project costing. The sensitivity of results to changes in key assumptions is analyzed to test the robustness of the results. Finally, the fiscal impact of the project is assessed. Two farm models are considered:

- Subsistence model: 80 percent of targeted beneficiaries are expected to grow primarily food crops for their own-consumption and a small proportion of cash crops.
- Semi-commercial model: 20 percent of beneficiaries are expected to grow a higher proportion of cash crops in agro-climatic zones where this is possible, in addition to some food crops.

Financial and economic benefits

Table 5.12 shows the summary results of the cost–benefit analysis. Financial and economic costs are assumed to be the same, because financial costs are generally free of taxes and transfer payments. However, it is only the financial benefits that include a small component of incremental taxes (derived from tax on agricultural inputs) and the linkage effects of changes in farm income, since economic benefits have to be net of taxes/subsidies and transfer payments such as interest. These benefits have little impact in the subsistence model, but a much greater one in the semi-commercial.

As the project is piloting new approaches to land redistribution – market-based land transactions and community-driven approaches in particular – a high proportion of the total project costs (43 percent) were for 'overhead costs', that is, costs not in the land acquisition and farm development component. The analysis considered the project net benefit for just this component, and the results indicate that the economic benefits are much higher.

The results presented in Table 5.13 show that the LAFD component, which is the key component for the project, was economically and financially viable since it generates positive financial and economic net present values, and the rates of return are all well above the threshold of 12 percent. The LADF component is found to generate ERR and FRR of 33 percent and 40 percent respectively, suggesting that there is a much higher return for every dollar spent in LAFD, mainly due to the resulting higher productivity of the land.

Table 5.12 Cost–benefit analysis results based on scenario II (80 percent subsistence and 20 percent semi-commercial farm households)

	Subsistence	Semi-commercial	Total project (US$ million)
Proportions of households (%)	80%	20%	100%
Number of households	12,114	3,028	15,142
Uniform grant ceiling	$1,050	$1,050	
Area per households	2	2	
Total area	24,227	6,057	30,284
Land price	$175	$175	
Area under cultivation	1.5	1.8	
Annual revenue/ha planted	$165	$422	
Financial analysis			
NPV of total costs	$1,289	$1,289	$13.0
NPV of total benefits	$2,366	$3,825	$20.6
NPV of net financial benefits	$1,078	$2,536	$7.6
Economic analysis			
NPV of incremental taxes	$14	$15	$0.2
NPV of linkage effects	$232	$1,405	$6.3
NPV of net economic benefits	$1,324	$3,957	$14.2
FRR	28%	42%	17%
ERR	28%	55%	20%

Source: Own computation.

5.5 Conclusions

The analysis of the impact of the CBRLDP was conducted using a four-year household unique panel survey dataset collected from 1194 households in six pilot districts (Mulanje, Thyolo, Mangochi, Machinga, Balaka and Ntcheu) in southern Malawi between 2006 and 2009. Before-and-after and treated-and-control groups comparisons were used in order to estimate the causal impact of the land project on household-level outcomes such as land acquisition, agricultural output, productivity, income and expenditure. Both the selection bias problem and the problem of missing data for the counterfactual were tackled by using propensity score matching combined with a difference-in-difference technique, whereby changes of outcomes of welfare for beneficiaries was compared over time to those of similar households who did not participate in the project.

Results show that the project significantly increased land holdings, agricultural output and crop-specific land productivity (maize and tobacco) of beneficiary groups in the six southern districts in Malawi.

Table 5.13 Project net benefits for the land acquisition component

Land acquisition and farm development component: 80 percent subsistence 20 percent semi-commercial, based on Scenario II			
Financial	NPV	$18.9	Million
	FRR	32%	
Economic	NPV	$25.2	Million
	ERR	38%	

Moreover, beneficiary households significantly improved their agricultural income levels after the project. In general, these impacts were higher in the short term, while they slightly decreased over time, when they remain significant.

The financial and economic analyses indicate that the project has been financially and economically viable under all scenarios tested, given the positive net present values and the financial and economic rates of returns which are above the 12 percent threshold. The economic rate of return (ERR) for the 15,142 households is 20 percent. A farm income analysis revealed a substantial increment in incomes, mainly attributed to a sharp rise in production leading to a substantial marketable surplus for the major crops (maize and tobacco). Our results are consistent with the MTRfindings in that the LADF component is found to generate ERR and FRR of 33 percent and 40 percent, respectively, suggesting that there is a much higher return for every dollar spent in LAFD, mainly due to the resulting higher productivity of the land.

Overall, the findings suggest that there is scope for reducing poverty and inequality in developing countries by implementing decentralized community-based, voluntary and market-assisted approaches to land reform through the provision of land to the landless and land-poor households. Such reforms should, however be coupled with improved access to reliable markets, increased extension services, and links to financial and credit institutions, in order to make a land reform effective in boosting both agricultural productivity and household well-being.

Notes

1. This is the total land that is either underutilized or unutilized as of the mid 1990s; and since there has been no recent study, this might have changed considerably in recent years.
2. Each tranche of money was released to the group as a whole, and then allocated among households. Project administrators often requested a report

of how the money had been spent before releasing subsequent tranches. Beneficiaries could use the money for farm inputs, and some money for hired labor and food. It was a requirement that purchases by BGs should be based on procurement guidelines.
3. A caliper is a predefined propensity score radius.

References

Aghion, P., Caroli, E. and García-Peñalosa, C. (1999) 'Inequality and Economic Growth: The Perspective of the New Growth Theories', *Journal of Economic Literature* .

Binswanger-Mkhize, H., Bourguignon, C. and van den Brink, R. (2009) 'Agricultural Land Redistribution: Towards Greater Consensus', Washington DC, The World Bank.

Birdsall, N. and Londono, J.L. (1998) 'No Tradeoff: Efficient Growth Via More Equal Human Capital in Latin America', in N. Birdsall, C. Graham, and R. Sabot (eds), *Beyond tradeoffs: Market Reforms and Equitable Growth in Latin America* (Washington, D.C.: Brookings Institution Press and Inter-American Development Bank).

Blundell, R. and Costa Dias, M. (2000) 'Evaluation Methods for Non- Experimental Data', *Fiscal Studies* 21(4), 427–68.

Caliendo, M. and Kopeinig, S. (2008) 'Some Practical Guidance for the Implementation of Propensity Score Matching', *Journal of Economic Surveys*, 22, 31–72. doi: 10.1111/j.1467–6419.2007.00527.

Chirwa, E.W. (2004) 'Access to Land, Growth and Poverty Reduction in Malawi', Report submitted to the North-South Institute, Canada.

Chirwa, E.W. and Chinsinga (2008) 'The Economics and Politics of Land Reform in Malawi: A Case Study of the Community Based Rural Land Development Program', IPPG Paper briefing No. 18.

Deininger, K., Lara, F., Olinto, P. and Maertens, M. (1999) 'Redistribution, Investment and Human Capital Accumulation: The Case of Agrarian Reform in the Philippines', Working Paper, World Bank.

de Janvry, A. and Sadoulet, E. (2001) 'Rural Poverty and Effective Rural Development Strategies', in H. Clemens and R. Ruben (eds), *Nueva Ruralidad y Politica Agraria*. Caracas (Venezuela: Editorial Nueva Sociedad).

Government of the Republic of Malawi (2002) 'Malawi National Land Policy', Government of the Republic of Malawi, Lilongwe.

Government of the Republic of Malawi (2008) 'Malawi Population and Housing Census', National statistical office, Malawi.

Heckman, James, R. Lalonde, and Smith, J. (1999) 'The Economics and Econometrics of Active Labor Market Programs', *Handbook of Labor Economics* , Volume 3, Ashenfelter, A. and D.

Holden, S., Kaarhus, R. and Lunduka, R. (2006) 'Land Policy Reform: The Role of Land Markets and Women's Land Rights in Malawi', Noragric Report No. 36 (October), Department of International Environment and Development Studies, Noragric, Norwegian University of Life Sciences (UMB), Norway.

Imbens, G.W. and Angrist, J.D. (1994) 'Identification and Estimation of Local Average Treatment Effects', *Econometrica*, 62, 467–76.

Lele, U. (1989) 'Sources of Growth in East African Agriculture', *World Bank Economic Review*, 3, 119–44.

Machira S. (2008) 'Pilot-Testing a Land Redistribution Program in Malawi', in H.P. Binswanger, C. Bourguignon and R. van den Brink (eds), *Agricultural Land Redistribution: Towards Greater Consensus*, The World Bank.

Robilliard, A.S., Sukume, C., Yanoma, Y. and Löfgren, H. (2002) 'Land Reform in Zimbabwe: Farm-level Effects and Cost-Benefit Analysis', Review report, World Bank Lilongwe.

Rosenzweig, M.R. and Binswanger, H.P. (1993) 'Wealth, Weather risk and the Composition and Profitability of Agricultural Investments', *Economic Journal*, 103, 56–78.

Saidi, Patrick M. (1999) Final Report of the Presidential Commission of Inquiry on Land Policy Reform, Malawi Government, Lilongwe.

Simtowe, F., Magisoni, J. and Mendola, M. (2011) 'Independent Project Impact Evaluation of the Community Based Rural Land Development in Malawi', Contract Nr. 013/IPC/CB/09/10.

Takane, Tsutomu (2007) 'Gambling with Liberalization: Smallholder Livelihoods in Contemporary Rural Malawi', Institute of Developing Economies Working Paper, JETRO.

Wooldridge, J.M. (2001) 'Instrumental Estimation of the Average Treatment Effect in the Correlated Random Coefficient Model', Department of Economics, Michigan State University, Michigan.

World Bank (2001) *World Development Report 2000/2001: Attacking Poverty* (New York: Oxford University Press).

World Bank (2007) *An Economic Analysis of the Malawi Land Project- A Mid Term* .

Part II

Tenure Security and Transfer Rights Enhancing Reforms

6
Welfare Impacts of Land Certification in Tigray, Ethiopia

Stein T. Holden and Hosaena Ghebru

6.1 Introduction

Earlier studies on the impacts of land certification in Ethiopia have identified significant positive investment and land productivity effects (Holden, et al., 2009; Deininger et al., 2008), a significant reduction in land border disputes (Holden et al., 2011a), and a significant enhancement of land rental market activity (Holden et al., 2011b; Deininger et al., 2011a). Female-headed households in particular appear to have become more tenure-secure after receiving land certificates, and have thus become more willing to rent their land through sharecropping contracts. These effects should also contribute to poverty reduction, but this has not yet been investigated thoroughly, and this is therefore the original contribution of this chapter.

This study has two related objectives that will fill gaps in the existing literature. First, the study will assess whether the increased land rental activity due to land certification is associated with higher land productivity on rented land, particularly for land with female landlords. An earlier study by Holden and Bezabih (2008) revealed that land productivity was lower for land owned by female landlords than for land owned by male landlords. They also found significant Marshallian inefficiency in the land rental market dominated by sharecropping in the Amhara region of Ethiopia. This study, therefore, first investigates whether a similar productivity difference can be detected in the Tigray region, and whether land certification has contributed to reducing such inefficiency in land use, if such use is found to have existed before certification.

Second, the study aims to measure the welfare effect of the land certification at the household level based on household panel data from the Tigray region, where the land certification process was first implemented in Ethiopia. The data covers the period of 1997 to 2006, from one year before the registration and certification reform was implemented till up to eight years after. Welfare effects may be delayed both because productivity impacts of investments may be delayed and grow over time and because of the consumption-smoothing behavior of households. In order to identify such delayed, and gradually increasing, effects the duration of land certificate ownership was considered, while welfare was measured by real household consumption expenditure per adult equivalent.

The study assesses whether there are signs of improved land productivity after the reform on rented land of female-headed households as compared to rented-out land of male-headed households. Furthermore, welfare improvements by years of land certificate ownership were significant and positive, especially for females.

The chapter is organized as follows. Section 6.2 provides an overview of land tenure reforms in Ethiopia since 1975. Section 6.3 gives an overview of studies on welfare impacts of land tenure reforms in general, as well as of earlier studies on tenure insecurity and land certification in Ethiopia. Data and methods of analysis are presented in Section 6.4, followed by the presentation of the results and discussion in Section 6.5, and then the conclusion.

6.2 The Ethiopian land tenure reforms

Ethiopia underwent a radical reform of land tenure in 1975, when all land was made state land. User rights to land were then distributed to individual households in each community (peasant association) in an egalitarian way, by providing each household with a fair share of each major land quality class in the community (Rahmato, 1984). The allocation depended on household size. Land sales, mortgaging, and rentals were made illegal, and so was the hiring of labor. The maximum farm size was set at 10 ha, and all resident households in the community had the constitutional right to land. This was based on the Land to the Tiller ideology inspired by experiences under the feudal tenancy system before the reform, and radical reforms in other countries; the reform thus resembled the reform in China but was less violent. The feudal landlords in Ethiopia were not killed, but were left with less than 10 ha of land each, and lost all power as they were excluded from local leadership positions. Collective farming was also promoted in the peasant associations, but did not succeed and was gradually phased out. Meanwhile such land was gradually distributed to individual households as the population increased, and new households that needed land were formed. To maintain the egalitarian land distribution further, land redistributions took place by taking land from the most land-rich households and giving it to the new households when other communal land was no longer available. This created a zero-sum game with enhanced tenure insecurity with possible negative investment and productivity effects (Alemu, 1999; Deininger and Jin, 2006; Holden and Yohannes, 2002).

Then the civil war in Ethiopia ended in 1991, when the military regime was overthrown and the new government, originating from the Tigray region, was established. Eritrea was separated out as an independent country. A more market-friendly land policy was introduced, allowing land renting (short-term contracts) and hiring of labor,– but the selling and mortgaging of land remained illegal. Continuation of the use rights also required continuing residence in the community, and implied an obligation to farm the land (Rahmato, 2003). Land redistributions were also halted, with a few exceptions (Ege, 1997). Stronger legal powers were devolved to the regional level.

A new Federal Land Proclamation was put in place in 1997 (FDRE, 1997), providing the basis for establishing regional land laws that were consistent with the federal land proclamation.

Tigray was the first region to have its own regional land proclamation (TRS, 1997). These new land laws formed the basis for implementing regional rural land registration and certification. This first started in the Tigray region in 1998, and followed in the Amhara region in 2003, then in the Oromia and SNNP regions in 2004.

Tigray implemented a low-cost land registration and certification reform covering more than 80 percent of the rural households during 1998 to 1999, but the war with Eritrea interrupted the process and delayed its completion. The rapid implementation was possible due to the low level of technology used (it required limited training and budget), the high level of local participation (minimizing the administrative costs) and motivation, and the focus on the land allocated to individual households, thus avoiding communal lands as well as pastoral areas. Land registration involved identifying the owners and neighbors of each individual plot, jointly inspecting and identifying or demarcating the plot borders, and having the owners and their neighbors agree on these. A form was filled out for each plot, which included this information as well as the plot location (by name), plot size (using local measurement methods and units), and land quality class. The information was registered in land registry books, where each household had a number. Each household was then provided a certificate which contained this same information for each of their farm plots. The certificate was issued in the name of the head of the household. It provided perpetual user rights to the land.

The three most populated regions, Amhara, Oromia and SNNP, followed up with a very similar approach to land registration and certification from 2003 and onwards; by 2006 more than 20 million plots and 6 million households had received land certificates (Deininger et al., 2008). The cost of the certification was estimated to be as low as US$1 per plot and US$3.5 per farm household, compared to the cost of US$150 in Madagascar, which uses the land titling upon demand approach (Deininger et al., 2008; Jacoby and Minten, 2007).

6.3 Literature review

6.3.1 Welfare effects of land reforms

We define land tenure reform as a formal change in a land tenure rights regime that also may include changes in the duties and restrictions of land rights holders. With this broad definition, we may identify a vector of sub-categories of land tenure reforms including: redistributive land reforms; classical land titling reform; low-cost land registration and certification; formalization of customary land rights; and changes in rights and duties of land rights holders. This study focuses only on a sub-category of land reform, which is the low-cost land registration and certification reform in Ethiopia that aimed to strengthen the use rights of land holders while restricting their transfer rights. These restrictions included prohibition of land sales and mortgaging while short-term renting was allowed, and provide important information on what types of welfare effects could be expected from this reform.

The three neoclassical focal points of land tenure reforms have included:

a) the tenure security and investment effect;
b) the transferability and allocative efficiency effect; and
c) the collateralization or credit access effect (Besley, 1995; Brasselle et al., 2002).

The land rights restrictions in Ethiopia imply that we can only expect the first two types of effects to be potentially significant as a result of the low-cost land registration and certification.

In addition to the productivity effects, many land reforms also emphasize achieving distributional effects. This has also been an important argument for new land reforms focusing on the legal empowerment of the poor, and has been promoted by the Commission for Legal Empowerment of the Poor, UN-Habitat and the World Bank, not to mention many of the national land redistributive reforms, including the radical reforms, Land to the Tiller reforms, and Market-assisted Land Redistributions (Deininger, 2003; Cotula and Mathieu, 2008; Singh, 2009). However, many land reforms have not succeeded in empowering the poor – on the contrary, they have seen many unintended effects such as élite capture, and have thus resulted in further marginalization of the poor (Benjaminsen et al., 2009; Otsuka, 2007; Toulmin, 2009). Toulmin (2009) argues that most African governments do not have the administrative capacity to implement land registration and titling of land; however, given the sharp increases in the demands for land there is a need for a decentralized system for land registration and certification. Such systems may, however, also be vulnerable to élite capture and corruption. It is, therefore, not obvious that such systems will be more able to deliver land tenure reforms that benefit the poor.

It has long been agreed that improving the asset base of the poor helps reduce their poverty (Besley and Burgess, 2000). Many studies have revealed an inverse farm size–land productivity relationship and, based on this, it has been advocated that the redistribution of land from large landholders to small landholders could contribute to efficiency as well as equity (Binswanger et al., 1995). The many challenges that redistribution reforms face, however, and the mixed experiences with their implementation and impacts, imply that no consensus has been achieved on whether such land reforms could be a useful policy instrument for poverty reduction.

While there are quite a few studies on investment effects of land reforms, very few rigorous quantitative studies exist on welfare impacts of land reforms. This is because such studies require comprehensive data from before and after the reforms, and because they need to control for the endogeneity of access to rights (Besley and Burgess, 2000). Published studies include Feder and Nishio (1999) who found positive impacts of land registration and titling on income and land values in Thailand. Lopez (1996) also found a positive net return in the form of household income to land registration and titling in Honduras minus the cost of titling, which was US$600 per title. Meanwhile, Migot-Adholla et al. (1991) found no significant impact of land registration and titling on land productivity and investment in Ghana, Rwanda, or Kenya, and concluded that land registration and titling is unlikely to be economically worthwhile in much of sub-Saharan Africa. Yet Galiani and Schargrodsky (2009) found a positive effect of land titling on investment in human capital in a study in Buenos Aires.

While the focus on welfare effects of redistributive land reforms tends to be on the households that have received additional land, the study on the effects of land registration and titling or certification, as in Ethiopia, is quite the opposite; the study is on the effects of not running the risk of losing land through future redistributions. While such a reform that strengthens existing rights has negative effects on potential gainers of land from redistributions, they may have impacts beyond a zero-sum game if they contribute to enhanced investment and land use efficiency. Another impact is that households themselves have to bear the costs of increases in family size to a larger extent, since such increases no longer provide the basis for claims for additional land. This implies that the land's potential role as a safety net for the landless and near landless may have been reduced while, at the same time, the reliance on alternative safety net programs may have increased. It is also possible that such landless and near landless households can gain access to land through the land rental market if this market has been enhanced by the land registration and certification. Below, we review the evidence of impacts from the Ethiopian land registration on investment, productivity and land rental market activity.

6.3.2 Impacts of land certification in Ethiopia

Deininger et al. (2008) assessed the early impacts of low-cost land registration and certification, using a large cross-section dataset from Ethiopia. They estimated the cost of registration and certification to be about US$1 per farm plot or US$3.5 per household, while about 20 million plots and 6 million households had received land certificates within a period of seven years. Holden et al. (2009) used household plot panel data from 1998, 2001, and 2006 from the Tigray region in Northern Ethiopia to estimate investment and productivity effects of land certification while controlling for the potential endogeneity of land certificate allocation. The study focused only on owner-operated plots and therefore did not capture any potential benefits from increased productivity on rented land due to land certification. This implies that the study focused only on the tenure security-investment-productivity effects of certification. The study revealed that conservation technologies on owner-operated plots with land certificates were better maintained than conservation technologies on plots without such certificates. Land certification was also found to enhance tree planting on owner-operated land; in addition, productivity was found to be more than 40 percent higher on owner-operated plots with land certificates than on owner-operated plots without land certificates. Ghebru and Holden (2011), using a different sample of owner-operated plots with and without land certificates, found that the productivity increase related to land certification was due more to an outward shift in the production frontier than a reduction in technical inefficiency; the levels of technical inefficiency were similar for certified and uncertified plots, while overall productivity was higher for certified plots.

Holden et al. (2011a), using data from 400 local conflict mediators in 27 communities from the Tigray region, found that land registration and certification led to better plot border demarcation and a significant reduction in plot border disputes. This is also a clear indication of improved tenure security for owners of land, because the risk of encroachment by neighbors has been reduced.

Deininger et al. (2011a) used a four-round household panel data from the Amhara region to estimate the early impacts of land certification on tenure security, investment, and land rental activity. They found that certification consistently increased the amount of land rented out by one-tenth of a hectare and the propensity to rent out by 9–13 percent.

Meanwhile, several other studies have tried to identify the impacts of investments in soil conservation in Ethiopia (Shiferaw and Holden, 1999; Shiferaw and Holden, 2001; Gebremedhin and Swinton, 2003). These studies have identified the delayed productivity effect of soil conservation to be an important reason for underinvestment in conservation, although in the Tigray region there appeared to be stronger short-term effects of conservation due to the moisture conservation effect of soil conservation measures. Severe land degradation and low investment levels have been important reasons for government interventions to promote such investments. Large-scale programs have, therefore, promoted such investments, especially through Food for Work programs and the more recent Productive Safety Net Program that also covers much of the Tigray region. Individual households' responsibilities have been more to maintain and improve such structures that have been introduced through these programs. With this in mind, it is not surprising that investment effects resulting from land certification also can be delayed.

Holden et al. (2011b) investigated the impacts of gender and land certification on land rental market participation and degree of participation in the Tigray region. Using four rounds of a balanced household panel covering 16 communities over the period from the year before the reform and up to 7–8 years after registration and certification, they found a significant increase in the land rental market activity. Female-headed households with land certificates had become more willing to rent out their land, and did so significantly more after land certification. However, the study did not assess the potential improved allocative efficiency effects in the land rental market or their welfare implications. Some other studies, however, give some indications of what these effects may be.

A broad literature exists on the efficiency of use of rented land and how such land use efficiency is affected by contract choice (Marshall,

1890; Cheung, 1968; Stiglitz, 1974; Otsuka and Hayami, 1988). The issue of whether sharecropping contracts are associated with Marshallian inefficiency in form of lower input use intensity and land productivity on sharecropped land was first empirically studied in Asia. While some studies in Asia, such as the study by Shaban (1987) in India, found significant Marshallian inefficiency, this finding was far from universal (Otsuka et al., 1992; Otsuka, 2007). More recently, this issue has also been studied in Africa, including in Ethiopia (see Holden et al. (2008) for a review). We give a brief overview of earlier studies in Ethiopia.

Pender and Fafchamps (2006) found no significant Marshallian inefficiency in a study in Arsi in Ethiopia, but the lack of significance could be due to the small sample size. Kassie and Holden (2007, 2008) found that productivity on sharecropped parcels could even be higher than on owner-operated parcels for the same tenants, and associated this with threats of eviction that motivated tenants to work harder to renew their contracts in a study in Gojjam in Amhara Region. In another study in the Amhara Region of Ethiopia, Holden and Bezabih (2008), using household plot panel data from the Amhara region in Ethiopia, found that land productivity was significantly lower on owner-operated as well as rented plots with female landlords as compared to male landlords. They found that female landlords (usually widows or divorced women) were less able to obtain efficient tenants due to higher eviction costs, particularly related to in-law tenants that were less productive. Strengthening of the land rights for women through land certification may therefore make female landlord households more willing to rent their land and enable them to find more efficient tenants; and this should also have welfare-improving effects as they share the productivity gains with the tenants through sharecropping contracts. The improved allocative efficiency of the land rental market should, therefore, potentially lead to higher production efficiency and welfare gains for both tenant and landlord through transfer of land to more efficient producers. This study will assess whether land registration and certification has had such an effect in the Tigray region.

Ghebru and Holden (2012) used matched landlord and tenant data from the Tigray region of Ethiopia in 2006 and, after controlling for observable and unobservable tenant characteristics with household fixed effects, found Marshallian inefficiency to be associated with kin female landlords.

We may conclude from findings that the degree of existence of Marshallian disincentive effects depends on the degree of tenure insecurity of landlords, their ability to select good tenants and evict bad tenants, terminate or renew contracts, and monitor and enforce contracts, as well as the social distance between landlords and tenants. We propose that in our study area land certification has strengthened the tenure security of landlord households, especially of female landlords, and we assess whether this has enhanced the land productivity on sharecropped land. If so, such a reduction in tenure insecurity should enhance the welfare of households through the positive investment effects and the reduction in Marshallian inefficiency.

6.4 Theory and hypotheses

We assume that households aim to maximize their welfare given the constraints they face, and this includes making inter-temporal choices that involve inter-temporal trade-offs. Households face shocks and risks that may cause their incomes as well as their resource access to fluctuate over time, while their basic needs must be satisfied in every period of time in order for them to survive. This implies that they will typically aim to smooth consumption over time, that is to compensate for periods of lack by depleting their asset base to maintain their consumption in such periods, rebuilding their asset base in periods with more favorable outcomes.

Tenure security over assets provides an opportunity for investment and asset resource allocation that enhances future expected welfare flows from this asset base. Land certification should, therefore, enhance investment and future expected welfare from the asset base. Such tenure security provided by land certificates should also make it possible to rent out land to more productive households for households that are less productive themselves because they have limited access to complementary resources that are important for land productivity. With land renting dominated by sharecropping, both parties of the sharecropping contract benefit from productivity increases on sharecropped land.

Drawing on this basic theoretical framework and the earlier studies of the reviewed land certification in Ethiopia, we formulate the following hypotheses for empirical testing in this study:

H1: Land certification has contributed to enhanced land productivity over time on rented land, especially for female-headed households.

H2: Land certification has enhanced household welfare over time.

H3: Land certification has also enhanced household welfare of female-headed households that depend more on renting out their land.

The testing of these hypotheses will fill important gaps in the existing literature and contribute to creating a more complete picture of the overall impacts of low-cost land certification in Ethiopia.

6.4.1 Data and estimation methods

The data used in this study comes from a survey that sampled 400 households in 16 communities in the Tigray region. The first round of the survey took place in 1998, just before the land registration and certification reform was implemented. The sample villages were stratified to capture the main variation in market access, population density, irrigation access, and zonal agro-ecological variation in the highland areas of the region where most of the population lives. The survey, as well as the land certification reform, did not include the lowland, mainly pastoral, areas of the region. Data were collected not only for a wide range of household-level variables but also for each farm plot of households, including land characteristics, input use, investments, and outputs.

The households were resurveyed in 2001, 2003, and 2006 and this gives a four-round household panel that is used for the analysis at the household level. The surveys used the same format for the data collection of household expenditures and plot-level production in the different rounds. Household expenditures were deflated using a local consumption price index generated for a typical basket of consumer goods. Household adult equivalents were calculated based on the standardized energy intake of household members by age and gender.

6.4.2 Land productivity estimation on rented land

For the plot-level analysis, data from 1998, 2001, and 2006 were used. Plot-level data for 2003 were dropped because of the severe drought that year. Land productivity was measured by the value of crops produced on a plot in a year; land productivity is assumed to be a function of the plot, farm, and household characteristics. Our analysis first focused on whether there were any productivity differences between rented plots of male- and female-headed households before and after the land certification, based on the identification of such differences in another region of Ethiopia by Holden and Bezabih (2008). Plot-level data were used for this purpose to estimate the following model year by year.

$$q^r_{pht} = \alpha_{0t} + \alpha_{1t} A^r_{pht} + \alpha_{2t} S^r_{ht} + c^r_{ht} + u^r_{pht} \qquad (1)$$

q^r_{pht} is the log of the output value on the rented-out plot p of household h in a specific year t, A^r_{pht} is a set of plot characteristics for the rented plots, S^r_{ht} is a dummy variable for the sex of the owner of the rented-out plot, c^r_{ht} represents unobservable household and farm characteristics that are controlled using household random effects, and u^r_{pht} is the error term. It was not possible to use household fixed effects in this estimation because many households rented out only one plot. This formulation is also more flexible than a model that forces the parameters to be constant over time. In particular, we hypothesized (*H1*) the parameter on the sex of the household head to change over time.

To control for selection bias (due to observables), propensity score matching was used to compare the land productivity of rented-out plots of male- and female-headed households before and after certification. The balancing requirement was satisfied in these estimations and the common support requirement was invoked. The same approach was attempted for the comparison of rented-out plots with and without certificates within years after certification – but this attempt failed since the balancing requirement could not be satisfied; there were very few rented-out plots without land certificates.

A further test for selection bias due to unobservables was implemented by use of a Heckman selection model. No significant selection bias was detected with this model. The results are presented in Table 6.1.

6.4.3 Welfare impact models

For the analysis of the possible welfare effects of land certification, we were able to use the full four-round household-level panel. Some attrition was experienced, such that our analysis is based on a balanced household panel of 292 households for which we have complete data for all variables in all years. While this could potentially lead to attrition bias, our tests did not reveal any such significant bias in the models presented in this chapter, where household fixed effects were used to control for unobserved household heterogeneity.

The welfare effects of land certification are not likely to appear immediately after a reform, and it may take time for them to grow stronger. It may therefore be appropriate to use an indicator variable capturing this accumulation effect. For this purpose, we used the time period (in years) over which the individual households have possessed their land certificates.

The specification of the estimated model is as follows

$$\begin{aligned} y_{ht} = {} & \beta_0 + \beta_1 A_{ht} + \beta_2 CY_{ht} + \beta_3 S_{ht} + \beta_4 D_t \\ & + \beta_5 CY_{ht} * S_{ht} + \beta_6 OP_{ht} / A_{ht} + \vartheta_h + e_{ht}, \end{aligned} \tag{2}$$

Table 6.1 Land productivity on rented-out plots: Heckman selection and pooled OLS models

	Heckman selection model		OLS
Explanatory variables	Second stage: productivity on rented-out plots	First stage probit model: Decision to rent out plot	Cluster robust standard errors
Dummy for year = 2001	0.192	–0.095	0.196
Dummy for year = 2006	0.145	–0.121	0.155
Sex of household head (female = 1, male = 0)	–0.338	0.576***	–0.434**
Sex of household head*Dummy for 2001	–0.119		–0.119
Sex of household head*Dummy for 2006	0.522**		0.518*
Years with certificate	0.002	–0.009	0.004
Plot size	–0.255***	0.050	–0.261***
Soil depth shallow	–0.048	0.083	–0.048
Soil depth medium	–0.058	–0.01	–0.061
Flat slope	0.004	–0.012	–0.024
Low hill slope	0.123	0.032	0.107
Mid hill slope	0.152	0.159	0.122
Soil type Cambisol	0.116	–0.037	0.122
Soil type Vertisol	0.11	–0.045	0.112
Soil type Regosol	–0.286**	–0.044	–0.288*
Distance to plot from home	0.001	0.007***	0.001
Age of household head		0.003	
Education of household head		–0.152***	
Log of female labor force		0.190**	
Log of male labor force		–0.259***	
Log of oxen endowment		–0.303***	
Log of other livestock endowment		–0.460***	
Farm size, tsimdi		–0.024**	
Constant	6.845***	–0.779***	7.088***
Athrho		0.153	
Ln sigma		–0.148***	
Number of observations	389	2621	389
R-squared			0.17
Log likelihood		–1364.789	
Chi2		73.77962	
Prob		2.15E-09	
Rho		0.1522949	

Source: Survey data.

Note: Significance levels: *** $p<0.01$, ** $p<0.05$, * $p<0.1$.

The dependent variable (y_{ht}) was specified as the real (deflated) value of total household annual expenditure per adult equivalent. A_{ht} is the farm size per adult equivalent, CY_{ht} is the number of years the household has had its land certificate, S_{ht} is a dummy for the sex of household head, D_t is a vector of year dummies, OP_{ht} / A_{ht} is the operational holding size divided by the own holding size, ϑ_h is the unobservable time-invariant household, farm, and village characteristics that can be controlled for using household fixed effects, and e_{ht} is the error term. Models were run with and without the interaction term between the sex of household head and years, with certificate variables to assess whether a difference in impacts between male- and female-headed households could be detected. Models without and with the ratio between operational and own holding sizes were also run to assess the impact of land rental market participation.

The impact of certification is identified with the years with a certificate variable, which can capture a delayed and gradual effect of land certification, if it exists. This also resembles a pipeline approach where variation in the timing of allocation of certificates is utilized to identify the impacts. This variation in timing was caused primarily by administrative constraints. The year dummy variables are a control for the general trend effect such that the effect of certification on those households that received certificates can be identified (test of *H2*). A further test of the impact of certification on female- vs. male-headed households is achieved with the interaction variable between the years with certificate and sex of household head variables; *H3* is tested with this variable. The tests rest on there not being any time-varying unobservable variables causing households with certificates to have a stronger trend in welfare improvement than households without certificates (common trend assumption). The same assumption is required for female vs. male landlord households. We cannot. however, think of any such variables that would cause stronger welfare improvement over time for female landlord households.

Finally, the model specifications allow for the assessment of whether changes in land rental market participation are associated with welfare changes and changes in the land endowment per adult equivalent (caused by changes in household composition or land endowment). We would expect that increases in operational holding are associated with welfare improvements, while a reduction in land endowment per adult equivalent (when, say, due to an increase in household size) is associated with a reduction in household welfare.

6.5 Results and discussion

6.5.1 Land productivity on rented-out land

Table 6.2 provides a comparison of land productivity on rented-out and owner-operated plots of male and female landlord households by year with simple *t*-tests. Productivity was measured as log-transformed output value. Gendered land productivity differences are weakly significant in 1998 (10 percent level) and more significant in 2001, but become insignificant for rented-out plots in 2006.

Table 6.3 provides information about the number of plots by rental status, certificate status and year. As can be seen, the number of rented-out plots with certificates was small, and we were unable to perform a proper assessment of productivity differences between rented-out plots with and without certificates using propensity score matching.

The results of the propensity score matching for rented-out plots of female versus male landlord households, with kernel and nearest neighbor methods that control observable plot characteristics, are presented in Table 6.4. The balancing requirement was satisfied and common support was invoked to eliminate potential outlier observations. The results show that after controlling for observables the productivity differences between rented-out plots of female- and male-headed households in 1998 have become highly significant, with female-headed households having lower land productivity on their rented-out plots. The same finding was found in 2001, about two years after land certification. However, in 2006 the land productivity on rented-out plots

Table 6.2 Land productivity on owner-operated and rented-out plots by sex of household head and year [a]

Year ->		1998	1998	2001	2001	2006	2006
Sex of household head		**Owner-operated**	**Rented-out plots**	**Owner-operated**	**Rented-out plots**	**Owner-operated**	**Rented-out plots**
Male-headed (m)	Mean	6.766	6.641	6.930	6.930	7.378	6.954
	St. err.	0.039	0.100	0.027	0.091	0.034	0.105
	N	619	83	951	96	737	61
Female-headed (f)	Mean	6.588	6.322	6.605	6.408	7.117	7.074
	St. err.	0.120	0.166	0.102	0.149	0.062	0.109
	N	73	31	86	48	230	72
t-test, f < m	t-value	1.41	1.65	3.0736	2.9967	3.701	−0.7943
Prob (f < m)		0.0815	0.0525	0.0014	0.0018	0.001	0.7858

Source: Survey data.

Note: [a] Land productivity is log-transformed from the value of crops produced on the land; f = female, m = male.

Table 6.3 Number of plot observations by renting out and certificate status by year

		Year and rented-out dummy					
		1998		2001		2006	
		0	1	0	1	0	1
Certificate,	0	552	115	167	22	201	31
1= Yes	1	0	0	721	122	647	108

Source: Survey data.

Table 6.4 Yield comparison on rented-out plots of female and male landlords, matching on observable plot characteristics

Year	Matching method	Number of treated observations: female landlords	Number of control observations: male landlords	ATT	Std. Err.	t
1998	Kernel	31	59	0.602	0.208	-2.892
1998	Nearest neighbor	31	25	-0.790	0.246	-3.216
2001	Kernel	48	90	-0.478	0.191	-2.499
2001	Nearest neighbor	48	34	-0.549	0.236	-2.325
2006	Kernel	70	56	0.072	0.176	0.407
2006	Nearest neighbor	70	35	0.094	0.198	0.474

Source: Survey data.

Note: [a] Kernel matching based on bootstrapped standard errors with 300 replications.

of female-headed households was no longer lower than that of male-headed households. This may be an effect of the land certification since it may take some time till the reform starts to affect the ability of landlord households to either select better tenant households or to enforce better management by existing tenants. Based on this, we are not able to reject *H1*. This is consistent with the findings by Holden et al. (2011), that female-headed households have become more willing to rent out land after land certification; the certification may have strengthened their bargaining power in relation to their land rental contract partners.

The results of the parametric econometric models of land productivity on rented plots, using household random effects to control for

Table 6.5 Factors correlated with land productivity on rented-out plots, models with household random effects and village fixed effects by year

Explanatory variables	1998	2001	2006
Sex of household head (1 = female, 0 = male)	–0.545**	–0.356*	0.022
Homestead plot dummy	–0.101	0.177	0.059
Plot size, tsimdi	–0.336***	–0.208**	–0.124
Soil depth shallow	–0.21	–0.361	0.04
Soil depth medium	0.04	–0.223	–0.019
Flat slope	–0.118	0.143	0.376
Low hill slope	0.098	–0.029	0.426
Mid hill slope	–0.191	–0.386	0.599
Soil type Cambisol	–0.149	0.15	0.127
Soil type Vertisol	0.011	–0.36	–0.087
Soil type Regosol	–0.446*	0.476**	–0.361
Distance from home to plot (minutes' walk)	–0.002	0.007***	–0.001
Village fixed effects	Yes	Yes	Yes
Constant	7.623***	7.257***	6.717***
Number of observations	114	144	131
Rho	0.157	0.451	0.301
R-squared, overall	0.414	0.423	0.393

Source: Survey data.

Note: Significance levels: *** $p<0.01$, ** $p<0.05$, * $p<0.1$.

household unobservables, are found in Table 6.5. As can be seen, the results are similar to those found with propensity score matching. The sex of household head variable turned from significant at 5 percent and negative in 1998, to significant at 10 percent and negative in 2001, and to insignificant in 2006. Further tests with Heckman selection and pooled OLS models are presented in Table 6.1. Together, these findings demonstrate that the key results are robust to alternative specifications; female-headed households who rent out their land seem to have become able to achieve higher land productivity on their rented-out land after land certification.

6.5.2 Welfare effects of land certification

Table 6.6 provides descriptive statistics for variables included in the regressions for households with and without certificates. It can be seen that on average the welfare levels are higher for households with certificates; about 20 percent of the households were female-headed, and a larger share of female-headed households (22.5 percent) had land

Table 6.6 Descriptive statistics for key variables by households with certificate or not, all years

Have certificate	Statistic measure	Real consumption expenditure per adult equivalent, Eth. Birr	Years with certificate	Sex of household head, 1 = female, 0 = male	Operational farm size/own farm size	Own farm size (ha)
No	Mean	624.208	0.000	0.158	0.990	1.088
	Std. error	32.872	0.000	0.018	0.047	0.063
	N	400	400	400	400	400
Yes	Mean	759.538	4.578	0.225	1.014	0.938
	Std. error	19.318	0.090	0.015	0.020	0.031
	N	768	768	768	768	768
Total	Mean	713.192	3.010	0.202	1.006	0.989
	Std. error	17.069	0.087	0.012	0.021	0.030
	N	1168	1168	1168	1168	1168

Source: Survey data.

Table 6.7 Descriptive statistics for key variables by year, all households

Year	Statistic measure	Consumption expenditure per adult equivalent	Years with certificate	Sex of household head, 1= female, 0 = male	Operational farm size/own farm size	Own farm size (ha)
1997	Mean	534.917	0.000	0.127	0.974	1.137
	Std. error	37.321	0.000	0.020	0.058	0.082
	N	292	292	292	292	292
2000	Mean	658.130	1.394	0.120	1.041	0.980
	Std. error	27.634	0.040	0.019	0.044	0.053
	N	292	292	292	292	292
2003	Mean	765.889	4.009	0.260	1.015	0.933
	Std. error	31.201	0.093	0.026	0.019	0.042
	N	292	292	292	292	292
2006	Mean	893.833	6.639	0.301	0.995	0.908
	Std. error	36.084	0.149	0.027	0.036	0.052
	N	292	292	292	292	292
Total	Mean	713.192	3.010	0.202	1.006	0.989
	Std. error	17.069	0.087	0.012	0.021	0.030
	N	1168	1168	1168	1168	1168

Source: Survey data.

certificates. Households with certificates also had smaller farm sizes, on average, than households without certificates.

Table 6.7 shows descriptive statistics by year for the same key variables. Average household welfare improved over time; the share of female-headed households also increased over time (influenced by the Eritrea–Ethiopia war); and average farm sizes declined over time. These time trends may, therefore, explain much of the variation between households with and without certificates, as seen in Table 6.6. Careful econometric analysis is required to control for these trends and to gain more reliable estimates of the welfare effects of land certification. The years with certificate variable and the interaction variable between years with certificate and sex of household head are used to obtain such welfare impact measures and test whether such impacts are different for female- and male-headed households. Table 6.8 presents the results of the welfare impact models with two-way fixed effects. Household fixed effects were used to control for time invariant unobserved household,

Table 6.8 Welfare effects of land certification with household fixed-effects models

Explanatory variables	**Model 1**	**Model 2**	**Model 3**	**Model 4**
Years with certificate	41.695*	32.527	42.423*	32.998
Sex of household head (female = 1, male = 0)	148.87***	0.26	154.24***	1.01
Farm size per adult equivalent	103.58***	105.65****	104.70****	106.92****
Sex of household head*Years with certificate		34.990**		36.170**
Operational holding size/Farm size			41.813***	44.817****
Dummy for year = 2000	79.815	86.353	76.197	82.695
Dummy for year = 2003	64.677	85.492	59.562	80.711
Dummy for year = 2006	78.627	96.415	72.237	90.166
Constant	378.64****	394.73****	335.75****	349.30****
Prob > chi2	0.000	0.000	0.000	0.000
Number of observations	1168	1168	1168	1168
R-squared	0.156	0.163	0.159	0.166

Source: Survey data.

farm, and village heterogeneity, while year dummies were used to control for time-specific effects.

Model 1 is without the interaction variable and the operational land/own farm size variable. The years with certificate variable is significant at 10 percent and with a positive sign, possibly indicating a positive effect of land certification on household welfare. The sex of household head variable is significant at 1 percent and with a positive sign, indicating that female-headed households have a higher welfare level than male-headed households after controlling for time-invariant observable and unobservable differences. The farm size per adult equivalent variable was also significant at 1 percent and with a positive sign, showing the importance of land for household welfare.

Model 2 includes the interaction effect between years with land certificates and sex of household head. The interaction variable became significant at 5 percent and with a positive sign, while the two variables' separate effects became insignificant. The coefficient for the years with certificate variable was reduced from 41.7 to 32, while the coefficient on the interaction variable was close to 35, which may imply that the welfare effect of land certification on female-headed households is about double that for male-headed households. The coefficient on the sex of household head variable switched from 148 to close to zero, possibly indicating that the entire positive-gender effect is linked to land certification. The farm size per adult equivalent variable became even more highly significant (0.1 percent) and positive in this specification.

Models 3 and 4 deviate from Models 1 and 2 only because they include the operational farm size/own farm size ratio variable. This was done as a robustness check, and to assess whether adjustments in the land rental market had any impact on household welfare. The results show that adjustments toward larger operational holding relative to own holding were associated with positive welfare gains; none of the other significant effects in Models 1 and 2 had any dramatic changes in Models 3 and 4. The coefficients of the key variables increased slightly, and so did some of the significance levels. We interpret the results as solid evidence of positive welfare effects of land certification, particularly for female-headed households. This implies that we cannot reject *H2* or *H3*.

As an additional robustness check, we ran Models 1 to 4 again after removing the years with certificate variable. The results are included in Table 6.9. With this change, the annual dummy variables all became highly significant and positive. The interaction variable between sex of household head and years with certificate (implying that we have assumed that this effect is insignificant for male-headed households) in

Table 6.9 Welfare effects of land certification with household fixed-effects models, models without the years with certificate variable

Explanatory variables	Model 1	Model 2	Model 3	Model 4
Sex of household head (female = 1, male = 0)	154.289***	−28.114	159.462***	−27.792
Farm size per adult equivalent	105.901***	107.797***	106.997***	109.067****
Sex of household head*Years with certificate		42.606***		43.869***
Operational holding size/ Farm size			39.596***	43.837****
Dummy for year = 2000	138.299****	130.601****	135.840****	127.651****
Dummy for year = 2003	231.554****	212.217****	229.470****	209.337****
Dummy for year = 2006	354.983****	302.649****	353.503****	299.459****
Constant	374.877****	395.474****	334.195****	351.045****
Prob > chi2	0.000	0.000	0.000	0.000
Number of observations	1168	1168	1168	1168
R-squared	0.148	0.158	0.15	0.161

Source: Survey data.

Note: Significance levels: *** $p<0.01$, ** $p<0.05$, * $p<0.1$.

Models 2 and 4 became significant at 1 percent and with coefficients in the range 42.6–43.9. These coefficients represent an increase in household welfare of about 7 percent for each additional year that households have kept their certificates. These welfare impact estimates are also close to the land productivity impacts found by Holden et al. (2009) using the same household panel.

6.5.3 Overall reflections of the significance of land certification

One might question why we find such positive effects of the Ethiopian land registration and certification program given that many other land reform programs have failed to meet their objectives or to produce significant positive welfare effects. Such projects have often been implemented in a top-down way, without sufficient recognition of local rights and without sufficiently broad-based information campaigns, and this has often resulted in a race for the rights that has favored the powerful élites (Easterly, 2008; Deininger et al., 2011; Benjaminsen et al., 2009; Jacoby and Minten, 2007). Important reasons for the success of the Ethiopian land certification include:

a) broad local participation in the implementation which also contributed to the low cost;
b) no local élite existed that was against the reform or that could resist or control the process;
c) the past policy with land redistributions had created tenure insecurity and there was a demand for the reform;
d) Ethiopia has quite strong local institutions in the form of peasant associations that were able to support the land registration and certification process; and
e) women at long last had a chance to show what they could achieve when freed up to make their own decisions.

6.6 Conclusions

Our study provides new evidence on the productivity and welfare impacts of low-cost land certification in Ethiopia. Land productivity of the rented land of female landlords appears to have improved relative to that of male landlord households after the certification. This is consistent with the findings of Holden et al. (2011b), that land certification has enhanced tenure security and land rental market participation, especially by female landlord households. It is also consistent with the findings of Deininger et al. (2011) who also found that land rental activity was stimulated by land certification.

In order to identify the possible delayed impact of land certification on household welfare, measured as real consumption expenditure per adult equivalent, we used the duration of ownership of land certificates in a four-round household panel data covering the period from just before certification up to seven years afterwards. After controlling for unobserved household and farm heterogeneity using household fixed effects, the duration of certificate ownership was significant and positive, especially for female-headed households. These results were robust to alternative specifications. The welfare measure increased by about 7 percent per year of ownership for female-headed households, and this is reasonable given that Holden et al. (2009) estimated that land certification has enhanced land productivity by about 45 percent on owner-operated land in the same study areas. Our study provides evidence of significant tenure security-investment and transferability/allocative efficiency effects resulting from the low-cost land certification, and the second effect has been particularly important for the welfare improvement of female landlords, who constituted a large share of landlord households.

The study also reveals that household welfare is highly dependent on the farm size per adult equivalent of the households, demonstrating the high dependence on farming and high welfare costs of population growth if off-farm income opportunities and migration cannot be facilitated. The majority of the households in the studied areas are net buyers of food, and are strongly dependent on employment through the government's Productive Safety Net Program. The strong restrictions on land transfer rights that are included in the revised land proclamation of 2006 (TRS, 2006) include a restriction stating that no more than 50 percent of the land can be rented out. These restrictions also state that the land will be confiscated without compensation from households that have migrated and been away for more than two years.

These restrictions are likely to increase the burden on the Productive Safety Net Program, and reduce the chance that households will be able to graduate from it. So, with continued population growth and technological stagnation in agriculture, poverty will in fact get worse unless new off-farm employment opportunities emerge.

6.6.1 Funding

The initial baseline survey was funded through a research project, Incentives for Land Conservation, under the Research Council of Norway. The second-round survey was funded by the Norwegian Ministry for Foreign Affairs as part of the support to the project Policies for Sustainable Land Management in Ethiopia and Uganda, and managed by the International Food Policy Research Institute. The third- and fourth-round surveys were funded through a Master program in Development and Resource Economics at the Norwegian University of Life Sciences, with support from NORAD and partly with funding from the World Bank for the analysis of impacts of land registration and certification.

6.6.2 Acknowledgements

We acknowledge the contributions of Dr Fitsum Hagos and two groups of MSc students in managing the surveys, collecting, cleaning and organizing the data. Good collaboration with Mekelle University in Tigray and its president, Professor Mitiku Haile, was essential for the success and served as our base during the surveys. The regional Land Administration was supportive and facilitated good information access at district and community levels. Special thanks go to Klaus Deininger and Alain de Janvry, who inspired and encouraged our work. Valuable comments were received during the presentation of an earlier draft of this chapter at the World Bank Land and Poverty Conference, 19–20 April 2011 at the World Bank, Washington, DC.

References

Alemu, T. (1999) 'Land Tenure and Soil Conservation: Evidence from Ethiopia', PhD dissertation, Göteborg University, Göteborg.

Benjaminsen, T.A., Holden, S.T., Lund, C. and Sjaastad, E. (2009) 'Formalisation of Land Rights: Some Empirical Evidence from Mali, Niger and South Africa', *Land Use Policy*, 26, 28–35.

Besley, T. (1995) 'Property Rights and Investment Incentives: Theory and Evidence from Ghana', *Journal of Political Economy*, 103(5), 903–37.

Besley, T. and Burgess, R. (2000) 'Land Reform, Poverty Reduction, and Growth: Evidence from India', *Quarterly Journal of Economics*, 115(2), 341–88.

Binswanger, H.P., Deininger, K. and Feder, G. (1995) 'Power, Distortions, Revolt, and Reform in Agricultural Land Relations', in J. Behrman, and T.N. Srinivasan (eds), *Handbook of Development Economics*, Vol. 3, North-Holland, Amsterdam.

Brasselle, A.S., Gaspart, F. and Platteau, J.-P. (2002) 'Land Tenure Security and Investment Incentives: Puzzling Evidence from Burkina Faso', *Journal of Development Economics*, 67, 373–418.

Cheung, S.N.S. (1968) 'Private Property Rights and Sharecropping', *Journal of Political Economy*, 76, 1170–22.

Cotula, L. and Mathieu, P. (2008) 'Legal Empowerment in Practice: Using Legal Tools to Secure Land Rights in Africa', FAO and IIED, London.

Deininger, K. (2003) *Land Policies for Growth and Poverty Reduction* (Washington D.C.: World Bank).

Deininger, K., Ali, D.A. and Alemu, T. (2011) 'Impacts of Land Certification on Tenure Security, Investment, and Land Market Participation', *Land Economics*, 87, 312–34.

Deininger, K., Ali, D.A., Holden, S.T. and Zevenbergen, J. (2008) 'Rural Land Certification in Ethiopia: Process, Initial Impact, and Implications for Other African Countries', *World Development*, 36, 1786–812.

Deininger, K. and Jin, S. (2006) 'Tenure Security and Land-related Investment: Evidence from Ethiopia', *European Economic Review*, 50, 1245–77.

Easterly, W. (2008) 'Institutions: Top down or bottom up?' *American Economic Review, Papers and Proceedings*, 98(2), 95–9.

Ege, S. (1997) 'The Promised Land: The Amhara Land Redistribution of 1997', SMU-rapport 5/97, Centre for Environment and Development, Norwegian University of Science and Technology, Dragvoll, Trondheim.

FDRE (1997) *Federal Rural Land Administration and Utilization Proclamation*, Federal Democratic Republic of Ethiopia, 89/1997.

Feder, G. and Nishio, A. (1999) 'The Benefits of Land Registration and Titling: Economic and Social Perspectives', *Land Use Policy*, 15(1), 25–43.

Galiani, S. and Schargrodsky, E. (2009) 'Property Rights for the Poor: Effects of Land Titling', Working Paper No. 7, Ronald Coase Institute, St. Louis, Missouri.

Gebremedhin, B. and Swinton, S.M. (2003) 'Investment in Soil Conservation in Northern Ethiopia: The Role of Land Tenure Security and Public Programs', *Agricultural Economics*, 29(1), 69–84.

Ghebru, H. and Holden, S.T. (2011) 'Efficiency and Productivity Differential Effects of Land Certification in Ethiopia', Paper presented at the CSAE 25th Anniversary Conference on Economic Development in Africa, Oxford, UK, 20–22 March 2011.

Ghebru, H. and Holden, S.T. (2012) 'Reverse Share Tenancy and Marshallian Inefficiency: Bargaining Power of Landowners and the Sharecroppers' Productivity', Paper presented at the International Association of Agricultural Economists (IAAE) Triennial Conference, Foz de Iguazu, Brazil, 18–24 August, 2012.

Holden, S.T. and Bezabih, M. (2008) 'Gender and Land Productivity on Rented Out Land: Evidence from Ethiopia', in S.T. Holden, K. Otsuka, and F. Place (eds), *The Emergence of Land Markets in Africa: Assessing the Impacts on Poverty, Equity and Efficiency* (Washington, D.C.: Resources for the Future Press).

Holden, S.T., Deininger, K. and Ghebru, H. (2009) 'Impacts of Low-Cost Land Certification on Investment and Productivity', *American Journal of Agricultural Economics*, 91(2), 359–73.

Holden, S.T., Deininger, K. and Ghebru, H. (2011a) 'Impact of Land Registration and Certification on Land Border Conflicts in Ethiopia', *CLTS Working Paper*, No. 5. Centre for Land Tenure Studies, Norwegian University of Life Sciences, Ås, Norway.

Holden, S.T., Deininger, K. and Ghebru, H. (2011b) 'Tenure Insecurity, Gender, Low-cost Land Certification and Land Rental Market Participation', *Journal of Development Studies*, 47(1), 31–47.

Holden, S.T., Otsuka, K. and Place, F. (2008) *The Emergence of Land Markets in Africa: Impacts on Poverty, Equity and Efficiency* (Washington D.C.: Resources For the Future Press).

Holden, S.T. and Yohannes, H. (2002) 'Land Redistribution, Tenure Insecurity, and Intensity of Production: A Study of Farm Households in Southern Ethiopia', *Land Economics*, 78(4), 573–90.

Jacoby, H.G. and Minten, B. (2007) 'Is Land Titling in Sub-Saharan Africa Cost-Effective? Evidence from Madagascar', *The World Bank Economic Review*, 21(3), 461–85.

Kassie, M. and Holden, S.T. (2007) 'Sharecropping Efficiency in Ethiopia, Threats of Eviction and Kinship', *Agricultural Economics*, 37, 179–85.

Kassie, M. and Holden, S.T. (2008) 'Kinship, Tenure Insecurity, Input Use, and Land Productivity', in S.T. Holden, K. Otsuka, F. Place (eds), *The Emergence of Land Markets in Africa: Assessing the Impacts on Poverty, Equity and Efficiency* (Washington, D.C.: Resources for the Future Press).

Lopez, R. (1996) 'Land Titles and Farm Productivity in Honduras', Department of Agricultural and Resource Economics, University of Maryland, College Park, MD.

Marshall, A. (1890) *The Principles of Economics, Vol. I* (MacMillan: London).

Migot-Adholla, S., Hazell, P., Blarel, B. and Place, F. (1991) 'Indigenous Land Rights Systems in Sub-Saharan Africa: A Constraint on Productivity?' *The World Bank Economic Review*, 5(1), 155–75.

Otsuka, K. (2007) 'Efficiency and Equity Effects of Land Markets', *Handbook of Agricultural Economics*, Vol. 3, chapter 51 (Elsevier), pp. 2671–703.

Otsuka, K., Chuma, H. and Hayami, Y. (1992) 'Land and Labour Contracts in Agrarian Economies: Theories and facts', *Journal of Economic Literature*, 30, 1965–2018.

Otsuka, K. and Hayami, Y. (1988) 'Theories of Share Tenancy: A Critical Survey', *Economic Development and Cultural Change*, 37(1), 32–68.
Pender, J. and Fafchamps, M. (2006) 'Land Lease Markets and Agricultural Efficiency in Ethiopia', *Journal of African Economies*, 15(2), 251–84.
Rahmato, D. (1984) *Agrarian Reform in Ethiopia*, Scandinavian Institute of African Studies, Uppsala.
Rahmato, D. (2003) 'Access to Resources and Livelihood Insecurity', Forum for Social Studies, Addis Ababa.
Shaban, R.A. (1987) 'Testing between Competing Models of Sharecropping', *Journal of Political* Economy, 95(5), 893–920.
Shiferaw, B. and Holden, S.T. (1999) 'Soil Erosion and Smallholders' Conservation Decisions in the Highlands of Ethiopia', *World Development*, 27(4), 739–52.
Shiferaw, B. and Holden, S.T. (2001) 'Farm Level Benefits to Investments for Mitigating Land Degradation: Empirical Evidence from Ethiopia', *Environment and Development Economics*, 6, 335–58.
Singh, N. (2009) Fighting Rural Poverty, Inequality and Low Productivity through Legal Empowerment of the Poor', *The Journal of Peasant Studies*, 36(4), 871–92.
Stiglitz, J.E. (1974) 'Incentives and Risk Sharing in Sharecropping', *Review of Economic Studies*, 41(2), 219–55.
Toulmin, C. (2009) 'Securing Land and Property Rights in Sub-Saharan Africa: The Role of Local Institutions', *Land Use Policy*, 26(1), 10–9.
TRS (1997) *Rural Land Administration and Utilization Proclamation*, Tigray Regional State, Ethiopia.
TRS (2006) *Rural Land Administration and Utilization Proclamation*, No. 97, Tigray Regional State, Ethiopia.

7

Access to Land: Market and Non-Market Land Transactions in Rural Vietnam

Luu Duc Khai, Thomas Markussen, Simon McCoy and Finn Tarp

7.1 Introduction

In a country as densely populated as Vietnam, land is a scarce resource. This is even more so because 70 per cent of the population still reside in rural areas. Therefore, achieving efficiency and equity in the allocation of land in this context is a key priority. Furthermore, in a rapidly developing economy such as that of Vietnam, there is a pressing need to facilitate a process whereby land can change hands without large inefficiencies. For example, to ensure an efficient flow of labor resources from rural to urban areas, it is necessary that households (HHs) in rural areas are able to transfer land rights without incurring excessive transaction costs. It is also important to ensure that agricultural land can be transformed into land for residential and industrial purposes without friction, and without imposing heavy costs on farmers. Evidence from other countries on the ability of land markets to perform these functions efficiently is mixed. The studies on land markets in four African countries in Holden et al. (2008) show considerable friction in the operation of land rental markets, but also, for example in Uganda, some positive effects on allocative efficiency. Similar results are reported in Holden et al. (2011), who find that land certification stimulated the rental markets in Northern Ethiopia, and those increased rental market activities, in turn, improved the efficiency of land use. On the other hand, Deininger et al. (2003) find land markets in Nicaragua to be largely ineffective in terms of improving equity as well as efficiency.

This chapter investigates the importance of both market and non-market modes of land transactions in rural Vietnam, using a 2008 dataset from 12 provinces, supplemented with information from surveys conducted in 2004 and 2006. Non-market land transactions include administrative land allocation and confiscation by the state, land inheritance transactions and clearing of public forest land for private agricultural use. In line with other studies (Brandt, 2006), we find that activity levels in Vietnamese land markets, following the legalization of these markets in 1993, have been rather slow to pick up speed, and that the cumulative effect of markets on overall land allocation is moderate. However, our results on recent developments in land transactions suggest that this pattern might be changing. Between 2004 and 2008, the importance of market-based transactions increased while, in contrast, the role of state-administered land transactions went down. This may partly be interpreted as a result of the 2003 Land Law, which was intended to streamline land transaction processes.

We find that land markets generally improve the efficiency of land use without increasing inequality. The evidence of these positive effects is stronger for rental than for sales markets; however, not all findings are equally positive. We show that both rental and sales markets remain stagnant and underdeveloped in the poorest region of the country (the North-Western Highlands). Also, we investigate the effect of informal, political and bureaucratic connections on land allocation processes. Results indicate that such connections have a significant effect on government land allocation decisions.

The chapter is organized as follows. Section 7.2 provides an overview of the nature and effects of land reforms in Vietnam and Section 7.3 describes the datasets used in the analyses. Section 7.4 compares the prevalence of different modes of land acquisition across provinces and Section 7.5 discusses recent developments in land transactions. Section 7.6 presents the analysis of the effects of land transactions on equity and efficiency. Section 7.7 concludes.

7.2 Overview of land reforms in Vietnam

During the second half of the twentieth century, Vietnam experienced several waves of highly radical land reform. During colonial times, the land distribution had become increasingly unequal as large landowners gradually expanded their holdings (for example, Gourou, 1936). Already during the War of Independence, the Viet Minh had started expropriating land from large land owners and transferring it to tenants.

This Land to the Tiller reform was broadly implemented in the North after victory over the French in 1954. But by around 1957, however, collectivization had already begun to be implemented, following the example of China. In the South of Vietnam, Land to the Tiller reforms were also implemented near the end of the American War, and after the Communist victory in 1975, collectivization started to be implemented in the South. This met with significant resistance from farmers and in fact only a minority of Southern farms was ever fully collectivized. Also in the North, local resistance to collectivization was growing in response to disappointing levels of output.

From the late 1970s some communes were illegally implementing contract systems (known as 'sneaky contracts') whereby control over land was effectively granted to households who delivered output to communes on terms settled by informal contracts. Following severe food shortages around 1980, this system was legitimized in 1981 through the so-called Directive 100 of the Communist Party. Before that year, farmer compensation was based on the number of hours worked, but after the implementation of Directive 100, farmers were responsible for delivering a set quota of grain to the cooperative, and then allowed to market any surplus above quota – so in effect, the farmers were turned into residual claimants of crop profits. Pingali and Xuan (1992) analyzed the effects of this reform, and found a significant effect on yields of rice.

Following the introduction of the Doi Moi reform program in 1986, a new land law was introduced in 1987. The implementation directive of this law, known as Resolution 10, came into effect in 1988. Together with the 1993 land law, this was the key event of pro-market land reforms in Vietnam. Resolution 10 provided for dissolution of agricultural collectives and transfer of land user rights to households. Use rights were guaranteed for 15 years for land under annual crops, and for one to two planting cycles for forestry and land under perennial crops. Land market transactions, however, remained illegal, until the 1993 land law, which provided for the issuance of Land Use Right Certificates (LURCs), endowing holders with the rights to exchange, transfer, lease, inherit and mortgage land.[1] Also, the duration of use rights were extended to 20 years for annual, and 50 years for perennial, land. The law states that in general households should be able to renew their use rights when the 20- or 50-year term expires. Although land officially remains the property of the 'whole people', LURCs therefore in effect function much like proper land titles.

One restriction, however, is the presence of a quasi-land ceiling. A significant land tax is imposed on holdings above a certain 'land use limitation'; the tax varies according to the designated land use purpose and the quality of land. The limitation is two hectares for land under annual crops (three hectares in some provinces), and 10 hectares for perennial land in lowland communes, or 30 hectares in upland communes. During the five-year period after 1993, more than 11 million LURCs were distributed to households, making this one of the fastest large-scale land titling programs in the World (Do and Iyer, 2008).

A number of authors have investigated the effects of the 1987 and 1993 land laws. Ravallion and Van de Walle (2004) analyzed the effects of the administrative allocation of plots to households following decollectivization. They conclude that while the administrative allocation differs from a hypothetical market-based allocation, the deviation is relatively small and can largely be explained as the price paid for achieving a highly egalitarian land distribution. They find little evidence that the land allocation process was captured by local officials. Ravallion and Van de Walle (2006) investigated whether land market transactions functioned to reduce the inefficiencies that did result from administrative land allocation, and find that markets did indeed play that role. Similar results are obtained by Deininger and Jin (2008), who find that land markets, especially rentals but also sales, allocate land on average from large to small land owners and from low-ability to high-ability farmers. The analytical section of this chapter follows up on these results with analyses of more recent data. Do and Iyer (2008) analyze the effects of the land titling program, exploiting the fact that it was rolled out faster in some provinces than in others. They find that titling led to increased investment in perennial crops and to more time spent on off-farm activities. The latter effect, to a large extent, follows from the former, because cultivation of perennial crops is typically less labor-intensive than cultivation of rice, the main annual crop. Ravallion and Van de Walle (2008a) note that liberalization of land markets has led to increasing levels of landlessness, especially in the South. However, they also argue that increased landlessness is correlated with falling poverty. A panel analysis reveals that in the North poverty fell more rapidly among households who became landless during the period of study than among others. This is circumstantial evidence that many people have sold land to take up non-farm enterprises, as it is unlikely that households on average would increase their incomes by selling land and becoming farm workers.

Markussen et al. (2011) highlight the fact that while rights to transfer land have largely been liberalized, the local state continues to intervene heavily in crop choice decisions. Most importantly, a large share of plots (more than 45 per cent in the sample analyzed by Markussen et al. (2011), are designated for paddy rice farming.

The Land Law was further revised in 1998 and 2003. The 2003 law aims to smooth land transaction procedures and facilitate the orderly acquirement of land by domestic and foreign enterprises. It also revises rules on land titling. Whereas LURCs used to be in the name of the household head only, the names of both the head and his or her spouse are now supposed to be entered.

Important current issues in land management include the prevalence of disputes following land recovery by the state for infrastructure or investment purposes and, sometimes related to this, corruption in land management. One piece of evidence on the importance of corruption in land management is provided in World Bank (2009, ch. 3). It shows that 55 per cent of respondents in a representative household survey perceive LURC issuance procedures as being affected by corruption. But despite recent attempts to regularize the processes of land confiscation and compensation, the compensation levels are often viewed as arbitrary and inadequate, and a number of conflicts related to land confiscation have occurred (Anderson and Davidsen, 2011).[2] Common reasons for complaining about land recovery, or even resisting it, include the perceptions that

(i) the rate of compensation per unit of area is too low;
(ii) compensation rates are inconsistent over time (land recovered earlier was compensated less);
(iii) compensation rates differ across locations within the same province; and
(iv) household expectations of finding employment in enterprises built on recovered land were not met.

A particular source of conflict is the fact that compensation is often based on the designation of a plot as agricultural land. Hence the entire rent resulting from its upgrade to residential or enterprise land is captured by the state and the land developer (World Bank, 2008).

While these issues are important, it should also be stressed that recurrent administrative land redistribution, which is common in some parts of China, plays a very insignificant role in Vietnam, and is not authorized by the Land Law;[3] the main motives for land confiscation are land requirement for infrastructure and industrial or other economic development projects.

Reforms of forest land management have to a large extent followed the same pattern as reforms for agricultural land, although generally at a slower pace. While almost all agricultural land has been allocated to households and individuals, and more than 75 per cent of this land is titled, only about 25 per cent of forest land has been handed over to households and individuals. Around 45 per cent of forest land has been allocated to corporate entities, including State Forest Enterprises. Around 55 per cent of the forest land allocated to users is titled (World Bank, 2009, figure 2.2). Community-based titling has been piloted in some areas dominated by ethnic minorities, but only a small fraction of land is held under this form of tenure. (World Bank, 2008, ch. D).[4] While the land ceiling for forestry land, 30 hectares, is higher than for agricultural land, land rights are in other ways more limited; most importantly, the sale of forest land is not allowed.

Vietnam experienced significant deforestation during the 1980s. Impressively, especially in the light of the rapid population growth, this deforestation trend was reversed in the 1990s and 2000s. This was partly the result of direct government efforts to plant more forest and improve incentives for communes and state economic enterprises to plant and preserve forest, for example through the important Program 661. However, Tachibana et al. (2001) argue that the strengthening of individual land rights also contributed positively to reforestation. First, rights to agricultural land in the lowlands induced farmers to shift their resources from extensive and shifting cultivation in the uplands to intensive farming in the lowlands. Second, improved rights to upland plots strengthened incentives to plant tree crops instead of annual crops, in line with the findings in Do and Iyer (2008).

For comprehensive reviews of land issues in Vietnam, see Kerkvliet (2006), Brandt (2006), Ravallion and Van de Walle (2008b) and Kirk and Nguyen (2009).

7.3 Description of datasets

We make use of a panel dataset collected in the Vietnam Household Living Standards Survey (VHLSS) and the Vietnam Access to Resources Household Survey (VARHS). We analyze data on households interviewed for the comprehensive (expenditure) version of the 2004 VHLSS. This is attractive because the 2004 round of the VHLSS contained a module collecting detailed information about land issues, which we can exploit. Furthermore, in 12 provinces, the rural households interviewed in the 2004 VHLSS were re-interviewed in the 2006

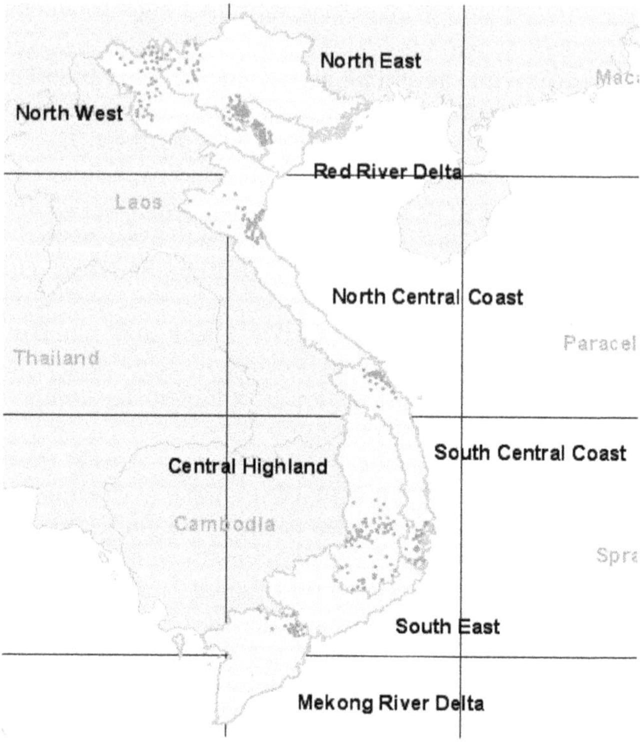

Map 7.1 VARHS survey sites

and 2008 rounds of the VARHS.[5] Our sample is statistically representative at the provincial but not at the national level. Map 7.1 shows the VARHS survey sites. The number of households available for analysis is 1312.

We mainly report results from the 2008 round of the VARHS. The other two surveys are very useful in terms both of exploring changes over time, and for measuring certain variables with a time lag. All statistical analyses conducted make use of the sampling probability weights for the 2004 VHLSS. This procedure corrects for biases in the original sampling procedure. However, the fact that only households already existing in 2004 are included in the analysis gives rise to a moderate bias in the estimates, since the households sampled in 2006 and 2008 are slightly older than the population average.

7.4 Modes of land acquisition

Table 7.1 presents plot-level information about how agricultural land currently owned or operated by households was acquired. *State* includes plots where the use right was granted for free, and a small number of plots were acquired through commune auctions (though the latter category is very small). Hence, the *Bought* category includes only plots purchased from other, private agents.

The table presents statistics for each of four distinct geographical areas, namely the Northern Lowlands, the Northern Highlands, the Southern Lowlands and the Central (Southern) Highlands. The distinction between lowlands and highlands is drawn somewhat roughly, since some of the provinces categorized as lowland, for example Phu Tho and Nghe An, do contain areas best characterized as highland. However, the majority of the population in these provinces resides in the plains.

Looking first at the results for all households, we see that the state is by far the most important source of land. Rental and purchase are only the fourth- and fifth-most important means of land acquisition respectively – slightly less important than inheritance and forest clearing. Hence, the cumulative importance of market transactions on current land allocation is rather modest. Several alternative, and not mutually exclusive, interpretations of this fact are possible. On the one hand, the modest impact of market transactions probably indicates to some extent the continued presence of barriers to entering markets for land. In some Northern communities, field observations suggest that selling land remains almost taboo. This means that the mere *possibility* of trading land may simply be ignored by many households. Even if a household should want to sell or buy land, it is likely to meet with considerable difficulties because the price of land is not known (most Northern households in our survey state that they do not know the approximate sales market value of their plots), procedures for transacting land are not well-established, and land sales may be met with disapproval from fellow community members. On the other hand, the fact that the land allocation created by decollectivization has not been massively reversed is consistent with the view that this allocation was not highly inefficient. As described above, this is indeed the conclusion reached by Ravallion and van de Walle (2004, 2008b).

A further inspection of the results in Table 7.1 reveals wide variation between provinces and areas. Whereas the state is the overwhelmingly dominant source of land in the Northern Lowlands, it is significantly less important in the Southern Lowlands, and has played an even

Table 7.1 Mode of land acquisition, plot level (%)[a]

Province	**State**	**Inherited**	**Bought**	**Cleared**	**Rented**	**Exchanged or other**	**Total**
Northern Lowlands	77.8	7.4	2.4	3.4	8.2	0.8	100.0
Northern Highlands	27.6	12.9	0.4	57.8	0.9	0.4	100.0
Southern Lowlands	46.7	25.2	11.6	5.0	10.7	0.9	100.0
Central Highlands	11.1	13.0	36.1	33.0	6.5	0.3	100.0
Total	63.1	11.3	7.4	9.4	8.1	0.7	100.0

Source: Authors' calculations based on survey data.

Notes: [a] N = 5,708. Only 2004–2008 panel households included. All agricultural land owned or operated by the household included. Purely residential plots excluded. The 'four areas' variable is coded as follow: Northern Lowlands: Ha Tay, Phu Tho and Nghe An. Northern Highlands: Lao Cai, Dien Bien and Lai Chau. Central Highlands: Dak Lak, Dak Nong, and Lam Dong. Southern Lowlands: Quang Nam, Khanh Hoa and Long An. (We use the term 'Central Highlands' rather than 'Southern Highlands', because this is the standard name for the area in question.)

smaller role in the Highlands. Land sales are much more important in the South than in the North, and land rentals are much more important in the Lowlands than in the Highlands – whereas land reclamation is a significant source of land in the Highlands but plays next to no role in the Lowlands. These differences have deep historical roots. It is natural to think of the differences between North and South in terms of the relative importance of state and market as the result of differing experiences with communist rule; the Communist takeover, after all, happened more than 20 years earlier in the North than in the South, and the period between Communist victory in the South (1975) and the land law that ended collective agriculture (1987) was quite short. Indeed, as explained above, most land in the South was never fully collectivized.

It is interesting to note, however, that the significant differences between land arrangement in the North and South originated much earlier than the Communist era. Even in the pre-colonial Vietnam, the erstwhile Indo-China up to the nineteenth century, inter-village land transactions were very rare in northern and central regions, but much more common in the South. According to Popkin (1979), the reason was that the Northern Lowlands ('Tonkin' in the colonial language of the area) had been fully settled by the French centuries earlier (perhaps as early as the seventeenth century, Popkin, 1979, p. 167), whereas unused, fertile land continued to exist in the Mekong river area well into the twentieth century. This meant that in the South it was easier to move out of a village and start a new life elsewhere, and this in turn stimulated a more dynamic land market in the South. Conversely, a significant share of land (20–25 per cent) in pre-colonial villages in Northern and Central villages was communal land, periodically redistributed by local authorities, whereas this system had a much smaller role in the South (Popkin, 1979, p. 173). Hence, the use of land reallocation by public authorities has a much longer history in the North than in the South.

These historical differences indicate that different experiences with Communist rule and collectivized agriculture may not only be a cause but also an effect of differences in land relations. Also, the fact that differences are rooted hundreds of years in the past suggest that they may be more persistent than if they had resulted only from different experiences in the more recent past. It underlines that a convergence of land transaction patterns between Northern and Southern Vietnam would be a truly historical development.

7.5 Recent developments in land transactions

Table 7.1, which we have discussed above, shows the results for all plots owned or operated by households, regardless of when they were acquired. Therefore, the table shows the *accumulated* effect of various modes of land acquisition over a period of 15 years – or in some cases more – since some plots, especially in the South, have been owned by households from before collectivization. To obtain a more accurate description of more recent development in the importance of various modes of transactions, Table 7.2 presents results from both the 2004 VHLSS and the 2008 VARHS. For each survey, we focus on households who acquired land during the two-year period prior to the year of the survey. We include households who initiated rentals during this period. The table presents results for the entire 2004–2008 panel as well as for each of the four areas defined by the north–south and highland–lowland distinctions. Note, however, that the numbers of observations in some of the latter cases are quite small, implying that results should be interpreted with care.

The overall results indicate that the share of households acquiring land is largely stable over the period of study (in fact a small, statistically insignificant, drop is recorded between the two surveys). The results, however,

Table 7.2 Recent land transactions, 2004 and 2008 (%)[a]

	Northern Lowlands		Northern Highlands		Southern Lowlands		Central Highlands	
	2004	2008	2004	2008	2004	2008	2004	2008
Share of households acquiring land in last two years before survey	15.4	13.5	17.2	12.1	16.9	29.6	7.1	9.5	21.4	20.8
Share of whom acquired land from										
State	40.4	14.0	58.8	25.5	21.9	4.7	12.1	0.0	3.4	2.7
Inheritance	5.4	3.9	5.1	3.2	9.7	5.1	4.7	3.6	5.5	5.1
Purchase	14.5	19.3	5.1	6.2	2.9	0.0	8.6	3.8	47.9	65.5
Clearing	13.2	14.4	8.0	1.8	49.4	88.8	17.4	15.7	19.5	13.7
Rental	36.0	54.9	34.8	71.3	5.4	6.3	52.5	73.8	37.2	23.5
Exchange or other	3.9	4.9	3.4	6.7	16.6	2.5	4.7	3.1	2.5	3.3
Total	100.0	100.0	100.0	100.0	100.0	100.0	100	100	100.0	100.0
Observations	195	185	91	65	30	42	22	29	52	49

Sources: Authors' calculations based on VHLSS 2004 and VARHS 2008.

Notes: [a]The unit of observation is households. The number of observations refers only to the households that acquired land in the last two years.

on the relative importance of different modes of land acquisition are much more remarkable. Among households who acquired land, the share who acquired it from the state is much smaller during the period 2006–2008 (14 per cent) than during 2002–2004 (40 per cent). In contrast, the relative importance of market transactions has increased. In the case of land purchases, the increase, from 15 to 19 per cent, is moderate and not statistically significant ($t=1.25$; $p = 0.21$). In the case of rentals, however, the increase is large, from 36 to 55 per cent, and statistically significant ($t = 3.76$; $p = 0.00$). The drop in the share of households acquiring land from the state may to some extent be a lifecycle effect: the state may give land primarily to young families, of which there are more in the 2004 survey than in the 2008 one. However, the increased importance of markets is not likely to result from such effects; hence, while the state retains a significant role in land allocation, the market is gaining ground.

Looking at the data for the four geographical areas, it is striking, in the light of the discussion above, that market transactions *in recent years* have in fact been as important in the Northern as in the Southern Lowlands. It is important to note, however, that the area referred to here as the 'Southern Lowlands' includes only one province in the populous Mekong river delta (Long An), and none from the South Eastern region. The group does include, on the other hand, two provinces from the region known as the South Central Coast, which did not belong to the historical area referred to above as the South (Cochinchina), but rather to central Vietnam (Annam). Also, the number of observations in the Southern Lowlands is quite small. Furthermore, when we focus on the highlands rather than the lowlands, we find that market transactions are much more important in the South (Central Highlands) than in the North.[6] It is particularly striking that rental markets play a much smaller role in the mountainous north than in any other region. It is also interesting to note that the role of land clearing does not appear to be decreasing. In fact, in the Northern Highlands the share of households who recently cleared land was actually much higher in 2008 than in 2004. In the latter period, land clearing appears to have been the overwhelmingly dominant mode of accessing new land in this region. It is beyond the scope of this chapter to explore whether or not this development should give rise to environmental concerns. It is fascinating to note, though, that the process of land clearing, which was essentially completed in the Northern Lowlands centuries ago, is still ongoing at full speed in the Highlands.[7]

Table 7.3 presents results on the supply side of the land market. It shows the share of households who rented out or permanently disposed of land during the two-year period before the 2008 VARHS.[8] Furthermore, it shows the relative importance of various modes of disposing of land. The variable describing modes of disposing of land combines information on *how* the land was handed over, and *who* it was handed over to. We distinguish between land handed over to the state or to relatives by any means, land sold to private non-relatives, land exchanged for other land with private non-relatives, and land disposed of in other ways. These distinctions reflect the view that exchanges with private non-relatives are of special interest, because such transactions are the hallmarks of a modern market economy.[9]

The first line of the table shows, as in Tables 7.1 and 7.2, that rental agreements are much less important in the Northern Highlands than in other regions. The second line shows that around 12 per cent of households permanently disposed of agricultural land, either voluntarily or involuntarily, during the two years before the survey.

Table 7.3 Land rented out or permanently disposed of

	All	Northern Lowlands	Northern Highlands	Southern Lowlands	Central Highlands
Share of households renting out land[b]	6.1	8.4	0.5	3.4	3.4
Share of households permanently disposing of land in last two years	11.7	12.4	7.6	9.2	14.3
Shares of whom land turned over to					
State	29.8	34.4	57.8	33.2	7.9
Relatives	48.0	50.8	25.2	45.1	45.4
Sold to non-state, non-relatives	17.0	5.2	7.4	24.9	48.0
Exchanged for other plot, with non-state, non-relative	8.9	12.6	0.0	0.0	7.1
Other	0.9	1.1	9.5	0.0	0.0
Total	100.0	100.0	100.0	100.0	100.0
Observations[a]	147	73	14	27	33

Source: Authors' calculations based on survey data.

Notes: [a] The number of observations refers to the number of households who have permanently disposed of land.
[b] Only contracts initiated in past two years before survey included.

The next rows in the table show the relative importance of different modes of disposing of land. Note again, that the number of observations for certain geographical areas is quite low. The results show that the most important way of disposing of land is to hand it over to relatives (most often children of the household head). The second most important mode of disposing of land, however, is to turn it over to the state; the state apparently plays a somewhat more important role as a receiver than as a donor/seller of land (compare with Table 7.2). In about two-thirds of plots handed over to the state, households were expelled from the land; in most cases, some compensation was received, but the transaction was involuntary on the part of the household (see CIEM et al., 2009, and tables 3.9 and 3.10).

The table shows that land sales play a larger role in the South than in the North, both in the lowlands and the highlands. Hence, when we look at the supply side, there is not much evidence of North–South convergence in the importance of land sales markets.

7.6 Land transactions, efficiency and equity

This section investigates the performance of different modes of land transactions in terms of their ability to generate efficiency and equity in land use. We investigate the propensity of each mode of transaction to transfer land to households with a high ability to farm, with abundant labor resources, with small initial landholdings, and with low income. Our approach follows, in important respects, the methodology used in Deininger and Jin (2008). However, we have added to their study in several ways. First, our results are based on data from 2008, rather than 1998. This is significant in an economy developing as rapidly as that of Vietnam. Second, we explore non-market as well as market transactions, focus on land fragmentation, and define some variables differently. Also, Deininger and Jin estimate farmers' agricultural abilities by retrieving the household fixed effects from agricultural production, whereas we proxy ability by the household head's years of schooling.

Tables 7.4 and 7.5 show how a number of household characteristics vary between households, depending on which types of land transactions they have participated in. Table 7.4 focuses on modes of acquiring land and Table 7.5 on modes of disposing of it.

Because there is a direct, almost mechanical, relationship between land transactions and household income (for example, a land sale generates

Table 7.4 Household characteristics by mode of acquiring land

HH acquired land from	Years of schooling, HH head	Land owned, sq. m.	Number of plots owned	HH members aged 15–64	HH income, 2006, 000 VND	HH connected with public official (per cent)[a]
State	6.9	5,932	5.3	3.2	26,055	38.0
Inheritance	6.4	6,979	4.4	3.1	30,872	37.2
Purchase	7.4	11,877	4.2	3.4	35,747	36.6
Clearing	5.3	14,232	4.8	3.4	25,697	28.0
Rental	7.7	6,831	4.4	3.4	30,764	40.4
Exchange	5.5	4,133	4.8	3.5	33,200	34.9
All	6.6	7,150	4.6	3.1	28,273	36.5

Source: Authors' calculations based on survey data.

Notes: [a] A household is defined as 'connected' with a public official if a household member, friend or relative holds hold an 'office or other trusted positions in the commune or higher levels of government'.

Table 7.5 Household characteristics by mode of disposing of land

	Years of schooling, HH head	Land owned, sq. m.	Number of plots owned	HH members aged 15–64	HH income, 2006, 000 VND	HH connected with public official (per cent)
HH rents out land	6.9	6,388	5.3	2.6	37,311	41.0
HH has disposed of land in last two years to:						
State	6.2	12,901	5.2	3.5	34,152	23.0
Relatives	7.1	6,044	4.3	2.7	28,710	37.7
Sold to non-state, non-relatives	5.7	16,098	3.1	3.1	31,758	26.3
Exchanged with non-state, non-relatives	5.9	4,615	5.2	3.1	18,160	33.4
All	6.6	7,150	4.6	3.1	28,273	36.5

Source: Authors' calculations based on survey data.

income), income for the year 2006 is used. While many of the results presented in these tables are interesting, care about how to interpret them is advisable, for several reasons: first, the analyses do not take regional differences into account. For example, the tables indicate that land sales typically take place between richer households with larger farms. This may simply be a result of the fact that land sales most often occur in the South, where households are on average richer and endowed with larger landholdings than those in the North. Second, results are sometimes affected by high outliers. Third, correlations between the different household characteristics are not taken into account. To deal with these issues, we turn to a multivariate, regression analysis of the relationship between modes of land transaction, equity and efficiency. Tables 7.6 to 7.9 present probit models for the probability that a household participated in each of a number of different types of land transactions. The independent variables include the variables analyzed in Tables 7.4 and 7.5, and a set of provincial dummies which take account of all differences between regions. To deal with outliers, we enter land owned, the number of working age household members, and household income in logarithms. As in Tables 7.4 and 7.5, income is lagged two years to take account of endogeneity.

Table 7.6 Land transactions, multivariate analysis, Northern Lowlands[a]

	Dependent variable					
	Acquired land from state	Bought land	Rents land	Disposed of land to state	Sold land	Rents out land
	Probit	Probit	Probit	Probit	Probit	Probit
Land owned, sq.m, log	–0.009	–0.022	–0.01	0.003	0.004***	0.022
Number of plots owned	0.020***	0.007	–0.006	–0.005*	–0.001**	0.023***
Working age HH members, log	0.014	0.011	0.128**	0.018	0.004*	–0.159***
Annual HH income, 2006, log	–0.003	0.041*	–0.034	0.003	0.002**	0.088**
Years of schooling, HH head	0.000	0.002	0.018**	–0.003	0.000	0.001
HH has connection with public official	–0.008	0.023	0.033	–0.027*		0.007
Observations	322	322	322	322	322	322

Source: Authors' calculations based on survey data.

Notes: [a] Province dummies are included in all regressions, results not reported. Marginal effects reported. The 'HH has connections' variable drops out of regression 5 because no households without connections sold land. Significance levels: *** $p<0.01$, ** $p<0.05$, * $p<0.1$.

To deal with potential autocorrelation within communes, we use standard errors corrected for commune level clustering. Note that for land acquired, we focus on all plots currently owned or operated. For plots disposed of, however, we only have information relating to the two years prior to the survey.

To take account of the profound regional differences described above, separate regressions are estimated for each region.[10] We focus first on the role of the state, then on the role of markets. Looking at Columns 1 and 4 in Tables 7.6–7.9, we see that in most cases neither acquiring land from the state nor losing land to it is significantly related to farm size; the only exception is the Northern Highlands, where large farms are more likely to lose land to the state. On the other hand, receiving land from

Table 7.7 Land transactions, multivariate analysis, Northern Highlands[a]

	Dependent variable				
	Acquired land from state	Bought land	Rents land	Disposed of land to state	Rents out land
	Probit	Probit	Probit	Probit	Probit
Land owned, sq.m., log	0.000	–0.032**	0.004	0.039***	0.000
Number of plots owned	0.037***	–0.007	–0.020***	–0.006	0.003
Working age HH members, log	0.049	0.023	0.000	0.047	–0.029
Annual HH income, 2006, log	0.038	0.016	–0.079***	–0.022	0.055***
Years of schooling, HH head	0.013*	0.003	0.017**	0.006*	0.005
HH has connection with public official	–0.112**	–0.002	0.047	0.059*	0.012
Observations	389	389	389	389	389

Note: [a] Same as Table 7.6.

the state is correlated with owning a large number of plots, consistent with the view that state land allocation policies are the strongest force behind high levels of land fragmentation.

The number of working age household members has a significant positive effect on the probability of receiving land from the state only in the Central Highlands. The estimated coefficient is positive but insignificant in the two Northern regions, and essentially zero in the Southern Lowlands. Hence, the evidence suggests that administrative land allocation procedures have tended to allocate land to households with abundant labor resources, but only in some areas. Household labor power, on the other hand, has no effect on the probability of losing land to the state. Household income is not correlated with either receiving land from, or losing land to, the state. Hence, the estimates provide no evidence that administrative land allocations play a progressive role in terms of decreasing income inequality. Receiving land from the state is not correlated with the level of education of the household head in the

Table 7.8 Land transactions, multivariate analysis, Southern Lowlands[a]

	Dependent variable					
	Acquired land from state	**Bought land**	**Rents land**	**Disposed of land to state**	**Sold land**	**Rents out land**
	Probit	**Probit**	**Probit**	**Probit**	**Probit**	**Probit**
Land owned, sq.m., log	-0.005	0.058***	0.008	0.005	-0.001	-0.008
Number of plots owned	0.045**	0.017**	-0.001	0.001	-0.004	0.002
Working age HH members, log	-0.026	0.012	0.002	-0.002	-0.039*	-0.107**
Annual HH income, 2006, log	-0.006	0.009	-0.017	0.012	0.004	0.060**
Years of schooling, HH head	-0.004	0.017**	0.017***	-0.001	0.002	0.003
HH has connection with public official	0.002	-0.019	-0.049	-0.033*	-0.022	-0.008
Observations	245	245	245	245	245	245

Note: [a] Same as Table 7.6.

lowland regions. In the Northern Highlands, better educated household heads are more likely to receive land from the state, but in the Central Highlands the opposite is true.

In both lowland regions, households with connections to a public official are significantly less likely than other households to lose land to the state, consistent with results reported in Markussen and Tarp (2011). On the other hand, in the Northern Highlands, well-connected households are *more* likely than others to lose land to the state. The explanation might be that in this region households in more isolated areas have little interaction with the state, and therefore neither develop connections with officials nor lose land to the state. We may conclude that in lowland regions political/bureaucratic connections work to protect households against land expropriation.

Table 7.9 Land transactions, multivariate analysis, Central Highlands[a]

	Dependent variable				
	Acquired land from state	**Bought land**	**Rents land**	**Sold land**	**Rents out land**
	Probit	**Probit**	**Probit**	**Probit**	**Probit**
Land owned, sq.m., log	-0.025	0.037	-0.01	0.000	0.012
Number of plots owned	0.031**	0.027	-0.032*	-0.001	0.009**
Working age HH members, log	0.199***	-0.036	0.033	-0.001	-0.040*
Annual HH income, 2006, log	0.022	-0.009	-0.028	0.02	0.022**
Years of schooling, HH head	-0.019**	0.047***	0.005	-0.003	0.006**
HH has connection with public official	0.131*	-0.046	0.085	0.029	0.021
Observations	270	270	270	270	270

Note: [a] Same as Table 7.6.

Now we turn to land sales markets. In the Northern Highlands, smaller farms are more likely than others to buy land. In contrast, in the Southern Lowlands it is the larger farms which tend to buy land. Then in the Northern Lowlands, larger farms are more likely than others to sell land. Hence, there is some evidence that land sales markets work to consolidate land holdings in the South, but not in the North, consistent with results in Markussen et al. (2012). This chapter also presents evidence that larger farms are more profitable than small farms when the much more intense use of labor on small farms is taken into account. Land concentration in the south may be interpreted as being partly motivated by these efficiency advantages of larger farms. In the Northern Lowlands, rich households are both more likely to buy and to sell land than other households. It thus appears that in the Northern Lowlands, poorer households are to some extent excluded from land sales markets. However, these effects are not present in other regions; in the Southern

Lowlands, households with more working age members are less likely than others to sell land. However, in the Northern Lowlands the opposite effect is found. Hence, land sales markets may contribute to allocating land away from households with few labor resources, but this is only the case in the South.

Meanwhile, the household head's duration of schooling is positively correlated with buying land. However, this effect is found only in the Southern regions. Hence, land markets allocate land to better educated households – but only in the South. Schooling apparently has no effect on the probability of selling land.

Turning to land rental markets, the multivariate analysis provides a set of interesting results. Household income has a positive and significant effect on the probability of renting land out in all regions, and a negative effect on the probability of renting land in, in three regions, although this effect is only significant in the Northern Highlands. This indicates that the function of the rental markets is to allocate land from rich to poor farmers. The number of plots owned has a negative effect on the probability of renting in, in all regions (statistically significant in Northern and Central Highlands), and a positive effect on renting out, in all regions (significant in Northern Lowlands and Central Highlands). This is consistent with the view that rental markets work to reduce land fragmentation, in the sense of moving plots from households owning many plots to households owning few. Furthermore, the number of working age household members has a positive and significant effect on renting in, in the Northern Lowlands and a positive effect on renting out in all regions (significant everywhere except the Northern Highlands). The implication is that rental markets move land from households with scarcity of labor to households with abundant labor resources. We also find that the household head's years of schooling has a positive significant effect on renting in for all regions except the Central Highlands. This may be interpreted as evidence that rental markets allocate land in favor of higher-ability farmers. The only evidence against this interpretation comes from the Central Highlands, where schooling has a positive effect on renting out. Participation in rental markets is not correlated with the amount of land owned. Hence, there is little evidence that rental markets operate to equalize operational holdings. Participation in rental markets is also not significantly correlated with connections to a public official.

In sum, one of the most striking results emerging from the analysis of land transaction modes is the benign effects of land rental markets in terms of efficiency and equity. We find that rental markets transfer land to high-ability households with low income and abundant labor resources. These findings are in line with those reported in Deininger and Jin (2008) for the 1998 VHLSS data. In contrast with the results in Deininger and Jin (2008) our results on land sales markets differ somewhat from those on rental markets. Sales markets tend to transfer land to well-educated households with abundant labor resources, but these effects are only found in the South. Sales markets do not transfer land from rich to poor, and in the Northern Lowlands poor households tend to be excluded from sales markets. In the Southern Lowlands, sales markets tend to increase land inequality, while the opposite effect is found in the Northern Highlands. There is some evidence that sales markets function to decrease land fragmentation; households typically sell the plots furthest away from the family home, whereas plots purchased are typically located close to the home.

Results on land given and taken by the state are mostly consistent with the view that administrative land allocation in Vietnam has been egalitarian and has taken variations in household size into account, as concluded in Ravallion and van de Walle (2004, 2008b). On the other hand, the view that state land allocation policies are in large measure responsible for the high degree of land fragmentation observed in Vietnam is also confirmed. There is no evidence that administrative land allocation has taken household endowments of human capital into account.

Ravallion and van de Walle (2008) argue that the massive-scale land allocation process that took place in the context of decollectivization is notable for the relatively small role played by nepotism and corruption at the local level. While we also conclude that state land allocation policies are mostly egalitarian, our results lead to a modification of these conclusions. We find that in lowland regions, households with informal connections to public officials are significantly less likely than others to have land taken away by the state, even when other household characteristics are controlled for. Hence, the local political economy of land allocation might have become somewhat less benign, as compared to the situation during the highly unusual period of decollectivization in the early 1990s (see Markussen and Tarp, 2011).

7.7 Conclusions

The results presented in this chapter show that the cumulative effect of land sales and rental markets on land allocation in rural Vietnam remains fairly moderate. Most plots operated by households were allocated by the state; most households have never participated in the land sales market; and the share of households participating in rental markets is not large. This is consistent with evidence from a number of other countries showing that even when they are legal, land markets tend to be thin. However, when we explore changes in land market activities between 2004 and 2008, interesting new evidence emerges, showing that in Vietnam some of these facts may be changing. Between 2004 and 2008, the importance of the state as a source of land acquisition declined, while the importance of markets significantly increased. The state continues to play a large part, but the relative importance of markets is rising. One of the factors behind this development may be the 2003 Land Law, which streamlined land transaction processes.

This appears to be good news. We find that rental markets in particular have positive effects on equity as well as on efficiency. While administrative land allocation in Vietnam has certainly contributed to a relatively egalitarian land distribution, our results clearly indicate that markets do better than the state at improving efficiency in land use. Not only do we find evidence that markets reduce land fragmentation, which to a large extent is brought about by state land allocation policies, but they also exhibit a tendency to allocate land to users with high levels of human capital. This tendency is generally absent from administrative state allocation procedures. While these results confirm the conventional economic theory that markets are the superior mechanism for efficient resource allocation, it is important to note that the benign effects of markets may well be conditional on the highly egalitarian, initial land distribution which resulted from the administrative land reforms; for example, Deininger et al. (2003) find much less benign effects of land markets in Nicaragua, where land is also much more unequally distributed than in Vietnam.

While generally confirming the view that the effects of land reform in Vietnam have been highly positive, we also point to some causes for concern: there is evidence that informal, political/bureaucratic connections may affect state land allocation activities; households with connections to public officials are less likely than other to have land taken away by the state, particularly in lowland areas; and whereas rental markets appear to have a number of benign effects, and activity levels in rental markets are increasing in most regions, in the poorest region, the mountainous Northwest, where improvements in land use efficiency are perhaps needed most, rental markets continue to play a minimal role and no increase in activity levels is recorded – instead, households rely more heavily than before on clearing new land. This calls for further studies of barriers to land market development in remote regions dominated by traditional forms of tenure.

Acknowledgements

We are grateful for financial support from Danida. Very helpful comments and suggestions from Nguyen Le Hoa and seminar participants at the Central Institute for Economic Management (CIEM) are also acknowledged. The usual caveats apply.

Notes

1. While land use rights can legally be bought and sold, a transfer does not imply that the time limit on use right is extended. If the original owner had 10 years of use right remaining, so will the new owner. Land rental contracts cannot extend beyond the time limit on use right, but otherwise rental markets are relatively unfettered.
2. Compensation in case of recovery is regulated in §42 of the Land Law, which states that households should be compensated with new land with the same land use purpose. If such land is not available, households should be compensated with 'the value of the land use rights at the time of recovery' (Land Law, §42, cl. 2). In practice, however, determining this value is often controversial.
3. The implementation directive of the land law provides for potential reallocation of land held by state farms or state forestry enterprises to poor members of ethnic minorities (Decision 198/2007/QD-TTg). However, this directive also does not authorize recovery of privately held land use rights for the purpose of redistribution to other farmers or to landless families.
4. The fact that more forest land than agricultural land is held by the state is of course common to most countries in the world.
5. See CIEM et al. (2009) for more background information and details. The sampled provinces are, by region: Red River Delta: Ha Tay. North East: Lao Cai and Phu Tho. North West: Lai Chau and Dien Bien. North Central Coast: Nghe Anh. South Central Coast: Quang Nam and Khanh Hoa. Central Highlands: Dak Lak, Dak Nong and Lam Dong. Mekong River Delta: Long An.
6. The high importance of land purchases in the Central Highlands is to a great extent driven by the immigration of ethnic Kinh from the North.
7. Some land in the Northern Lowlands has been reclaimed in modern times by draining wetlands. However, forest clearances seem to have played a very limited role for centuries (Popkin, 1979).
8. The 2004 VHLSS also contains a module on land disposed of. However, since question formulations are not directly comparable between the two surveys, we only present results for 2008.

9. In the case of land *purchases* – see Table 7.2 – the survey does not collect information about who the land was bought from, unless it was from the state.
10. Because only very few households sold land in the Northern Highlands, a regression for selling land could not be estimated in this region. For the same reasons, a regression for losing land to the state could not be estimated for the Central Highlands.

References

Anderson, J. and Davidsen, S. (2011) *Recognizing and Reducing Corruption Risks in Land Management in Vietnam* (Hanoi: National Political Publishing House (Su That)).

Brandt, L. (2006) 'Land Access, Land Markets and Their Distributive Implications in Rural Vietnam', Summary report, University of Toronto.

CIEM, DOE, ILSSA, and IPSARD (2009) *Vietnam Access to Resources Household Survey: Characteristics of the Vietnamese Rural Economy (2008 Survey)* (Hanoi: Statistical Publishing House).

Deininger, K. and Jin, S. (2008) 'Land Sales and Rental Markets in Transition. Evidence from rural Vietnam', *Oxford Bulletin of Economics and Statistics*, 70(1), 67–101.

Deininger, K., Zegarra, E. and Lavadenz, I. (2003) 'Determinants and Impact of Rural Land Market Activity: Evidence from Nicaragua', *World Development*, 31(8), 1385–404.

Do, Q.T. and Iyer, L. (2008) 'Land Titling and Rural Transition in Vietnam', *Economic Development and Cultural Change*, 56(3), 531–79.

Gourou, P. (1936) *Les Paysans du Delta Tonkinois* (Paris: Mouton & Co. and Maison des Sciences de l'Homme).

Holden, S., Deininger, K. and Ghebru, H. (2011) 'Tenure Insecurity, Gender, Low-Cost Land Certification and Land Rental Market Participation in Ethiopia', *Journal of Development Studies*, 47(1), 33–47.

Holden, S., Otsuka, K. and Place, F.M. (2008) *The Emergence of Land Markets in Africa: Assessing the Impacts on Poverty, Equity, and Efficiency* (Washington D.C.: Resources for the Future Press).

Kerkvliet, B.T. (2006) 'Agricultural Land in Vietnam: Markets Tempered by Family, Community and Socialist Practices', *Journal of Agrarian Change*, 6F(3), 285–305.

Kirk, M. and Nguyen, D.A.T. (2009) 'Land Tenure Policy Reforms: Decollectivization and the Doi-Moi System in Vietnam', IFPRI Discussion Paper 00927.

Markussen, T., Nguyen, D.A.T., Tarp, F. and Thiep, D.H. (2012) 'Inter- and Intra-Farm Land Fragmentation in Vietnam', Working paper, Central Institute for Economic Management, Hanoi.

Markussen, T. and Tarp, F. (2011) 'Political Connections and Investment in Rural Vietnam', WIDER Working Paper No. 37/2011.

Markussen, T., Tarp, F. and Van den Broeck, K. (2011) 'The Forgotten Property Rights: Evidence on Land Use Rights in Vietnam', *World Development*, 39(5), 839–50.

Pingali, P. and Xuan, V.T. (1992) 'Vietnam: Decollectivization and Rice Productivity Growth', *Economic Development and Cultural Change*, 40(4), 697–718.
Popkin, S.L. (1979) *The Rational Peasant: The Political Economy of Rural Society in Vietnam* (Berkeley: University of California Press).
Ravallion, M. and van de Walle, D. (2004) 'Breaking Up the Collective Farms: Welfare Outcomes of Vietnams Massive Land Privatization', *Economics of Transition*, 12, 201–36.
Ravallion, M. and van de Walle, D. (2006) 'Land Reallocation in an Agrarian Transition', *Economic Journal*, 116, 924–42.
Ravallion, M. and van de Walle, D. (2008a) 'Does Rising Landlessness Signal Success or Failure for Vietnams Agrarian Transition?' *Journal of Development Economics*, 87, 191–209.
Ravallion, M. and van de Walle, D. (2008b) *Land in Transition: Reform and Poverty in Rural Vietnam* (Washington DC: World Bank).
Tachibana, T., Nguyen, T.M. and Otsuka, K. (2001) 'Agricultural Intensification Versus Extensification: A Case Study of Deforestation in the Northern-Hill Region of Vietnam', *Journal of Environmental Economics and Management*, 41, 44–69.
World Bank (2008) *Land policy in Vietnam: Current Status and Key Challenges* (Ha Noi: World Bank in Vietnam).
World Bank (2009) *Vietnam Development Report 2010: Modern Institutions* (Hanoi: The World Bank in Vietnam).

8
Land Tenure Reforms, Land Market Participation and the Farm Size – Productivity Relationship in Uganda

Alex Tatwangire and Stein T. Holden

8.1 Introduction

Historical circumstances and colonial policies in Uganda are well known to have created land tenure insecurity and other unintended consequences, including establishment of the overlapping land ownership rights, conflicts on land, poor land management, and skewed land distribution (Rugadya, 1999; Coldham, 2000; Deininger, 2003, 2005; Green, 2006; Deininger and Ayalew, 2007; Ahene, 2009). Customary land is estimated to comprise at least 75 percent of land in Uganda (Busingye, 2002) and was for a long time not legally recognized (Bosworth, 2003; Hunt, 2004). It was administered based on traditional institutional arrangements that discouraged the functioning of land rental and sales markets, while focusing on preserving the cultural identity of different lineage groups.

The search for a solution to challenges in the land sector has led to several land law reforms in the history of Uganda. For example, the 1995 Uganda constitution emphasizes protection of the land rights of the poor, and the 1998 Land Act redefines and provides full protection of private land rights, including those of the underprivileged groups, women and children. It also aims at transforming the traditional land rights into a modern land tenure system that can cope with increasing population pressure and the need to ensure land tenure security, broad-based land access through better-functioning land markets, more sustainable land management, land use efficiency, and economic growth (Bosworth,

2003). While stronger land tenure security can enhance land access, investment in land, and land use productivity (Deininger and Ayalew, 2007), it can also reduce poverty by securing land access for the poor who have limited access to other sources of livelihood (Deininger, 2003, 2005; Finan et al., 2005).

Land tenure reforms can play an important role in stimulating land markets and thereby the labor supply in farm and off-farm activities (Deininger, 2005). Such reforms can also be a tool to break power traps ('élite capture') created by the minority powerful land-rich élites at the expense of the majority of land-poor households, who also tend to be vulnerable to shocks and more likely to lose their land through distress land sales (Deininger, 2005; Holden, 2009). Distress land sales may lead to land concentration in the hands of a few rich and inefficient owners who may have incentives to accumulate land but fewer incentives to utilize the land efficiently (Otsuka, 2007; Holden et al., 2008a). Skewed land distribution may therefore be associated with an inverse farm size–land productivity relationship. Several studies have detected such an inverse relationship in Asian and African countries (Aryal and Holden in ch. 3 (Nepal); Heltberg, 1998 (Pakistan); Lamb, 2003 (India); Barrett et al., 2010 (Madagascar); Carletto et al., 2011 (Uganda)). The inverse relationship has in many studies persisted after controlling for land quality (Barrett et al., 2010). Others have attributed the inverse relationship to pervasive market imperfections in land and labor markets (Heltberg, 1998), and this has been used as a basis for arguing for redistributive land tenure reforms or land tenure reforms that enhance land market development that would be good for both efficiency and equity (Holden et al., 2008b). However, some more recent studies have failed to attribute all the inverse relationship to soil quality and market imperfections, and have blamed the remaining inverse relationship on errors in farm size measurement (Lamb, 2003; Barrett et al., 2010). However, Carletto et al. (2011) used cross-section data from Uganda with GPS-measured plot and farm sizes; they suggested that farmers tend to overestimate small plots and underestimate large ones, and measurement error could therefore rather reduce the inverse relationship than strengthen it. This is the opposite of what Lamb (2003) and Barrett et al. (2010) found.

We have used three years of household farm plot panel data from Uganda where most of the farm plots and farms were measured with GPS. This should allow us to control for measurement error and soil quality by combining household fixed effects and random effects, and thus give more robust tests of the existence of an inverse farm size–productivity relationship which could be a sign of inefficient land use due to a skewed land distribution. We estimate this relationship separately in the freehold, *mailo*[1] and customary tenure systems. We expect the inverse relationship to be stronger in the mailo and customary systems, where there traditionally have been stronger restrictions on land transactions. However, the recent land tenure reforms strengthening tenure security and stimulating land sales and land rental markets may have reduced or eliminated the inverse relationship if better-functioning land markets have encouraged land transfers from the less efficient and able to the more skilled households. In particular, land rental markets may have provided an affordable means through which the land-poor can gain access to more land to promote productivity and welfare (Binswanger and Rosenzweig, 1986; Deininger and Feder, 1998; de Janvry et al., 2001; Deininger and Mpuga, 2008; Holden et al., 2008b).

While land rental and the sales markets are reported to be widespread and increasing in all regions of Uganda, the evidence shows that the land sales market did not lead to a more unequal land distribution during the 1990s (Deininger and Mpuga, 2008); in actual fact it provided the poor with opportunities to generate starting capital for other investments.

We also use the household panel data from 2001, 2003 and 2005 to assess the relationship between poverty and access to land, the functioning of land rental and sales markets in the different tenure systems and the extent to which an inverse relationship between farm size and land productivity still prevails in Uganda. Well-functioning land and labor markets should eliminate such an inverse relationship, and the relationship should *ceteris paribus* be less inverse where land markets function relatively better.

Our stochastic dominance analysis shows that household welfare measured through consumption expenditure is closely correlated with land access, because land still is such an important source of livelihood. Furthermore, we find that land sales markets work most efficiently in areas dominated by the freehold tenure system, while land rental and sales markets are least important as sources of land access in the mailo tenure system. Finally, we find a consistent strong inverse farm size–land productivity relationship in the freehold, mailo and customary tenure systems for which we had sufficient data, but the inverse relationship was less strong in the freehold system, consistent with the finding of better-functioning land markets there.

8.2 A historical summary of land policy reforms in Uganda

This section presents the evolution of land tenure systems and land policy reforms that have been adopted in Uganda since 1900 to resolve historical land tenure problems. In pre-colonial Uganda, communities and individual households in various kingdoms and tribes possessed larger chunks of land. Kings, local chiefs, and clan heads were the custodians of land on behalf of their subjects and members of the lineage groups.

8.2.1 The colonial period (1900–1962)

Land legislation in Uganda started in 1900 with the signing of the 1900 Buganda Agreement between the British Government and the Kingdom of Buganda, under which mailo land tenure was created in the Buganda region and parts of Bunyoro. Out of the estimated 19,600 square miles of total land in Buganda, 8958 square miles of mailo land were given to the Kabaka (king) of Buganda Kingdom, and his top chiefs and notables, to own it in perpetuity. The royal family of Buganda was granted 958 square miles of land as private mailo,[2] while his 1000 top chiefs and notables shared a total of 8000 square miles, with each getting eight square miles of land on average (West, 1972; Brett, 1973). The rest[3] (9000 square miles) of the uncultivated land was allocated to the protectorate as Crown land, to be administered by the colonial government. All the small landowners that had traditionally occupied these lands were declared tenants, were consequently unable to secure independent land rights, and were required to pay rent, *busulu*, to their landlords, who possessed the certificate of land title. Although this helped to stimulate surplus production from small farms and wage labor supply, the position of tenants was vulnerable and land tenure insecurity remained a serious concern of policymakers.

Under the 1900 Buganda Agreement, the colonial government created Freehold Land Tenure in the Western part (Ankole, Toro and Kigezi), parts of Buganda in the Central region, and Bugisu in the Eastern part of Uganda, following agreements between numerous kingdoms and the British government. Holders of freehold land included church missionaries and academic institutions; they now owned this type of land for an unlimited period of time, having sought land titles from the Crown or the Uganda Land Commission (ULC).

Leasehold Land Tenure was established in 1900 to allow holders of mailo and freehold land, including the Crown (ULC), to grant land ownership under a contract to another person for a specified period of time and on certain conditions such as the payment of rent. The holders of land under lease were also entitled to a certificate of lease title.

In 1900, Customary Land Tenure included land that was held and regulated under the traditional systems as defined by custom, the geopolitical location and lineage groups. It still includes:

(i) communal customary tenure that is predominant in Northern and Eastern parts of Uganda and
(ii) individual/family /clan customary tenure that exist in Central, Western, parts of the North and South Western Uganda (Busingye, 2002).

Occupants of customary land[4] could be on freehold, mailo, leasehold or public[5] land. Customary rules imposed different restrictions on the right to sell or mortgage this type of land. Approval of clan chiefs, elders, community, lineage and family membership is mandatory regarding any land transaction, and this keeps land resources within communities.

The Crown Land Ordinance of 1903 declared holders of all the land held under the customary system, but outside the mailo area, to be tenants on the will of the Crown. The continued land ownership of customary land was regarded as unlawful and on request from the state; holders of this type of land would easily be evicted. The *Busulu* (annual dues) and *Envujo* (levy per acre) Law of 1928 defined the rights of original occupants of customary land, who were being exploited by their landowners as a result of high economic gains from cotton production. The law put a limit on the rent tenants were to pay their landowners, and provided some protection against eviction without compensation for the land and improvements made on it. This, however, failed to resolve the challenges of the overlapping land rights. According to Deininger and Ayalew (2007) tenure insecurity on land continued to hamper investments and land market activity on tenanted land.

8.2.2 From independence (1962 to 1986)

The 1969 Public Land Act provided the customary tenants with more protection against evictions. Then the 1975 Land Reform Decree declared all land in Uganda to be public land, to be administered by the Uganda Land Commission. The decree abolished mailo and freehold land tenure, and converted land held under these two systems into government leases for a period of 99 years. Customary tenancy on mailo land was also converted into customary tenure on public land with a limited tenure security. Restrictions were imposed on the acquisition and disposal of customary land. Holders of customary land were prohibited from engaging in any land transfer, including land transfers into leasehold, without the consent of the ULC; if their occupation was to be terminated, they would be compensated. According to Deininger (2003), this attempt to nationalize land created unintended consequences such as land grabbing, unlawful evictions and resource dissipation, which reduced the level of investments on land, land transactions, access to credit, and increased the incidence of conflicts on land

8.2.3 Under the Museveni government (1986 to present)

The recent land reforms started with the promulgation of the 1995 Uganda constitution, which repealed the 1975 land reform decree that had been seen to be controversial, and declared all land in Uganda to belong to the citizens. The constitution reinstated the customary, mailo, freehold, and leasehold land tenure systems that had been in place during the colonial government, and made provisions aimed at strengthening land rights on customary land, especially the rights of the underprivileged groups, women and children. The Ugandan parliament enacted the 1998 Land Act seeking to define and entrench full land ownership, rights and tenure security to all Ugandans, including those on customary land, and to increase land use efficiency and economic growth (Bosworth, 2003). The Land Act set out procedures under which holders of customary land could apply and acquire certificates of customary land ownership, using the decentralized institutions of land administration including: Parish Land Committees, office of the Land Recorder at the Sub-county level, District Land Boards, and Land Courts (Tribunals) that also work with the High Court to resolve land disputes.

The 1998 Land Act also enables lawful and *bona fide* occupants[6] of mailo, freehold, and public land (land that is mainly in urban areas and owned by the government) to apply and acquire certificates of occupancy, on condition that they continue paying the landowner the annual nominal ground rent – but there was limited consensus on this provision, due to resistance by the existing landholders (Coldham, 2000). The Land Act also made provision on how the holders of customary land certificates, together with land leaseholders could apply and convert their certificates to freehold tenure using the office of Registrar of Titles. Individual freehold land tenure was adopted as a long-term system of land ownership, given its aptness in providing land holders with the most complete rights, and minimal restrictions on all modes of land transfer and access.

Under the 1998 Land Act, holders of freehold land now have the freedom to use their land for any lawful purpose, including lease, sale, mortgage, and bequest. Holders of leases are also free to use their land in any lawful way, including sub-leasing, during the lease period of 49 or 99 years. In the customary land system, the rights of land ownership, usufruct and bequest are considered to be secure, while the transfer of rights is primarily through inheritance. The holders of mailo land, on the other hand, still face the challenge of utilizing their land resource effectively without evicting and compensating the lawful and bona fide occupants that have statutory protection against such evictions as long as they continue paying rent of Ug. Shs 1000 (US$0.60) per year. The act further provides for the establishment of a land fund, to be used in resettling people that become landless as a result of government actions and natural disasters, but its implementation has been slow (Rugadya et al., 2008), probably due to the lack of resources and other administrative challenges. A comprehensive Land Sector Strategic Plan (LSSP) and new National Land policy were put in place between 2004 and 2010 to further improve land access through the market and the efficiency of the land administration, by modernizing the infrastructure, the processing of land information[7] and permit system.

These recent land law reforms were expected to increase tenure security, reduce inequality in landholding, increase land access through better-functioning land rental and sales markets, and enhance agricultural productivity and welfare. However, the implementation of the new law still faces the challenges of limited social legitimacy, opposing cultural interests, and institutional design limitations (Hunt, 2004; Rugadya et al., 2004). The Land Amendment Law was passed in 2009 to resolve cultural dissent and ethnic demands, especially in Buganda region (Green, 2006), to improve the implementation of the Land Law, and to stop evictions of tenants from registered land except on order of eviction from a court of law.

8.3 Theoretical framework

Land is one of the most important assets of rural households in Uganda and a primary basis for their livelihoods. The high transaction costs of labor supervision tend to reduce productivity on large farms, which rely more on hired labor than is the case on small and owner-operated farms that are very productive (Deininger, 2003). On the other hand, small farms tend to face more significant credit constraints than is the case on large farms, and this may explain higher productivity on large farms in areas with developed credit markets. To the extent, therefore, that land reforms become effective in improving tenure security and enhance access to additional land through better-functioning land markets, land-poor but otherwise resource-rich households can more easily move up the agricultural ladder to land ownership, access to credit, and higher productivity. In other words, land markets create a selection effect by attracting more efficient producers on the demand side. Evidence of such a selection effect should thus show up in form of higher marginal returns to land for tenants and buyers of land than for the average household inheriting land. On the other hand, if those who are able to buy land are not doing it for productive purposes, this type of productivity effect may not be seen, and land markets are not efficiency-enhancing.

We assume that households maximize their utility subject to a set of constraints where access to land from different sources is part of this constraint set. Households will attempt to get access to additional land when the benefits of doing so are expected to be higher than the costs. It is mainly through the market that households can adjust their farm size in the short run, while access to land through inheritance can be influenced to a small extent. And while the size of inherited land of individual households changes less frequently, household size and composition changes over time such that the amount of inherited land per adult-equivalent also changes over time. Cash and liquidity constraints may prevent households from accessing additional land through the market, and their labor endowment limits their ability to utilize the land.

We assumed that the households that are able to access land through the market have additional non-land resources and are therefore more able to improve their welfare through such land access. Based on this, we tested the following hypotheses:

H1: There is a positive correlation between household welfare levels and access to land through inheritance and through the market.

H2: There is an inverse farm size–land productivity relationship that is stronger in the customary and mailo tenure systems than in the freehold tenure system.

8.4 Data and variable generation

This study utilizes a three-period household panel dataset collected in 2001, 2003, and 2005 by two research projects. The first survey was conducted in 2001 by the International Food Policy Research Institute

(IFPRI), and covered two-thirds of the country, including Southwest, Central, and Eastern and some areas in Northern Uganda. A stratified sampling procedure was employed based on a classification of Uganda's territory according to the agricultural potential, market access and population density. A total of 450 households in 107 communities were interviewed in 2001. The subsequent two surveys were conducted in 2003 and 2005 as part of the Research on Poverty, Environment, and Agricultural Technologies (REPEAT) project, conducted by the Foundation for Advanced Studies on International Development (FASID).

In these surveys, three districts that were part of the earlier IFPRI study areas were dropped due to insecurity in the North and Northeastern parts of Uganda. Instead, 94 out of 107 communities that had previously been covered by the IFPRI survey in 2001 were selected. Only 333 households, out of the 450 in the baseline survey of 2001 were included in the 2003 REPEAT survey due to the change in the sampling frame in 2003. In addition, out of the 333 sample of households, 20 dropped out for various reasons in the 2005 survey, while four more households with outliers and conflicting values of land access were also dropped from data analysis. This study is therefore based on balanced panel data of 309 households. Data analysis was conducted on 927 observations from 26 districts that include: Mubende, Luwero, Nakasongola, Masaka, Mukono, Kayunga, Rakai and Mpigi in the Central region; Sironko, Tororo, Bugiri, Iganga, Mayuge, Jinja, Kamuli, Pallisa, Mbale, Busia and Kumi in the Eastern region; and Mbarara, Kabale, Kisoro, Kabarole, Kasese, Bushenyi and Rukungiri in the Western region of Uganda.

We computed expenditure per adult-equivalent as measures of household poverty levels. Distinctively, household total consumption expenditure was constructed from cash expenditure for consumption and value of consumption of home-produced goods. This measure of household poverty level was adjusted to 2005 prices. Problems with the household income data, especially in the initial period of 2001, compelled us to use the more reliable consumption expenditure data for the estimation of marginal returns to land access.

Land access includes land endowments in acres that farm households own or operate in their production process. Plot sizes were measured by GPS for most plots in the sample. Only for the more remote plots did we rely on farmers' own estimates of plot sizes. Land that farm households operate may include land that is accessed through inheritance and market modes of land access including purchases, renting-in and borrowing. Land acquired through the market is a limited dependent variable (LDV) while land owned and lands operated are continuous variables.

8.5 Econometric model estimation

Panel Tobit models with household random effects were used to assess the factors correlated with access to land through the land sales market, the land rental market and inheritance. Initial participation in each of the markets and initial inherited land were included as additional controls for unobservable household and farm characteristics that were time-invariant. Model results without these additional controls are shown in Table 8.1.

Models with household fixed effects and random effects were alternatively used on the three rounds of household panel data to test for an inverse farm size–productivity relationship. Household fixed effects should control for unobservable soil quality that could be correlated with farm size (small farms having better land quality) (Walker and Ryan, 1990; Binswanger et al., 1995; Benjamin, 1995; Bhalla and Roy, 1998; Heltberg, 1998; Lamb, 2003; Barrett et al., 2010). Barrett et al. (ibid.) were unable to explain all of the inverse relationship with market imperfections and soil quality variation (using soil quality measurements). But even soil quality measurements are subject to measurement error, and similarly farm sizes. Measurement errors could therefore be an additional reason for the inverse relationship. Lamb (2003) used household random effects and fixed effects to indirectly assess the extent of measurement error. We have used GPS recorded plot and farm sizes which should be less subject to measurement error than self-reported farm sizes. While household fixed effects should control for unobservable soil quality and should therefore eliminate an inverse relationship caused by soil quality being higher on small farms, Lamb (2003) found that fixed-effects models could become both inconsistent and more biased due to measurement error. Carletto et al. (2011) used cross-section data from Uganda with GPS-measured plot and farm sizes; interestingly, they suggested that if farmers tend to overestimate small plots and underestimate large plots, measurement error could reduce the inverse correlation rather than strengthen it, which is the opposite of the effects found by Lamb (2003) and Barrett et al. (2010). By combining fixed-effects and random-effects models with more reliable measures of farm sizes we believe we have gone a long way in controlling for unobservable land quality and measurement error.

8.6 Descriptive statistics

Tables 8.2 and 8.3 provide descriptive statistics for key variables on land access and poverty indicators across rural households.

Table 8.1 Results of the first-stage estimation of a panel Tobit random-effects regression model of land access without further controls of initial conditions [a]

	Specific land access normalized to total land owned		
	Land purchased	**Land rented-in**	**Land inherited**
Right hand side (RHS) variables	(1)	(2)	(3)
Inherited land (acres) normalized to land owned	−1.173***	−1.095	
Sex of the household head (1 = Male; 0 = Female)	0.016	0.653	0.108
Education (years) of household head normalized to land owned	−0.007**	0.024	0.011**
Tropical Livestock Units (TLUs) normalized to land owned	0.008	−0.845***	−0.082***
Number of male adults (>=16 yrs) normalized to land owned	−0.012**	−0.328***	−0.012
Number of female adults (>=16 yrs) normalized to land owned	0.018*	1.660***	−0.023
Age of household head (years)	0.015**	−0.011	−0.040***
Age of household head squared	−0.000**	−0.001	0.000***
Tenure system 2: Leasehold	−0.112	4.160***	−0.063
Tenure system 3: Mailo	−0.258***	−2.984***	−0.098
Tenure system 4: Customary	−0.104***	−0.690	0.143***
Distance to primary market (in miles)	0.013*	−0.086	0.013

Continued

Table 8.1 Continued

	Specific land access normalized to total land owned		
	Land purchased	**Land rented-in**	**Land inherited**
Right hand side (RHS) variables	(1)	(2)	(3)
Dummy for high population density in a community (1 = high; 0 = otherwise)	–0.026	–2.005***	0.068
Dummy for high rainfall in a community (1= bi and uni high, 0 = otherwise)	0.089***	–1.814***	–0.060
Proportion of households in the LC1 that can afford at least two meals a day	0.008	1.797	0.088
Dummy variable for year 2001	0.168***	–2.264**	–0.156**
Dummy variable for year 2003	0.075**	–1.494**	–0.005
Constant	0.360**	–1.923	1.141***
Panel level standard deviation (sigma_u)	0.122***	0.743	0.333***
Standard deviation error term (sigma_E)	0.313***	5.299***	0.528***
Number of observations	927	927	927
Number of households	309	309	309
Uncensored observations	559	164	551
Left–censored observations	368	763	376
Wald chi2	1122.463	338.918	74.309
Prob > chi2	0.000	0.000	0.000
Rho (Panel fraction of variance)	0.132	0.019	0.285
Log likelihood	–372.034	–692.706	–792.881

Note: [a] Significance levels: *** $p<0.01$, ** $p<0.05$, * $p<0.1$.

Table 8.2 Household land access, land market participation and poverty indicators by yeara

Variables	N	Mean
Land owned (acres)	309	6.33 (0.25)
Land purchased (acres)	269	3.58 (0.23)
Land rented-in (acres)	118	0.67 (0.06)
Land inherited (acres)	256	2.84 (0.16)
Households with land under freehold tenure system	200	0.57 (0.02)
Households with land under leasehold tenure system	23	0.33 (0.06)
Households with land under mailo tenure system	97	0.58 (0.03)
Households with land under customary tenure system	235	0.56 (0.02)
Distance in miles to primary market	309	2.97 (0.06)
Real household expenditure/10,000 (Ug. Shs)	309	220.18 (7.51)

Source: REPEAT survey data.

Note: [a] Standard errors are in parentheses.

There can be limitations of research instruments that depend on recall information over a long period. Besides, enumerators may fail to effectively probe all information from the households during data collection. This creates significant data limitations in form of hidden and undisclosed information. It is widely agreed that consumption is a better measure of lifetime welfare than is current income (Deaton, 1997). Thus, the welfare estimates of land access in this study rely on the more plausible consumption expenditure per adult-equivalent as the measure of household welfare.

The first-order stochastic dominance analysis (FOSDA), that is cumulative density functions (CDFs), was conducted to assess the statistical differences in the distribution of land endowment across households with varying levels of welfare. Graphically, the curve for the CDF of a dominated quartile will be to the left of the CDF for the dominating alternative quartile. This implies that a dominating quartile has a lower

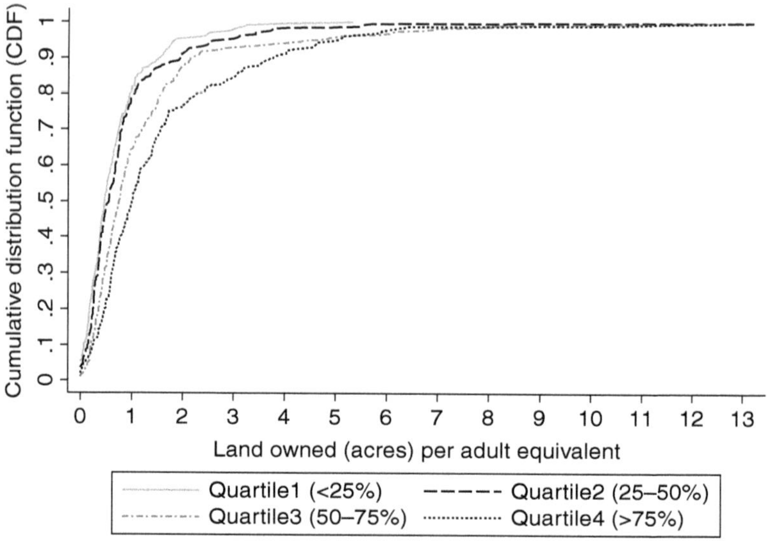

Figure 8.1 First-order stochastic dominance graph comparing land owned and welfare levels (quartiles) in terms of household expenditure per adult-equivalent, 2001–2005

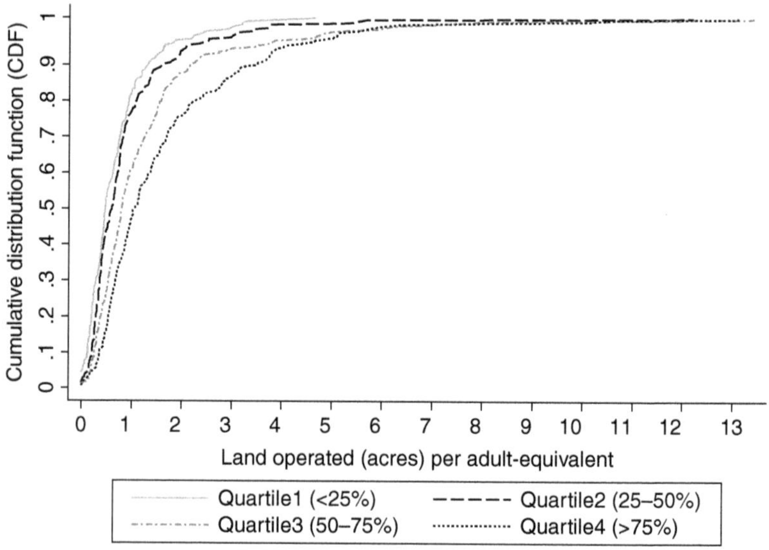

Figure 8.2 First-order stochastic dominance graph comparing land operated and welfare levels (quartiles) in terms of household expenditure per adult-equivalent, 2001–2005

cumulative density than a dominated alternative. Figures 8.1 and 8.2 show results of the FOSDA for land owned and land operated per adult-equivalent. Notice that households in the poorest two quartiles (quartile 1 and 2) are dominated by households in quartiles 3 and 4. The land distribution of households in quartile 4 clearly dominates all other land endowment (owned and operated) distributions in quartiles 1 to 3. Thus, land owned and land operated are statistically highest for households in quartile 4, followed by households in quartile 3, lower for households in quartile 2 and lowest for households in quartile 1.

8.7 Results and discussion

8.7.1 Land market participation

Table 8.3 presents the results for models assessing the factors that are associated with access to land through the land sales market, the land rental market, and inheritance, while controlling for unobservable household and farm characteristics with the initial year-dependent variable status. We see a strong negative correlation between the amount of inherited land and the amounts of purchased and rented-in land. This shows that it is the land-poor, who have inherited little land, who access land through these markets. It is particularly livestock-poor (significant at 1 percent level) and labor-rich households, with more female labor (significant at 1 percent level) but also more male labor (significant at 10 percent level), who access additional land through the land rental market. Land purchases were higher for household heads with less education and more livestock (significant at the 5 and 10 percent levels). Land inheritance was higher for male-headed households (significant at the 10 percent level) and household heads with more education (5 percent level of significance), and was negatively associated with male labor in the household (5 percent level of significance).

To assess the effect of the tenure system on mode of land access, three dummy variables were included, for the leasehold, mailo and customary systems, using the freehold system as the benchmark. As one might expect, access to land through the sales market was significantly higher for the benchmark freehold system than for the three other systems. The differences were significant at 5 percent (leasehold system) and 1 percent levels (mailo and customary systems). Even access to land through inheritance was significant lower in mailo land than in the other tenure regimes.

Table 8.3 Factors associated with land access through purchases, rentals and inheritance[a]

	Specific land access normalized to total land owned		
	Land purchased	**Land rented-in**	**Land inherited**
Right hand side (RHS) variables	(1)	(2)	(3)
Inherited land (acres) normalized to land owned	−1.139***	−1.649***	
Sex of the household head (1= Male; 0 = Female)	0.020	0.766	0.108*
Education (years) of household head normalized to total land owned	−0.006**	0.018	0.008**
Tropical Livestock Units (TLUs) normalized to land owned	0.011*	−0.958***	−0.023
Number of male adults (>=16 yrs) normalized to land owned	−0.003	0.355*	−0.044**
Number of female adults (>=16 yrs) normalized to land owned	0.010	1.309***	0.028
Age of household head (years)	0.007	−0.051	−0.023**
Age of household head squared	−0.000	−0.000	0.000**
Tenure system 2: leasehold	−0.123**	0.442	−0.086
Tenure system 3: mailo	−0.228***	−2.047**	−0.113**
Tenure system 4: customary	−0.073***	−0.122	−0.002
Distance to primary market (in miles)	0.004	0.035	0.006
Dummy for high population density in a community (1 = high; 0 = otherwise)	0.002	−1.529***	0.065
Dummy for high rainfall in a community (1= bi and uni high; 0 = otherwise)	0.090***	−1.582***	0.000
Proportion of households in the LC1 that can afford at least two meals a day	0.065*	2.228**	0.079

Initial conditions (2001)			
Land (acres) purchased in 2001 normalized to total land owned	−0.156**		
Dummy for households with purchased land in 2001	2.523		
Land (acres) brought in through renting-in in 2001, normalized to total land owned		−0.521	
Dummy for households with rented-in land in 2001		117.202	
Land (acres) inherited in 2001, normalized to total land owned			0.994***
Dummy for households with land inherited in 2001			2.384
Dummy variable for year 2001	−2.049	−113.116	−2.728
Dummy variable for year 2003	0.076***	−1.502***	0.035
Constant	0.480***	−1.296	0.763***
Panel level standard deviation (sigma_u)	0.139***	1.514***	0.393***
Standard deviation error term (sigma_E)	0.207***	3.681***	0.292***
Number of observations	927	927	927
Number of households	309	309	309
Uncensored observations	559	164	551
Left-censored observations	368	763	376
Wald chi2	1695.995	662.885	375.322
Prob > chi2	0.000	0.000	0.000
Rho (Panel fraction of variance)	0.310	0.145	0.643
Log likelihood	−116.552	−576.128	−472.314

Notes: [a]The freehold tenure system is the omitted tenure system (benchmark).Significance levels: *** $p<0.01$, ** $p<0.05$, * $p<0.1$.

8.7.2 The farm size–land productivity relationship

Figure 8.3 shows a scatter plot and lowess regression of the relationship between log of farm size and log of land productivity. The inverse relationship is evident. Table 8.4 presents the results from regression models with household fixed effects and household random effects separately for the freehold, mailo and customary tenure systems. We see that the coefficients in the random-effects models are slightly lower than in the fixed-effects models, but all are negative and highly significant. The fixed-effects models may do a better job in controlling for unobserved time-invariant farm characteristics such as land quality. We cannot rule out that the fixed-effects models also are biased due to measurement error (Lamb, 2003) but the dominant use of GPS measurement of plots should limit such bias, and the study by Carletto et al. (2011) in Uganda indicated that measurement error led to a downward rather than an upward bias in the inverse relationship. As a further sensitivity analysis of this we reran the models by adding observable time-varying

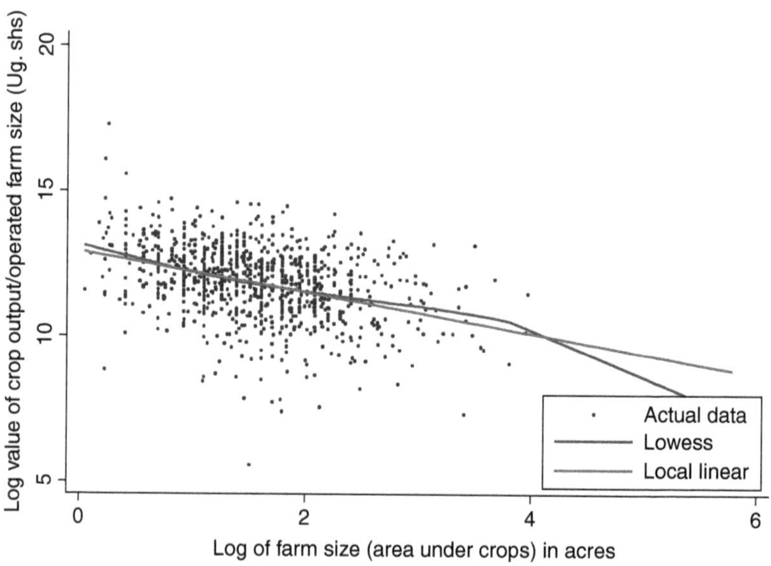

Figure 8.3 Scatterplot and nonparametric regression between log of total value of crop production per acre operated farm size (Ug. shs) and log of farm size (area under crops) in acres

Notes: [a] Significance levels: *** $p<0.01$, ** $p<0.05$, * $p<0.1$. The leasehold land tenure system was not modeled due to fewer observations (only 23) in the data.

Table 8.4 Farm size–productivity relationship by tenure system in Uganda, fixed-effects and random-effects models[a] (Dependent variable: log of farm size)

	Log of total value of crop production per acre operated farm size (in Ug. Shs)					
	Panel fixed-effects (FE) models			Panel random-effects (RE) models		
	Different land tenure systems			Different land tenure systems		
	Freehold	Mailo	Customary	Freehold	Mailo	Customary
Right-hand side (RHS) variables	(1)	(2)	(3)	(4)	(5)	(6)
Log of farm size (area cultivated/under crops) in acres	−0.480***	−0.885***	−0.757***	−0.441***	−0.735***	−0.616***
Dummy variable for year 2001	−1.246***	−0.376	−0.992***	−1.195***	−0.505***	−1.033***
Dummy variable for year 2003	−0.538***	−0.355**	−0.516***	−0.577***	−0.326**	−0.515***
Constant	13.262***	13.371***	13.468***	13.154***	13.110***	13.258***
Number of observations	342	168	394	342	168	394
Number of households	200	97	235	200	97	235
F statistic	21.201	11.545	32.979			
Wald chi2				104.459	37.465	143.170
Prob > F/chi2	0.000	0.000	0.000	0.000	0.000	0.000
R2-within	0.343	0.456	0.374	0.341	0.450	0.371
R2-between	0.147	0.177	0.232	0.150	0.191	0.234
R2-overall	0.207	0.278	0.259	0.208	0.285	0.264
Panel level standard deviation (sigma_u)	1.074	0.911	0.961	0.685	0.610	0.586
Panel level standard deviation (sigma_E)	0.994	0.792	0.898	0.994	0.792	0.898
Rho (Panel fraction of variance)		0.539	0.570	0.534	0.322	0.298

Notes: [a]Significance levels: *** $p<0.01$, ** $p<0.05$, * $p<0.1$. The leasehold land tenure system was not estimated due to too few observations (only 23) in the data.

Table 8.5 Farm size–productivity relationship in Uganda, sensitivity analyses with additional control variables: summary of key results [a]

	Dep. var.: log of total value of crop production per acre operated farm size (in Ug. Shs)					
	Panel fixed-effects (FE) model			Panel random-effects (RE) model		
	Different land tenure systems			Different land tenure systems		
Right-hand side (RHS) variable	Freehold	Mailo	Customary	Freehold	Mailo	Customary
Log of farm size (area cultivated/under crops) in acres	(1)	(2)	(3)	(4)	(5)	(6)
Model with additional household characteristics	–0.616***	–0.911***	–0.781***	–0.539***	–0.815***	–0.688***
Random-effects models with additional household characteristics and village fixed effects				–0.616***	–0.935***	–0.724***

Notes: [a]Significance levels: *** p<0.01, ** p<0.05, * p<0.1. Leasehold land tenure system was not modelled due to fewer observations (23 observations) in the data.

household characteristics, and also combined this with village fixed-effects in the random-effects models. The specific farm size coefficients for these additional models are presented in Table 8.5. We see that the addition of these variables led to an increase rather than a reduction in the inverse relationship. This seems like convincing evidence of an inverse farm size–land productivity relationship in these three tenure systems in Uganda.

We see that the inverse relationship was less negative in the freehold system than in the mailo and customary systems; we cannot therefore reject Hypothesis 2. The difference may be due to the better-functioning land market in the freehold system than in the mailo and customary systems. The inverse relationship seemed also to be stronger in the mailo than in the customary system, because the coefficients were larger in all model specifications although the coefficients were not significantly different.

8.8 Conclusion

The existing land tenure systems in Uganda are influenced by cultural norms as well as by its colonial history. The most recent tenure reforms have aimed to strengthen tenure security and land market development even in the customary and mailo tenure systems. Our stochastic dominance analysis shows that land access is closely correlated with the consumption welfare of rural households in Uganda, demonstrating the high dependence on land and agriculture as a source of livelihood. Land-poor and labor-rich households were more likely to have accessed land through the land markets; livestock-poor and labor-rich households were more likely to access land through the land rental market, while livestock-rich and less educated households accessed more land through the land sales market. Land markets as a source of land access were significantly more important in the freehold and leasehold tenure systems than in the mailo and customary tenure systems, where land sales and rental markets were apparently less well developed, even though the recent land tenure reforms also promoted land markets in these systems.

Finally, we found robust evidence of an inverse farm size–land productivity relationship in the freehold, mailo and customary systems. The relationship was less inverse in the freehold system, consistent with the evidence of better-functioning land markets there.

Acknowledgement

The authors thank the International Food Policy Research Institute (IFPRI Kampala office), the Foundation for Advanced Studies on International Development (FASID), and Makerere University, Faculty of Agriculture, for allowing us to use their rich datasets on: 'Project on Policies for Improved Land Management' and 'Poverty, Environment, and Agricultural Technologies (REPEAT)'.

Notes

1. For more information, see Section 8.2.1.
2. The Kabaka (King) of Buganda kingdom was given 350 square miles of private mailo land.
3. This land was later surveyed and found to be less than previously estimated; the size of Crown land was reduced to 8307 square miles (West, 1972; Green, 2006).
4. The term *Kibanja* represents occupants (*Bibanja* holders) on land under customary tenure. Under the 1998 Land Act, the statutory Bibanja holders are guaranteed protection against any eviction without compensation, and can also purchase the stake of the registered landowner to become a mailo or freehold land title holder.
5. Public land included land that was not owned in either freehold or mailo tenure and out of which public leasehold and freeholds would be granted by the ULC.
6. A lawful occupant refers to customary tenants and any other person that had peacefully entered the land (mailo, freehold or public land) with the consent of the owner, while the bona fide occupant includes households that had been in unfavorable possession of the land, including those that were resettled on government land, at least 12 years before the 1995 Uganda Constitution came into force (Coldham, 2000).
7. Inadequate information about the land regulations and inefficient delivery of services provided by the land sector in Uganda may discourage land transactions and make land transfers risky and prone to opportunistic tendencies that further increase the transaction costs of engaging in land market activity (Ahene, 2009).

References

Ahene, A.R. (2009) Measures to Improve Equal Access to Land Resources and Related Benefits in Uganda, Proceedings: Land Governance in Support of the MDGs: Responding to New Challenges, FIG-World Bank Conference, Washington, DC, USA, 9–10 March 2009, International Federation of Surveyors, FIG and the World Bank, 1–13.

Barrett, C.B., Bellemare, M. and Hou, J.Y. (2010) 'Reconsidering Conventional Explanations of the Inverse Productivity–Size Relationship', *World Development*, 38(1), 88–97.

Benjamin, D. (1995) 'Can Unobserved Land Quality Explain The Inverse Productivity Relationship?' *Journal of Development Economics*, 46, 51–84.

Bhalla, S.S. and Roy, P. (1988) 'Mis-Specification in Farm Productivity Analysis: The Role of Land Quality', *Oxford Economic Papers*, 40, 55–73.

Binswanger, H.P., Deininger, K. and Feder, G. (1995) 'Power, Distortions Revolt and Reform in Agricultural Land Relations', in J. Berhman and T.N. Srinivasan (eds), *Handbook of Development Economics*, Vol. IIIB, Amsterdam: Elsevier, pp. 2659–772.

Binswanger, H.P. and Rosenzweig, M. (1986) 'Behavioural and Material Determinants of Production Relations in Agriculture', *Journal of Development Studies*, 22, 503–39.

Bosworth, J. (2003) 'Integrating Land issues into the Broader Development Agenda: Uganda', Land Reform, Land Settlement, and Cooperatives – Special Edition, 11, 233–48.

Brett, E.A. (1973) *Colonialism and Underdevelopment in East Africa: The Politics of Economic Change* (London: Heinemann). Available at: http://www.getcited.org/pub/101453454.

Busingye, H. (2002) Customary Land Tenure Reform in Uganda: Lessons for South Africa. International symposium on communal tenure reform, Land reform in Africa: lessons for South Africa, Johannesburg, 12–13 August 2002, pp. 1–12: Uganda Land Alliance.

Carletto, C., Savastano, S. and Zezza, A. (2011) 'Fact or Artefact: The Impact of Measurement Errors on the Farm Size-Productivity Relationship', Policy Research Working Paper No. 5908, The World Bank, Washington, D.C.

Coldham, S. (2000) 'Land Reform and Customary Rights: The Case of Uganda', *Journal of African Law*, 44, 65–77.

Deaton, A. (1997) *The Analysis of Household Surveys: A Microeconometric Approach to Development Policy* (Baltimore and London: Johns Hopkins University Press).

Deininger, K. (2003) 'Land Policies for Growth and Poverty Reduction', A World Bank Policy Research Report 26384, a copublication of the World Bank and Oxford University Press.

Deininger, K. (2005) 'Land Policy Reforms', in A. Coudouel and S. Paternostro (eds), *Analyzing the Distributional Impact of Reforms: A Practitioner's Guide to Trade, Monetary and Exchange Rate Policy, Utility Provision, Agricultural Markets, Land Policy, and Education*, Vol. 1 (Washington D.C: The World Bank).

Deininger, K. and Ayalew, A.D. (2007) 'Do Overlapping Land Rights Reduce Agricultural Investment? Evidence from Uganda', Policy Research Working Paper 4310, The World Bank Development Research Group and the Sustainable Rural and Urban Development Team.

Deininger, K. and Feder, G. (1998) 'Land Institutions and Land Markets', Policy Research Working Paper 2014, prepared as background for the forthcoming *Handbook on Agricultural Economics*, 1–44.

Deininger, K. and Mpuga, P. (2008) 'Land Markets in Uganda: What is Their Impact and Who Benefits?' In T.S. Holden, K. Otsuka and M.F. Place (eds), *The Emergence of Land Markets in Africa: Impacts on Poverty, Equity and Efficiency* (Washington, DC: Resources for the Future).

de Janvry, A., Platteau, J.-P., Gordillo, G. and Sadoulet, E. (2001) 'Access to Land and Land Policy Reforms', in A. de Janvry, G. Gordillo., J.-P. Platteau and S. Elizabeth (eds), *Access to Land, Rural Poverty and Public Action* (Oxford: Oxford University Press).

Finan, F., Sadoulet, E. and de Janvry, A. (2005) 'Measuring the Poverty Reduction Potential of Land in Rural Mexico', *Journal of Development Economics*, 77 (1), 27–51.

Green, D.E. (2006) 'Ethnicity and the Politics of Land Tenure Reform in Central Uganda', *Commonwealth and Comparative Politics*, 44, 370–88.

Heltberg, R. (1998) 'Rural Market Imperfections and the Farm Size-Productivity Relationship: Evidence from Pakistan', *World Development*, 26(10), 1807–26.

Holden, S.T. (2009) 'Power Traps or Poverty Traps? Institutions, Markets, and Environmental and Livelihood Restoration', Paper presented at the NFU Conference, 23–24 November 2009, University of Agder, Kristiansand, pp. 1–22.

Holden, S.T., Otsuka, K. and Place, M.F. (2008a) 'Land Markets and Development in Africa', in T.S. Holden, K. Otsuka and M.F. Place (eds), *The Emergency of Land Markets in Africa* (Washington, DC: Resources for the Future).

Holden, S.T., Otsuka, K. and Place, M.F. (2008b) 'Land markets and Poverty in Perspective', in T.S. Holden, K. Otsuka and M.F. Place (eds), *The Emergence of Land Markets in Africa: Assessing the Impacts on Poverty, Equity and Efficiency* (Washington, DC: Resources for the Future).

Hunt, D. (2004) 'Unintended Consequences of Land Rights Reform: The Case of the 1998 Uganda Land Act', *Development Policy Review*, 22(2), 173–91.

Lamb, R.L. (2003) 'Inverse Productivity: Land Quality, Labor Markets, and Measurement Error', *Journal of Development Economics*, 71, 71–95.

Otsuka, K. (2007) 'Efficiency and Equity Effects of Land Markets', in R. Evenson and P. Pingali (eds), *Handbook of Agricultural Economics*, 3, 2671–703.

Rugadya, A.M., Nsamba-Gayiiya, E. and Kamusiime, H. (2008) 'Analysis of Post Conflict Land Policy and Land Administration: A Survey of IDP Return and Resettlement Issues and Lesson: Acholi and Lango Regions', in Northern Uganda Land Study, for the World Bank to input into Northern Uganda Peace, Recovery and Development Plan (PRDP) and the draft national land policy.

Rugadya, M. (1999) 'Land Reform: The Ugandan Experience', paper presented at Land Use and Villagisation Workshop, Hotel De Mille Collines, Kigali, Uganda, 20–21 September 1999.

Rugadya, M., Obaikol, E. and Kamusiime, H. (2004) 'Gender and the Land Reform Process in Uganda: Assessing Gains and Losses for Women in Uganda', Associates for development: Land Research Series No. 2.

Walker, T.S. and Ryan, J.G. (1990) *Village and Household Economies in India's Semi-arid Tropics* (Baltimore: Johns Hopkins University Press).

West, H.W. (1972) *Land policy in Buganda* (London: Cambridge University Press).

Part III

Forest Tenure Reforms

9

From Deforestation to Reforestation: The Evolution of Community Forest Management in the Dang District of Nepal

Narayan Raj Poudel, Nobuhiko Fuwa and Keijiro Otsuka

9.1 Introduction

Massive deforestation and degradation of forest conditions have been taking place in developing countries for several decades.[1] Since the capacity of governments to protect and manage forests are limited, and the incentives to do so are even more so, state-owned forests tend to become severely degraded (Somanathan, 1991; Ostrom, 1990; Jodha, 2001). An alternative system is community management even though the forest may be owned by the state, as in the case of Nepal. Since the protection of forests is often costly, however, socially excessive extraction of resources, or the 'free rider' problem, may arise under community management, which may lead to 'the tragedy of the commons', as described by Hardin (1968). Such a bleak scenario, however, is not inevitable. In particular, if secure property rights on forests are provided to the community, it may then have incentives to protect and manage forests effectively.

Indeed, there is accumulated evidence that community management, as opposed to public or private management, may be an effective system for managing the commons, even though the question of the conditions under which it works has been debated in the literature (Baland et al., 2010; Edmonds, 2002). Hayami (1997) argues that community management of common pool resources, including communal irrigation and forests, is efficient in traditional communities where everybody knows everybody else, so that mutual trust – and swift and certain feedback loops – can serve as effective enforcement mechanisms. In fact, many studies reveal that community management is a viable and effective institutional arrangement to attain the efficient use of natural resources as long as the user rights are granted to the community (Ostrom, 1990; Bromley, 1992; Baland and Platteau, 1996). In their study on the efficiency of timber forest management under community and private forestry in Nepal, Sakurai et al. (2004) found that community management was more efficient than private management in protecting the forest resources, since the cost of protection can be saved by the community mechanism of enforcing agreements, as argued by Hayami.[2]

There is widespread agreement among researchers that the community management system is successful in the management of non-timber forests in the hill regions of Nepal (Gilmour and Fisher, 1991; Tachibana et al., 2001). However, there is no consensus on the success of community forestry in the Tarai region of Nepal, where the major tree resource is timber. Some researchers argue that forest characteristics such as the production of high-value timber trees and the socio-economic context of the Tarai region, plus good access to roads and markets and high population pressure, are the main factors causing the mismanagement of forests by community forest user groups (Gautam et al., 2004). Existing studies, however, can be criticized for methodological flaws such as lack of rigorous econometric analysis, lack of ground-level data, and choice of endogenous management regime in explaining the forest conditions. Furthermore, the determinants of forest management under the community management regime have seldom been analyzed.[3] Another point worth mentioning is that the literature is relatively weak in the analysis of reforestation, as distinct from that of deforestation and degradation. This is a serious omission, since how to reforest is becoming a critical issue given the degradation of so many forest areas in developing countries.

This study focuses on three issues. First, it explores the determinants of deforestation, as well as forest degradation, in the past in Tarai. Second, it explores the determinants of forest management intensity at present. Third, it attempts to assess the effect of handing over forest use rights to the community on forest conditions by comparing the determinants of deforestation, which took place before the handover, and forest management after the handover. Our basic hypothesis is that before the forest use rights were handed over to the community, forest land was basically open access, so that the larger the demand for forest resources, the greater the extent of deforestation and forest degradation. More specifically, because of the population pressure, the large demand for grazing land and firewood resulted in deforestation, whereas favorable access to markets led to the felling of large timber trees for sale, which leads to forest degradation. However, the regeneration of new trees has also been taking place recently in forests near market towns. We also postulate the hypothesis that once the forest use rights have been handed over, the larger the demand for forest resources, the greater the incentives to undertake silvicultural operations, thereby leading to the swifter rehabilitation of forest conditions. In addressing the above issues, this study tries to avoid some of the methodological shortcomings of the existing studies by considering wider explanatory variables such as demographic (population pressure), biophysical (soil type and slope of the forest), accessibility (distance to market and distance from village) and socio-cultural (cast composition) factors. Since we use cross-section data, our analysis has limitations in exploring the determinants of dynamic changes in forest conditions.

This chapter is structured as follows. Section 9.2 briefly discusses how the deforestation and forest degradation in Nepal are related to Nepal's forest policy. Section 9.3 presents information about sample forests and their user groups, while Section 9.4 postulates the hypotheses guiding this study and presents the estimation strategy. Section 9.5 examines the estimation results. Finally Section 9.6 concludes the chapter.

9.2 An overview of forest policy in Nepal

People in Nepal are heavily dependent on forest products such as firewood, fodder, timber and leaf litter for their survival. However, for the last few decades, forest resources in Nepal, especially in the Tarai region, have been facing the problem of unsustainable exploitation. The Nepalese government implemented a resettlement program from 1950 to 1980 by converting the forest into agricultural land in the Tarai region (Regmi, 1994). After the eradication of malaria in the 1960s, migration from the hills to Tarai was accelerated due to better employment opportunities and the availability of cultivable forestlands in the lowlands (Gautam et al., 2004). Therefore, since the 1950s the Tarai region has faced increasing population pressure, leading to massive deforestation as well as the degradation of forests.

Tarai forests are dominated by high-valued timber trees such as sal (*Shorea robusta*), which is valuable for timber. An important trait of the sal tree is its ability to regenerate after harvesting; unless sal trees are repeatedly felled and the ground is wrecked by overgrazing, regeneration usually takes place.

There were three landmark policy regimes in Nepal regarding the ownership and management of forests, namely the private regime until 1957, the nationalization regime between 1957 and the 1970s, and the decentralization regime after the late 1970s (Hobley, 1996). Since the population was small and forest resources were abundant, earlier governments had encouraged people to convert forestland into agricultural land to increase tax revenue (Mahat et al., 1986). This was the case during, for instance, the Rana dynasty period (1846–1950); many forestlands, as well as agricultural lands developed by clearing forest land, were distributed to Rana family members and other influential people as birta[4] tenure by 1950 (Joshi, 1993), thereby creating an extensive landlord system. In practice, however, some forests were managed informally by community members.

The ownership of forestland was shifted from individuals or communities to the government after the promulgation of the Forest Nationalization Act in 1957. This immediately led to rapid deforestation, because the act destroyed the incentives for local people to manage the forests (Hobley, 1985). As the pace of deforestation became faster, it became clear that the government had to consider changing the policy quickly to protect the forest from severe deforestation and forest degradation. And then, although the government policy did not actually change, a spontaneous and participatory approach to forest management by local people dependent on forest resources started to evolve in the 1970s.

Eventually, in the late 1970s, the government fully realized that it could not arrest deforestation and forest degradation, and official efforts to engage the local people in forest protection and management were started. Following the recommendations of the Ninth Forestry Conference that had been held back in 1974, the government of Nepal drafted a national forestry plan to combat the severe deforestation and forest degradation. For the first time, the plan officially recognized the role of local people in forest management activities (Pokharel, 1997). In response, the government enacted Panchayat Forest Rules and Panchayat-Protected Forest Rules in 1978, which allowed the locally elected body, the village Panchayat, to manage the degraded forestland. The Decentralization Act in 1982 introduced the concept of the user group, and promoted it as an effective means to combat the deterioration of the stock of forest resources.

Another landmark development in community forestry was the preparation of the 25-year master plan in 1988, which emphasized the importance of forest user group management provisions, revitalizing the age-old indigenous practices of forest resource management.

In response to the master plan, in 1993 the Forest Act was passed, for the proper management of community forests. It specifies the number of provisions of community forests and the procedure for the formation of community forest user groups (CFUGs). Community forestry was given high priority, and CFUGs were identified as self-governed autonomous entities (Gautam et al., 2004). A revision of the Forest Act in 1999 devised the provision of investing 25 per cent of forest income for forest development; it also specified the control mechanism for the CFUG members. A second amendment of the community forest development guidelines (2005) focused more on the rights of poor people, and specifies the detailed role of forest stakeholders such as foresters, CFUGs and NGOs/INGOs.

The handover of forest use rights from government to local community begins with a discussion between the local forest users and the local forest officers. A general assembly meeting must be held wherein the Forest User Group Committee (FUGC) members and its president must be elected by all the community members. Foresters help them prepare a constitution and an Operational Plan of Forest Management. Then the CFUG submits these documents to the District Forest Office for the handover; if all the requirements are fulfilled, the District Forest Office hands over the forest use rights to the CFUG. State control of forest management remains in place, as there are many restrictions on the management, including the prohibition of the excessive harvesting of forest products.

As a result, community forest management by CFUGs has become a widespread practice in Nepal. By 2009, about one-third of the total population of Nepal were participating in the community forestry programs, and about a million hectares of forest (one fourth of the total) had been handed over (Ojha et al., 2009). It is widely recognized that the community forestry regime is successful in Nepal. However, evidence from existing studies shows that there are wide variations in the success of community forestry between the hill region and the Tarai region of the country. About 90 per cent of all user groups and 83 per cent of all areas under community forestry are located in the hill region, and only 10 per cent of all user groups and 17 per cent of areas under community forestry are located in the Tarai region (Hobley, 1996). There is deep controversy regarding the success of community forestry in the Tarai region, which needs to be settled by careful empirical studies.

9.3 Characteristics of sample forests and user groups

We conducted a case study of community timber forest management in the Dang district, which is situated in the south-western part of Nepal.[5]

It lies in the Rapti zone of the Western Development Region, and the area of the district is nearly 300,000 ha. The elevation of the district ranges from 213 meters (Sishniya Village Development Committee (VDC)) to 2058 metres (Hansipur VDC) above sea level. The Dang district is divided by Churia Hills into two valleys and their peripheral areas; the Dang Valley lies towards the northern side of the mid-Churia Hills, which is also called inner Tarai, while the Deukhari Valley is situated in the southern part of mid-Churia Hills and extends to the south. The district headquarters is located in the Dang Valley, which is more developed than the Deukhari Valley. In the northern part of the district, the Mahabharat Range extends from east to west. The district has a subtropical monsoon climate in the valleys and the Churia Hills, and a temperate climate in the Mahabharat Range. Loam and clay soils can be found in the valleys, whereas rock, slate and mixed soils are found in the hill area. The former is considered to be more favorable for tree growth than the latter. Sal is the main tree species in the forests in the Churia Hills and the valleys; other main tree species in the forests are asna (*Terminalia tomentosa*), sissoo (*Dalbergia sissoo*), khair (*acacia catechu*) and jamun (*Syzigium cumini*). Meanwhile, important species found in the Mahabharat Range include salla (*Pinus roxburghii*) and tooni (*Toona ciliata*). The basic characteristics of this district are summarized in Table 9.1.

The Dang district is recognized as a pioneer district in initiating community forestry in the Tarai region of Nepal. In this district, communities have resumed timber forest management informally since around

Table 9.1 Basic characteristics of the Dang district

Total population (2000 census)	462,380
Total number of households	82,495
Total area of district (ha)	295,500
Total forest area (ha)	192,155
Community forest area (ha)	95,226
Number of community forests	447
No. of households involved in community forestry[a]	88,076
Average forest area per community user group (ha)	213.0
Average forest area per household (ha)	1.08
Average no. of households per user group	197

Source: DFO monitoring report, 2008.

Note: [a]Some households are involved in the management of more than two forests.

1980 (Sakurai et al., 2004). Since the inception of the scheme, 95,226 hectares of national forest area have been handed over to 447 CFUGs (DFO Dang monitoring report, 2008).

Of the 447 community forests which have been handed over and registered in the district forest office, we have excluded the planted community forests whose management is qualitatively different from the sal-based community forests. Also, the forests handed over later than 2005 have been excluded as they are too new for an assessment to be made of the impact of the handover. Then 200 community forests were randomly selected. Community forest and CFUG data were collected from both primary and secondary sources. The secondary sources are the constitutions[6] and operation plans[7] of the CFUGs, which they have to submit to the district forest office. The forest inventory data was collected by the community people with the help of technicians using a standard forestry approach: first, they divide the forest into different blocks on the basis of the forest conditions, species, and natural borders; then they sub-divide the block into smaller parcels depending on the forest conditions; they select sample plots of different sizes from the sub-blocks, depending on the conditions of the forest and size of the sub-block; and finally they count the number of trees of different sizes and calculate the number of trees per hectare. In addition to these forest inventory data, other information about silvicultural activities (such as pruning, thinning, weeding and singling) was collected by our own survey, in which CFUGs were requested to fill out a questionnaire.

Table 9.2 provides the indicators of forest conditions and management. For expository purposes, we have divided the samples into 'nearby' and 'remote' relating to the nearest market town, and 'high' and 'low' household density (the number of households per hectare of community forestland area), with the division at the mean, because we consider that market access and population density are two of the most important variables explaining the extent of forest management.[8] Since some data items are missing, however, the sample sizes are different for different items.

Forest condition has a range of dimensions, so is difficult to measure with a single indicator. In this study, we basically use two types of measure for the forest conditions.

The first variable pertains to the extent of deforestation, represented by the area where trees were planted and replanted, the area of barren land, and the area of encroachment for agriculture and human settlement purposes. As mentioned earlier, the sal tree is dominant

Table 9.2 Indicators of forest conditions, management and year of handover by distance to market town and household density

	Distance to market town[b]				Household density[c]			
	Nearby		Remote		High		Low	
	Mean	No. of samples	Mean	No. of samples	Mean	No. of samples	Mean	No. of samples
% of severely degraded area[a]	1.53	94	1.17	106	1.79	54	1.17	146
No. of small trees per hectare	12372.51	91	11806.83	98	11151.85	51	12421.91	138
No. of large trees per hectare	285.0	78	304.6	85	319.3	46	285.7	117
% of managed area in the past 5 years	46.47	92	37.38	104	63.20	53	33.66	143

Notes: [a] Proportion of the sum of planted and encroached areas and barren area.
[b] Distance to market town is grouped into two categories: 'nearby' indicates nearer than the mean distance from the market and 'remote' indicates farther than the mean distance.
[c] Household density is the total number of households per hectare of forest land. Household density is also grouped into two groups: 'low' represents lower household density than the mean, and 'high' represents higher than the mean.

and has a high regenerative capacity, so unless the sal trees have been completely uprooted or the ground heavily grazed, regeneration will have taken place. Therefore, we can safely assume that all areas of community forest which are barren, planted artificially and encroached on have been completely and severely degraded at least once due to complete felling of trees and over-heavy animal grazing, and then subsequently, some part of the barren area will have been replanted by CFUGs. As is shown in Table 9.2, such areas tend to be larger in forests nearer to market towns and other areas of higher population density.[9]

A second measure of forest condition is the average number per hectare of small trees of diameter less than 10 cm, and that of large trees with a diameter of more than 20 cm at chest height. A larger number of small trees indicates not only reforestation but also the extent of forest degradation before. It is important to note that small coppices are regenerated if the larger trees are felled. Table 9.2 shows that a larger number of small trees are found in places near market towns and areas of low household density.

Similarly, the higher the number of large trees, the better the forest condition. Roughly speaking, these large trees are older than 20 years at least. The average time elapsed since the forest was handed over is about 12 years, so that the presence of such large trees in the community-managed forests is very unlikely to be a result of reforestation after the handover. Rather, it is more reasonable to assume that they have been protected since before the handover. According to Table 9.2, a slightly larger number of large trees is found in remote forests and forests with high household densities.

To measure the intensity of forest management in recent years, we used the percentage of the total area of forest where the CFUG members carried out silvicultural activities during the five-year period, from 2005 to 2009, before the time of data collection; silvicultural activities comprise weeding, signaling, thinning, pruning and planting, as well as other activities such as constructing fire lanes and fences. The proportion of forest area where silvicultural operations took place is significantly higher in forests with high household densities. In our field survey, we found that when forest users carried out forest management activities, they were not in general paid, but were allowed to collect firewood, poles and fodder. They work together for several days per year, and failure to participate is often penalized by instituting a fine amounting to the prevailing daily wage.[10]

While Table 9.2 shows the values of the dependent variables in the regression analysis, Table 9.3 exhibits the characteristics of sample community forests, which are used as explanatory variables. Conspicuous differences are found in forest area, the number of households per CFUG, and the number of households per community forest area between high and low household density areas. The same tendency, though less pronounced, can be found between nearby and remote areas.

It is also noteworthy that government managed forests still exist in some areas. According to our informal interviews, community forest users illegally felled large timber trees in government forests, particularly before the handover when the government forests were not strictly protected. Since the handover of a large number of forests, the role of the local forestry officers has changed from that of guardian of all the forests to facilitator for the community forest management and protector of the remaining government forest.

Table 9.3 Characteristics of sample community forests by distance to market town and household density

	Distance to market town[e]				Household density[f]			
	Nearby		Remote		High		Low	
	Mean	N	Mean	N	Mean	N	Mean	N
Distance to market town (km)	5.5	95	13.5	106	8.9	55	10.0	146
Distance from center of village to forest (km)	0.50	95	0.63	106	0.44	55	0.62	146
Distance to headquarters from VDC (km)[a]	14.0	95	19.1	106	15.4	55	17.2	146
Forest area (ha)	286.4	95	328.1	106	138.9	55	372.2	146
No. of households	298.0	95	213.6	106	329.6	55	224.8	146
No. of households per hectare of forest land	1.64	95	1.16	106	0.69	146	3.23	55
Slope of forest land	11.70	89	14.10	94	10.7	53	13.9	130
Brahmin/Chetri HH ratio	0.35	84	0.41	93	0.45	48	0.35	129
Soil dummy[b]	0.70	86	0.78	91	0.74	50	0.74	127
Dang valley dummy[c]	0.64	95	0.75	106	0.89	55	0.62	146
Ratio of government managed forests in VDC[d]	0.27	95	0.35	106	0.27	55	0.33	146

Source: District Profile of Dang, Central Bureau of Statistics, Nepal.

Notes: [a] Distance from the border of the Village Development Committee (VDC) in which the forest is located, to the municipality (Tribhuvan) where the district headquarters, including the district forest office, is located.

[b] Soil dummy means the clay and loam type of soil in the forest land. Base of comparison includes stony and gravel type of soil.

[c] Valley dummy represents the Dang valley and their surrounding VDCs in which the district headquarters is located. The Deukhari valley is the base for comparison.

[d] Area of forests under government management in VDC divided by total VDC area.

[e] Distance to market town is grouped into two categories: 'nearby' indicates nearer than the mean distance from the market and 'remote' indicates farther than the mean distance.

[f] Household density is the total number of households per hectare of forest land. Household density is also grouped into two groups: 'low' represents lower household density than the mean, and 'high' represents higher than the mean.

9.4 Hypotheses and estimation method

Since the forest was likely to be basically open access under the state management regime before the handover,[11] deforestation would have occurred due to firewood collection, agricultural expansion, the extension of settlement areas, and grazing in areas where the population density is higher. Hence, the demand for firewood, agricultural land, land for settlements and grazing per unit of land is higher.[12] Based on this consideration, we postulate the following hypothesis:

> *H1*: Higher population density resulted in more severe deforestation because of the larger demand for minor forest products, land for agriculture and settlements and grazing.

Although a fair amount of timber is used for the construction of buildings, serious degradation of forest conditions would not have occurred unless timber had been sold in massive quantities to the markets. In fact, according to our informal interviews the local demand for timber could have been satisfied by community forests in a sustainable manner if the forests had been managed properly. If the purpose of felling mature timber trees is sale at the markets, it is likely that large trees would have been felled in those forests with favorable access to markets.

If the large trees are felled, coppices are regenerated from the roots, especially in sal forests. Such coppices need to be protected from grazing and premature harvesting in order to grow into small trees. If protected effectively, the number of small trees increases in degraded forests. Thus, it seems reasonable to postulate the following hypothesis:

> *H2*: Better access to markets resulted in more active harvesting of mature trees, but also the subsequent active regeneration of small trees after the handover, so that there remain fewer large trees but more small trees per unit of land at present.

Although *H1* asserts that higher population density results in more deforestation, this is unlikely to hold after forests were handed over, because the higher the demand for forest resources, the greater would have been the incentives for community forest users to manage community forests collectively (Otsuka and Place, 2001). In fact, given the cost of organizing collective action to manage forests, the greater the demand for forest products, the greater the net benefit of such action. Therefore, it makes sense to postulate the following hypothesis:

> *H3*: Higher population density leads to more intensive management of community forests after the forest use rights had been handed over.

Ideally we would have liked to examine how much forest conditions have changed since the handover. It was difficult to do so, however, partly because we could not obtain data on forest conditions at the time of the handover, and partly because the timing of the handover was endogenous. As a first step, nevertheless, towards formulating the more comprehensive simultaneous equation systems, this study attempts to identify the determinants of severe deforestation, the number of large trees and small trees, and the management intensity at present by estimating the reduced-form functions. Denoting the proportion of severely deforested areas, the average number of large trees and small trees per hectare, and the proportion of managed areas in the last five years by y, the reduced-form function is specified as

$$y_i = \alpha_0 + \alpha_1 \text{ Household density}_i + \alpha_2 \text{ Market access}_i + \gamma X_i + \varepsilon_i \qquad (1)$$

where subscript *i* refers to the *i*-th forest, αs and γ are regression parameters, X is a vector of other explanatory variables, and ε is an error term. Other explanatory variables include the community forest area or the number of forest user households, which is supposed to capture the transaction cost of collective community forest management; the distance from the village centre to the edge of the community forest; the distance from the village to the district headquarters, which is expected to measure the extent of monitoring of forests by the district forest officers; the average slope of the forestland and a clay and loam soil dummy, which measure the quality of the forestland;[13] the proportion of Brahmin and Chetri households, (which are the highest castes); the Dang Valley dummy, which may capture, among other things, the higher opportunity cost of labor, as there are more favorable non-farm employment opportunities in this valley than in other places; and the ratio of the government forest area to total area of VDC. The last variable is supposed to measure the availability of tree and other resources from forests other than the community's own forests.[14]

Note that in the regression analysis we have alternated between the community forest area and the number of households, and we have estimated the functions with and without the proportion of Brahmin and Chetri households and the soil dummy, as the data on these two variables are unavailable in 29 of the sample community forests.

9.5 Estimation results

9.5.1 Determinants of severe deforestation

According to Table 9.4, a major determinant of severe deforestation is household density, whose coefficients are positive and significant. This finding clearly supports *H1*, that population pressure is a major cause of severe deforestation through grazing, the clearance of forest for agricultural fields and settlements, and the repeated collection of young trees for firewood. Another significant variable is the total area of forest, which may mean that, everything else being equal, the larger the total forest area, the smaller the proportion of the severely deforested area. In

Table 9.4 Determinants of severe deforestation[a]

	Model 1	Model 2	Model 3	Model 4
Household density	0.232**	0.220**	0.335***	0.288***
Area of forest	–0.002**	–0.001*	–	–
Number of households	–	–	–0.001	0.0004
Distance to market town	–0.022	–0.030	–0.033	–0.037
Distance to village	0.156	0.054	0.098	0.006
Distance to headquarter	0.028	0.033*	0.029	0.034*
Slope of forest land	–0.033	–0.029	–0.036	–0.029
Brahmin/Chetri HH ratio	0.092	–	0.196	–
Soil dummy	0.020	–	–0.014	–
Dang valley dummy	–0.198	0.149	0.065	0.308
Ratio of government managed forests in VDC	0.282	0.543	0.485	0.717
Constant	1.646**	1.198*	1.195	0.788
N	154	182	154	182
F	2.73	3.23	2.32	2.83
Prob>F	0.0043	0.0019	0.0145	0.0057
R-squared	0.1601	0.1298	0.1398	0.1156

Notes: [a] Dependent variable is the proportion of the sum of planted and encroached areas and barren area.
Significance levels: *** $p<0.01$, ** $p<0.05$, * $p<0.1$.

two of the regressions, the coefficients of distance to headquarters are positive and weakly significant, which may indicate that district forest officers monitored deforestation in areas relatively close to their offices. The other variables are insignificant.

9.5.2 Determinants of the number of large trees per hectare

In the case of the determinants of the number of large trees per hectare shown in Table 9.5, neither household density nor area of forest, nor the number of forest user households, is significant. But what is highly significant instead is, unsurprisingly, the distance to the market town; its positive coefficients imply that large trees were felled in areas with good access to markets. This finding gives clear support for *H2*, that market access is positively associated with the felling of mature trees for commercial purposes. It is worth emphasizing that the determinants of deforestation due to grazing, firewood collection and the expansion of agricultural land are very different from those due to the felling of large trees.

Consistent with the results in Table 9.4,[15] the effect of the distance to the headquarters is negative and significant, suggesting that the headquarters played a certain part in preventing the felling of large trees in areas near its location. Thus, community forests near the headquarters were not totally open access, but were subject to the supervision of the district forest officers to some extent.

It is intriguing to observe the positive and significant effects of the ratio of government forests in VDC. One possible interpretation is that community forest users went to the government, rather than the community, forests, and felled mature trees there, to sell them; as a result, the large trees in the community forests were preserved. This might indeed have been possible if the protection of government forests had been less draconian than that of community forests, and also if government forests had generally been located in areas with favorable access to roads and markets. This point needs further scrutiny.

9.5.3 Determinants of the number of small trees per hectare

According to Table 9.6, the coefficients of the distance to market town are negative and significant in all models when the dependent variable is the number of small trees per hectare. Small trees generally grow naturally after large trees have been harvested; indeed, it is difficult for small trees to grow in the presence of large trees, because they need enough sunlight and space to grow. Therefore, in places near market towns, the larger the number of small trees per hectare, the higher the extent of degradation of large trees beforehand, which is also consistent

Table 9.5 Determinants of the number of large trees per hectare[a]

	Model 1	Model 2	Model 3	Model 4
Household density	6.296	3.686	6.752	5.761
Area of forest	−0.025	−0.039	–	–
Number of households	–	–	0.053	0.007
Distance to market town	13.300***	12.607***	13.576***	12.523***
Distance to village	45.742	40.797	44.115	39.026
Distance to headquarter	−6.569**	−4.965*	−6.666**	−4.955*
Slope of forest land	−1.415	−1.879	−1.168	−1.830
Brahmin/Chetri HH ratio	127.393	–	133.069	–
Soil dummy	42.650	–	40.682	–
Dang valley dummy	54.387	89.183	50.625	93.938
Ratio of government managed forests in VDC	309.014**	275.130**	318.074**	284.818**
Constant	39.645	111.683	14.722	89.685
N	144	162	144	162
F	2.74	3.1	2.76	3.07
Prob>F	0.0042	0.0028	0.004	0.0031
R-squared	0.1709	0.1396	0.1717	0.1384

Note: [a] Significance levels: *** $p<0.01$, ** $p<0.05$, * $p<0.1$

with Table 9.5. However, the growth of small trees is possible only when the grazing and harvesting of small trees is controlled. Actually, in most community forests both grazing and the harvesting of small trees are prohibited, so it can be claimed that reforestation is taking place in forests near market towns as a result of community forest management.

The area of forest is negatively significant in Model 1, which indicates that the larger the forest area, the less the forest degradation that had taken place earlier. Similarly, consistent with the analyses reported in Tables 9.4 and 9.5, the distance to headquarters is positively significant in two models, indicating that the headquarters has a positive role in protecting the large trees.

9.5.4 Determinants of forest management intensity

According to Table 9.7, the effect of household density on forest management intensity is positive and highly significant, which is diametrically

Table 9.6 Determinants of the number of small trees per hectare

	Model 1	Model 2	Model 3	Model 4
Household density	-695.34	-294.756	-292.799	-26.707
Area of forest	-5.787**	-3.719	–	–
Number of households	–	–	-4.614	-4.855
Distance to market town	-318.586**	-322.52**	-361.868**	-368.448**
Distance to village	-315.787	-150.09	-527.031	-304.221
Distance to headquarters	123.811	158.082*	127.518	165.776*
Slope of forest land	95.152	83.511	81.175	70.413
Brahman/Chetri HH ratio	946.721	–	1298.161	–
Soil dummy	1184.461	–	1047.559	–
Dang valley dummy	-3631.715*	-1607.825	-2564.943	-856.401
Ratio of government managed forests in VDC	1749.711	3438.048	2556.99	3479.094
Constant	15839.377***	13504.530***	14287.328***	13259.844***
N	148	173	148	173
F	2.5047	2.2212	2.2254	2.3041
Prob>F	0.0085	0.0283	0.0197	0.0229
R-squared	0.1546	0.0978	0.1397	0.1010

Note: Significance levels: *** $p<0.01$, ** $p<0.05$, * $p<0.1$.

opposed to its effect on severe deforestation. These findings strongly suggest that the large demand for forest resources contributes to the deforestation and degradation of forests if they are open access and to the rehabilitation if they are managed communally with clear communal use rights. The unusually high *t*-statistics for the coefficients of household density strongly support the validity of *H3*.

The coefficients of both the area of forest and the number of households are negative and significant, suggesting that there is a high cost of managing large forest areas or high transaction costs of organizing a large number of community members. The effect of the distance to market town is largely insignificant, indicating that the selling of forest products to the market may not be a major motive for the community management of forests. Although the significance level is low, the effect of the distance to the headquarters is negative, which is reasonable if the district forest office assists and monitors the management of community forests in nearby areas. In Models 1 and 2, the Dang Valley

Table 9.7 Determinants of forest management intensity[a]

	Model 1	Model 2	Model 3	Model 4
Household density	11.369***	10.551***	13.529***	12.649***
Area of forest	-0.031***	-0.032***	–	–
Number of household	–	–	-0.024**	-0.023**
Distance to market town	-0.130	-0.268	-0.376	-0.550
Distance to village	0.969	3.484	-0.134	2.179
Distance to headquarter from VDC	-0.388	-0.393	-0.370	-0.349
Slope of forest land	0.188	0.186	0.134	0.150
Brahmin/Chetri HH ratio	1.338	–	3.024	–
Soil dummy	1.868	–	1.338	–
Valley dummy	-18.372***	-18.508***	-12.822*	-13.140**
Ratio of gov. managed forest in VDC	-3.948	10.843	0.133	14.036
Constant	51.798***	51.810***	43.456***	43.455***
N	150	179	150	179
F	12.66	17.2	11.33	15.13
Prob>F	0	0	0	0
R-squared	0.4767	0.4473	0.4492	0.4159

Notes: [a]Dependent variable is the proportion of forest management area in the last 5 years. Significance levels: *** $p<0.01$, ** $p<0.05$, * $p<0.1$.

dummy is negative and significant, which may suggest that due to the higher opportunity cost of labor, the participation of forest user group members in the collective management of community forests is lower in the Dang Valley area.

9.6 Concluding remarks

While much is known about the ability of local communities to manage non-timber forests, much less is known about their abilities to manage timber forests. According to Otsuka and Place (2001), unlike non-timber forests, whose conditions can be maintained and rehabilitated by preventing the excessive extraction of resources, the production of timber is management intensive, so that incentives to manage forests by pruning, thinning, and weeding are important. Thus, whether the local communities are equipped with the ability to organize collective action to manage timber forests is a critical issue. Another critical issue is the extent to which the devolution of land use rights from the government to local communities contributes to the improvement of forest conditions.

According to the results of our analyses on the management of timber forests in the Dang district of Nepal, the handover of the forest use rights to the local community has desirable impacts on community forest management. Indeed, the population pressure, measured by household density, contributed to severe deforestation before the handover and to intensive management of forests afterwards, which in turn must have contributed to the rehabilitation of forest conditions over the longer run. It seems clear that the handover of the forest use rights to the local community is the main driver for reversing the trend from deforestation to reforestation.

Whether the local community has the ability to grow valuable timber tress is a major question remaining. While the incentive to harvest mature trees seems to have been positively associated with market access before the handover, the management intensity of forests is unrelated to the market access after the handover; this may suggest that local communities are interested in the rehabilitation of forests to provide minor forest products, rather than growing valuable timber trees for sale at the market. Timber trees which have been grown under community management after the handover are still immature. Further enquiry into the management and sale of timber tress by communities is called for in the future, in order to shed more light on the ability of local communities to manage their timber forests.

Notes

1. Deforestation refers to the conversion of forest to another land use (e.g., agricultural land and permanent pasture).
2. According to Sakurai et al. (2004), private management allocates more labor for the intensive care of trees than does community management.
3. In this study, 'management' refers to silvicultural operations such as weeding, pruning, thinning, singling and harvesting.
4. Birta is the land provided by the state to privileged individuals primarily for religious, economic, and political reasons.
5. Unlike copse forests in which the major forest resources are minor forest products such as firewood and leaf litter, timber is by far the most important product in the forests in the Dang district. In order to produce valuable timber trees, appropriate silvicultural operations are crucially important.
6. Every community group has to submit its constitution at the time of handover, but they can be revised later. The constitutions contain information about the number of user households, the functions, duties and powers of the user groups and user committees, and the financial regulations.

7. The community forest user group must submit their operational plans at regular intervals of, usually, five years. This report contains information about the objective of the forest management, forest development activities that have to be carried out in the plan period, and forest characteristics such as the number of trees in the forest by size and type, slope, soil type and so on. The operational plan is prepared by the CFUGs with the technical support of the district forest office and other supporters such as NGO/INGOs.
8. The number of households is the proxy for population. The extent of forest management is measured by the proportion of managed area during the last five years.
9. The proportion of severely degraded areas ranges between 1 and 2 per cent. In our view, this seems to be an underestimate – importantly, because small degraded areas are generally excluded from barren land. We assume, however, that the reported degraded areas are largely proportional to the true degraded areas.
10 Continuous failure to participate may be panelized by the prohibition to use forest products or even by social exclusion.
11. This point is based on a number of informal interviews. Also see Sakurai et al. (2004).
12. In extreme cases, people harvested even the roots of trees and very young trees, leading to complete degradation. Heavy grazing also resulted in deforestation.
13. Clay and loan soil is considered more favorable for tree growth than stony and gravel soil.
14. Alternatively we also used the government forest area per household in VDC, but the estimation results remain largely unchanged.
15. Also see Table 9.6.

References

Baland, J., Bardhan, P., Das, S. and Mookherjee, D. (2010) 'Forests to the People: Decentralization and Forest Degradation in the Indian Himalayas', *World Development*, 38(11), 1642–56.

Baland, J. and Platteau, J.-P. (1996) *Halting Degradation of Natural Resources: Is There a Role of Rural Communities?* (Oxford: Clarendon Press).

Bromley, D.W. (1992) 'The Commons, Property, and Common-Property Regimes', in D.W. Bromley (ed.), *Making the Commons Work* (San Francisco: ICS Press).

Edmonds, E. (2002) 'Government-Initiated Community Resource Management and Local Extraction form Nepal's Forests', *Journal of Development Economics*, 68, 89–115.

Gautam, A.P., Shivakoti, G.P. and Webb, E.L. (2004) 'A Review of Forest Policies, Institutions, and Changes in the Resources Condition in Nepal', *International Forestry Review*, 6(2), 136–48.

Gilmour, D.A. and Fisher R.J. (1991) *Villagers, Forests and Foresters: A Philosophy, Process and Practices of Community Forestry in Nepal* (Tripureswor, Kathmandu, Nepal: Sahayogi Press).

Hardin, G. (1968) 'The Tragedy of the Commons', *Science*, 162, 1243–8.

Hayami, Y. (1997) *Development Economics: From the Poverty to the Wealth of Nations* (Oxford: Clarendon Press).

Hobley, M. (1985) 'Common Property Does Not Cause Deforestation', *Journal of Forestry*, 83, 663–4.
Hobley, M. (1996) 'Participatory Forestry: The Process of Change in India and Nepal', Rural Development Forestry Study Guide 3, Overseas Development Institute, London.
Jodha, N.S. (2001) 'Common Property Resources and the Rural Poor', *Economic Political Weekly*, 21, 1169–81.
Joshi, A.L. (1993) 'Effects on Administration of Changed Forest Policies in Nepal', in K. Warner and H. Wood (eds), *Policy and Legislation Overseas Development Institute in Community Forestry*, Proceedings of a Workshop held in Bangkok.
Mahat, T.B.S., Griffin, D.M. and Shepherd, K.R. (1986) 'Human Impacts on Some Forests of the Middle Hills of Nepal: Part 1. Forestry in the Context of the Traditional Resources of the State', *Mountain Research and Development*, 6, 223–32.
Ojha, H., Persha, L. and Chhatre, A. (2009) 'Community Forestry in Nepal: A Policy Innovation for Local Livelihoods', IFPRI Discussion Paper 0913.
Ostrom, E. (1990) *Governing the Commons: The Evolution of Institutions for Collective Action* (Cambridge: Cambridge University Press).
Otsuka, K. and Place, F. (2001) *Land Tenure and Natural Resource Management: A Comparative Study of Agrarian Communities in Asia and Africa* (Baltimore and London: Johns Hopkins University Press).
Pokharel, B.K. (1997) 'Foresters and Villagers in Connection and Impacts', Ph.D. Thesis (Norwich, UK: University of East Anglia).
Regmi, R.R. (1994) 'Deforestation and Rural Society in the Nepalese Terai', *Occasional Papers in Sociology and Anthropology*, Volume 4.
Sakurai, T., Rayamajhi, S., Pokharel, R. and Otsuka, K. (2004) 'Efficiency of Timber Production in Community and Private Forestry in Nepal', *Environment and Development Economics*, 9(4), 539–61.
Somanathan, E. (1991) 'Deforestation, Property Rights and Incentives in the Central Himalayas', *Economics and Political Weekly*, 26, 37–46.
Tachibana T., Upadhyaya, H.K., Pokharel, R., Rayamajhi, S. and Otsuka, K. (2001) 'Common Property Forest Management in the Hill Region of Nepal', in K. Otsuka and F. Palace (eds), *Land Tenure and Natural Resource Management: A Comparative Study of Agrarian Communities in Asia and Africa* (Baltimore and London: Johns Hopkins University Press).

10

Tenure and Forest Management in India: Impacts on Equity and Efficiency of Van Panchayats in Uttarakhand

Ashokankur Datta and Gunnar Köhlin

10.1 Introduction

Environmentalists and conservationists have often advocated communal control of natural resources as a way to ensure its judicious and sustainable use (Colchester, 1994; Kothari, 2011). Since the early 1980s, economists, sociologists and cultural anthropologists have documented cases of sustainable natural resource management by local communities (Acheson, 1988; Ostrom, 1990; Berkes, 1986). This was followed by sophisticated theoretical models that showed that 'commons' – resources that are jointly managed – often follow trajectories that are not 'tragic' (Sethi and Somanathan, 1996; Chichilnisky, 1994). Once Ostrom and others had demolished the infallibility of the Tragedy of the Commons, policymakers around the world started viewing communal control as a panacea to solve all kinds of natural resource problems.

South Asia also followed the trend by adopting policies promoting communal or joint management of natural resources. The forestry sector saw major action in terms of transfer of managerial authority, and in some cases even ownership, to local communities. In India, this took the form of joint forest management (JFM) in the early nineties. JFM involves local communities in conservation of forest with the promise of pecuniary and non-pecuniary benefits on successful completion of such efforts. However, JFM was viewed with skepticism by proponents of community forestry, as the state still played a substantial role in forest management (Sarin et al., 2003). The failure of JFM in achieving its objectives (Lele and Borgoyary, 2008; Banerjee, 1997)[1] contrasted sharply with the success stories of true community management in the form of Van Panchayats in Uttarakhand and informal community forest management in Orissa (Somanathan et al., 2005; Baland et al., 2010; Singh et al., 2005).

However, in most of these studies success was defined in terms of the ability of these management regimes in achieving their *conservation* objectives. While only a few of the studies measured forest quality directly (for exceptions, see Somanathan et al., 2005; Baland et al., 2010), others studied the impact of decentralization on forest resource collection with the implicit assumption that reduced resource collection improved forest quality (Edmonds, 2002; Bandhyopadhyay and Shyamsundar, 2004).

The issue of intra-community *distributional* fairness was rarely the criterion to measure success. In the highly unequal and stratified societies of South Asia, it is important to measure the success of a policy in terms of its distributional effects. In this chapter, we try to evaluate community management of forest in terms of its intra-community distributional outcomes. Related to the question of intra-community equity is the question of *economic efficiency* of a natural resource management regime. Economic efficiency is a metric that is distinctly different from the conservation metrics usually used to judge community management regimes. Given the focus on conservation objectives, most analyses emphasize the role of institutions in reducing resource extraction. The question of efficient economic management is, however, usually ignored. It should be noted that the metrics of conservation and economic efficiency are often not directly related. A forest from which no resource is extracted and on which no silvicultural management is practised can have high canopy cover and basal volume. However, given its low-intensive management (primarily protection), such a forest is unable to achieve its economic potential, and is hence inefficient. In this chapter, we focus on two issues of interest: the first is the implications of assets and caste on access to firewood in villages with differences in forest management. The second aspect is how local forest management affects the efficiency of collection. More specifically, we test if the marginal productivity of firewood collection with respect to labor is systematically higher in locally managed forests than in forests under state control. We do this by using the specific example of Van Panchayats in Uttarakhand, India, local forest management institutions that are uniquely longstanding.

10.2 Hypotheses with respect to equity and efficiency implications of local forest management

There might be several reasons for a change in distributional outcome due to a change in resource regime. It has been widely documented that the history of state control of forests is also a history of widespread forest degradation. It is suggested that heavy deforestation occurs during nationalization, as people feel that their forests are being taken away from them (Gilmour et al., 1989; Guha, 1989; Tamuli and Choudhury, 2009). Since the government does not have the ability to monitor and control collection, forests are in effect converted to open access resources; it might be the case that as free entry ensures zero rents, the village élite have no incentive to monitor and control collection. Analogously, restrictions on entry imposed by communitarian regimes create possibilities for rent and hence create an environment where the community élite has an incentive to restrict forest use by the marginalized within the community.

Studies on the impact of a resource control regime on the intra-community distribution of resource collected are not very common. Most studies on this issue look at inequities across income levels, often neglecting inequities across social groups. Sundar (2000) argues that community forestry schemes, such as JFM in India, adversely affect the poor by closing access to nearby forests. The rich, who have access to alternate sources of firewood and can afford non-biomass fuels, are not affected. Sarin et al. (1998) and Kumar (2002) support the view of Sundar (2000). Meanwhile, Agarwal (2001) studies issues of gender equity and observes that women, who have no role in the decision-making process of JFM, is the group that is most adversely affected by JFMs. In Nepal,[2] studies have shown that many of the forest user groups suffer from élite capture (Banjade et al., 2004; Malla et al., 2003; Timsina, 2003; Adhikari, 2008).

Although these studies highlight the existing inequities under communal management of resources, they do not study how such systems perform in terms of equity compared to other modes of resource control, like centralized state control or private ownership. Given the predominant orientation of the literature, the hypotheses to be tested in this study with regard to equity are that asset-poor and low-caste households are made worse off with respect to firewood collection under Van Panchayat management than under government management.

The literature on the economic efficiency of alternative forest regimes is even leaner. Sakurai et al. (2004) compare 'the management performance of timber production among three management regimes in Nepal:

private forestry, community forestry with collective management and community forestry with centralized management'. They find that centralized management leads to higher revenue and profit from timber production when compared to community management. In fact, Sakurai et al. (2004) identifies a negative trade-off between conservation objective and economic efficiency: 'while collective management is more efficient for protection of trees due to mutual supervision, profit seeking private management or centralized management is more efficient than collective management for silvicultural operations due to superior work incentives'. Chand (2011) also shows that production is not organized efficiently in the community forests of Nepal. Köhlin and Amacher (2005) estimate the firewood production functions for different firewood sources and different categories of labor, to calculate the marginal productivity of labor for each of these categories. The comparison between collection in plantations under local management ('social forests') and natural forests (government controlled but *de facto* open access) reveals that the marginal productivity of men from villages with natural forests *alone* is systematically lower than the marginal productivity of men from villages with social forests. While men seem to be able to equate the marginal productivity between different sources of fuel, women had significantly higher productivity in their collection in the nearby managed plantations. Caste was also a significant factor in explaining collection behavior; Köhlin and Amacher (2005) found two efficiency gains from the social forestry intervention – a direct improvement through the increased access to fuel in the plantations, and also an indirect effect through increased productivity in collection from the subsequently less degraded natural forests.

Our hypothesis with regard to efficiency is that the long-term protection of Van Panchayat forests, with its demonstrated positive effects on forest quality (Baland et al., 2010), has been at the expense of forest collection.

10.3 Van Panchayats in Uttarakhand

Since the Van Panchayats in Uttarakhand are geographically distinct and have historic roots, we need to explain their background. Prior to India's independence in 1947, British rule extended to all the districts of Uttarakhand except Uttarkashi and Tehri Garhwal; these two districts constituted the princely state of Tehri Garhwal.[3] The British-ruled part of the state was broadly divided into the British Garhwal district and Kumaon district.[4]

The Van Panchayats in Uttarakhand owe their origins to the British Colonial Forest policy. After the British took control over Kumaon and British Garhwal, between 1840 and 1910, they brought most forest areas of the Kumaon division under their control to exploit the forest resources commercially. The introduction of railways in India and the process of rapid capitalist industrialization in Britain had generated a huge demand for Indian timber; this demand pressure forced the British colonial government to establish the sole authority of the colonial state on forest resources. In 1910–1917, the British government tightened its control over forest resources by designating 7500 square kilometers of commons as 'reserve forests', thus restricting the local people's access to forest produce. The increased presence of the forest department also led to an increase in *collie utar* (forced labor) and *bardaish* (the mandatory supply of provisions from villagers to colonial bureaucrats). Popular resistance in the form of rebellions and incendiarism made the state pass the Van Panchayat Act in 1931, according to which 30 percent of the forests (Class I Forests and Civil Forests) were given back to the villagers, to be controlled and managed by the relatively autonomous panchayats. Today, more than 6000 Van Panchayats control the use of 13.63 percent of the forest areas in Uttarakhand.

Agarwal (1999) lists the functions of Van Panchayats as follows:

a) Prevent indiscriminate felling and tempering of fencing by villagers.
b) Ensure equitable distribution of forest produce amongst members.
c) Earmark eligible trees for felling.
d) Prevent encroachment on forest land by villagers for agricultural and other purposes.
e) Fix boundary pliers and ensure proper maintenance of pillars.
f) Carry out forestry operations as per advice of forest experts from the forest department.

In the process of discharging these functions, Van Panchayat committees are allowed to impose fines, seize and impound cattle and confiscate weapons of violators/offenders. In addition to such formal measures, informal social sanctions can also be used. The Van Panchayats also have the ability to raise revenues by selling grass, fallen twigs, stones and slates to local markets, tapping resins and felling trees with the prior approval of the forest department, and auctioning mature trees.

Thus, the nature of Van Panchayat rules is such that it is conceivable that they can be used to protect the interests of the élite. The fact that application can be made by 20 percent of the population and that elections to the managing committee are not done formally through secret ballot, can conceivably lead to a capture of such institutions by the powerful village élite, who in turn can enact rules that go against the interests of the marginalized. For example, Agarwal (1999) notes: 'In Uttarakhand, women are responsible to carry fuelwood and fodder from forests, and they know forests more than men, still their participation in Van Panchayats and its decision-making process is negligible. As a result, fodder and fuelwood yielding species are neglected and commercial ones encouraged'.

10.4 Data

In this paper, we have used data collected by the Planning and Policy Research Institute of the Indian Statistical Institute, New Delhi.[5] The objective of this survey was to study 'a large number of villages within a fairly common agro-climatic region with similar ecological characteristics but with disparate socio-economic structure, market access and governance patterns with enough independent variation in each of these factors'. The survey restricted its focus to villages at an average altitude of 1800 meters to 3000 meters, and the sampling frame was adjusted accordingly. On the basis of census data, villages with less than 20 households were dropped, and the remaining set of villages were stratified on the basis of altitude, number of households in a village, and distance to the nearest town. Villages were selected randomly from each stratum.

The sample villages for Uttarakhand are from the six districts of Uttarkashi, Chamoli, Nainital, Bageshwar, Champawat and Pithoragarh. Household surveys were done in 83 villages over a period of three years. A stratified sample of 20 households was surveyed in each village. Stratification was based on land holding and caste.

10.5 Results with respect to intra-community equity

The hypothesis that we want to test is whether the presence of a communally controlled forestry regime in a village (in the form of Van Panchayats) adversely affects the asset-poor and low-caste households in terms of resource collection.

Figure 10.1 shows the collection of firewood (the most widely collected forest product) by households belonging to different asset quintiles in the sample villages. The asset quintiles are constructed by undertaking a principal component analysis of a set of 19 assets; the list of assets

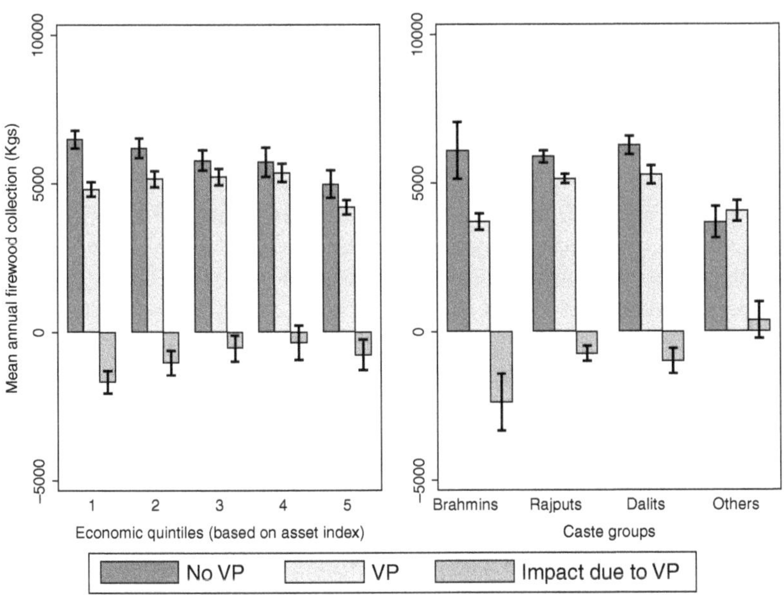

Figure 10.1 Firewood collection for different socio-economic groups (asset quintiles) in Van Panchayat and non-Van Panchayat villages

includes quantity of land owned, number of independent rooms in the house, 10 varieties of consumer durables, 6 varieties of livestock and a certain amount of non-farm business assets.

It is evident from Figure 10.1 that all quintiles except the fourth experience a statistically significant reduction in firewood collection due to the presence of Van Panchayats. However, the quantum of reduction and the proportion of reduction are highest for the lowest two quintiles. The asset-poor experience the largest decline in absolute and proportionate terms. Figure 10.1 also shows the distribution of firewood collection across castes for the two regimes. All caste groups, apart from 'other castes', suggest a statistically significant decline in firewood collection. However Brahmins – the group at the top of the Hindu caste hierarchy, show the largest drop, both in terms of absolute values and percentage. Thus, the social élite seems to bear the cost of 'conservation'. This is interesting, as a much smaller percentage of the Brahmin population is 'poor' compared to Rajputs, Dalits and 'Other Castes'. According to Guha (1989), the social structures of Uttarakhand are somewhat different from the caste hierarchies of the rest of India.

Thus, the classification of the data into only four caste categories might restrict our ability to accurately capture the impact of caste hierarchies on forest management.

The descriptive statistics discussed above do not establish any causal link between VP status and the poverty-collection relationship. For example, if Van Panchayats are formed in villages with better infrastructure, the lower collection of firewood in VP villages might be an artifact of the fact that villages with better infrastructure are expected to have greater access to alternatives to firewood. Similarly, if the poor have larger family sizes, it might exaggerate the impact of Van Panchayat status on firewood collection. In our effort to establish causality, we take recourse to simple linear regressions with additional controls; we do this by controlling separately for assets and caste before combining them into a full specification.

In Table 10.1, Column 1, we start by regressing firewood collection on Van Panchayat Status, our Asset Index, the interaction of the two, and a host of other controls.[6] The coefficient of the VP variable is negative and significant throughout the specifications. We also have a number of significant controls, such as household size (+) and composition, forest quality (+), presence of a primary health centre (–) (an indicator of public infrastructure and prosperity in a village) and availability of the substitute Liquid Petroleum Gas (LPG) (–). The coefficient of the interaction term between VP and asset index is the one of interest, but it has very low statistical significance in this specification. The coefficient of the asset index term is, however, negative and significant. Thus in villages without VP, we have a confirmation of the poverty–environment hypothesis.[7] The poor collect more forest resources, in this case firewood, than do the rich. However, in Column 2, when we add dummies for castes, the coefficient of the interaction term is positive, indicating that the negative relationship between asset ownership and firewood collection is dampened in the presence of a VP.

Recall that Figure 10.1 indicated a non-linear relationship between assets and collection in VP villages. In Column 3 we therefore divide the households into five quintiles to capture non-linearities that might exist in this relationship. We include dummies for each quintile (the lowest quintile being the omitted group) and interactions of each with the Van Panchayat dummy. This way, we capture the significant reduction in collection by the quintile with the most assets. Among the interaction terms, it is only a positive interaction between VP and the fourth asset quintile that is significant (+). These results remain as we add on the caste dummies in Column 4.

In Column 5 we include caste dummies and their interaction with VP status while dropping the asset variables. *Brahmins* are considered to be the omitted category. The dummies for *Rajput* and *Dalit* are insignificant, indicating that these two castes collect firewood in amounts similar to *Brahmins* in a non-VP regime. However *Other castes* consume much less in such a situation. The interaction terms are highly significant when VP status is interacted with *Other castes* while it is only significant at a 10 percent level when interacted with *Dalits* and *Rajputs*. Thus, as observed in Figure 10.1, the negative impact of VP on firewood collection is the highest for *Brahmins*. However, this result has to be interpreted cautiously; *Brahmins* as a group is not unambiguously higher in ritual purity than *Rajputs* (Guha, 1989).

In Specification 6, we allow for interaction of VP status with both asset quintile dummies as well as caste dummies. In this full specification, we replicate all the previously mentioned significant results, and those with higher overall significance.

Until now, our analysis has been based on the fact that the location of VP villages is exogenous. However, the history of Van Panchayats points to possibilities that the choice of Van Panchayats might be endogenous; for example, the fact that the application for Van Panchayats had to be signed by 66 percent of adult population (later reduced to 20 percent) shows that it is likely that the villages with a homogenous population and strong leadership could apply for the status. To the extent that these factors also affect firewood collection patterns in a village, the non-inclusion of such village characteristics might have led to biased estimates. Since we have no historical data about village conditions prior to VP formation, we use village-level fixed effects to control for village heterogeneity.[8] However, the use of fixed effects makes it impossible to identify the impact of village-level variables – most importantly, *VP (Village)* – on firewood collection. However in the context of this paper we are more interested in the interaction of *VP (Village)* with asset indices and caste dummies.

The first two columns of Table 10.2 provide the fixed-effects estimates of specifications discussed in Columns 1 and 2 of Table 10.1. In both specifications, the asset index is negatively significant while the interaction is positively significant. This reinforces the previous results. In Columns 3 and 4 we have fixed-effect estimates of a specification similar to those in Columns 3 and 4 of Table 10.2, respectively.

The estimates mimic the results obtained from the OLS estimations; however, in the specifications that involve interaction between caste and VP status (Columns 5 and 6 of Table 10.2), we do not find any differential impact across castes. This is different from our results in the OLS estimations; Columns 5 and 6 of Table 10.1 show *Brahmins* bearing the biggest burden of reduction in firewood collection. The introduction of

Table 10.1 Linear regressions of annual firewood collection[a]

	Dependent variable: annual firewood collection in kilograms				
	(1)	(2)	(3)	(4)	(5)
VP (village)	–741.33***	–753.52***	–807.15***	–792.93***	–635.11***
Asset index	–030.89***	–912.15***			
VP (village) × asset index	1197.46	1308.40*			
Second asset quintile			–55.02	–44.51	
Third asset quintile			–296.30	–281.08	
Fourth asset quintile			–372.72	–347.22	
Fifth asset quintile			–236.84***	–188.03***	
VP(village) × second asset quintile			169.07	143.70	
VP (village) × third asset quintile			426.09	421.09	
VP (village) × fourth asset quintile			625.96**	641.98**	
VP (village) × fifth asset quintile			349.28	379.11	
Rajput		293.57		326.05	–407.80
Dalit		380.67		448.02	–192.21
Other castes		–97.83		–136.44	–829.92***
VP (village) × Rajput					1172.34*
VP (village) × Dalit					1134.34*
VP (village) × Other caste					2066.9***
Adjusted household size	668.76***	661.46***	661.76***	653.72***	605.23***
Share of men (>16 years)	945.92***	902.62**	812.50**	760.72**	959.70***

Share of women (>16 years)	1469.0***	1377.6***	1321.7***	1215.9***	1429.0***
Share of boys (≥6 yrs & ≤ 16 yrs)	976.17*	880.53*	908.29*	793.81	1287.58**
Share of girls (≥6 yrs & ≤ 16 yrs)	1968.2***	1865.0***	1893.0***	1767.5***	2278.3***
Male headed household	302.00**	273.01*	342.65**	305.49**	503.32***
Education of household head	4.25	5.56	−2.01	0.16	−23.10
No. of private trees	0.59	0.71	0.44	0.60	−0.31
Per capita forest area	−65.22	−28.31	−83.81	−37.66	−60.06
Forest quality: basal area	7.64**	7.02*	8.30**	7.55*	7.92**
Distance to forest	−38.05	−45.30	−39.89	−47.69	−33.05
Altitude of village	0.12	0.15	0.19	0.22	0.16
Electricity in village	−155.04	−165.59	−192.84	−207.56	−202.50
PHC in village	−521.81***	−529.67***	−574.03***	−581.74***	−671.32***
Link to motorable road	−59.59	−52.31	−5.53	0.98	−4.88
Availability of LPG	−386.52***	−374.20***	−419.40***	−404.34***	−526.27***
Constant	2647.0***	2414.1***	2157.0***	1906.9**	2428.0**
Observations	1552	1552	1552	1552	1555
R^2	0.35	0.35	0.35	0.35	0.33
Adjusted R^2	0.34	0.34	0.34	0.34	0.32

Note: [a] ***Significant at the 1% level, **at the 5% level, *at the 10% level.

Table 10.2 Linear regression of annual firewood collection with village fixed effects[a]

	Dependent variable: Annual firewood collection in kilograms				
	(1)	(2)	(3)	(4)	(5)
Asset index	−3161.59***	−3149.44***			
VP (Village) × asset index	1596.39**	1639.58**			
Second asset quintile			51.69	50.19	
Third asset quintile			−76.17	−77.41	
Fourth asset quintile			−46.45	−47.89	
Fifth asset quintile			−865.32***	−860.91***	
VP (village) × second asset quintile			234.93	224.47	
VP (Village) × third asset quintile			445.98	440.18	
VP (village) × fourth asset quintile			628.68**	625.09**	
VP (village) × fifth asset quintile			543.80	545.02	
Rajput				23.19	−242.04
Dalit				23.54	−175.47
Other castes				−308.73	−222.08
VP (village) × Rajput					364.44
VP (village) × Dalit					340.88
VP (village) × other caste					−282.66
Adjusted household size	630.21***	627.89***	615.56***	613.90***	585.10***
Share of men (>16 years)	726.33*	732.58*	633.41	636.49	755.62*
Share of women (>16 years)	1250.53***	1235.35***	1095.89***	1082.58***	1259.96***
Share of boys (≥6 yrs. & ≤ 16 yrs.)	406.69	409.08	389.92	388.11	650.39
Share of girls (≥6 yrs. & ≤ 16 yrs.)	1699.59***	1683.01***	1648.13***	1630.54***	1891.22**
Male headed household	238.16	233.96	275.67*	269.89*	388.64**
Education of household head	11.64	11.57	5.21	5.58	−5.92
No. of private trees	0.41	0.40	0.18	0.19	−0.59
Constant	2166.71***	2202.50***	1769.74***	1780.76***	1795.10***
Observations	1552	1552	1552	1552	1555
R^2	0.22	0.22	0.22	0.23	0.20
Adjusted R^2	0.17	0.17	0.18	0.17	0.15

Note: [a] *** Significant at the 1% level, ** at the 5% level, * at the 10% level.

fixed effect washes away all the caste effect we saw earlier. However, the results regarding differential impact across asset quintiles are robust to introduction of fixed effects.

The above results are suggestive of the fact that it is the poor who bear a disproportionate level of cost in the process of conserving forests. But the marginalized caste groups, on the other hand, do not experience additional costs compared to groups at the top of social hierarchy; introducing fixed effects ensures that all the effects on the caste axis that we obtain under OLS are washed away. Thus it is economic rather than social disadvantage that conditions the costs of conservation borne by households.

10.6 Results with respect to efficiency of firewood production

In this section, we try to test the economic efficiency of different forest governance regimes. In particular, we want to test if the average productivity of firewood collection from VP forests with respect to labor is higher than the average productivity of labor in collection from non-VP forests. On one hand, communitarian regimes have the possibility of decreasing the average productivity of labor by introducing restriction on collection from nearby forests or by regulating the nature of lopping. Government Forests, which are often *de facto* open access forests, do not have such restrictions. However by reducing firewood collection, communitarian regimes might facilitate forest regeneration (assuming that the forest was degraded to begin with) and enhance the biomass availability in the long run. Baland et al. (2010) showed the importance of the institution of Van Panchayats in improving the quality of forests, measured in terms of canopy cover, basal area and basal volume. Since both the effects are possible in Uttarakhand, the dominance of one over the other is a question that needs to be tested empirically by estimating the labor productivity.

In this dataset, we have detailed information on time allocation by different members of a household on an average day, and we have explicit information on the time spent in collection activities. Using this information, we can calculate the total hours spent by the various members of a household in firewood collection. Unfortunately, we have no information about the allocation of firewood collection time across different forests or different type of forests; thus, to estimate the marginal productivity of labor in the two regimes, we restrict our attention to only those villages that have access to only one kind of forest: either Van Panchayat (VP) forests or non-Van Panchayat forests. Villages that have access to both kinds of forest are dropped from the sample. This restricts our sample to 46 villages (916 households) of which 9 villages (178 households) have Van Panchayats. Using this sample we have tried to estimate the firewood production function in both of those regimes.

In Table 10.3, we compare the labor hours allocated to firewood collection by households every day in the firewood collection season. We find that for every asset quintile and caste group, households spend more time on collection when they are in a non-VP regime. The differences are higher for the lowest asset group and *Dalits*. *Rajputs* experience very little reduction in the time allocated; as mentioned earlier, the source of this reduction might be exogenous (due to restrictions on time spent in forests) or endogenous (restrictions on the kind of trees that can be lopped, mode of lopping and area where lopping is allowed), and either form of restriction might reduce the productivity of labor spent on firewood collection. Reduced productivity will reduce time allocation if we assume the opportunity cost of time to be unchanged. It might also be the case that VPs improve the quality of forest, thereby ensuring that a certain quantity of firewood might be collected in less time. This explanation is based on the assumption that a household has a fairly fixed demand for firewood, which it tries to collect efficiently. The analysis below tries to disentangle these effects.

Table 10.4 shows the mean average product of firewood production across different socio-economic groups for the two regimes. There is no statistically significant difference between the two regimes except in the fourth quintile and two caste groups: *Dalits* and *Other castes*; for these three groups, the average product is much higher in the VP regimes. Now average productivity can rise due to increase in productivity (upward shift of the production function) or due to reduction in labor use (the production function remaining unchanged). We know from Table 10.5 that the labor spent on firewood collection is lower in VP villages and, as mentioned earlier, this might be because of exogenous or endogenous reasons. We try to plot the average product as a function of labor to find out the source of increase in AP_L in VP villages.

We use local polynomial regression to non-parametrically plot the relationship between average product and time spent on firewood collection (Figure 10.2); we do this separately for the two regimes. The average product curve for the VP regimes lies entirely below the curve for non-VP regime, lending credence to the hypothesis that restriction imposed on nature of extractions (either on the kind of trees that can be lopped, or through insistence on ecologically sustainable lopping methods) reduces the returns from labor spent on collection. However the 95 percent confidence intervals of the two curves overlap each other

Table 10.3 Labor allocated per household to firewood collection during an average day in the firewood collection season[a]

	Non-VP	VP	p-value for test of equality (adjusted Wald Test)
Asset quintiles			
1	8.45	5.80	0.02**
2	8.59	6.70	0.01**
3	8.34	6.68	0.02**
4	8.93	6.35	0.00***
5	8.39	6.51	0.02**
Caste			
Brahmins	9.34	6.40	0.03**
Rajputs	8.47	7.41	0.03**
Dalits	8.58	5.53	0.00***
Others	7.91	5.16	0.01**
Total sample	8.53	6.47	0.00***

Notes: [a] The third columns show the t-statistic for the equality of means test. *** Significant at the 1% level, ** at the 5% level.

Table 10.4 Average product of firewood collection[a]

	Non-VP	VP	p-value for test of equality (Adjusted Wald Test)
Asset quintiles			
1	887.81	989.49	0.44
2	804.99	897.54	0.30
3	828.04	854.12	0.76
4	726.96	878.42	0.02**
5	672.86	802.26	0.2
Caste			
Brahmins	715.94	752.81	0.68
Rajputs	797.16	830.93	0.58
Dalits	846.50	991.53	0.01**
Others	566.35	1008.47	0.04**
Total sample	800.74	878.37 (43.43)	0.10*

Notes: (= Annual Firewood Collection/Time Spent by household on an average day in firewood collection season).
[a] Significant ** at the 5% level, * at the 10% level. The last column shows the t-statistic for the equality of means test.

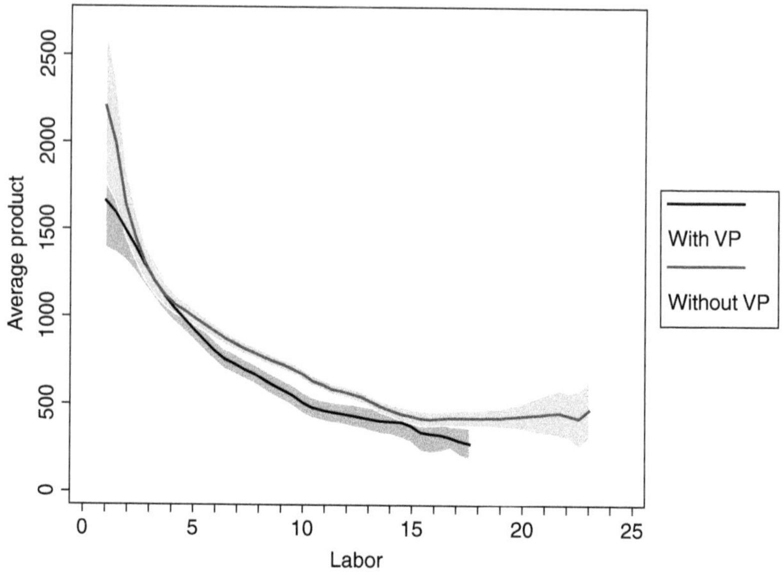

Figure 10.2 Relationship between average product and labor spent on firewood collection

Note: Curve fitted non-parametrically using locally weighted scatter plot smoothing.

at very high and very low values of labor spent. Figure 10.3 above does not control for any variable other than labor; we try to control for these other variables using parametric models.

Let us assume that the production function has a functional form like:

$$F = A(x)L\alpha \tag{1}$$

where F is the firewood collected, L is labor spent in collection and A is the productivity parameter which is a function of x. Note that the function $A(x)$ and the parameter α can be different for VP and non-VP households. The average product is given by:

$$AP_L = F/L = A(x)L\alpha^{-1} \tag{2}$$

or,

$$log(F/L) = log\ A(x) + (\alpha - 1)log\ L \tag{3}$$

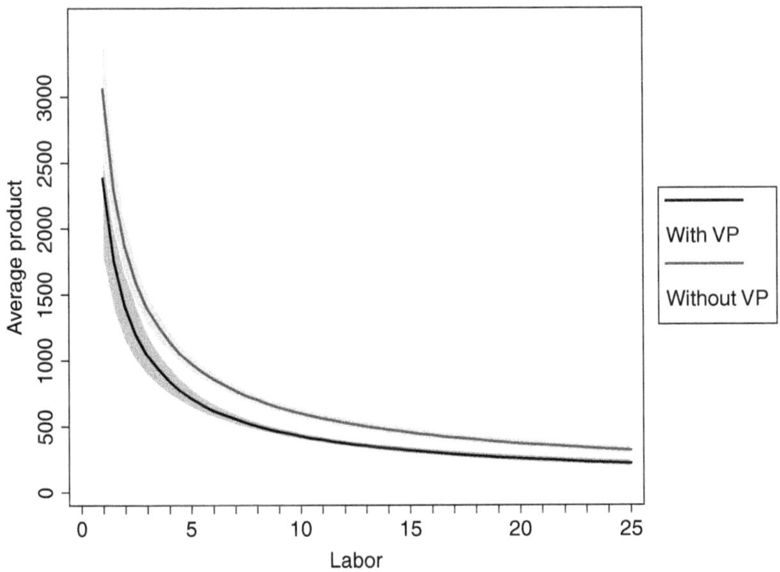

Figure 10.3 Graphical representation of Table 10.6

Note: Variables other than Labor held constant at their means.

Thus we estimate the population regression function:

$$log(F/L) = b_0 + b_1VP + b_2logL + b_3(VP * log\ L) + \varepsilon \quad (4)$$

Table 10.5 has the coefficients estimated for different functional forms. The coefficient of the VP dummy and its interaction with the labor is negative but never significant. Thus, everything else being constant, the average product schedule is identical for VP households and non-VP households. This implies that there is no upward shift in the firewood production function as a result of a shift in the VP regime. Hence the higher average product for VP households that we observe in earlier tables is in fact due to reduced time spent on firewood collection and not due to productivity shifts. It should be noted that earlier work by Baland et al. (2010) shows that VP forests are of better quality than non-VP forests. However, our results are robust to the inclusion (or exclusion) of forest quality as a control. It is conceivable that the improvement in forest quality does not translate to higher productivity due to extraction rules that aims to maximize the conservation objective.

Note that in the above regressions, we don't allow controls other than the log of labor for firewood collection to have differential impact on the

Table 10.5 Relationship between average productivity of labor and labor hours[a]

Dependent Variable: log(AP_L)	**(1)**	**(2)**	**(3)**	**(4)**	**(5)**	**(6)**
Dummy: VP household	−0.086	−0.082	−0.100	−0.091	−0.095	−0.083
log (firewood labor)	−0.691***		−0.699***	−0.710***		
Interaction: log (firewood labor) × VP household dummy	−0.047		−0.063	−0.037		
Log (age adjusted firewood labor)		−0.687***			−0.692***	−0.703***
Interaction: log (age adjusted firewood labor) × VP household dummy		−0.050			−0.067	−0.043
Llog (distance to forest)			−0.092	−0.112*	−0.096	−0.115**
log (per capita forest area)			−0.029	−0.024	−0.028	−0.024
log (basal area)				0.238**		0.238*
log (altitude of forest)			0.174	−0.083	0.184	−0.075
Constant	7.989***	7.990***	6.709***	7.798***	6.631***	7.728***
Observations	916	916	857	857	857	857
R2	0.48	0.48	0.49	0.50	0.49	0.50

Note: [a] *** Significant at the 1% level, ** at the 5% level, * at the 10% level.

log of average product (AP_L) for the two regimes. In Table 10.6, we estimate the functions separately for the two regimes. In addition to labor, distance to forest has a negative and significant coefficient for the VP regime. However, this is not the case for the non-VP regime. Also, forest quality has a positive and significant effect in the non-VP regime, but not in the VP regime. This suggests that restrictions imposed in VP regimes are not sensitive to forest quality. The overall Chow test rejects the null hypothesis. In Figure 10.3, we plot the result obtained in Table 10.6, holding variables other than labor constant at their mean values. The average productivity curve of VP regime lies consistently below that for the non-VP regime. This suggests that restrictions imposed in VP regimes shift the average productivity schedule downwards. However, reduced labor allocation to firewood collection ensures higher average productivity of labor for VP households compared to non-VP households.

Table 10.6 Relationship between average productivity of labor and labor hours (using a flexible functional form)[a]

Dependent variable: log (AP_L)	**VP**	**Non-VP**	**t-test**
log (firewood labor)	−0.754***	−0.712***	0.61
log (distance to forest)	−0.242***	−0.087	1.47
log (per capita forest area)	−0.003	0.002	0.17
log (basal area)	−0.123	0.344***	2.36
log (altitude of forest)	1.078**	−0.11	2.15
Constant	0.14	7.58***	1.99
Observations	139	718	
R2	0.62	0.47	
Chow test (p-value)	0.00		

Note: [a] *** Significant at the 1% level, ** at the 5% level.

10.7 Conclusion

In the larger political economy literature, the impact of devolution of power on within-community distribution of benefits has often been studied and questioned (Dasgupta and Beard, 2007; Prinsen and Titeca, 2008). The issue of distributional impact of devolution has, however more rarely been studied in the context of natural resource management reform. While studies have analyzed issues of inequality and injustice within specific management regimes (Omvedt, 1997; Kumar, 2002), comparison has rarely been made across regimes. This specific question achieves great importance in South Asia, as the poor depend heavily on common natural resources for survival in this region (Jodha, 1986; Kumar, 2002). South Asia has high levels of economic and social inequality. In the Hindu majority countries of India and Nepal, social inequality expresses itself in the form of caste distribution. Thus, this essay tries to understand the distributional effects of devolution of natural resource management by studying the specific example of Van Panchayats in Uttarakhand.

In this chapter, we do find some evidence that presence of Van Panchayats leads to reduced firewood collection by households. The reduction in collection is significantly higher at the lower end of the household distribution. 'Poor' households (that is, households with low assets) experience a large reduction in collection in both absolute and proportionate terms. In fact, in Van Panchayat villages, the relationship between firewood collection and asset holding becomes positive for the lower half of asset distribution. However, we find no such adverse effect on grounds of caste; Brahmins, who are at the top of the social hierarchy, experience the largest decline in firewood collection, compared to other caste groups when fixed effects are not used.

However, the use of fixed effects washes away all caste effects of the impact of VP management. This result has important implications for policy. While creating communitarian forest institutions like JFM, government has tried to ensure equity by mandating representation of marginalized identity groups like *Dalits*, *Other Backward Castes*, tribal peoples and women. However, this study shows that economic status rather than caste is the major axis around which the differential impact of a communitarian regime is felt. Reservations for *Dalits* or *Backward Castes* might indirectly ensure representation of the poor since such categories are most often poorer than upper castes. However, ensuring representation of the economically marginalized might be a more direct way of achieving intra-community equity.

While this paper suggests that community forestry might have adverse distributional consequences, some issues require further investigation. The initial results in this paper (obtained using classical regression techniques) are based on the assumption of exogeneity of Van Panchayat location. However, as villages have to initiate the process of Van Panchayat formation, the location of VPs might be endogenous. Later, we try to control for such endogeneity by using village fixed effects. However, in the process of estimation using fixed effects, we lose the information about the impact of variables defined at village level. To control for that, we need credible instruments for VP location. Prior to 1947, only British-controlled areas could formally form VPs, and besides this, the Kumaon Association played an important role in organizing people to assert their forest rights. Thus, even within British-controlled areas, villages in Kumaon should have a higher probability of forming VPs. This can be used to create instruments for VP location. As villagers had to come to Nainital to apply for VP formation, it is also likely that villages closer to Nainital will have higher chance of forming VPs. We plan to do further research on this after collecting secondary information to create such instruments.

Acknowledgement

The authors would like to thank Professor Dilip Mookherjee of Boston University, for generous access to the data used in this chapter, and the editors Kei Otsuka and Stein T. Holden for constructive comments on previous drafts. We would also like to thank E. Somanathan, Debraj Ray, Sudha Vasan and Anirban Kar for their useful comments. Financial support from the Environment for Development initiative and the Centre for Land Tenure Studies for participation in workshops and financial support by the FORMAS funded program Human Cooperation to Manage Natural Resources (COMMONS) is gratefully acknowledged.

Notes

1. Banerjee writes '...although the potential of JFM is high, in the overall Indian forestry situation, the impact is small. Only 2% of the forests of India have been covered by JFM so far. Only degraded forests are being offered for joint forest management. Leaving out the closed and high forests from the JFM operation is counterproductive as the degraded forests of to-day are the closed forests of yesteryear. And the fate of the present day closed forests will be the same over time unless the people are involved in their management' (p. 16).
2. Nepal has a lot of similarity with Uttarakhand in terms of its geography. Both the regions have parts that overlap the Greater Himalayas, the Middle Himalayas, Shivaliks and the Terai. They share demographic similarity as well with more than 80 percent of the population being Hindus. However, Uttarakhand has a higher percentage of 'untouchable' castes (*Dalits*) (around 17 percent) compared to Nepal (12 percent). Nepal, on the other hand, has a higher percentage of tribal peoples (*Janajatis*). While informal communal forestry institutions are old in both Uttarakhand and Nepal, formal institutions evolved much earlier in Uttarakhand than Nepal. Van Panchayats were set up by the British–Indian government in the 1930s as a response to protest movements by people who felt threatened by the colonial forestry policy. The community forestry program in Nepal was initiated by the government in the late 1970s in response to high rates of deforestation due to the nationalization of forests. Unlike JFM committees in India, both Van Panchayats in Uttarakhand and FUGs in Nepal enjoy substantial autonomy in decision making.
3. Champawat, Almora, Bageshwar and Pithoragarh constituted the erstwhile British district of Almora (Kumaon Division). Nainital and Udham Singh Nagar were a part of the British district of Nainital (Kumaon Division). Chamoli, Rudraprayag and Pauri constituted the British Garhwal District (Kumaon District). Haridwar and Dehradun were neither a part of the princely state of Tehri Garhwal nor a part of the Kumaon Division of United Provinces.
4. Certain parts of the state of Uttarakhand were neither a part of Tehri Garhwal nor a part of Kumaon division (British Garhwal district and Kumaon district).
5. We are extremely grateful to Prof. Dilip Mookherjee of Boston University for allowing us to use this data.
6. Only two households report no firewood collection. Thus we do not have a serious problem regarding censoring.
7. The poverty–environment Hypothesis states that natural resource extraction falls as households become richer.

8. Hausman tests suggest in most cases fixed effects to be the correct specification, as compared to a random-effects model.

References

Acheson, J. (1988) *The Lobster Gangs of Maine* (New England Universities Press).

Adhikari, B. (2008) 'Caste and Social Justice in Common Property Forest Management in Nepal', Presented at the 16th Annual Conference of European Association of Environmental and Resource Economists (EAERE), Gothenburg, Sweden.

Agarwal, B. (2001) 'Participatory Exclusions, Community Forestry, and Gender: An Analysis for South Asia and a Conceptual Framework', *World Development*, 29, 1623–48.

Agarwal, R. (1999) 'Van Panchayats in Uttarakhand: A Case Study', *Economic and Political Weekly*, 34(39), 2779–81.

Baland, J.M., Bardhan, P., Das, S. and Mookherjee, D. (2010) 'Forests to the People: Decentralization and Forest Degradation in the Indian Himalayas', *World Development*, 38(11), 1642–56

Bandhyopadhyay, S. and Shyamsundar, P. (2004) 'Fuelwood Consumption and Participation in Community Forestry in India', World Bank Policy Research Working Paper 3331.

Banerjee, A. (1997) Decentralization and Devolution of Forest Management in Asia and the Pacific. FAO Working Paper No: APFSOS/WP/21. ftp://ftp.fao.org/docrep/fao/W7712E/W7712E00.pdf (accessed on 2 April 2012).

Banjade, M., Luintel, H. and Neupane, H. (2004) 'An Action and Learning Process for Social Inclusion in Community Forestry', Proceedings of the Fourth National Workshop on Community Forestry, 480–88.

Berkes, F. (1986) 'Local Level Management and the Commons Problem: A Comparative Study of Turkish Coastal Fisheries', *Marine Policy*, 10, 215–29.

Chand, N.B. (2011) 'Production Efficiency of Community Forestry in Nepal : A Stochastic Frontier Analysis', Ph.D. Thesis. Lincoln University, Christchurch.

Chichilnisky, G. (1994) 'North South Trade and the Global Environment', *American Economic Review*, 84(4), 851–74.

Colchester, M. (1994) 'Sustaining the Forests: The Community-Based Approach in South and South-East Asia', *Development and Change*, 25, 69–100.

Dasgupta, A. and Beard, V. A. (2007) 'Community Driven Development, Collective Action and Elite Capture in Indonesia', *Development and Change*, 38, 229–49.

Edmonds, E. (2002) 'Government Initiated Community Resource Management and Local Resource Extraction from Nepal's Forests', *Journal of Development Economics* 68(1), 89–115.

Gilmour, D., King, G. and Hobley, M. (1989) 'Management of Forests for Local Use in the Hills of Nepal: Changing Forest Management Paradigms', *Journal of World Forest Resource Management*, 4, 93–110.

Guha, R. (1989) *The Unquiet Woods*, Oxford University Press.

Jodha, N.S. (1986) 'Common Property Resources and Rural Poor in Dry Regions of India', *Economic and Political Weekly*, 21(27), 1169–81.

Köhlin, G. and Amacher, G.S. (2005) 'Welfare Implications of Community Forest Plantations in Developing Countries: The Orissa Social Forestry Project', *American Journal of Agricultural Economics*, 87(4), 855–69.

Kothari, A. (2011) 'Stories of Hope: Towards a Radical Ecological Democracy', Common Voices, Foundation of Ecological Security, 6, 38–48.

Kumar, S. (2002) '"Does" "Participation" in Common Pool Resource Management Help the Poor? A Social Cost-Benefit Analysis of Joint Forest Management in Jharkhand, India', *World Development*, 30, 763–82.

Lele, S. and Borgoyary, M. (2008) 'Governing Local Forests: JFM and Beyond', National Workshop on Beyond JFM: Rethinking the Forest Question in India, CISED and Winrock International India.

Malla, Y., Neupane, H. and Branney, P. (2003) 'Why aren't Poor People Benefiting More from Community Forestry?' *Journal of Forest and Livelihood*, 3, 78–93.

Omvedt, G. (1997) 'Why Dalits dislike environmentalists?' *The Hindu*, 24 June 1997, Section: Opinion.

Ostrom, E. (1990) *Governing the Commons: The Evolution of Institutions for Collective Action* (Cambridge, Massachusetts: Harvard University Press).

Prinsen, G. and Titeca, K. (2008) 'Uganda's Decentralised Primary Education: Musical Chairs and Inverted Elite Capture in School Management Committees', *Public Administration and Development*, 28(2), 149–64.

Sakurai, T., Rayamajhi, S., Pokharel, R.K. and Otsuka, K. (2004) 'Efficiency of Timber Production in Community and Private Forestry in Nepal', *Environment and Development Economics*, 9, 539–61.

Sarin, M., Ray, L., Raju, M., Chatterjee, M., Banerjee, N. and Hiremath, S. (1998) 'Who is Gaining? Who is Losing? Gender and Equity Concerns in Joint Forest Management', SPWD, New Delhi.

Sarin, M., and Singh, N.M., Sundar, N. and Bhogal, R.K. (2003) 'Devolution as a Threat to Democratic Decision-making in Forestry? Findings from Three Sates in India', Working Paper 197, Overseas Development Institute.

Sethi, R. and Somanathan, E. (1996) 'The Evolution of Social Norms in Common Property Resource Use', *The American Economic Review*, 86(4), 766–88.

Singh, K.D., Sinha, B. and Mukherjee, S.D. (2005) 'Exploring Options for Joint Forest Management (JFM) in India', Rome, FAO and Washington DC, World Bank.

Somanathan, E., Prabhakar, R. and Mehta, B.S. (2005) 'Does Decentralization Work? Forest Conservation in the Himalayas', BREAD Working Paper No. 096.

Sundar, N. (2000) 'Unpacking the "Joint" in Joint Forest Management', *Development and Change*, 31, 255–79.

Tamuli, J. and Chowdhury, S. (2009) 'RE Looking at Forest Policies in Assam: Facilitating Reserved Forests as de Facto Open Access', MPRA Paper No. 29560, posted 11 May 2011.

Timsina, N.P. (2003) 'Promoting Social Justice and Conserving Montane Forest Environments: A Case Study of Nepal's Community Forestry Programme', *The Geographical Journal*, 169, 236–42.

11

Tenure Security and Investment Effects of Forest Tenure Reform in China

Stein T. Holden, Yuanyuan Yi, Xuemei Jiang and Jintao Xu

11.1 Introduction

Tenure security in land is considered crucial in order to stimulate investment and create economic growth, for three reasons; higher expected returns from investment, better functioning land markets allowing land transfers to more efficient producers, and better access to credit (Demsetz, 1967; Besley, 1995; Brasselle et al., 2002). Land allocation has played a special role in China as a key resource that has been shared based on strong equity principles in rural areas where land has been the main resource pillar of the economy (Carter and Yao, 1998; Jacoby et al., 2002). Various forms of collective and individual management have been tested with varying success, but a breakthrough came with the Household Responsibility System from the late 1970s which has stimulated strong economic growth since the 1980s. This reform primarily focused on agricultural land which was allocated to individual households and enhanced private production incentives. A similar reform, the 'Three Fixes' policy, was started for forest land from 1981, and by 1986 nearly 70 percent of the collectively-owned forest land had been transferred to individual household management (Xu and Jiang, 2009). The experiences from this reform were mixed and less positive in southern China, causing a partial reversal of the reform. However, the subsequent relatively poor performance of the forestry sector leading to low generation of revenues and poor forest management led to a second forest tenure reform after year 2000, again with a stronger emphasis on forest management by individual households.

This study aims to provide new evidence on the logic of forest land allocation to households in three provinces in southern China; Fujian, Jiangxi, and Yunnan. While all these three provinces have large forest areas, there were important historical differences between them in how they dealt with the forest tenure reforms in the 1980s, and this may also affect how they deal with the new reform based on past experience. First, we assess what factors affected the allocation of forest land to individual households in the 1980s reform, as well as in the 2000 reform, to see if these factors have changed. This includes assessing the importance of the equity motive in forest land allocation, and the effect of local village elections. Second, we assess households' perceived tenure security for individual forest plots and group-controlled plots and factors influencing this level of tenure security. In particular, we assess whether the difference in past policies in the three provinces may have created differences in tenure security across provinces. We also assess whether provision of forest land certificates has contributed to the enhancement of tenure security and investment in forest land, and whether past agricultural land readjustments and the quality of village leaders have impacts on tenure security. Finally, we assess how the bundle of property rights on household forest plots for households / plots with or without a certificate is related to investment on forest land. The main finding of policy relevance is that provision of written proof of time-restricted ownership in the form of a forest land certificate has increased tenure security and forestry investment. In addition, the effects are significant and strong beyond the impact of the bundle of rights on household plot level tenure security and investment. No significant impact was, however, found from past agricultural land adjustments on tenure security, while there was a negative correlation between past land adjustments and the amount of forest land allocated to households, possibly indicating a negative effect on the demand for forest land. Democratic village elections did not have any positive effect on tenure security but appear to have stimulated forest land allocation during the New Forest Tenure Reform.

The structure of the chapter is as follows. Section 11.2 puts tenure security into a theoretical and empirical context; Section 11.3 gives a brief review of past experiences with forest and agricultural tenure reforms in China. The New Forest Tenure Reform is explained in Section 11.4, followed by the descriptive statistics of the data this study is going to use in Section 11.5. The analysis of forest land allocation is conducted in Section 11.6, and the analyses of tenure security and investment on forest land in Sections 11.7 and 11.8. Finally, Section 11.9 concludes.

11.2 Tenure security in theory and practice

Tenure security is one of the three fundamental neoclassical arguments for land tenure reform (Besley, 1995; Brasselle et al., 2002), the others being transferability (gains from trade) and credit access (using land as collateral), all important to stimulate investment, more efficient land use and economic growth. Land tenure reform may explicitly aim to enhance tenure security, as an important catalyst which in turn stimulates investment. Expected additional important benefits from land reform are equity and poverty-reduction effects. The positive mutual relationship between tenure security and investment implies an endogenous bias problem and thus creates a challenge for empirical analyses.

Broadly we think that land tenure security at farm plot level depends on many factors, including the specific farm plot characteristics, the household owner or operator characteristics, the land tenure characteristics, the local institutional (including market) characteristics, past and present land policies, cultural norms and the historical context.

We can broadly distinguish between three types of approaches to the assessment of tenure security or insecurity: these approaches are known as the bundle of rights, the hazard analysis of individual plot tenures, and the direct inquiry or perception.

Examples of applications of the bundle of rights approach include Brasselle et al. (2002) who developed a ranking based on a hierarchy of rights at household level in a study in Burkina Faso. The hazard analysis relates the predicted 'hazards of expropriation' to some land-specific investment, or earlier land redistributions, or other proxies, as an indicator of tenure insecurity. Studies using this approach include Carter and Yao (1998), Jacoby et al. (2002), Brandt et al. (2002) and Rozelle et al. (2002) in China. Meanwhile, Brandt et al. (2002) analyzed explanations of frequency and intensity of land readjustments. Then Carter and Yao (1998) used household panel data and simulations to show that reducing the number of reallocations by one would increase investment to an extent that in the end would raise output by about 5 percent. Jacoby et al. (2002) assessed the impact of expropriation risk on investment in organic fertilizer use. Studies using the direct perceptions of tenure security approach include Holden and Yohannes (2002) in Ethiopia.

In this study we combine the three approaches and specifically assess how earlier land readjustments are related to current perceptions of future tenure security at the household forest plot level. Also we assess how a disaggregated bundle of land rights at household forest plot level as well as an aggregated index of these rights are associated with the perceptions of future tenure security. Furthermore, we assess how the New Forest Tenure Reform and distribution of forest land certificates has affected the perceptions of future tenure security. Finally, the impact of tenure security perceptions and forest land rights, as well as the individualized certification of forest land on forestry investment are evaluated.

11.3 Tenure security and forest tenure reforms in China: a review

There have been many dramatic changes in the land tenure systems in China over the last 60 years. For forest lands, these changes include collectivization of private forests of farm households in 1956, the taking of private trees around homesteads by the communes in 1958, returning the trees around homesteads to households in 1961–1962, and then taking these private trees from households again in the period 1966–1980 (Liu and Edmunds, 2003). It is obvious that such frequent policy changes create tenure insecurity among households.

Forest areas in China before 1981 may be classified into state-owned forests and collective forests, of which the collective forests accounted for 61 percent. From 1981, China started experimenting with new forms of management for its collective forests by establishing three forms of tenure; family plots, 'responsibility hills' (also managed by individual households), and collective management.

The collective owns the family plots but the use rights are distributed to households, and trees planted on the plots are owned by the households. For responsibility hills, the collective owns both the land and the trees, and decision making is shared by the collective and households. For collective management, ownership is collective for land and trees, and decision making is by village leadership (Liu and Edmunds, 2003). Initially it was illegal to transfer the use rights of family plots, but such transfers started in the early 1990s and were legalized by the Revised Forest Tenure Law of 1998. In the early 1980s, 31 million ha of forest land was transferred to 57 million households. This area of family plots remained steady for the rest of the century, while there was a slight decline in responsibility hill areas from 1984 to 1990. This was partly due to a conversion to family plots and partly due to a conversion back to collective management.

Forest tenure and tax policies were quite different in Northern China vs. Southern China (Yin et al., 2003). In Northern China households were assigned nearby forest areas and bare lands for re-forestation, and this has almost doubled the contracted forest area. Households were allowed to sell trees at market prices, harvest permits were not required and taxes were low, stimulating households to plant trees.

In Southern China, the experience with the tenure reform of the early 1980s was that it caused a decline in forest stocks, and this caused some responsibility hill areas to be taken back into collective management. No clear duration was at first given for the family forest plots, while responsibility hills were contracted for just 5–15 years, which was too short for most timber species. Most of the forest land allocated as family plots had been deforested already and was given to the household on condition that they plant trees there. This was similar to the responsibility to use the agricultural land that had been allocated to individual households. Lack of use or lack of planting of trees therefore resulted in higher tenure insecurity as such lands were recovered by the collectives and either redistributed to other households, or leased out, or converted back to collective management. According to Liu and Edmunds (2003) this policy did not succeed in enhancing investment but in fact had the opposite effect of discouraging the replanting of trees after harvesting. This may also have been a result of the frequent changes in earlier policies, and may have initiated myopic harvesting strategies (Albers et al., 1998; Yin, 1998).

Other types of policy that may affect tenure security is the logging bans that have been introduced in the upper watersheds of the Yellow and Yangtze rivers, plus logging quotas, taxes and fees on harvesting, and marketing restrictions. Whether these affect expected profitability only directly, or indirectly as well through an effect on tenure insecurity would have to be examined more carefully. In either case they may affect investment and harvesting behavior of individual households.

The agricultural land contracts under the Household Responsibility System were renewed in the late 1990s, and this should have contributed positively to the feeling of tenure security for forest lands as well. The reallocation of village land has been an instrument to ensure equitable land distribution, and has been a substitute for missing land markets in China and several other countries. It has also been used to facilitate the collection of taxes and production quotas, and may be used in rent-seeking by local cadres (Brandt et al., 2002). There is, however, large local variation in the extent of tenure insecurity as a consequence of the variation in the ways local governments have practised land adjustments (Brandt et al., 2002). It is also possible that such adjustments may have affected forest land distribution to households; for example, villages with a more stringent adjustment philosophy for agricultural land may have the same for forest land. This would imply that household size is an important determinant of forest land allocation to households. On the other hand, if land adjustments create tenure insecurity, this may also reduce the demand for forest land and lead to a negative effect from such readjustments to forest land distributions. However, recent law reforms like the Rural Land Contracting Law of 2003 may have reduced the impact of past land adjustments on current perceptions of tenure security. This may, however, depend on the degree to which the new laws have become locally known and implemented.

The introduction of the Villager Committee Organization Law in 1988 allowed villages in China to conduct competitive elections of a village leader and a village committee consisting of four to seven members. Considerable variation has been identified in the speed with which this law has been implemented and also in the ways in which it has been implemented (Kennedy et al., 2004); they found, in a study in Shaanxi province, that more open elections were related to perceptions of fairer land reallocations.

Wang (2008) found in a nationwide study that higher quality village elections have improved the quality of rural governance by holding village cadres more accountable to peasants' demands, as demonstrated in the higher level of peasant satisfaction with the performance of village committees in the provision of public services; the effect of village elections in holding cadres accountable was significantly higher in villages that owned substantial collective resources.

Our data contain variables for trust in village leader, the number of village leaders since 1990, and the year the current village leader took up position. Our basic hypothesis is that popular leaders have favored distribution of more forest land to individual households. But the reverse causality could also be true – more distribution of village forest land to households could have made village leaders more popular. A larger number of village leaders may be an indicator of democratic elections, and this may also be the case if the current village leader has taken office very recently.

11.4 The New Forest Tenure Reform in China

11.4.1 First steps

In the spring of 2003, the provincial government of Fujian formally approved the reform – but in fact the precedents had already been established as early as 1998[1] when a rural village, suffering from severe deforestation due to ineffective collective management, had decided to reform forest tenure for itself. In 2002, another village individualized user rights to villagers, and transferred some of the forests to people outside the village, in return for payment. In the latter case, the individualization of forest management helped eliminate village debt and provided significant rents for the first time since the first year of reform. The reason was that the farmers who accepted the forest user rights were required to pay a land rental fee to the villages. The forest plots sold off to outsiders earned village revenues in the form of lump sum stumpage (payment per tree stump at harvest) payments. In our survey, many villages in Fujian were enjoying similar gains through forest tenure decentralization. A separate survey (Kong et al., 2006) confirms these findings in Fujian.

The political rationale behind the support of the provincial government is also noteworthy. Historically, there had been provinces, such as Fujian, that had resisted tenure decentralization to a certain extent. So, why the renewed interest in reform? The answer may be found partly in the fact that due to the declining contribution of the forest sector in regional economies, fiscal incentives for the provincial government have changed; while forestry has declined in economic importance, particularly in harvests of state-owned forests and shipping industry, there has been concurrent growth in other sectors and the creation of private economies. As a result of these transformations, the cost of reforming the forest tenure system has been greatly reduced.

Moreover, national leaders have devoted much greater attention to rural development over the past few years. The New Countryside Development Initiative has become a more benevolent policy, since it includes the gradual elimination of agriculture taxes and fees as well as increasing investment in rural infrastructure and basic education. Also, farmers' rights over agricultural land have made major progress after the enactment of the Rural Land Contract Law. These changes in the agricultural sector have made the still-stringent policies in the forest sector more susceptible to criticism.

11.4.2 The nature of Collective Forest Tenure Reform since 2000

By the end of 2007, more than ten provinces had announced plans for collective forest tenure reform that provides stronger individual or group rights to forestland. As will be seen later, the magnitude of the current forest land reallocation is not as great as that of the first round of reforms in early 1980s. What makes the second wave reform important can be summarized as follows:

(i) The once-resistant Fujian province has adopted mainstream forest tenure reforms aiming at individualization;
(ii) Provincial decrees have stated that decisions regarding forest land reallocation should be made by village representative committees or by village assemblies requiring a 2/3 vote majority;
(iii) Redistribution of plots will be accompanied by legal contracts and/or forest certificates;
(iv) The allowable contract period is extended to 30, 50 or 70 years;
(v) Adoption of the Rural Land Contract Law has enabled expanded rights, including those of forestland transfer, inheritance and mortgaging.

11.4.3 Approach and variation with the three provinces in mind

Fujian started out from a situation which emphasized collective management. Having failed the test during the period from the mid-1980s to the early 2000s, this time the provincial government issued a document calling for tenure reform of individualization, setting the precedent for the second wave reform. Much of the forestland that had previously been managed collectively was distributed to individual farmers for management. But in Fujian, farmer partnership had been a favored management model by many villages, probably as a result of a long tradition of collective management. So Fujian province allowed the village collectives to collect a forest land rental fee in return for redistributing forest land to individuals, as such forest land had belonged to the village collectives before the reform. This facilitated the decision to reform being made by the village leadership and the local forest authorities.

Jiangxi individualized the majority of the forest land in the early 1980s. In the late 1980s it is believed that much of the forest land was reclaimed by the collectives, setting the foundation of the pressure for a new reform in the early 2000s. Jiangxi basically followed the footstep of Fujian, and issued its reform document in 2004; the basic plan of the reform was broadly similar to that of Fujian, with the exception of disallowing a forest land rental fee by the village collectives. Instead, to compensate the village committee and local government, the provincial government provided funds to the local authorities as an incentive to carry out the reform.

Yunnan is a province with great ethnic diversity. It is generally believed that in Yunnan a large number of rural villages are accustomed to community management; many villages in Yunnan are under the influence of the Natural Forest Protection Program, which basically banned commercial harvests in affected areas. It is conceivable that in the reform process there might be a tendency towards re-collectivization instead of individualization. Our survey data demonstrate that the outcomes are mixed; there was significant individualization, but re-collectivization also occurred in a number of villages, probably due to ethnic preference for community management – or it could be that the prevention of excessive extraction was the main task in the non-timber copse forestlands (Kijima et al., 2000). Whatever the case, Yunnan province issued its reform document in 2006 and also started experimenting in nine of its counties that same year; full scale reform started in 2007.

11.4.4 Description of tenure categories

Based on the information collected in the survey areas, we identified more than ten different tenure types (or management arrangements). For purposes of analysis, we grouped them into six broad categories of tenure type. Of these types, 'Private Plot' and 'Individual Household Management', as well as 'Outsider Management Contract held by individuals or private organizations' are classified as Individual Management, while the other types – 'Partnership', 'Villager Group', 'Outsider Management Contract held by collectives', 'Collective Management' and 'Ecological Reserve Forest' – are classed as Collective Management.

It is generally understood that since the reforms the Individual Management tenure type provides direct benefits to ordinary farmers, while the various levels of village leadership are the primary beneficiaries of the Collective Management. To what degree the reforms have redistributed welfare within villages hinges largely upon these two broad divisions of management.

11.4.5 Evolution of forest land allocation

The principal transfer took place in the early 1980s, while at the time of our survey the New Forest Tenure Reform had transferred less land to households. There is also a small share of forest land that households have kept since the 1950s. In Jiangxi and Yunnan there was a more concentrated transfer of land to households in the early 1980s than in Fujian, where the allocation was more gradual. Group management is relatively more common on the more recently allocated forest land (after the year 2000), while individual management was relatively more common on land allocated in the early 1980s. A major reason is that the group management includes not only collective management but also the natural village and partnership management. In particular, during the New Forest Tenure Reform period, village leaders sometimes decided to retain natural village leadership (also known as village cluster), as it was regarded as better in efficiency of scale than individual management.

11.5 Descriptive analysis

We refer to Holden et al. (2011) and Yi (2011) for more descriptive details. This study focuses on the three provinces: Fujian, Jiangxi and Yunnan. Table 11.1 provides descriptive statistics for the household level variables disaggregated by province from the survey in 2005/2006. The New Forest Tenure Reform started first in Fujian and last in Yunnan. There was more total forest land available in the villages surveyed in Fujian and Yunnan than in Jiangxi, but the average forest land allocated to households was nevertheless higher in Jiangxi than in Yunnan.

Table 11.2 provides information at household forest plot level. The mean forest plot size is largest in Fujian and smallest in Yunnan; however, the distribution of plot sizes is skewed and thus in all provinces the median plot size is much smaller than the average plot size. Collective plots are much larger than the average individual plots, and constituted 50 percent of the forest land in 2000, based on the household level data from the three provinces.

A very large proportion of forest land plots was under individual management: 92 percent in Fujian, 85 percent in Jiangxi and 99 percent in Yunnan. Households had received forestland certificates for 13.2 percent of the plots in Jiangxi, 13.8 percent of the plots in Yunnan and 15.6 percent of the plots in Fujian. Tenure security at plot level was assessed by asking each household for their plot whether they thought they would still have the plots five years into the future. A score of 2 was given if they were confident that they would still keep it, a score of 1 if they were uncertain, and a score of 0 if they thought they would not keep the plot after five years. The average scores were high in all provinces; 1.90 in Fujian, 1.93 in Jiangxi and 1.89 in Yunnan – significantly higher in Jiangxi than in the other two provinces. This score is the variable used as the dependent variable for the analysis of tenure security.

The average number of agricultural land adjustments was higher (1.6) in Fujian than in Jiangxi (1.2) and in Yunnan (0.9). Yunnan had a higher average score for trust in village leader, 7.35 – on a scale from 1 (lowest) to 10 (highest) – against 6.35 in Fujian and 6.65 in Jiangxi. The number of village leaders since 1990 was higher in Fujian.

Table 11.3 contains data on households' perceptions of their bundle of forestland rights which had been disaggregated into different types of management rights and transfer rights within the village and to outsiders. The management rights were generally perceived to be very strong, except when it came to the conversion of forest land to agricultural land for crop production (allowed on about 50 percent of the plots), while intercropping

Table 11.1 Summary statistics for household-level variables

Variable	Fujian		Jiangxi		Yunnan	
	Mean	St. Error	Mean	St. Error	Mean	St. Error
Household size 2000	4.789	0.066	4.683	0.090	4.628	0.044
Hukou type 2000, 1 = Agricultural, 2 = Non-agricultural, 3 = Not registered	1.015	0.005	1.030	0.011	1.021	0.004
Household does farm work 2000, 1 = Yes, 0 = No	0.953	0.009	0.983	0.007	0.954	0.006
Average education of household members 2000; years	4.756	0.077	5.130	0.104	4.933	0.066
Age of household head 2000; years	45.023	0.445	46.003	0.621	43.389	0.342
Education of household head 2000; years	4.914	0.130	5.826	0.155	5.565	0.097
Member of communist party or not 2000, 1 = Yes, 0 = No	0.150	0.015	0.163	0.021	0.115	0.009
Head of household is village head 2000, 1 = Yes, 0 = No	0.050	0.009	0.037	0.011	0.058	0.007
Household has job in forestry sector 2000, 1 = Yes, 0 = No	0.013	0.005	0.000	0.000	0.010	0.003
New Forest Tenure Reform started, 1 = Yes, 0 = No	0.950	0.009	1.000	0.000	0.867	0.010
Time of start of Forest Tenure Reform	2003.1	0.062	2004.7	0.027	2006.3	0.012
Forest land per capita in village 2000	18.211	0.748	4.310	0.664	17.657	0.747
Agricultural land per capita in village 2000	1.149	0.024	1.050	0.022	1.703	0.032
Forest area allocated to household, mu	46.449	4.174	40.000	7.544	33.733	2.833

Source: Peking University survey data.

Table 11.2 Descriptive statistics for variables used in the plot-level analysis by province

Variables	Fujian		Jiangxi		Yunnan	
Forest plot characteristics	**Mean**	**St. Error**	**Mean**	**St. Error**	**Mean**	**St. Error**
Forest plot size in mu	16.164	1.066	12.848	2.313	8.308	0.577
Irrigation dummy	0.122	0.008	0.160	0.012	0.122	0.006
Slope (1=<15%, 2=15–25%, 3=>25%)	2.612	0.015	1.541	0.022	1.475	0.016
Distance to home, km	2.053	0.046	2.097	0.068	2.351	0.060
Distance to road, km	1.270	0.035	1.579	0.060	1.801	0.049
Tenure variables						
Individually controlled plot (dummy)	0.916	0.007	0.853	0.012	0.991	0.002
Share of plot controlled by household, group tenure	0.171	0.013	0.279	0.014	0.136	0.036
Forest type (1 = Commercial, 2 = Ecological)	1.014	0.003	1.037	0.006	1.107	0.006
Has forest certificate dummy	0.156	0.009	0.132	0.011	0.138	0.007
Year when plot was contracted	1987.6	0.329	1986.0	0.268	1986.1	0.175
Tenure security: expect to keep plot after 5 years, 2 = Yes, 1 = Uncertain, 0 = No	1.898	0.008	1.934	0.010	1.892	0.008
Village level variables						
Number of land adjustments	1.631	0.025	1.193	0.031	0.857	0.020
Trust in village leader (score 1–10)	6.351	0.030	6.645	0.033	7.535	0.016
Number of village leaders since 1990	4.339	0.027	3.719	0.056	3.740	0.030
Start year of current village leader	2001.3	0.064	2000.6	0.172	2000.2	0.134

Table 11.3 Disaggregated land rights at household forest plot-level by province

	Fujian		Jiangxi		Yunnan	
Type of land right	**Mean**	**St. Error**	**Mean**	**St. Error**	**Mean**	**St. Error**
Right to convert forest land to cropland	0.493	0.012	0.528	0.016	0.548	0.010
Right to change forest type	0.811	0.009	0.826	0.012	0.821	0.007
Right to decide tree species	0.845	0.008	0.856	0.011	0.845	0.007
Right to intercrop trees and agric. crops	0.960	0.004	0.914	0.009	0.945	0.004
Right to abandon forest	0.669	0.007	0.826	0.008	0.840	0.005
Right to transfer plot to other villagers	0.751	0.010	0.740	0.014	0.659	0.009
Right to transfer plot to outsiders	0.634	0.011	0.724	0.014	0.590	0.009
Property rights index (sum of rights scores)	5.177	0.041	5.438	0.061	5.255	0.036

Note: Right = 1 if yes, Right = 0.5 if yes but requires village approval, Right = 0 if no.

Source: Peking University survey data.

trees and agricultural crops was allowed on more than 90 percent of the plots. Transfer rights were perceived to be weaker in Yunnan than in the other two provinces. Not much difference was found in the average property rights index (the aggregate score of individual management rights) for the three provinces. The following analysis shows the disaggregated rights alternating with the property rights index related to the perception of tenure security at household plot level and whether a written documentation in form of a forestland certificate enhances the perception of tenure security beyond the contribution of the perceived property rights in form of the disaggregated rights or the property rights index. Their correlation with or effect on households' investment on forest land is assessed.

11.6 Allocation of forest land

Based on the context described above we have, in relation to the process of allocating forest land to households, tested the following hypotheses:

HA1: The equity principle used for agricultural land is important for the allocation of forest land. This implies that it is household size that is the main determinant of forest land allocated to households within a village.

HA2: Local power and influence helps to improve access to forest land. Being a village leader or party member therefore enhances access to forest land. Such leaders are more influential, because the provincial decrees stated that decisions regarding forest land reallocation should be made by village representative committees or by village assemblies requiring a 2/3 vote majority.

HA3: Democratic village elections have contributed to enhancing the forest land allocation to households. This is based on the assumption that there is popular demand for more individualized land rights and there is a demand from those that had lost land during collectivization.

HA4: Good (trusted) local leaders have distributed more forest land to households.

HA5: Frequent agricultural land adjustments have reduced the demand for forest land among households and thus reduced the allocation of forest land.

HA6: The more valuable the forest land, the more likely it is to be converted to individual land.

Table 11.4 presents the results of the regression models testing these hypotheses. The first two models (columns 2 and 3) used *total forest area of households* as the dependent variable. The last two models (columns 4 and 5) used *forest land allocated to households after year 2000* as the dependent variable; this is because of the interest in exploring whether there existed a different logic for forest land allocation in the New Forest Tenure Reform period than in the previous one, as the new one probably lays less emphasis on the equity principle. Models with and without the village level, potentially endogenous, variables were used due to lack of good instruments for their prediction. Panel data Tobit models with village random effects were used. The extent of left-censoring was more serious in the models with new forest land allocated after year 2000, but some interesting results still came out of these models.[2]

Hypothesis HA1 was supported in the models for total forest land allocation but not for forest land allocation after year 2000. Since *household size in year 2000* was used as a test variable, we may conclude that the equity motive was important in the past, not only in agricultural land allocation but also in forest land allocation. However, this motive seems not to have been important in the recent Forest Tenure Reform.

Table 11.4 Determinants of household forest areas: results from RE Tobit models

Variables	Total area of forest plots	Total area of forest plots	New forest area after 2000	New forest area after 2000
Household size in 2000	5.554***	5.435***	1.158	1.226
Jiangxi province	31.989**	28.338*	−57.579**	−44.641*
Yunnan province	−2.989	−11.005	−37.929	−12.730
Hukou 2000 = Non-agricultural household	6.930	5.299	47.493	45.539
Hukou 2000 = Unregistered	−4.272	−2.557	−447.896	−426.361
Household does farm work	−9.994	−9.510	−12.757	−13.241
New Forest Tenure Reform started dummy	169.622**	180.437**	87.267	102.308
Time of start of Forest Tenure Reform; year	−4.242	−3.395	−1.769	−5.992
Forest land per capita in village	1.949****	1.839****	0.628	0.558
Agricultural land per capita in village	3.072	4.722	9.871	9.988
Member of communist party or not, dummy	18.756**	18.944**	21.125*	21.309*
Head of household is village head, dummy	−9.952	−9.318	0.569	1.486
Household has job in forestry sector, dummy	−3.786	−3.435	23.784	22.543
Average education of HH members, years	0.946	0.876	−0.981	−0.929
Age of household head	−0.180	−0.186	−0.480	−0.486
Education of household head	0.188	0.134	−0.933	−1.009
Number of land adjustments in village		−10.660**		−2.096
Trust in village leader		4.582		6.218
Number of village leaders since 1990		3.852		20.375****
Start year for current village leader		−0.649		−2.949
Constant	8309.368	7872.375	3391.675	17616.267
Prob > chi^2	0.000	0.000	0.062	0.007
Number of observations	1795	1795	1795	1795
Rho	0.157	0.144	0.263	0.237
Left-censored observations	217	217	1262	1262

Significance levels: **** $p<0.001$, *** $p<0.01$, ** $p<0.05$, * $p<0.1$. Models with village random effects.

This provides evidence that in the past the equity principle had been adopted, since there was no scale advantage in forest management as in the case of agriculture land. During the New Forest Tenure Reform, the democratically elected leaders preferred individual management, and allocated forest land to individuals. Household size is likely to be quite stable over time, but we should be aware that there can be some reverse causality causing households that received more forest land to also have a larger household size.

Neither education nor age was found to have any effect on the recent allocation of forest land, so there is no evidence showing the improvement on access to forest land by skill and ability. Hypothesis HA2 cannot be rejected, as a positive and significant relationship was found between membership in the Communist Party and forest land allocation, both for total forest land and for recent forest land allocation.

Hypothesis HA3, that democratic village elections have stimulated forest land allocation to households, is strongly supported by the analysis, as the new forest area allocated is strongly positively correlated (significant at 0.1 percent level) with the number of village leaders since 1990. But it was insignificant for total forest land. Trust in Village Leader was not significantly correlated with forest land allocation, so hypothesis HA4 is rejected, while there was a significant negative correlation between the number of land adjustments and the forest land allocated to households. This lends support for hypothesis HA5 that land adjustments have caused a reduction in demand for forest land.

When comparing the three provinces, significantly more forest land was allocated to households overall in Jiangxi than in the other two provinces, while significantly less was allocated to households in the same province after 2000. This fits into the overall picture, where the forest tenure reform went further in allocating land to households in the early 1980s in Jiangxi, leaving less forest land available for additional distribution after year 2000.

Quite surprisingly, we found a positive significant correlation between forest land allocated to households and the dummy variable for whether the New Forest Tenure Reform had started in the village in the models with total forest area – but no such significant effect was found in the recent forest area allocation models. This may be interpreted such that those villages where the reform contributed to more forest land allocation in the past were also more eager to start the New Forest Tenure Reform, implying a reverse causality in the first two models. Finally, we found a significant positive effect of total forest land per capita in the village on forest land allocated, as would be expected.

Hypothesis HA6, that more valuable forest land is transformed to individually managed, is tested first by running a panel probit model with a dummy for individually versus collectively managed land as the dependent variable. Right-hand side variables were key land characteristics as indicators of land value; that is distance to road, slope (dummy) and irrigation (dummy). The more valuable land is assumed to be closer to roads, less likely to have steep slopes, and more likely to have access to water for irrigation. Initial investment on the land could also be correlated with land value and individualization of the forest land rights. Town dummies were included, as the individualization of forest land was initiated at town level. The results are presented in Table 11.5; we see that 16,525 plot observations were used in the analysis.

The results are consistent with hypothesis HA6. Forest plots closer to roads, on flatter slopes and with irrigation water access are more likely to have been transferred to individual management.

11.7 Forest plot level tenure security

Based on property rights theory and earlier studies of tenure security and insecurity in China and elsewhere, we have also launched a number of hypotheses about the relationship between perceived forest plot

Table 11.5 Factors correlated with plots being individually or collectively managed

Explanatory variables	Tenure choice
Year 2005 (dummy)	–0.117
Irrigation dummy	2.341***
Slope (dummy: 1 =>25 and 0 =>25)	–0.505***
Distance to road (km)	–0.266***
Start year of managing forest plot	–0.030***
Length of contract for forest plot (years)	0.004**
Number of times of small land adjustment in the village	–0.042
Log of investment on forestland in year 2000	0.460***
Town dummies	Yes
Constant	61.450***
Lnsig2u constant	2.775***
Number of observations	16525

Notes: Panel probit model town dummies. The dependent variable is a dummy variable with individual tenure = 0 and collective tenure = 0. Significance levels: **** $p<0.001$, *** $p<0.01$, ** $p<0.05$, * $p<0.1$. Models with village random effects.

tenure security and various variables, *inter alia* forest plot characteristics, tenure characteristics, village and policy characteristics where we can draw on the existing local variation. The benefit of having data on perceived forest plot tenure security and forest land rights at forest plot level allows us to use panel data methods that can control for observed as well as unobserved household heterogeneity by using household random-effects and fixed-effects models. Our hypotheses are as follows:

HB1: Tenure security is higher on plots that have been allocated to individual households than on plots with shared (group) ownership.

HB2: Forest land certificates enhance tenure security.

HB3: Frequent land readjustments in agricultural land reduce tenure security of forest plots.

HB4: Trust in village leaders (good ones, at least) is positively correlated with tenure security.

HB5: Tenure security is higher in villages with more democratic elections.

HB6: Stronger property rights in terms of the score of the rights index representing the bundle of rights that households enjoy are correlated with higher tenure security.

We have tested these hypotheses using the household forest plot data from the three provinces. The dependent variable was whether households believed they would still keep the plot five years into the future, with three possible outcomes. The regression results are presented in Table 11.6, and the key findings are summarized below.

No significant differences were found for individually vs. group-managed plots with respect to the perception of tenure security, and the same was the case for the share of the plot that the household controls, meaning also that group size did not significantly affect the feeling of tenure security. The findings therefore lend no support for hypothesis HB1.

Households were found to feel significantly more tenure secure on plots for which they had received forest land certificates. This variable was highly significant (1 percent level) in the random-effects as well as the fixed-effects models. The fixed-effects models should control for unobserved household heterogeneity that could cause selection in getting certificates, but the parameters in the fixed-effects models were even higher than those in the random-effects models, and remained highly significant. This represents strong evidence on the importance

Table 11.6 Factors correlated with tenure security: household RE and FE models with rights index vs. disaggregated rights variables

	Dependent variable: household still owns plot after 5 years			
Variables	**RE**	**FE**	**RE**	**FE**
Has certificate for plot	0.054***	0.062***	0.055***	0.062***
Year when plot was contracted	0.002	0.003	0.002	0.003*
Share of plot controlled by HH	0.220	0.410	0.218	0.414
Individually controlled plot	–0.137	–0.257	–0.130	–0.259
Rights index (sum of rights score)	0.031****	0.031****		
Right to convert forest land to cropland			0.013	–0.007
Right to change forest type			0.078	0.131
Right to decide tree species			–0.101	–0.150
Right to intercrop trees and agric. crops			0.122**	0.036
Right to abandon forest			0.002	0.056
Right to transfer plot to other villagers			0.125**	0.168*
Right to transfer plot to outsiders			0.014	0.054
Number of land readjustments	–0.001		0.001	
Trust in village leader	0.007		0.008	
Number of village leaders since 1990	–0.010*		–0.009	
Start year of current village leader	–0.007****		–0.007****	
Jiangxi province	0.018		0.027	
Yunnan province	–0.034*		–0.023	
Plot level characteristics	Yes	Yes	Yes	Yes
Constant	11.787****	–3.564	12.314****	–3.815
Prob > chi^2	0.000	0.001	0.000	0.001
Number of observations	4706	4706	4706	4706

Note: RE is random-effects models using xtmixed with household random effects, deriving bootstrapped standard errors with 500 replications, re-sampling households to control for clustering at household level. FE is fixed-effects models using xtreg and applying fixed effects at household level and correcting standard errors for clustering at household level. Significance levels: **** $p<0.001$, *** $p<0.01$, ** $p<0.05$, * $p<0.1$.

of written documentation for the ownership of forest plots. Forest land certificates had been distributed only recently, with a duration of 30 to 70 years, far beyond the five-year perspective applied in this analysis. So Hypothesis HB2 cannot be rejected.

The 'number of land adjustments' variable that could only be included in the random-effects models was insignificant. Hypothesis HB3 may therefore be rejected in our case. Experience of earlier land adjustments for agricultural land appears not to affect the current tenure security on forest land. Likewise, the 'Trust in village leader' variable (Hypothesis HB4) did not significantly affect the feeling of tenure security. The 'Number of village leaders since 1990' variable was only significant (at the 10 percent level) in one of the models, and with a negative sign. If this variable is a reasonable indicator of democratic elections, Hypothesis HB5, that democratic elections have enhanced tenure security, may be rejected. The 'Start year of current village leader' variable was highly significant (at 0.1 percent level) in the random-effects models and with a negative sign. This indicates that recently elected leaders had a significant negative impact on tenure security – apparent evidence that local leaders were still considered to have substantial power over local land tenure rights, as it appears difficult to explain this result as a reverse causality or a spurious correlation.

In addition, the property rights index was found to be highly significant (at the 0.1 percent level) in both the random and fixed-effects models and with a positive sign, demonstrating a strong positive correlation between the number and strength of rights and the feeling of tenure security. For the models with disaggregated rights, only the local transfer right was significant in both models, and with a positive sign, while the right to intercrop agricultural crops with trees on the forest plot was significant and positive in the random-effects model only. The aggregate combination of rights may be more significant because of the synergy between the disaggregated rights. We cannot therefore reject hypothesis HB6.

Putting these findings into context, it may be concluded that perceptions of a bundle of rights can be a good indicator of tenure security, but it does not tell the whole story. Provision of written documentation of rights in the form of forest land certificates strengthened the feeling of tenure security as a separate and additional effect. This is a lesson of substantial policy relevance, and it provides support for land certification in settings where there is tenure insecurity that can be reduced by such written documentation. It should be added that this is not necessarily the case in all settings, as local political economy factors could subvert such effects.

11.8 Determinants of investment on forest plots

Besley's (1995) three neoclassical arguments – tenure security, transferability, and credit access – are suggested to stimulate investment in land. In this section, we present the results of our test regarding the three fundamentals on forestland-related investment. The (monetized) investment variable was composed by adding up all forms of physical inputs, including family labor and capital investment on the forestland plot within the year, including afforestation, re-forestation after tree harvesting, silviculture, labor etc. We took its logarithmic form as our dependent variable. Panel Tobit models with household random effects were used for the analysis based on exogenous switching, such that separate models were run for households with and without forestland certificates, and separate models were run for forestland plots with and without certificates for households having at least one forestland plot certificate. The lagged (log of) the investment variable for year 2000 was included as an additional control for unobserved forestland plot heterogeneity and initial investment level. As a first stage, panel probit models were run to identify the factors associated with households with or without forestland certificates; and for the households with forestland certificates, panel probit models were run for the factors associated with forestland plots with certificates. The inverse of the predicted probabilities were included in the investment models as an attempt to control for selection bias. As an identification strategy, county dummy variables were included in the panel probit models, because forestland certification is largely decided at this administrative level. The results from the panel probit models are available from the authors upon request. A range of plot and household variables were included as controls.

We then aimed to test the following hypotheses:

HC1: Tenure security increases forest investment. We use possession of forest land certificates and the perceived rights on forest land as indicators of tenure security, by assessing how specific rights were correlated with investments on certified and uncertified plots and for households without certificates.

HC2: The transferability of forest land plots stimulates investment in said plots. We assessed how the transfer rights for plots were associated with investment in different types of plots.

HC3: Access to credit encourages investment in the forest land plot. We assessed how mortgaging rights were associated with investment on different types of plots.

Table 11.7 presents the results. For households with forestland certificates the results are clearly different for forestland plots with certificates compared to the forestland plots without certificates for the same households. The right to change forest type was positively correlated with investment, and so were the rights to transfer plots to other villagers and to outsiders. On the other hand, rights to abandon forestland and to convert it to cropland were negatively associated with forestland investments on certified plots. The right to mortgage forestland with certificate was also negative and significant on plots with certificate. Few of these rights variables were significantly associated with investment in the uncertified forest plots belonging to the same households.

Another model, including the rights index variable, gave a significant and positive correlation between the index on plots with certificates, while it was insignificant on the plots without certificate. This seems to indicate that stronger rights and forestland certificates jointly enhance investment unless the land can be converted to other uses or abandoned. So we cannot reject hypothesis HC1. Transfer rights were also positively associated with investment on certified plots. However, on plots without certificates, transfer rights were partly negatively associated with investment. We therefore have mixed evidence regarding hypothesis HC2. Mortgaging rights were on the other hand negatively associated with investment on certified plots; this indicates that such rights may not stimulate investment, and so we have to reject hypothesis HC3. Households with forestland certificates that had borrowed money were also investing significantly less in their certified forestland.

For households without forestland certificates, the right to convert forestland to cropland and the right to transfer plots to outsiders were significantly negatively associated with investment, while the right to select tree species and the right to use non-timber forest products were positively associated. Household heads that were village leaders invested significantly more than other households in their certified plots, while village leaders without forestland certificates invested significantly less in their forestland than did other households. Household income was significantly negatively associated with forest investment on certified plots but not on uncertified ones. This may imply that poorer households are more likely to see forestland investment as a future livelihood opportunity and therefore invest more – and they invest more where the tenure security is higher.

Table 11.7 Factors correlated with plot-level investment for plots with and without certificate for households with and without certificate

Dependent variable: log of value of investment in 2005	Households with certificate		Households without certificate
	Plots with certificate	Plots without certificate	
Right to convert forestland to cropland[d]	–3.770***	0.778	–0.851**
Right to change forest type	5.653***	1.089	–0.769
Right to select tree species	–1.245	0.094	0.733
Right to use non-timber products	0.514	–1.798	2.610***
Right to abandon forestland	–3.267**	0.165	0.487
Right to transfer plot to other villagers	3.393**	–0.576	0.273
Right to transfer plot to outsiders	3.675***	1.260	–1.266***
Right to mortgage forestland with certificate	–2.700**	–0.420	–0.317
Right to mortgage forestland without certificate	–0.709	0.468	0.155
Year 2005 (dummy)	0.448	–0.352	–0.187
Household size, number of people	0.371	–0.230	–0.053
Age of household head (years)	–0.027	0.019	0.023*
Educated years of household head	–0.431**	–0.079	0.050
Gender of the household head	–0.473	–4.508	–0.343
Household head is member of the Communist party	0.187	0.685	–0.594
Household head is village leader	4.097***	–1.770*	–1.620***
Household head once has job in forestry sector	5.416	3.891**	0.429
Log of total household income	–0.472**	0.064	–0.264**
House value in 2005 (yuan)	0.078	–0.096	0.026
Borrowed money or not, dummy	–0.775**	–0.034	0.104

Can successfully borrow 500 yuan within one week	–0.051	0.251	0.118
Forestry income share	–2.110	0.024	1.617**
Forest plot area (mu)	–0.006	–0.009**	–0.007**
Household's total plot number (in year 2005)	0.315**	–0.453**	0.342***
Irrigation dummy	1.890*	1.278*	1.299***
Slope (dummy: 1 =>25 and 0 =>25)	0.062	–0.310	–1.048***
Distance to home (km)	–0.035	0.053	0.101***
Distance to road (km)	0.027	–0.109	–0.188***
Length of one rotation period (years)	0.061	–0.250	–0.045
Start year of managing forest plot	0.053*	–0.029*	0.017**
Length of contract for forest plot (years)	0.001	0.004	–0.007***
Household's total cropland area (mu)	–0.006	–0.007	–0.003
Household's total working days in off-farm jobs	0.000	0.002**	0.001**
Number of times of small land adjustment in the village	–0.253	–0.655	–0.033
Log of investment on forestland in year 2000	0.636***	0.370***	0.727***
Fujian (dummy)	0.205	1.921	–3.765***
Jiangxi (dummy)	–8.185***	–22.298	–8.706***
Inverse of predicted certificate	0.004	–0.027***	
Constant	–108.404*	66.073*	–31.738**
Sigma u constant	7.073***	2.960***	4.816***
Sigma e constant	1.263***	1.467***	1.529***
Number of observations	1859	840	7480

Note: Panel probit models with household random effects.

Significance levels: *** $p<0.01$, ** $p<0.05$, * $p<0.1$.

11.9 Conclusion

This study has revealed that the equity principle was important in the process of forest land allocation to households in the 1980s, but the principle appears not to have played an important part in the forestland allocation to households that took place after year 2000. Democratic elections appear to have stimulated the recent allocation of forestland to households for individual household management. More valuable forest land; that is, forest plots located closer to roads, less sloping, and with access to irrigation water; were more likely to have been allocated to individual households. Forestland certificates strengthened the feeling of tenure security on plots and stimulated investment in forestry, which may be the most significant finding of policy relevance. Such certificates represent a written documentation that appeared to provide security additional to that of the perceived rights that households enjoyed in their land, whether these were captured in a disaggregated way or through an aggregate index.

Since the households surveyed only had forestland certificates for about 15 percent of all forest plots, expanding such certification can be recommended. It is likely that such certification will further enhance tenure security which again should stimulate investment in the longer run, along with further reform being rolled out. It is expected to lead to better management of forestland and will be the subject of future research. This is in line with recent findings in Ethiopia, where land certification has been found to stimulate tree planting and maintenance of soil conservation structures (Holden et al., 2009).

Notes

1. Hongtian Village, Yongan County of Fujian Province, individualized forestland tenure in 1998.
2. In the estimation of allocated forest land, we also included individual characteristics such as age, education of household head, as indicators of skill and ability. The rationale is that they might improve people's bargaining power in a way similar to that of being a village leader/cadre or Communist Party member, etc., and so have influence on the decision process of forest land allocation.

References

Albers, H.J., Rozelle, S. and Guo, L. (1998) 'China's Forests under Economic Reform: Timber Supplies, Environmental Protection, and Rural Resource Access', *Contemporary Economic Policy,* 16, 22–33.

Besley, T. (1995) 'Property Rights and Investment Incentives: Theory and Evidence from Ghana', *Journal of Political Economy*, 103(5), 903–37.
Brandt, L., Rozelle, S. and Turner, M.A. (2002) 'Local Government Behavior and Property Rights Formation in Rural China', *Working Paper* No. 02–004, Department of Agricultural and Resource Economics, University of California, Davis.
Brasselle, A.S., Gaspart, F. and Platteau, J.P. (2002) 'Land Tenure Security and Investment Incentives: Puzzling Evidence from Burkina Faso', *Journal of Agricultural Economics*, 67(2), 373–418.
Carter, M. and Yao, Y. (1998) 'Property Rights, Rental Markets, and Land in China', *Working Paper*, Department of Agricultural and Applied Economics, University of Wisconsin-Madison.
Demsetz, H. (1967) 'Towards a Theory of Property Rights', *The American Economic Review*, 57(2), 347–59.
Holden, S.T., Deininger, K. and Ghebru, H. (2009) 'Impacts of Low-cost Land Certification on Investment and Productivity', *American Journal of Agricultural Economics*, 91(2), 359–73.
Holden, S. T., Xu, J. and Jiang, X. (2011) 'Collective versus Individual Property: Tenure Security and Forest Tenure Reforms in China', *Centre for Land Tenure Studies Working Paper* No. 04/11. Centre for Land Tenure Studies, Norwegian University of Life Sciences, Ås.
Holden, S.T. and Yohannes, H. (2002) 'Land Redistribution, Tenure Insecurity and Input Intensity: A Study of Farm Households in Southern Ethiopia', *Land Economic*, 78(4), 573–90.
Jacoby, H., Li, G. and Rozelle, S. (2002) 'Hazards of Expropriation: Tenure Insecurity and Investment in Rural China', *The American Economic Review*, 92(5), 1420–47.
Kennedy, J.J., Rozelle, S. and Yaojiang, S. (2004) 'Elected Leaders and Collective Land: Farmers' Evaluation of Village Leaders' Performance in Rural China', *Journal of Chinese Political Science*, 9(1), 1–22.
Kijima, Y., Sakurai, T. and Otsuka, K. (2000) 'Iriaichi: Collective vs. Individualized Management of Community Forests in Postwar Japan', *Economic Development and Cultural Change*, 48(4), 867–86.
Kong, X., Guo, Y. and Li, S. (2006) 'On Influence of Collective Forest Property Reform to Economy at Village Level', *Forestry Economics*, 171(10), 17–21.
Liu, D. and Edmunds, D. (2003) 'Devolution as a Means of Expanding Local Forest Management in South China. Lessons from the Past 20 Years', in Hyde, W.F., Belcher, B. and Xu, J. (eds), *China's Forests: Global Lessons from Market Reforms* (Washington D.C. Resources for the Future Press).
Rozelle, S., Brandt, L., Gou, L. and Huang, J. (2002) 'Land Rights in China: Facts, Fictions, and Issues', *China Journal*, 47, 67–97.
Wang, X. (2008) 'Making Sense of Village Politics in China: Institutions, Participation, and Governance', PhD dissertation, Department of Political Science, Georgia State University, Georgia.
Xu, J. and Jiang, X. (2009) 'Collective Forest Tenure Reform in China: Outcomes and Implications', Paper presented at the *World Bank Conference on Land Governance*, 9–10 March.
Yi, Y. (2011) 'Property Rights, Tenure Security and Forest Investment Incentives: In the Context of China's Collective Forest Tenure Reform Since 2003', MSc

thesis, School of Business, Economics and Law, University of Gothenburg, Gothenburg.

Yin, R. (1998) 'Forestry and the Environment in China: The Current Situation and Strategic Choices', *World Development*, 26(12), 2153–67.

Yin, R., Xu, J. and Li, Z. (2003) 'Building Institutions for Markets: Experiences and Lessons from China's Rural Forest Sector', *Environment, Development and Sustainability*, 5(3–4), 333–51.

12
Community Forest Management and Tree Planting on Farms in Kakamega, Kenya

Maurice Juma Ogada, Wilfred Nyangena and Geophrey Sikei

12.1 Introduction

The decentralized forest management regime has gained currency in developing countries in recent years (Agrawal et al., 2008), being viewed as a means of enhancing economic efficiency, public accountability, community and individual empowerment, and allocative efficiency in the forest sub-sector (World Bank, 2009). These reforms are expected to reconcile conservation and livelihood needs. In particular, forest decentralization is aimed at enhancing people's livelihoods, alleviating poverty and preserving the forest condition.

Decentralization policies, however, do not affect forest users' behavior directly. Rather, they change local incentive structures by altering security, access and the power structure of local governance, which in turn lead to behavioral change. The expected outcomes of regime change are mediated by forestry regulations that impose conditions for the use of forest resources, and by the capacities of small holders and communities to adapt to those regulations. For instance, communities are required to implement workable systems of governance for their collective lands, exclude third parties and engage in competitive conditions with the forest markets. Indirectly, the outcomes of the reform are also influenced by access to financial and non-financial services; in the absence of these conditions, forest tenure reforms are unlikely to achieve their livelihood and conservation goals. Thus, decentralization policies may produce a variety of outcomes, both desirable and undesirable. For example, many of the Community Forest Associations (CFAs) formed in Kenya were driven by expectations beyond what the legislation provided (Ongugo, 2007; Ongugo et al., 2007). Indeed some CFAs anticipated converting forests into farmlands for production of cash and food crops (Ongugo and Njuguna, 2004). Basically, the diverse outcomes are dependent on community experiences and traditions, and the capacity of the local communities to take advantage of the prevailing market conditions (Monterroso, 2008).

Numerous benefits are expected to accrue to individuals from participating in community forest associations through increased access to forest products such as fuel wood, herbal medicine, honey, tree seedlings, thatch grass and fodder. Other activities allowed within the co-management framework include ecotourism, bee-keeping, fish farming and the growing of crops. With these benefits, it would be expected that communities would fast embrace the system and participate effectively. However, progress has been slow, and in some cases CFAs have been formed, only to collapse after a short while (Ongugo et al., 2007). But it is also important to note that decentralization of forest management may not necessarily yield desirable environmental outcomes, as has been revealed by evaluation studies elsewhere in the World (Agrawal and Ribot, 1999). Thus, it is critical and urgent to understand what drives individual households to participate in community forest associations, and how this participation impacts on specified environmental outcomes in Kenya, where forest cover is only 3 percent, much lower than the globally recommended rate of 10 percent.

Several studies have been conducted on community participation in forest management, the effects of Participatory Forest Management (PFM) on household poverty and the opportunity cost of forest conservation (Emerton, 1999; Mogaka et al., 2001; Colfer, 2005; Mbuvi et al., 2007; Ongugo, 2007; Guthiga et al., 2008 and Borner et al., 2009). Decentralization policies interact with numerous context-specific pressures and interactions to change governance institutions and forest user behavior, and the resulting forest conditions and livelihood outcomes (Andersson et al., 2008). While there are several theoretical arguments relating to benefits and costs of forest decentralization, these fail to generate consistent predictions (Andersson et al., 2008). These studies ignore behavioral changes resulting from decentralization among forest users in their empirical investigations.

This study contributes to the literature on forest decentralization and devolution in Kenya by first examining the drivers of households' participation in community forest associations (CFA), which is the framework through which communities take part in forest management, before analyzing how this participation impacts on household farm forestry investment decisions. We seek to understand how decentralization policies filter down to local forest users. Economic theory does not provide clear predictions about the effects of decentralization policies on forest users' behavior. Instead, using studies of the way in which such policies interact with existing biophysical socio-demographic variables such as age, gender and educational variables, we must derive how wealth and other factors change incentives at the local level. We test the effects of forest decentralization, arguing that the effects of decentralization need to be understood according to specific contexts. Data for the analysis came from field research between May and July 2010 in several villages around Kakamega forest in Kenya, where decentralization of forest management has been implemented.

The study employs Propensity Score Matching (PSM) to measure the impact of household's participation in CFA on farm forestry decisions, and checks the robustness of the results with an Endogenous Switching Regression (ESR). We find that participation in CFA by households is influenced broadly by socio-economic and institutional factors. Participation in CFA is positively correlated with farm forestry development. Our results suggest that policy makers need to devise and implement interventions that would promote development of community forest associations, with the ultimate goal of increasing forest cover in the country. The rest of the chapter is organized as follows: in the next section we review the history of decentralized forest management in Kenya. In Section 12.3 we draw on existing literature to derive factors that influence household farm forest investment decisions. Section 12.4 examines methodological issues, while Section 12.5 outlines the study area and provides summary statistics of the variables used. In Section 12.6, we report and discuss our empirical results, and in Section 12.7 we conclude and draw policy implications.

12.2 Forest decentralization trends in Kenya

The colonial government of Kenya created a forest department in 1902, alienating most of the then existing community-managed forests. The Forest Department managed and controlled all forests in the country, with policies focused on conservation. Following independence in 1963, a series of donor-funded forestry programs focused on afforestation and reforestation on farms, with the goal of alleviating firewood shortages. The Forest Department managed the forests without consultation outside the relevant government ministry, and without concerns for social issues and the interests of local communities. The consequences of this central forest control were an increase in deforestation, forest degradation and loss of biodiversity, leading to resistance by local people. Conflicts increased in the late 1980s between communities who needed firewood from neighboring forests and the Forest Department (Ongugo and Njuguna, 2004).

The Forest Act of 2005 saw the formation of the Kenya Forest Service (KFS), a semi-autonomous government agency with representation from various government ministries. Unlike its precursor, the act provides a framework and incentives for community and private sector involvement in the forestry sector. Community participation is achieved primarily through CFAs, and integrated management of forests is the central principle motivating the new policy (Ongugo et al., 2007).

With CFAs entering into partnerships with KFS, local communities are given some leeway to directly participate in protection, conservation and management of a given forest area, subject to the provision of a management plan for the forest. The new act has granted user rights, albeit limited, to the associations, provided the rights do not conflict with the conservation objectives (GoK, 2007). Under the new arrangement, the association members may collect non-timber forest products (NTFP). In addition, they are granted the rights to undertake ecotourism and recreational activities, scientific and educational activities, contracts to assist in undertaking specified silvicultural operations and other benefits that might be agreed on from time to time with the KFS.

The CFAs' roles have been changing over time, and it is expected that they will become more and more involved in decision-making processes. They have also expanded their roles from lobbying to conflict management, involvement in fundraising activities, negotiating with KFS during most of the meetings, and initiating rural development and forestry development activities. In addition, they are increasingly getting involved in putting in place systems designed to ensure equitable resource distribution. CFAs have successfully pioneered projects like butterfly farming, bee-keeping, farm forestry initiatives, environmental awareness programs, and ecotourism activities (Ongugo et al., 2008).

Mogoi et al. (2012), however, observe that forest user rights are not fully implemented as stipulated in the Forest Act 2005, and that communities still lack access to valuable forest products. Table 12.1 shows the structure of property rights to forests before and after decentralization. The government still reserves the right to decide on what CFAs are supposed to do and what section of the forest they will manage,

Table 12.1 The structure of property rights to forests before and after decentralization

Type of rights	Rights holder before decentralization	Rights holder after enactment of Forest Act	On the ground situation
Access rights	Government (Forest department and KWS) for forest reserves and forest national parks. Local councils (for trust land). Local communities (community forests). Any citizen or non-citizen with permission from above authorities.	Government, CFAs and all other stakeholders with vested interest.	All stakeholders have access but permission is required from KFS for non-locals whether they have vested interests or not.
Use rights	Citizens/community members had rights to harvest selected NTFPs, and firewood in form of dead fallen wood. For some products, they had to purchase licenses from the FD. Total exclusion from KWS-managed forests.	KFS and communities (although communities must write management plans subject to approval by KFS).	Very few management plans have been approved, and no contracts have been signed; therefore communities still have use rights limited to NTFPs and dead wood.
Rights to earn income from a resource by using it directly or indirectly	Forest department (FD); local councils.	KFS, local councils, and CFAs through approved management plans.	Very few communities can access meaningful income from the forest.
Management rights	FD; KWS.	KFS, CFAs and stakeholders with vested interests through approved. management plans.	KFS still holds overall power since it is the final decision-making body; community rights limited to protection, conservation and monitoring, with no economic returns.
Exclusion rights	FD; KWS; Minister of Forestry.	KFS and CFAs through approved management plans; Parliament.	KFS still hold these rights waiting for the act's operationalization.
Alienation rights	Courts; Minister of Forestry.	KFS; judiciary system; communities may be consulted but do not make final decision; Parliament.	Courts still hold these rights; communities may only act as witnesses.

Source: Mogoi et al. (2012).

and most of the financial benefits accruing from productive units of the forests still belong to the government. Communities have been limited to subsistence and NTFPs with low financial value, with extraction being limited to only a few forests, plausibly explaining the low rate of CFA formation/uptake in the country. In some instances, non-members of CFAs blame their lack of involvement on the argument that government still has considerable power in forest management.

A number of CFAs have been formed through sensitization of communities adjacent to the major forests in the country by the Kenya Forest Action Network (FAN), the Kenya Forests Working Group (KFWG) (Ongugo et al., 2007) and the Laikipia Wildlife Forum (LWF). Lately, the Kenya Forest Service has also been spearheading the formation of CFAs as a step towards meeting the requirements of the Forest Act (2005). Members of a forest community and the locals adjacent to forest ecosystems who form such associations are required to apply to the Kenya Forest Service (KFS) for certain privileges in relation to management of the said forests. The CFAs rely on membership fees and subscriptions as their main sources of funds (Kinyanjui, 2007).

Within the region of the current study, the introduction of participatory forest management through the Forest Act (2005) led to the formation of the Kakamega Community Forest Association (KACOFA). This association was formed to enable the local communities participate in forest management and enjoy the associated benefits; it is an umbrella association comprised of about 31 forest user groups located around the forest. Membership to the user groups is open to all, although it involves payment of membership fees and periodic subscriptions to run the group activities; the members also have to contribute some of their time. Besides coordinating activities of the different user groups, KACOFA is at the centre of management and conservation of Kakamega forest, with activities ranging from the establishment of tree nurseries to afforestation. It also helps raise community awareness relating to conservation, monitoring the forest condition, monitoring activities carried out by user groups, training groups on tree nursery management and forest policing.

With the participation of its members, the CFA crafts the rules governing the harvesting of forest resources (see Table 12.2 for example of rules), members' participation in forest conservation, rehabilitation and management, and the sharing of benefits; some of the forest products that may be harvested include firewood, thatch grass, mushrooms, fodder, herbs, honey and butterflies. Some groups engage in ecotourism and the propagation of tree seedlings for sale. Although membership of a CFA is open to all who are ready to conform to the rules and requirements, the kind of forest products that can be harvested are more pro-poor.

Table 12.2 Example of CFA rules for grazers

(i)	All grazers must be registered with a user group and pay membership dues.
(ii)	Grazers may not graze on young plantations.
(iii)	Grazers will participate in forest management activities such as firebreak clearing, pruning, tending to young seedlings in the forest, etc.
(iv)	Grazers will pay 10 KES per sheep and 40 KES per cow.
(v)	Goats are not allowed into the forest.
(vi)	A fine equivalent to 1 ram will be charged to offenders.

12.3 A review of farm forestry decisions by rural households

This section reviews the link between participation in community forest management groups and households' investment decisions relating to farm forestry. It also explores other factors that may motivate households to undertake on-farm tree growing.

12.3.1 Community forest association-farm forestry nexus

Because participatory management allows communities to access a number of forest products, it could seen as a disincentive to on-farm tree planting. The literature, however, indicates that this may not be true; participation in forest management groups has been shown to influence decisions to plant more trees on farms (Emtage and Suh, 2004). Perhaps this is because such participation enhances people's attached value to forest ecosystems and the need to protect them, which in turn results in their desire to increase forest cover on their farms. Moreover, participation in community-based conservation groups enhances farmers' access to diversity, quality and quantity of tree species (Boffa et al., 2005). For instance, in Kenya the community forest associations train their members in tree planting and care, and tree nursery establishment. As a result, the group members have easy access to tree seedlings, either from group-managed or their own nurseries for planting in their own farms; this could accelerate on-farm tree planting practices. Moreover, the range of forest products allowed by the act to be extracted by communities is restricted to non-timber and dead wood. Because community participation in forest management improves forest policing, the community members may be compelled to plant trees for timber and related products on their own farms. While this may apply to all community members, CFA members and non-members alike, the CFA members could have an edge over the non-members because of the training they get and their easy access to tree seedlings.

12.3.2 Other factors that explain on-farm tree growing

Various factors explain the differences in farm tree-growing decisions by smallholder farmers. However, the specific socio-economic and institutional variables affecting those decisions differ across countries, regions, villages, and farms. Moreover, the direction of influence of a given variable is often inconsistent across studies.

Household decisions to plant trees may be directly influenced by household-specific, plot-specific and institutional factors. For instance, farm forests have enormous environmental advantages above direct benefits to the farm households. To comprehend these indirect benefits, the decision maker at household level requires some education, either formal or informal, obtained through schooling or extension services. Thus, better educated household heads, or households with access to government or farmer-farmer extension services, are better adopters of farm forestry (Muneer, 2008), either because they view tree planting as a means of improving the land (Dewees, 1995) or because they are able to appreciate other non-quantifiable benefits such as ambiance, microclimate modification or carbon sequestration. This also explains why households with good social networks may have a higher possibility of planting trees; because they are able to get extension services through such networks (Muneer, 2008; Gebreegziabher et al., 2010).

Institutional factors have also been shown to influence the decision by households to plant trees. Secure land tenure arrangements, for example, have been found to influence tree planting decisions among farmer groups. Trees take a long time to come to maturity, and only farmers who are confident of continued use of a given plot would be encouraged to plant them (Warner, 1995; Deininger and Feder, 2001; Bannister and Nair, 2003; and Gebreegziabher et al., 2010). However, some studies do not agree with the idea that secure tenure may encourage tree planting, and cite cases where communal ownership of land has been more conducive to development of farm forestry (German et al., 2009). Perhaps tree planting in areas with an ambiguous land tenure system is a means used by households to place a claim of legitimacy of ownership and/or access to a given piece of land.

12.4 Methodology

This section has twin objectives: to identify the determinants of a household's participation in CFA, and to estimate the impact of participation in CFA on farm forestry investment decisions. We discuss the approaches used to achieve these objectives in this section.

12.4.1 Factors associated with participation in CFA

Participation in CFA has potential costs and benefits which are perceived uniquely by different households. Costs may include membership fees, monthly/annual subscriptions, and time to undertake the association's activities; while benefits may include access to forest products, contracts to undertake specified activities within the forest, grazing in the forest, access to information on care for trees and general benefits of maintaining forests, and better access to quality tree seedlings. The individual decision to participate in a CFA can be modeled in a random utility framework, popular in analyzing innovation adoption under uncertainty (see Feder, Just and Zilberman, 1985). This implies that participation in CFA can be modeled as a binary choice based on utility maximization subject to household resource constraint (Manski, 1977). The utility function of the household can be expressed as:

$$U_i = f(\beta X_i) + \varepsilon_i \tag{1}$$

where X_i is a vector of exogenous variables and β is a vector of parameters to be estimated. The unobserved part of the household's utility is represented by ϵ_i which is assumed to be independently and identically distributed with a mean of zero. A farm household will choose to participate if the utility derived from participation, U_i^p is higher than the utility derived from non-participation, U_i^n. The probability of a household being a member of CFA is given by $P(\epsilon_i < \beta X_i)$. Thus, the participation model to be estimated is:

$$P(p_i = 1) = P(\varepsilon_i < \beta X_i) = \beta X_i + \varepsilon_i, \tag{2}$$

$$\text{where } p_i = \begin{cases} 1 & if \quad U_i^p > U_i^n \\ 0 & otherwise \end{cases}$$

The behavior of each household is influenced by its transaction costs, which are influenced by its access to information, assets, services and markets (Barrett, 2008). Whether a household participates in a CFA or not is dependent on the household's evaluation of the costs and benefits.

Literature indicates that human capital is important for receiving and processing information with regard to new developments (Schultz, 1982). It is therefore important to include in the analysis the household's decision makers' education and experience, captured by their level of education and age. A better educated household head is exposed to more information, and so has the capacity to interpret information received appropriately, and thus turn it into an opportunity. Experience may come with education or age, and has an important influence on the activities of an individual. Other important factors are the physical assets such as land, labor and cash (Boahene, Snijders and Folmer, 1999). Thus we include the landholding size, household size (to proxy for access to labor), and access to credit (to proxy for cash constraints). Whether a household owns cows or oxen is also important in the analysis as they indicate the household wealth level. Moreover, ownership of such livestock may motivate a household to participate in CFA so as to access the forest for grazing. Ownership of oxen may also proxy for transport cost. Because households participate in CFAs as a result of perceived benefits (Ongugo et al., 2007), distance to the forest and the forest management agency are likely to influence participation. Households that are close to the forest are more likely to participate because they are impacted more directly by the forest condition. Moreover, they are likely to gain more from harvesting the bulky forest products which are less economical for households that live far from the forest to extract and transport for domestic use. Even with community participation in forest management, the different management agencies in charge of different portions of Kakamega forest still pursue different objectives. For instance, the main objective of the Kenya Wildlife Service (KWS) is conservation; it does not allow communities to extract any forest products, whether or not they participate in forest management. Thus, the scope of private benefits of participatory forest management is limited from KWS-managed forest areas. Consequently, KWS as a forest management agency is likely to discourage participation in CFAs. But on the other hand, the KFS permits the harvesting of a specified range of forest products as well as allowing regulated grazing and crop cultivation in the forest by registered CFA groups.

The gender of the household head may influence participation. Men and women have different opportunities, motivation and abilities to involve themselves in collective action (Pandolfelli, Meinzen-Dick and Dohrn, 2007). Domestic responsibilities may also reduce the chances of women to participate in groups (Meinzen-Dick and Zwarteveen, 1998). Because of this, we include the gender of the household head in the analysis.

The influence of social networks in decision making among the smallholder households has been recognized in the literature. Such networks are for farmer-to-farmer extension, and may accelerate the diffusion of new ideas (Matuschke and Qaim, 2009; Conley and Udry, 2010). As a result, we include the number of social groups, other than CFA, that a household participates in.

12.4.2 Analyzing the impact of participation in CFA on farm forestry

The main interest here is to estimate the average treatment effect on the treated (ATT); that is, the way in which participation in community forest association affects the on-farm growing of trees. Because we are not able to observe what the results would have been without participation, we have to deal with data missing from the counterfactual; the remedy is to identify non-participating households and use them as counterfactual. But we must also deal with selection bias, because households take deliberate decisions whether or not to participate in a CFA. This self-selection implies that the mere comparison of outcomes of CFA members and non-members cannot yield reliable results.

Selection bias may arise from systematic differences between participants and non-participants. These arise from observable characteristics such as asset ownership and education. We use propensity score matching (PSM) to control for the observable characteristics; PSM constructs a suitable comparison, using non-participants that are similar to the participants in all relevant observable attributes (Caliendo and Kopeinig, 2008). Another potential source of bias is differences between participants and non-participants in terms of the unobservables. PSM cannot control for this kind of bias, and therefore we conduct a sensitivity analysis of our impact results. We further use endogenous switching regression (ESR) to verify the existence of selection bias due to unobserved household effects.

The execution of PSM is undertaken in two stages. The first stage involves generation of the propensity scores, $P(X)$, from the probit model; these scores indicate the probabilities of respective households being members of CFAs. From the scores, we construct a control group by matching participants to non-participants according to their propensity scores. Participants for whom no matches are found and the non-participants that are not used as matches are excluded from further analysis. At the second stage, we compute the effect of membership to CFA on land size that a household devotes to tree growing (ATT), using the matched observations. PSM estimator of the ATT is obtained by computing the difference in land size under trees between households participating in

CFA and the non-participating ones which are appropriately matched by the propensity scores, expressed as:

$$\tau_{ATT}^{PSM} = E(P(X)\big|p=1)\left\{E\left[Y(1)\big|p=1, P(X)\right] - E\left[Y(0)\big|p=0, P(X)\right]\right\}, \tag{3}$$

where $Y(1)$ and $Y(0)$ represent acreage under trees for participating households and non-participating households respectively. $p=1$ indicates treated/participating households while $p=0$ indicates control/non-participating households. We use all the variables in the PSM probit in the outcome analysis, in the belief that the inclusion of even non-significant variables cannot bias the estimates nor can they make them inconsistent (see Caliendo and Kopeinig, 2008 for details).

12.5 The study area and data

The study site for this survey was around Kakamega Forest, situated in the ethnically homogenous Kakamega county of Kenya. It lies north-east of Lake Victoria, between latitude 00°10′N and 00°21′N and longitude 34°47′E and 34°58′E, at about 1600 meters above sea level. The forest area is drained by two main river systems: the Isiukhu to the north and the Yala to the south. The forest is the only remaining rainforest in Kenya, and is the furthest east remnant of the Guinea-Congolean rain forest. According to the 1994 welfare monitoring survey, 52 percent of the population in the district lives below the poverty line (US$1 per day). As a result, there is heavy reliance on the forest for livelihood and income generation. This region has also been considered by the Kenya Woodfuel and Agro-forestry Programme (KWAP) as one of the areas that could benefit most from policies that target improvement of forestry projects due to its high population and agricultural potential.

12.5.1 Data

The data for this study was collected from communities around Kakamega forest in western part of Kenya. A random sample of 318 households was interviewed using a detailed semi-structured questionnaire. The households were randomly selected across the villages in the study area. Information was collected on household demographics, household assets, location, participation in social groups other than CFA, access to credit facilities, land size planted with trees, management agency in charge of the neighboring forest portion, and knowledge of the forest management reform envisaged in the Forest Act (2005). Table 12.3 captures the descriptive statistics of the variables used in this analysis.

Table 12.3 Basic descriptive statistics for participants and non-participants in CFAs

	Participants in CFAs			Non-participants		
Variable	**Obs.**	**Mean**	**Std. dev.**	**Obs.**	**Mean**	**Std. dev.**
Individual attributes						
Age of head	153	48	13.2	182	46.6	15.07
Education level of the household head (0 = no education, 1 = primary, 2 = secondary, 3 = tertiary)	153	2.4	0.81	182	2.43	0.87
Number of household members	149	6	1.8	187	5	1.90
Proportion of male-headed households	153	0.79	0.40	182	0.69	0.46
Farm characteristics						
Farm size (acres)	150	1.9	1.77	179	2.32	2.44
Value of total assets	153	18791	33779	195	21156.8	71025
Distance to nearest forest edge (minutes)	153	22.2	59.0	195	24.6	23.6
Proportion of households owning cows	153	0.79	0.40	186	0.76	0.42
Proportion of households owning oxen	153	0.37	0.48	186	0.32	0.47
Access to credit facilities (1 if yes, 0 otherwise)	150	0.27	0.44	178	0.08	0.27
Household land size (acres) under trees	153	0.41	0.45	195	0.26	0.29
Institutional attributes						
Number of social groups other than CFAs that a household participates in	153	1.74	1.20	195	0.91	0.98
Proportion of households whose neighboring forest is managed by KFS	153	0.91	0.29	195	0.8	0.40
Proportion of households aware of the Forest Act (2005)	150	0.85	0.35	165	0.37	0.48

Source: Authors' computation based on *Field Survey of Kakamega Forest* (2010).

The mean age of household head is 48 years and 47 years for participating and non-participating households, respectively. The education level of both participants and non-participants was secondary school, on average. The household size for participants and non-participants is six and five, respectively. 79 percent of the households participating in CFAs were male-headed. It is presumed that male-headed households may be better resourced and informed, enabling them to participate more in CFAs. Of the non-participating households, 69 percent were male-headed.

On farm characteristics, participants in CFAs had smaller land sizes (average 1.9 acres/0.77 ha) relative to that owned by non-participants (2.3 acres/0.93 ha). Another variable of significant interest is access to credit facilities; 27 percent of CFA participants had access to credit, compared to a paltry 8 percent of non-participants.

With regard to institutional attributes, households not participating in CFAs belonged, on average, to one social group, while participating households belonged to two social groups other than the CFA. Participation was also informed by the management agency of the neighboring forest portion; 91 percent of the participating households were closer to forest portions managed by the KFS. Awareness of the household of Forest Act (2005) also appears to have had influence on the decision to participate in CFA; 85 percent of the participating households were aware of the act even before joining, whereas of the non-participating households, only 37 percent were aware of the act.

Notably, the difference in mean land size under tree cultivation between the participating and the non-participating households is different from zero with a *t*-statistic of 3.64. This makes it important to investigate whether this difference does indeed originate from CFA membership. Notice that we only considered trees planted after 2005, when community participation in forest management was initiated in the country.

12.6 Results and discussion

In this section, we show and discuss the results of our analysis of the determinants of household participation in CFA, and how this participation impacts on household farm forestry behavior.

12.6.1 Determinants of household participation in CFA

We estimate the probit model of household membership to CFAs as described in Equation 2. The results are displayed in Table 12.4.

Table 12.4 Probit model of CFA membership

Variable	Marginal effect	Standard error	Z
Distance to forest (in minutes)	–0.006	0.004	–1.70*
Access to credit	0.253	0.097	2.43**
Owning cow(s)	0.049	0.091	0.53
Owning oxen	–0.002	0.079	–0.03
Household size	0.034	0.020	1.72*
Landholding size (acres)	–0.048	0.021	–2.31**
Male household head	0.039	0.088	0.44
Education level of head	0.017	0.051	0.34
Social capital (no. of social groups)	0.107	0.037	2.85***
Distance to forest, squared	0.00002	0.00004	0.70
Age of head	0.004	0.003	1.47
Log of household assets value	–0.009	0.034	–0.28
Aware of Forest Act	0.487	0.062	6.77***
KFS Management	0.217	0.096	2.10**
No. of observations	297		
Pseudo R-squared	0.33		

Source: Authors' computation based on *Field Survey of Kakamega Forest* (2010).

Note: * Significant at 10%, ** Significant at 5%, *** Significant at 1%.

Distance to the forest is negatively correlated with the probability of a household participating in CFA; each additional minute of walking time to the forest reduces the probability by 0.6 percentage points. This is reasonable, because if households join a CFA to benefit from the extraction of forest products, households that are far from forests will have less impetus to participate, it being more expensive for them to travel to the forests for such products.

Access to credit is positively associated with household participation in a CFA; it increases a household's chance of participating in a CFA by about 25.3 percentage points. This is plausible, because such households are better endowed to hire labor or purchase equipment that would maximize their gains from participating in a CFA. As a result, they would be more motivated to participate in CFAs.

Households with more members have a higher chance of participating in CFAs; each additional member increases the chance of a household participating in CFA by 3.5 percent. The reason for this is fairly straightforward. Household size is a proxy for labor endowment at the household level, so larger households have labor time to devote to CFA activities, besides being better placed in terms of labor for the extraction of forest products. Larger households may also have a higher demand for forest products which they may not satisfy by on-farm production. Thus, participating in CFAs and benefiting from forest products could be viewed as a viable livelihood alternative for the larger households.

Household landholding size is negatively correlated with CFA membership. Each additional acre (0.4 ha) of land owned reduces the probability of participating in CFAs by 4.8 percentage points. A possible explanation for this is that households with larger pieces of land may produce a number of forest products on farm; if this is the situation, such households would not be motivated to join CFAs. Moreover, if a larger proportion of the land owned is put under crop cultivation or livestock farming, the household may lack the time to devote to CFA activities.

Participation in other social groups positively correlated with household participation in CFA. This is understandable, because through such groups information on CFA is disseminated. Of course, herd behavior may also lead members of a given social group to jointly decide to participate in a CFA. Furthermore, trust built from the previous social groups may encourage households to quickly accept new ways of cooperating.

Those households that were aware of the Forest Act (2005) had a 48.7 percent higher chance of participating in a CFA. This could have been because such households were aware of the benefits that could be derived from participating in CFAs, and wanted to take advantage of these. But management agency is also important in determining participation of households in CFAs. Those households that are closer to forests managed by the Kenya Forest Service (KFS) have a 21.7 percent higher probability of participating in CFAs than do households closer to forests managed by the Kenya Wildlife Service (KWS). This could in part be because the KFS has been at the forefront of educating and encouraging communities to join CFAs. However, it must also be noted that management by KWS is more restrictive, limiting forest entry by communities and thus reducing potential benefits. People are less willing to participate in CFAs if doing so does not give them any advantages in terms of extraction of forest products.

12.6.2 Impact of CFA membership on farm forestry

As indicated earlier, the matching process is preceded by specification of the propensity scores for the treatment variable. A probit model was employed to predict the probability of a household being a member of CFA, as outlined and discussed in Section 12.6.1. The

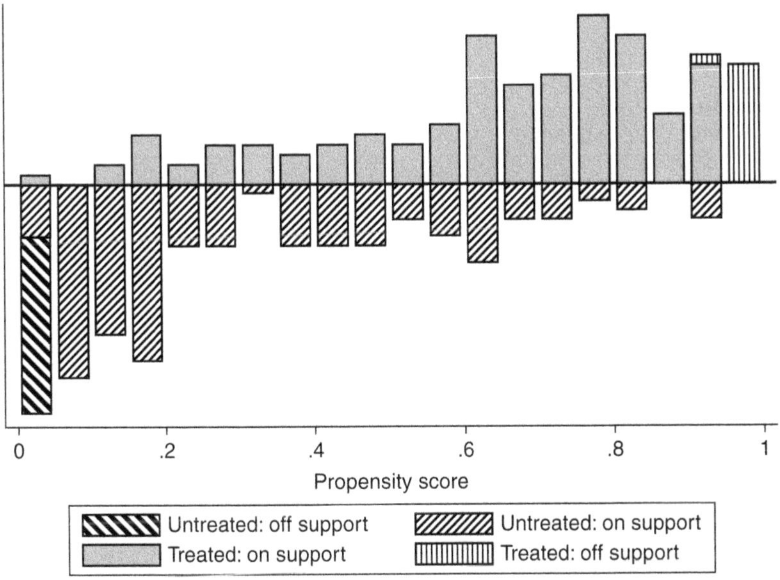

Figure 12.1 Propensity score distribution and common support for propensity score estimation

effect of participation in CFA on a household's land area under trees (farm forestry) was estimated with Nearest Neighbor Matching (NNM) and Kernel-Based Matching (KBM). Matching was done in the region of common support. Figure 12.1 presents the distribution of propensity scores and the region of common support. The figure indicates the bias in the distribution of propensity scores between members and non-members of CFA; it reveals the significance of proper matching and imposition of the common support condition to avoid bad matches.

Treated on-support shows CFA-member households which found suitable matches while *treated off-support* shows CFA-member households which did not find suitable matches. Similarly, *untreated on-support* represents non-CFA member households which found suitable matches whereas *untreated off-support* shows the non-CFA member households which did not find suitable matches. We present the average treatment effects and sensitivity analysis in Table 12.5.

The results indicate that household participation in CFA is positively correlated with the size of land that the household devotes to tree planting. Specifically, the NNM and the KBM causal effects of CFA membership on size of household land under trees suggest that

Table 12.5 Average treatment effects and sensitivity analysis

Matching algorithm	Outcome	ATT	Critical level of hidden bias (Γ)	Number of treated	Number of control
NNM	Acreage under trees	0.428*** (4.43)	2.65–2.70	140	157
KBM	Acreage under trees	0.428*** (4.13)	2.00–2.05	140	157

Source: Authors' computation based on *Survey of Kakamega Forest* (2010).
Note: t-values in parentheses; *** Significant at 1%. ATT = Average Treatment Effect for the treated.

households that participate in CFA have 0.428 acres (0.17 ha) more land under tree cultivation than do the non-CFA members. A casual examination may give the impression of perverse results here, because it would appear that farm households should plant *fewer* trees once they are able to access forest products from the government forest. There are, however, critical factors that could lead the participants to initiate and/or intensify on-farm tree growing:

1. CFAs train members in the need to manage and conserve forests, not just as a source of livelihood products but also as a source of income. The members are encouraged to initiate alternative income sources, such as bee-keeping, which may necessitate allocating part of the household's land to trees;
2. Not all forest products may be obtained from the government forest. For instance, the forest users may harvest wood fuel, but they can never be allowed to cut down trees for, say, building or fencing poles. In any case, involvement of communities in forest management implies a remarkable reduction in the cases of cheating; this means that community members have no option but to run on-farm forests for extraction of the products that cannot be accessed from the government forest. While this may apply to all the community members, CFA participants and non-participants alike, the CFA participants may have the advantage of accessing tree seedlings more cheaply from the association than their non-participating counterparts;
3. Because the CFAs have increased access to the forest, there could be stiffer competition for certain valuable forest products such as medicinal plants. This could drive community members to develop their

own farms with such species. Indeed, medicinal plants were found to be some of the most popular on-farm tree species during the survey;

4. Participatory forest management allows communities to graze their animals in the forest or to harvest grass for livestock. It also allows the communities to grow crops within the forest through the Plantation Establishment and Livelihood Improvement Scheme (PELIS). This could free more household land for tree growing among the participating households; and
5. Through training by the community forest association and direct engagement in forest management, the CFA-participating households may develop a sense of appreciation of forests. For instance, the group involved in ecotourism such as the Kakamega Environmental Education Programme (KEEP) would be more interested in forest conservation and would encourage members to plant trees on their farms rather than disturb the condition of the government forest.

The results of the sensitivity analysis for the presence of hidden bias are presented in the fourth column. Because the sensitivity analysis for insignificant effects is not meaningful, we computed Rosenbaum bounds, given by gamma (Γ), only for the treatment effects that were significantly different from zero (Hujer et al., 2004). Our results indicate the highest values of Γ of 2.05 and 2.70 for KBM and NNM, respectively; this shows that our results are less sensitive to unobserved confounding selection effects. Notice that Γ=1 implies absence of hidden bias. Thus, for our results to be rendered invalid, an unobserved variable must increase the odds of a household choosing to participate in CFA by 105 percent for KNM and 170 percent for NNM. This shows that even fairly large amounts of unobserved heterogeneity are not likely to alter the inference about the estimated effects of CFA membership on size of land devoted to trees by households. The robustness of these results is further confirmed by results of Endogenous Switching Regression (ESR), which indicate that there is no selectivity arising from unobserved factors (see Table 12.6). Correlations between the error terms of the selection equation and the outcome equations of the CFA participation and non-participation regimes (as measured by $\rho_{1\mu}$ and $\rho_{0\mu}$, respectively) are positive but statistically insignificant. This suggests that households that choose to participate or not to participate in CFA do no better or worse than any randomly picked household in terms of their acreage devoted to trees. The model fulfils the necessary condition for consistency that $\rho_{1\mu} < \rho_{0\mu}$. The likelihood ratio test for the independence of the three

Table 12.6 Results of endogenous switching regression model

	Selection equation		CFA participants		CFA Non-participants	
	Coefficient	Z-score	Coefficient	Z-score	Coefficient	Z-score
Land size	−0.14***	−2.67	0.17***	5.36	0.04***	2.62
Asset value	0.01	−0.11	0.01	0.41	0.02	0.98
Social capital	0.92***	3.76	0.05	0.37	0.01	0.10
Age of head	0.01	1.24	−0.004*	−2.04	−0.001	−0.58
Household size	0.05	0.98	−0.01	−0.43	0.003	0.19
Male head	0.15	0.70	−0.04	−0.62	0.07	0.86
Credit access	0.67***	2.65	−0.08	−1.00	0.01	0.05
Secure tenure	0.26	1.35	−0.02	−0.40	0.03	0.57
Own cows	0.21	1.01	−0.20***	−1.92	0.08	1.56
Own oxen	−0.04	−0.19	−0.02	−0.44	−0.16**	−2.35
Access to extension	0.02	0.08	−0.02	−0.24	0.13*	1.71
KFS mgt	0.36	1.35	−0.04	−0.31	0.01	0.21
Intercept	−2.82***	−3.01	0.39	0.39	0.01	0.02
Distance to forest edge	−0.001	−0.65				
Aware of forest rules	1.38***	7.43				
ln σ_1			−1.11***	−2.61		
$\rho_{1\mu}$			0.077	0.22		
ln σ_0					−1.29***	−2.86
$\rho_{0\mu}$					0.645	0.96
Wald χ^2	91.13***					
Log likelihood	−192.04					
LR test of indep. eqns: $\chi^2(1)$ 1.04						

Source: Authors' computation based on *Survey of Kakamega Forest* (2010).
Note: *, **, *** mean significant at 10%, 5% and 1%, respectively.

equations could not be rejected. These findings confirm the reliability of the PSM results.

The main objective of PSM estimation is to balance the distribution of relevant variables in the groups of CFA and non-CFA members rather than making a precise prediction of selection into treatment. We use the reduction in the median absolute standardized bias between the matched and unmatched models to examine the balancing power of our estimations. We show these results in Table 12.7.

As indicated by the third and fourth columns, substantial reduction in bias was achieved through matching. *P*-values show that joint significance of the regressors was rejected after matching, and never rejected at any level of significance before matching. This suggests that there was no systematic difference in the distribution of the covariates between members and non-members of CFAs after matching.

Table 12.7 Indicators of covariate balancing before and after matching

Matching Algorithm	Median absolute bias before matching	Median absolute bias after matching	% bias reduction (total)	Pseudo R^2 (unmatched)	Pseudo R^2 (matched)	P-value of LR (unmatched)	P-value of LR (matched)
NNM	21.5	7.9	63.3	0.325	0.054	0.000	0.164
KBM	21.5	2.9	86.5	0.325	0.017	0.000	0.963

Source: Authors computation based on *Survey of Kakamega Forest* (2010).

12.7 Conclusion and policy recommendations

The direct effect of households participating in community forest associations (CFA) is that more household land gets devoted to farm forestry. The study employed combined Propensity Score Matching (PSM) and Endogenous Switching Regression (ESR) to examine the direct effect of CFA membership on acreage under tree cultivation, using cross-sectional data from a survey of farm households adjacent to Kakamega forest. The analysis considered the causal relationship between participation in CFA and household land area that has been put under trees since 2005. It also examined the factors that drive households to participate in CFAs.

Empirical results indicate that CFA-member households, on average, have 0.428 more acres (0.17 ha) of land under tree cultivation than non-members. The implication of this is that decentralized forest management is a viable approach towards increasing private forest cover while conserving public forests in the country. This may appear less practicable in very land-scarce regions, but through a program like PELIS even the land-poor may be able to free some private land for tree growing. To ensure that households effectively participate in the community forest associations, policymakers must devise alternative livelihood and income-generation mechanisms to ease financial constraints among the forest-adjacent communities. Alternatively, funding mechanisms for the CFA operations may need to be devised so that they are less burdensome particularly to the poor participating and/or intending-to-participate segments of society.

Campaigns for participation in CFA by households should target education of the households about the relevant components of the Forest Act (2005), because those who understand the act have a higher probability of joining CFAs. Moreover, the campaigns should motivate communities to form other social groups as well, because those who participate in other social groups are more likely to join the CFAs later. More importantly, forest management agencies should guarantee entry into forests for the extraction of specified forest products, because restricting entry discourages households from joining CFAs and participating in the devolved forest management arrangements.

In a nutshell, promising policies include:

1. Increased access to information, especially with regard to the content of the Forest Act (2005);
2. Increased access to formal credit among the forest communities;
3. Promotion of formation of social groups, other than CFAs, among the forest communities;
4. Improvement of infrastructure to link communities with the forests so as to minimize transport cost that individuals incur on harvesting forest products; and
5. Provision of increased access to forests by the adjacent communities. The range of products harvested and other activities allowed in the forest could perhaps be expanded to cater for the varying interests of households; this would make participation in CFAs more rewarding to households.

References

Agrawal, A.A., Chhatre, A. and Hardin, R. (2008) 'Changing Governance in the Worlds' Forests', *Science*, 320, 1460–2.

Agrawal, A.A. and Ribot, J.C. (1999) 'Accountability in Decentralization: A Framework with South Asian and West African Cases', *The Journal of Developing Areas*, 33, 473–502.

Andersson, K.P., Bauer, J., Jagger, P., Luckert, M., Meinzen-Dick, R., Mwangi, E. and Ostrom, E. (2008) *Unpacking Decentralization*. Paper presented at the SANREM CRSP Annual Meeting, Los Banos, Philippines, May 2008.

Bannister, M.E. and Nair, P.K.R. (2003) 'Agroforestry Adoption in Haiti: The Importance of Household and Farm Characteristics', *Agroforestry Systems*, 57, 149–57.

Barrett, C.B. (2008) 'Smallholder Market Participation: Concepts and Evidence from Eastern and Southern Africa', *Food Policy*, 33(4), 299–317.

Boahene, K., Snijders, T.A.B. and Folmer, H. (1999) 'An Integrated Socioeconomic Analysis of Innovation Adoption: The Case of Hybrid Cocoa in Ghana', *Journal of Policy Modelling,* 21(2), 167–84.

Boffa, J. M., Turyomurugyendo, L., Barnekow-Lillesø, J. and Kindt, R. (2005) 'Enhancing Farm Tree Diversity as a Means of Conserving Landscape-based Biodiversity: Insights from the Kigezi Highlands, Southwestern Uganda', *Mountain Research and Development,* 25(3), 212–17.

Bolfor (2004) *Bolivia Sustainable Forest Management Project Report.* Chemonics International Inc., April 2004.

Borner, J., Mburu, J., Guthiga, P. and Wambua, S. (2009) 'Assessing Opportunity Costs of Conservation: Ingredients for Protected Area Management in the Kakamega Forest, Western Kenya', *Forest Policy and Economics,* 11(7), 459–67.

Caliendo, M. and Kopeinig, S. (2008) 'Some Practical Guidance for the Implementation of Propensity Score Matching', *Journal of Economic Surveys,* 22(1), 31–72.

Colfer, C.J.P. (2005) *The Complex Forest: Communities, Uncertainty and Adaptive Collaborative Management,* Resources for the Future, Washington, DC, and Center for International Forestry Research, Bogor, Indonesia.

Conley, T.G. and Udry, C.R. (2010) 'Learning About a New Technology: Pineapple in Ghana', *American Economic Review,* 100(1), 35–69.

Deininger, K. and Feder, G. (2001) *Land Institutions and Land Markets: Handbook of Agricultural Economics,* 1, 288–331.

Dewees, P.A. (1995) 'Trees on farms in Malawi: Private Investment, Public Policy, and Farmer Choice', *World Development,* 23(7), 1085–102.

Emerton, L. (1999) *Mount Kenya: The Economics of Community Conservation.* Evaluating Eden Series, Discussion Paper No. 4.

Emtage, N. and Suh, J. (2004) 'Socio-Economic Factors Affecting Smallholder Tree Planting and Management Intentions in Leyte Province, the Philippines', *Small-Scale Forest Economics, Management and Policy,* 3(2), 257–71.

Feder, G., Just, R.E. and Zilberman, D. (1985) 'Adoption of Agricultural Innovations in Developing Countries: A survey', *Economic Development and Cultural Change,* 33(2), 255–98.

Gebreegziabher, Z., A. Mekonnen, M. Kassie and G. Kohlin (2010) *Household Tree Planting in Tigrai, Northern Ethiopia: Tree Species, Purposes and Determinants.* EfD Discussion Paper Series. RFF.

German, G., Akinnifesi, F.K., Edriss, A.K., Sileshi, G., Masangano, C. and Ajayi, O.C. (2009) 'Influence of Property Rights on Farmers' Willingness to Plant Indigenous Fruit Trees in Malawi and Zambia', *African Journal of Agricultural Research,* 4(5), 427–37.

Guthiga, P.M., Mburu, J. and Holm-Mueller, K. (2008) 'Factors Influencing Local Communities' Satisfaction Levels with Different Forest Management Approaches of Kakamega Forest, Kenya', *Environment Management,* 41(5), 696–706.

Hujer, R., Caliendo, M. and Thomsen, S.L. (2004) 'New Evidence on the Effects of Job Creation Schemes in Germany: A Matching Approach with Threefold Heterogeneity', *Research in Economics,* 58(4), 257–302.

Kinyanjui, J.M. (2007) The readiness of community forest Associations to take up Participatory Forest Management. *Proceedings of the 1st National Conference on Participatory Forest Management.* June 6th-8th. KEFRI, Kenya.

Manski, C.F. (1977) 'The Structure of Random Utility Models', *Theory and Decision*, 8(3), 229–54.

Matuschke, I. and M. Qaim (2009) 'The Impact of Social Networks on Hybrid Seed Adoption in India', *Agricultural Economics*, 40(5), 493–505.

Mbuvi, M.T.E., Ongugo, P.O., Maua, J.O. and Koech, C.K. (2007) *Emerging Values of Forests: A Blessing for Participatory Forest Management (PFM)-The Case of Kenya*. Paper presented to the 3rd International PFM Conference. Addis Ababa, Ethiopia.

Meinzen-Dick, R. and Zwarteveen, M. (1998) 'Gendered Participation in Water Management: Issues and Illustrations from Water Users Associations in South Asia', *Agriculture and Human Values*, 15(4), 337–45.

Mogaka, H., Simons, G., Turpie, J., Emerton, L. and Karanja, F. (2001) *Economic Aspects of Community Involvement in Sustainable Forest Management in Eastern and Southern Africa*. IUCN – The World Conservation Union, Eastern Africa Regional Office, Nairobi, Kenya.

Mogoi, J., Obonyo, E., Ongugo, P., Oeba, V. and Mwangi, E. (2012) 'Communities, Property Rights and Forest Decentralisation in Kenya: Early Lessons from Participatory Forestry Management. Conservat Soc [serial online]', 10, 182–94. Available from: http://www.conservationandsociety.org/text.asp?2012/10/2/182/97490 [Accessed 24 Sep 2012].

Monterroso, I. (2008) *Institutional change and community forestry in Mayan Biosphere Reserve, Guatemala*. In the 12th Biennial Conference of the International Association of the Study of Commons. Cheltenham: IASCP

Muneer, S.E.T. (2008) 'Factors Affecting Adoption of Agroforestry Farming System as a Mean for Sustainable Agricultural Development and Environment Conservation in Arid Areas of Northern Kordofan State, Sudan', *Saudi Journal of Biological Sciences*, 15(1), 137–45.

Ongugo, P.O. (2007) *Participatory Forest Management in Kenya: Is There Anything for the Poor?* Proceedings: International Conference on Poverty Reduction and Forests. September, 2007. Bangkok, Thailand.

Ongugo, P.O, Mogoi, J.N., Obonyo, E. and Oeba, V.O. (2008) *Examining the Roles of Community Forest Associations (CFAs) in the Decentralization Process of Kenyan Forests*. Paper presented to the IASC Conference in England, July 2008.

Ongugo, P.O., Mbuvi, M.T.E., Maua, J.O., Koech, C.K. and Othim, R.A. (2007) *Emerging Community Institutions for PFM process Implementation in Kenya*. Paper presented to the 3rd International PFM Conference. Addis Ababa, Ethiopia.

Ongugo, P.O and Njuguna, J.W. (2004) *The Potential Effects of Decentralization Reforms on the Conditions of Kenya's Forest Resources*. Paper presented to the Biennial Conference of the International Association for the Study of Common Property (IASCP) on 3–13 August 2004. Oaxaca, Mexico.

Oyono, P.R. (2004) 'Resources Management Decentralization in Cameroon', *The Journal of Modern African studies*, 42(1), 91–111.

Pandolfelli, L., Meinzen-Dick, R. and Dohrn, S. (2007) *Gender and Collective Action: A Conceptual Framework for Analysis*. CAPRi Working Papers 64. Washington D.C.: International Food Policy Research Institute.

Schultz, T.W. (1982) *Investing in People: The Economics of Population Quality* (Berkeley: University of California Press).

Warner, K. (1995) 'Patterns of Tree Growing by Farmers in Eastern Africa', in J.E.M. Arnold and P.A. Dewees (eds), *Tree Management in Farmer Strategies: Responses to Agricultural Intensification* (London: Oxford University Press).
The World Bank (2009) *Community Driven Development*, available at: http://go.worldbank.org/24k81HVVso [accessed 8 December 2009].

13

The Impact of Land Certification on Tree Growing on Private Plots of Rural Households: Evidence from Ethiopia

Alemu Mekonnen, Hosaena Ghebru, Stein T. Holden and Menale Kassie

13.1 Introduction

Many environmental problems such as soil degradation and forest depletion can be characterized as being a result of incomplete, inconsistent, or non-enforced property rights (Bromley and Cernea, 1989). It has been long observed that easily transferable and secure property rights have been identified as a key element to bring about higher levels of investment and access to credit, to facilitate the reallocation of production factors to maximize allocative efficiency in resource use, and to allow economic diversification and growth (Deininger and Jin, 2006; Place, 2009).

More recently, the importance of land tenure has been given considerable attention. For instance, it has been mentioned as important in the Commission for Legal Empowerment of the Poor (2008), Commission for Africa (2005), NEPADs Comprehensive African Agricultural Development (2003), and the UN Millennium Project (2005). It has also received attention in the Poverty Reduction Strategy Papers produced by many African countries, and a number of African countries have passed legislation related to land reform. However, implementation of such legislation has been either very slow or non-existent in most of these countries; this makes it difficult for benefits from such legislation to be realized and the potential benefits for the poor are therefore likely to be lost (Deininger et al., 2008b).

In Ethiopia, to enhance tenure security and reduce land disputes in rural areas, a low-cost land certification and registration was launched in four major regions from 1998/99 (the reform started in one region in 1998/99, it started in the next region in 2003, then in 2004 and 2005 in the third and fourth region), and is currently being carried out. This is the largest land certification program in the last decade in Africa, and possibly in the world (Deininger et al., 2008b). The cost of the land certification program is also considered to be an order of magnitude lower than what could be found elsewhere in the literature (Deininger et al., 2008b). The program started in Tigray region (one of our study areas) in 1998/99, while in the Amhara region (the other region covered in this study) the program began in 2003. There are limited studies on the impact of this new program on investment in land and agricultural productivity (Deininger et al., 2009; Holden et al., 2009). Holden et al. (2009) assessed the investment (tree and soil and water conservation) and crop productivity impact of land certification in Tigray region of Ethiopia using panel data; they found that the program has positive impact on investment and productivity. Similarly, Deininger et al. (2009) assessed soil and water conservation and productivity impact of this program in the Amhara region and they also found positive impacts. The impact of land tenure security or the lack of it depends on the types of investment, the available infrastructure and the political setting of each region/country (Place, 2009; Deininger and Jin, 2006). Thus, the results of empirical studies of impacts of land tenure insecurity or land titling are not uniform (Deininger and Feder, 2009).

This chapter is therefore expected to contribute to the growing but limited literature by focusing on impacts of land certification on the number of trees grown, using household plot-level data in the Amhara and Tigray regions of Ethiopia. The specific objectives of the study are: to analyze the effects of land certification on tree-growing behavior on private plots of rural households in the Amhara and Tigray regions of Ethiopia, and factors other than land certification that have significant effects on the number of trees planted on private plots of rural households. Unlike most other studies looking at impacts on tree growing, we use household and plot panel data in the analysis.

We find that land certification has a positive impact on tree growing on private plots of rural households in both the Tigray and the Amhara regions. We also find that other variables influence tree growing by rural households. The rest of the chapter is structured as follows. Section 13.2 presents a brief review of related literature. The analytical framework and data used in the study are briefly described in Section 13.3. Section 13.4 presents descriptive statistics, while Section 13.5 describes the methodology used. Section 13.6 presents results and discussion focusing on the effects of land certification on tree growing while Section 13.7 concludes the chapter.

13.2 Brief literature review

Increased tenure security could encourage farmers to invest in land and improve land productivity through its expected effects on the possibilities of using land as collateral and on land transfer to those who use it more productively (Besley, 1995). However, individual land titling may not always be appropriate for countries in Africa, as apart from anything else it may be too costly, and improper implementation could mean more confusion and conflict (Deininger et al., 2008b). On the other hand, there is demand in some African countries to introduce some formal means to enable and encourage farmers to ensure that proper land transactions take place and farm boundaries are demarcated with some formal enforcement mechanism. For example, a recent study by Deininger et al. (2008a) in Uganda showed that more than 90 percent of households wanted to get a certificate, and 87 percent were willing to pay. Principles to be followed in addressing these issues include protection of women's rights and local level documentation of land rights – which is less demanding and less costly than title, but with possible external enforcement and an improved state of certification in the future. Examples of attempts to implement these principles in Africa include new land laws or policies in Tanzania (Sundet, 2004), Malawi (Peters and Kambewa, 2007), Mozambique (Tanner, 2002), and Uganda (McAuslan, 1998). Meanwhile, Sikor and Muller (2009) argue that state-led land reforms encounter significant problems in practice; two main reasons for this are reliance on top-down initiatives and bureaucratic implementation. They note that empirical and conceptual insights suggest the benefits of a shift in emphasis from state to community in land reform.

Studies on the effect of land tenure insecurity (measured in different ways) on investment in land in Africa have found different results (Brasselle et al., 2002; Deininger and Jin, 2006). A recent work by Place (2009) notes significant heterogeneity of findings of studies in Africa that examine the productivity effects of tenure systems and recommend paying attention to local context, and overarching macro and sectoral conditions. Deininger and Feder (2009) also note, in a recent review of work on potential gains from land titles, that existing evidence is not uniform. For example, a study in Madagascar suggests that there is no effect of formal title on plot-specific investment (Jacoby and Minten, 2007). On the other hand, in Uganda a shift to full ownership from plots merely occupied by owner-cum-occupants increased the likelihood of investment in trees fivefold, and doubled that of soil conservation

(Deininger and Ali, 2008). In Ghana, Pande and Udry (2005) find that tenure insecurity reduced investment in the form of fallowing, leading to an estimated reduction in output by about one-third and very large losses in aggregate efficiency.

In Ethiopia, earlier studies have used measures of land tenure insecurity such as perceived insecurity by farmers or the length of time the farmer has worked on the land. Some of these earlier studies have focused on soil and water conservation investments (for example, Gebremedhin and Swinton, 2003; Deininger and Jin, 2006) while others have looked at tree growing (Holden and Yohannes, 2002; Deininger and Jin, 2006; Mekonnen, 2009).

Holden et al. (2003) found that there was a large potential for more tree planting on private land with good market access that was unsuitable for crop production due to steep slopes and shallow soils in the Amhara region of Ethiopia. Stimulation of such investments could both reduce the pressure on communal lands and provide a good source of income for households without having any significant negative impact on household food production.

Ethiopia's recent implementation of a large-scale and low-cost land certification program is an important example of attempts to formalize land rights with low cost while also addressing other related issues. Using community- and household-level data collected recently from the four major regions of Ethiopia, Deininger et al. (2008b) document such certification. As the study by Deininger et al. (2008b) is a first description of such a process, they recommend that such a study be complemented by more detailed evidence of certification impacts, preferably using panel data.

Recent studies on Ethiopia have focused on the impact of land certification on investment and productivity in agriculture (Deininger et al., 2008b; Deininger et al., 2009; Holden et al., 2009). These studies were motivated by a large-scale low-cost land certification program that has been undertaken in the four major regions of Ethiopia. Holden et al. (2009) use household- and plot-level panel data collected from the Tigray region of Ethiopia to assess the investment and productivity impacts of the recent low-cost land certification. They find significant positive impacts, including effects on the maintenance of soil conservation structures, investment in trees, and land productivity. Using panel data from the Amhara region of Ethiopia, Deininger et al. (2009) assess the effects of the low-cost land registration program in Ethiopia on soil and water investment. They find that despite policy constraints the program increased soil and water -related investment.

In addition to land certification, other variables are also expected to influence tree growing. One such variable is access to and availability of wood from communal land or forests. A study by Heltberg et al. (2000) finds that rural Indian households substitute fuels from private sources for forest fuelwood in response to forest scarcity and increased fuelwood collection time. Similar results were found by Van't Veld et al. (2006), who find that when biomass availability from communal areas decreases, households would be more likely to use privately produced fuel instead of increasing the time they spend to collect fuel from communal sources. Linde-Rahr (2003) also finds that in Vietnam higher shadow prices of fuelwood collection from open-access leads to more collection from private plantations. Amacher et al. (1993) find that when fuelwood is sufficiently scarce on communal land, households eventually begin growing wood on their own private land. Amacher et al. (2004) also find that in Tigray region of Ethiopia, distance to the main fuelwood collection area positively affects the decision to plant eucalyptus on own agricultural land and on microdam land. After a review of studies on household responses to fuel wood scarcity, Cooke et al. (2008) conclude that in the presence of sufficient scarcity, the empirical results generally reinforce the contention that households change their behavior in ways that are least costly to them.

This brief review suggests that more evidence is needed on the impacts of land certification on investment in land and agricultural productivity, including tree growing behavior.

13.3 Analytical framework and data

The analytical approach for this research will draw on the previous literature on the economics of farmer participation in tree-planting activities. Previous research on tree-planting activities has modeled farmers' participation in tree planting as a function of a number of economic, social, demographic, institutional and plot variables, and other variables (such as agro-ecology indicator variables and village dummy variables) (for example Holden et al., 2009; Deininger et al., 2009; Mekonnen 2009). In developing countries where input and product markets are imperfect, consumption and production decisions are non-separable. So, a non-separable farm household model will be used as our theoretical framework.

We use household- and plot-level panel data. The data used for the Amhara region was collected in 2002 and 2007 by the Environmental Economics Policy Forum for Ethiopia together with its partners. It included over 1700 households and covers 7 districts and 14 communities in the Amhara region. The data from Tigray region includes 16 communities, and is stratified by market access, population density, access to irrigation and agro-ecology. From each community, 25 households were selected with information from all plots surveyed in 1998, 2001, 2003 and 2006.

13.4 Descriptive statistics

13.4.1 Amhara region

Table 13.1 presents mean and standard deviation of the variables used in the analysis of the Amhara region.

The results show that on average a household grows 159 trees with a very wide variation across households as reflected by a standard deviation of more than three times the mean. In terms of extent of certification, the data shows that about 40 percent of the households have received land certificates.

13.4.2 Tigray region

Table 13.2 shows the average number of trees by type, on plots with and without land certificates, irrespective of year, based on data from

Table 13.1 Descriptive statistics (Amhara region)

Variable	Mean	Std. Dev.
Dependent variable		
Planted trees (number)	158.623	547.319
Explanatory variables		
Certification (1 = yes)	0.405	0.491
Household age (year)	49.764	15.103
Family size (number)	5.328	2.131
Livestock (TLU)	5.579	39.758
Off-farm activity participation (1 = yes)	0.125	0.331
Education (year)	3.211	4.198
Farm size (ha)	1.615	0.946
Distance to Woreda town (minutes)	66.917	47.605
Distance to road (minutes)	35.084	35.009
Gender (1 = male)	0.849	0.358
Extension contact (1 = yes)	0.124	0.330
Credit access (1 = yes)	0.364	0.481
Time spent to collect wood from communal land (in hours per round trip)	1.67	1.24

Source: Survey data.

Table 13.2 Descriptive statistics for tree variables (Tigray)

	Certificate			No certificate			
Variable	Mean	St. Error	N	Mean	St. Error	N	t-test
Eucalyptus trees	5.05	1.26	924	1.37	0.71	168	>***
Indigenous trees	15.78	4.20	939	1.99	0.59	169	>***
Young trees	5.97	1.19	928	0.95	0.40	168	>***
Tree seedlings	9.08	1.18	933	3.86	2.01	167	>**

Source: Authors' survey data.

1998, 2001 and 2006. For *Young trees* and *Tree seedlings* we only had data from 2001 and 2006. Land certification took place in 1998–99. Plots that were on households' land certificates had significantly more trees than plots that were not included on households' land certificates. However, this does not say anything about the direction of causality between land certificates and planting of trees; further econometric analysis is required for the inference of impacts from land certification. Basic variable description and statistics for the variables included in the econometric models are presented in Table 13.3.

13.5 Methodology

13.5.1 Amhara data analysis and estimation methods

The choice of method partly depends on the nature of the outcome variable; our outcome variable has observations with both positive and zero values. Where a dependent variable contains both zero and positive values, a Tobit model and its variants could be used. In this chapter a random-effects Tobit model is adopted;[1] we assumed that household-specific unobserved characteristics would not affect impact of certification, as this intervention is exogenous to individual households, and all households within a village are well aware that they will receive the certificate. However, the decision to adopt tree planting may be influenced by the gain from adoption, and estimation without controlling for this problem may lead to biased results. A Heckman self-selection correction approach is also tried, in order to address this problem, but the inverse Mills ratio was not significant. Thus, we report results only for probit and Tobit models. For both of those models, to account for time-varying variables we also used a correlated random-effects model (the Chamberlain-Mundlak approach) where average values of these variables are included as additional variables. The characteristics of a household's plot may affect decisions on tree planting; however, for the Amhara data the analysis has been done at household level, as the outcome variable was not collected at plot level during the 2007 round of data collection. We included district-level (Woreda) fixed effects to address the district-level effects.

We also included the time spent by households in collecting wood from communal lands, for which a positive correlation with private tree planting is expected.

13.5.2 Tigray data analysis and estimation methods

We applied a two-step approach to data analysis by first using non-parametric matching to ensure that we have a sample of plots with and without land certificates that satisfies the balancing and common support requirements. This facilitates the elimination of selection bias due to observable plot and household characteristics. To assess the need for separation of planting of trees from how many trees to plant on a plot, we tested probit versus Tobit models, and assessed the pattern of signs and significance levels for the two types of model. We found a remarkably similar pattern in the two types of models and decided that there is little reason to use two-stage models after matching, and to worry about selection bias due to unobservables. We therefore used random-effects Tobit models on the matched sample. Fixed-effects models with limited dependent variables suffer from the incidental parameter problem, which leads to biased estimators (Greene, 2003; Wooldridge, 2002). The correlated random-effects (Mundlak-Chamberlain) model was also tried, but could not converge; this could be due to the problem that there were relatively few dependent variable observations with non-zero values.

Models for farm-plot level investments in trees have the following specification for estimation of factors associated with plot level tree stocks and tree planting, including the certification impacts:

$$\begin{aligned} I^{P}_{hpt} &= \alpha_0 + \alpha_1 Q_{hpt} + \alpha_2 CY_{hpt} + \alpha_3 I^{F}_{hpt} + \alpha_4 I^{F}_{hpt} * CY_{hpt} \\ &\quad + \alpha_5 DF_h + \alpha_6 Z_{ht} + \alpha_7 Z_v + \alpha_8 D_t + \zeta_h + e_{hpt} \end{aligned} \tag{4}$$

Table 13.3 Variables used in the analysis in Tigray region

Variables	Obs	Mean	Std. Dev.	Min	Max
Number of eucalyptus trees	1048	4.671756	36.0918	0	650
Number of indigenous trees on plot	1065	14.25915	120.8971	0	2200
Number of young trees (2–5 years) on plot	1051	5.313987	34.14669	0	580
Number of tree seedlings (0–2 years) on plot	1053	8.292498	35.15054	0	400
Log of number of eucalyptus trees	1048	0.252643	0.892815	0	6.48
Log of number of indigenous trees on plot	1065	0.425352	1.207831	0	7.70
Log of number of young trees (2–5 years) on plot	1051	0.348412	1.036651	0	6.36
Log of number of tree seedlings (0–2 years) on plot	1053	0.467652	1.266248	0	5.99
Public investment in conservation on plot (dummy)	1726	0.349942	0.47709	0	1
Years with certificate	1726	3.9763	3.199153	0	8.92
Distance to communal woodlot	1719	4.638967	1.891153	0.69	9.21
Time used to collect firewood	1726	5.435084	1.767046	1.099	9.21
Tree planting interest on any plot in 2006 (dummy)	1641	0.912249	0.283019	0	1
Perceived effect of land certificate on tree planting (dummy)	1641	0.831201	0.374689	0	1
Homestead plot (dummy)	1726	0.293743	0.455608	0	1
Sex of household head (dummy, 1 = female)	1726	0.169757	0.375528	0	1
Age of household head (years)	1726	54.26564	15.16672	0	100
Education of household head	1726	0.487833	0.762621	0	4
Female labor force (log)	1726	0.915345	0.531597	0	2.83

Male labor force (log)	1726	0.871548	0.623985	0	3.50
Number of oxen/ha (log)	1726	0.534374	0.566066	0	2.83
Tropical livestock units/ha (log)	1726	1.042118	0.785082	0	4.04
Own farm size, tsimdi	1726	4.513751	3.145199	0.25	19.5
Plot size, tsimdi	1726	1.123013	1.105606	0.0016	15
Soil depth (deep)	1726	0.393395	0.488645	0	1
Soil depth (medium)	1726	0.31518	0.464722	0	1
Flat slope	1726	0.714948	0.45157	0	1
Low hill	1726	0.192932	0.394714	0	1
Mid hill	1726	0.056199	0.230373	0	1
Soil type Cambisol	1726	0.279258	0.448765	0	1
Soil type Vertisol	1726	0.274044	0.446161	0	1
Soil type Regosol	1726	0.248552	0.432299	0	1
Distance to plot (minutes walk)	1702	24.02482	30.48366	0	360

Source: Authors' survey data.

Where:

I^{P}_{hpt} is the log(number of trees +1) on plot p of household h in period t,

Q_{hpt} is a vector of plot level time-varying biophysical characteristics,

CY_{hpt} is the duration of ownership of land certificate for plots with certificate,

I^{F}_{hpt} is a public investment dummy on plot p of household h in period t,

DF_h is the distance to nearest communal forest area in 2003 (used as time-invariant variable),

Z_{ht} is a vector of household characteristics,

Z_v represents zonal dummy variables

D_t represents time period dummy variables,

ζ_h is a household random effects error component,

e_{hpt} is the transitory error component.

The investment enhancement effect that may have accrued due to the land certification that has reduced plot level tenure insecurity is not likely to appear immediately after the receipt of land certificates, and is likely to grow stronger over time. First, the perceptions of stronger tenure security must sink in, and then these perceptions will gradually start to affect plot-level behavioral decisions. To capture this gradual effect, we used the time period (in years) during which the individual households have possessed their land certificates. This also resembles a pipeline approach, where variation in timing of allocation of certificates is utilized to identify the impacts. This variation in timing was caused primarily by administrative constraints. The land registration and certification took place all over the highlands of Tigray in a fairly short period of time in 1998–99, when more than 80 percent of the households received land certificates. Administrative errors caused some households or sections of communities to receive their certificates later than other households and sections of communities. It is this variation in timing of allocation of certificates that we can utilize to identify the impacts.

The plot-level characteristics include a dummy variable for homestead plots. We assume that tenure security is higher on homestead plots and that there are no restrictions on tree planting on those plots. Therefore we expect a positive sign for this variable. Another of the plot characteristics is the distance from the homestead to the plot. We assume that there is greater tenure insecurity on distant plots, and also a larger risk that planted trees can be stolen or damaged due to the higher costs of monitoring and protecting investments on distant plots than on nearby plots. We also expect tree planting to be positively associated with sloping land and shallow soils.

We expect the planting of trees to be negatively associated with public investments on the plot because of the prohibition of tree planting on land suitable for crop production (with the exception of homestead plots). In particular, we expect such a negative relationship for eucalyptus, for which restrictions on planting are most clear. It is possible, therefore, that land certification has not stimulated planting of eucalyptus even though certification may have reduced tenure insecurity. We therefore test for the interaction between public investment and years with certificate, expecting it to give a negative coefficient – particularly so in the eucalyptus model. However, there are also legal restrictions against cutting down of indigenous trees, and public investment in plots may be positively associated with the stock of indigenous trees on plots for that reason.

To assess the relationship between tree-planting incentives on private land and the availability of trees from communal land, we have included two variables: the distance to the nearest communal woodlot, and the time the household spent per week on collection of firewood. We expect tree-planting incentives to be stronger when the distance to the nearest communal woodlot is greater. Initially, we also expect that households that spend a considerable amount of time on collection of firewood will have stronger incentives to plant trees. Over time, however, it is possible that those who have planted more trees will have spent less time on the collection of firewood (negative feedback effect). Since these two variables are available for only one year, 2003, in our data – and we therefore use them as time-invariant variables – the expected sign for the collection time for firewood could be ambiguous due to the possible negative feedback effect.

13.6 Results and discussion: effects of land certification on investment in trees

13.6.1 Amhara region

The distribution of the outcome variable (number of trees planted) is highly skewed, with a skewness of 8.52 and a kurtosis of 108.2. We therefore transform the outcome variable by using a logarithm. The natural logarithm of the outcome variable has a skewness of 0.67 and a kurtosis of 1.90. Estimated results are presented in Tables 13.4 and 13.5. Bootstrapped standard errors are reported.

Results of the correlated random-effects Tobit model[2] (Table 13.5) show that land certification has a positive and statistically significant effect on the number of trees grown. Similarly, the effect of certification on the likelihood of tree growing in the correlated random-effects probit model is positive and statistically significant (Table 13.4). This suggests that tenure security is important, given the fact that the benefits from long-term investments accrue over time.[3] Deininger et al. (2009) found similar results using the same dataset but with soil conservation measures as the outcome variable.

On the other hand, the results of the Heckman correction approach suggest that the inverse Mills ratio is not significant. For this reason, we report and discuss the probit results for analysis of the decision to plant trees (Table 13.4) while the analysis of number of trees grown is handled using the results for the correlated random-effects Tobit presented in Table 13.5.

In addition to the certification variable, other variables also affect the tree growing by the rural households in our sample. Since the results differ across the different models used, we took the results of correlated random-effects Tobit model (Table 13.5) to briefly present the effects of other variables. Participation in off-farm activities, farm size, being a male head of household, and contact with extension agents were found to be positively correlated with number of trees grown. Households further away from roads planted fewer trees, signifying the role of market access. We also found that more educated households had fewer trees, which is generally not expected – but in fact, households who spend more time collecting fuelwood per trip from communal areas have more private trees.[4] The results from the correlated random-effects Tobit model also suggest that there are significant differences across districts, as these are jointly significant. We also find that time dummies and averages of time variant variables are jointly significant. Most of these results are similar in the probit as in the Tobit model.

Table 13.4 Tree investment decision: results of the correlated random-effect probit model

Variables	**Coefficient**
Certification (1 = yes)	0.378***
Household head age	0.002
Family size	0.011
Livestock (in Tropical Livestock Units)	–0.010
Off-farm activity participation	0.301*
Education	–0.038**
Farm size	0.052
Distance to district town (Woreda)	0.002
Distance to road	–0.003***
Gender of head (1 = male)	0.272***
Extension contact	0.370**
Credit access	0.090
Time dummy	0.268*
Time spent to collect wood from communal sources	0.068***
Constant	–1.327***
Joint significance of district dummies ($chi^2(6)$)	24.10***
Joint significance of average time-varying variables ($chi^2(7)$)	28.90***
Likelihood-ratio test of rho = 0: $chibar^2(01)$	27.98***
Log likelihood	–1384.688
Wald $chi^2(28)$	189.89***
Number of observations	3002

Source: Survey data.
Note: Significance levels: *** $p<0.01$, ** $p<0.05$, * $p<0.1$.

Table 13.5 Tree investment: correlated random-effects Tobit model (Chamberlain–Mundlak) approach

Variables	**Coef.**
Certification (1 = yes)	0.380**
Household head age	0.003
Family size	–0.015
Livestock (in Tropical Livestock Units)	–0.002
Off-farm activity participation	0.476**
Education	–0.040*
Farm size	0.107*
Distance to district town (Woreda)	0.002
Distance to road	–0.006***
Gender of head (1 = male)	0.683***
Extension contact	0.580***
Credit access	0.165
Time dummy	1.151***
Time spent to collect wood from communal sources	0.111***
Constant	–0.615*
Joint significance of district dummies (chi2(6))	70.12***
Joint significance of average time-varying variables (chi2(7))	45.46***
Rho	0.327***
Log likelihood	–6319.704
Wald $chi^2(28)$	665.57***
Number of observations	3002

Source: Survey data.
Note: Significance levels: *** $p<0.01$, ** $p<0.05$, * $p<0.1$.

13.6.2 Tigray region

The restrictions on tree planting, eucalyptus trees especially, on arable land caused us to launch an alternative hypothesis for the effects of certification on tree planting: that land certification has not stimulated tree planting, the planting of eucalyptus especially. However, eucalyptus may be the most profitable crop to grow for rural households in Ethiopia (Holden et al., 2003; Jagger and Pender, 2000), and local norms and attitudes towards tree planting may differ from the rules stated by the law. We cannot therefore rule out that land certification has also stimulated eucalyptus planting.

The results from four household random-effects panel Tobit investment models, including models with eucalyptus, indigenous trees, young trees (2–5 years old), and tree seedlings (< 2 years old) are presented in Table 13.6, using years that the household has held the land certificate as the variable for identification of the effect on land certification on investment in trees.

Table 13.6 shows that the years with certificate variable was significant at the 1 percent level and had a positive sign in the models with eucalyptus, young trees and tree seedlings while it was insignificant in the model with indigenous trees. There was a negative and significant correlation between public investments in conservation structures on plots and stocks of young trees and tree seedlings. This seems to indicate that the law restrictions on tree planting on arable land have an impact, and more so on land that has been exposed to public conservation investment. Furthermore the interaction variable between *public plot-level investment* and *years with certificate* was highly significant and with a negative sign. Assessing this effect jointly with the separate effects of the two interacted variables shows that land certification has stimulated the planting of eucalyptus – but less so (the net effect is only about half of that on other plots) on land that has been exposed to public conservation investment. We also found that households with more educated household heads had more eucalyptus trees on their land. This is not likely to be because they are less aware of the restrictions on tree planting, but rather that they are more aware of the advantages of eucalyptus.

We can therefore reject the hypothesis that land certification has not stimulated tree planting. Land certification has indeed stimulated tree planting, including planting of eucalyptus, even with the restrictions on tree planting on arable land.

Homestead plots had significantly more trees of all types, whereas the number of trees was significantly lower on distant plots, as indicated by

Table 13.6 Land certification on plot-level investments in trees in Tigray (RE Tobit)

Variables	Eucalyptus trees	Indigenous trees	Young trees	Tree seedlings
Public investment in conservation on plot (dummy)	0.057	–0.745	–1.871***	–2.334***
Years with certificate	0.653***	0.179	0.755***	0.793***
Public investment (years with certificate)	–0.345**	0.208	0.132	0.321
Distance to communal woodlot	0.115	0.03	–0.041	–0.175
Tree planting interest on any plot in 2006 (dummy)	0.755	1.034	–0.328	–0.376
Perceived effect of land certificate on tree planting (dummy)	–0.539	1.142*	–0.388	–0.536
Homestead plot (dummy)	1.895***	2.695***	2.829***	4.437***
Sex of household head (dummy, 1 = female)	–0.097	–0.224	0.365	–0.064
Age of household head (years)	0.024	0.01	0.011	0.024
Education of household head	0.669**	0.301	0.475	0.264
Female **labor** force (log)	–0.642	0.043	–0.517	–0.226
Male **labor** force (log)	0.191	–0.579	0.894*	0.91
Number of oxen/ha (log)	–0.808	–0.553	–0.735	–0.715
Tropical livestock units/ha (log)	0.480	0.002	0.113	1.024
Own farm size, *tsimdi*[5]	0.138	0.111	0.095	0.145
Plot size, tsimdi	–0.272	0.467***	–0.367	–0.196
Soil depth (deep)	–1.284**	–1.250***	0.05	–1.124
Soil depth (medium)	–0.006	–1.534***	0.54	0.392

Flat slope	−1.343	2.246	−0.785	−0.168
Low hill	−0.814	2.96	0.549	0.739
Mid hill	−0.395	5.429**	−2.371	−2.268
Soil type Cambisol	−0.197	0.336	1.846***	0.27
Soil type Vertisol	−0.542	−0.024	1.468**	−0.247
Soil type Regosol	0.697	0.911*	0.34	0.941
Distance to plot (minutes' walk)	−0.143***	−0.048***	−0.077***	−0.097***
Year dummies	Yes	Yes	Yes	Yes
Zonal dummies	Yes	Yes	Yes	Yes
Constant	−4.344	−6.387**	−7.133**	−12.417***
Household panel variance	1.377***	0.24	2.065***	2.120***
Residual variance	2.955***	3.022***	3.253***	3.931***
Number of observations	958	975	963	964
Log likelihood	−363.969	−484.181	−474.226	−546.308
Chi-square	99.1	194.2	103.3	111.4
P-value for model	1.36E-09	2.28E-26	2.91E-10	1.34E-11
Rho (Panel variance fraction)	0.178	0.006	0.287	0.225

Source: Authors' survey data.
Note: Household random-effects Tobit models. Significance levels: *** $p<0.01$, ** $p<0.05$, * $p<0.1$.

Table 13.7 Questions in 2007 Household Questionnaire in Tigray

43	Are you interested in planting trees on any of your plots? 1 = Yes, 0 = No	Code
44	Does having the land certificate increase your incentive to plant trees? 1 = Yes, 0 = No	Code
45	Are there restrictions on tree planting in your community? 1 = Yes, 0 = No	Code
46	If yes, what type of restrictions? 1 = Not allowed to plant trees on land suitable for food crop production, 2 = Not allowed to plant eucalyptus trees, 3 = Eucalyptus trees are only allowed to be planted on homestead plots, 4 = Other, specify:	Code More than one possible
47	Would you have planted more eucalyptus trees if there were no restrictions on where they could be planted? 1 = Yes, 0 = No, 2 = Don't know	Code
48	If yes, where would you plant more eucalyptus trees? 1 = On homestead plot, 2 = On poor quality cropland, 3 = On good quality cropland, 4 = On communal land if it were divided to individuals, 5 = Other, specify:	Code
49	If yes, why? 1 = Eucalyptus is profitable, good market, 2 = Need it for construction purposes, 3 = Need it for fuelwood, 4 = Other, specify:	Code
33	Do you believe that having a land certificate improves the tenure security of women? 1 = Yes, 0 = No, 2 = Not sure	Code

the strongly significant and negative effect of the distance to plots. This may be the result of lower land and tree tenure security on distant plots, and the higher monitoring costs related to protection of trees on distant plots. The variable distance to communal sources of wood was insignificant, however – contrary to our expectations that a long distance to communal forests should enhance tree planting.

13.4 Conclusions

In this chapter we have attempted to examine the impact of land certification on tree growing on the private plots of samples of rural households in the Amhara and Tigray regions of Ethiopia. The results show that land certification encourages tree growing, as it is found that those who have certificates grow more trees. Tree growing was negatively associated with public investment in plots in Tigray, and this may be related to the legal restrictions on tree planting on arable land, especially for eucalyptus. Nevertheless, these restrictions have not been able to prevent the positive incentive effects of certification on tree planting.

There is also a reason to question the rationale of restricting such tree planting on very marginal arable land where production of annual crops is likely to be less sustainable than growing of trees and where tree production is much more profitable than crop production. A stock of trees may also be more valuable to fall back on in case of drought to meet the immediate needs and food security of households. Gebregziabher and Holden (2011) found that the collection of firewood and the renting out of land for a low fixed rent were among the desperate coping strategies used by households after a severe shock. Allowing more tree planting on private land could therefore provide an alternative coping strategy that would reduce the pressure on communal lands.

In the Amhara region we found that households respond to scarcity of fuelwood from communal areas (measured by the time spent to collect wood from communal areas per trip), by planting trees on their plots. Involvement in off-farm activities is also positively associated with tree planting in the Amhara region suggesting the importance of such activities for increased private tree cover. Better access to markets, as reflected by shorter distance to motorable road, also encourages tree growing. The selling of trees can also be an important source of cash and a 'savings account' for households, that can be utilized at times of shocks; legal restrictions on tree planting on arable land, although intended to enhance household food security, may therefore have the opposite effect in the long run.

Notes

1. Given the nature of the data – two years of panel data – fixed effects and difference-in-difference (DID) methods could have been used. However, some households have just one observation per year, and a minimum of two points is required to implement fixed effects and DID methods. In addition to this, the application of fixed effects on non-linear models is tricky because of incidental parameter problems (Wooldridge, 2002).
2. We also run simple random-effects Tobit and simple probit models, but the results are similar. The results may be obtained from authors on request.
3. We also tried propensity score matching (PSM) method, and found the same qualitative results as in the Tobit model. However, although the bias is substantially reduced, use of PSM did not completely eliminate the bias, as some of the matching quality indicators such as the joint significance of covariates (the *p*-value of the likelihood value) are significant after matching.
4. It is important to note here that a majority of the households in the sample did not collect wood from communal lands. For these households we assigned the maximum amount of time in the dataset for the variable, assuming that the opportunity cost of collection from the commons for these households is very high.
5. *Tsimdi* are a unit of land measure in rural Ethiopia: the amount of land that can be ploughed by a pair of oxen in a single day. This varies depending on climate and terrain, but is approximately one quarter of a hectare (half to three-quarters of an acre).

References

Amacher, G., Ersado, L., Hyde, W. and Osorio, A. (2004) 'Tree Planting in Tigray, Ethiopia: The Importance of Human Disease and Water Microdams', *Agroforestry Systems,* 60(3), 211–25.

Amacher, G., Hyde, W. and Rafiq, M. (1993) 'Local Adoption of New Forestry Technologies: An Example from Pakistan's Northwest Frontier Province', *World Development,* 21(3), 445–53.

Besley, T. (1995) 'Property Rights and Investment Incentives: Theory and Evidence from Ghana', *Journal of Political Economy,* 103(5), 903–37.

Brasselle, A-S., Gaspart, F. and Platteau, J-P. (2002) 'Land Tenure Security and Investment Incentives: Puzzling Evidence from Burkina Faso', *Journal of Development Economics,* 67(2), 373–418.

Bromley, D. and Cernea, M. (1989) 'The Management of Common Property Natural Resources', *World Bank Discussion Paper* No. 57, The World Bank, Washington D.C.

Commission for Africa (2005) 'Our Common Interest: Report of the Commission for Africa', March, Commission for Africa.

Commission for Legal Empowerment of the Poor (2008) 'Making the Law Work for Everyone', Vol. 1 and 2, Commission for Legal Empowerment of the Poor, UNDP.

Cooke, P., Kohlin, G. and Hyde, W.F. (2008) 'Fuelwood, Forests and Community Management – Evidence from Household Studies', *Environment and Development Economics,* 13(1), 103–35.

Deininger, K. and Ali, D.A. (2008) 'Do Overlapping Property Rights Reduce Agricultural Investment? Evidence from Uganda', *American Journal of Agricultural Economics* 90(4), 869–84.

Deininger, K., Ali, D.A. and Yamano, T. (2008a) 'Legal Knowledge and Economic Development: The Case of Land Rights in Uganda', *Land Economics*, 84(4), 593–619.

Deininger, K., Ali, D.A., Holden, S. and Zevenbergen, J. (2008b) 'Rural Land Certification in Ethiopia: Process, Initial Impact, and Implications for Other African Countries', *World Development*, 36(10), 1786–812.

Deininger, K., Ali, D.A. and Alemu, T. (2009) 'Impacts of Land Certification on Tenure Security, Investment, and Land Markets', *EfD Discussion Paper* 09–11, a joint publication of the Environment for Development Initiative and Resources for the Future (www.rff.org), Washington D.C.

Deininger, K. and Feder, G. (2009) 'Land Registration, Governance, and Development: Evidence and Implications for Policy', *World Bank Research Observer*, 24(2), 233–66.

Deininger, K. and Jin, S. (2006) 'Tenure Security and Land-related Investment: Evidence from Ethiopia', *European Economic Review*, 50(5), 1245–77.

Gebregziabher, G. and Holden, S.T. (2011) 'Distress Rentals and the Land Rental Market as a Safety Net: Evidence from Tigray, Ethiopia', *Agricultural Economics*, 42, 45–60.

Gebremedhin, B. and Swinton, S.M. (2003) 'Investment in Soil Conservation in Northern Ethiopia: The Role of Land Tenure Security and Public Programs', *Agricultural Economics*, 29(1), 69–84.

Greene, W. (2003) *Econometric Analysis*, 5th edition (Upper Saddle River, NJ: Prentice Hall).

Heltberg, R., Arndt, T.C. and Sekhar, N.U. (2000) 'Fuelwood Consumption and Forest Degradation: A Household Model for Domestic Energy Substitution in Rural India', *Land Economics*, 76(2), 213–32.

Holden S.T., Benin, S., Shiferaw, B. and Pender, J. (2003) 'Tree Planting for Poverty Reduction in Less-Favoured Areas of the Ethiopian Highlands', *Small-scale Forest Economics, Management and Policy*, 2(1), 63–80.

Holden, S., Deininger, K. and Ghebru, H. (2009) 'Impact of Low-cost Land Certification on Investment and Productivity', *American Journal of Agricultural Economics*, 91(2), 359–73.

Holden, S. and Yohannes, H. (2002) 'Land Redistribution, Tenure Insecurity and Intensity of Production: A Study of Farm Households in Southern Ethiopia', *Land Economics*, 78(4), 573–94.

Jacoby, H., and Minten, B. (2007) 'Is Land Titling in Sub-Saharan Africa Cost Effective? Evidence from Madagascar', *World Bank Economic Review*, 21(3), 461–85.

Jagger, P. and Pender, J. (2000) 'The Role of Trees for Sustainable Management of Less-favored Lands: The Case of Eucalyptus in Ethiopia', *EPTD Discussion Paper* no. 65, IFPRI, Washington D.C.

Linde-Rahr, M. (2003) 'Property rights and Deforestation: The Choice of Fuelwood Source in Rural Vietnam', *Land Economics*, 79(2), 217–34.

McAuslan, P. (1998) 'Making Law Work: Restructuring Land Relations in Africa', *Development and Change*, 29(3), 525–52.

Mekonnen, A. (2009) 'Tenure Security, Resource Endowments and Tree Growing: Evidence from the Amhara Region of Ethiopia', *Land Economics*, 85(2), 292–307.

NEPAD (2003) 'Comprehensive Africa agriculture development programme', New Partnership for Africa's Development.

Pande, R. and Udry, C. (2005) 'Institutions and Development: A View from Below', *Working Papers* 928, Economic Growth Center, Yale University, New Haven, CT.

Peters, P.E. and Kambewa, D. (2007) 'Whose Security? Deepening Social Conflict over 'customary' Land in the Shadow of Land Tenure Reform in Malawi', *Journal of Modern African Studies*, 45(3), 447.

Place, F. (2009) 'Land Tenure and Agricultural Productivity in Africa: A Comparative Analysis of the Economics Literature and Recent Policy Strategies and Reforms', *World Development*, 37(8), 1326–36.

Sikor, T. and Muller, D. (2009) 'The Limits of State-led Land Reform: An Introduction', *World Development*, 37(8), 1307–16.

Sundet, G. (2004) *The Politics of Land in Tanzania* (Oxford: Oxford University Press).

Tanner, C. (2002) 'Law Making in an African Context: The 1997 Mozambican Land Law', *FAO Legal Papers Online*, 26, FAO, Rome.

UN Millennium Project (2005) 'Investing in Development: A Practical Plan to Achieve the Millennium Development Goals', *Report to the UN Secretary-General*, Earthscan, London.

Van ' t Veld, K., Narian, U., Gupta, S., Chopra, N. and Singh, S. (2006) 'India's Firewood Crisis Re-examined', *Discussion Paper* 06–25, Resources for the Future.

Wooldridge, J.M. (2002) *Econometric Analysis of Cross Section and Panel Data* (Cambridge, Mass.: MIT Press).

Part IV

New Challenges and the Future of Land Tenure Reform

14

The Rise of Large Farms in Land-Abundant Countries: Do They Have a Future?

Derek Byerlee and Klaus Deininger

14.1 Introduction

After a long period of neglect, policy makers have recently re-discovered the importance of agriculture for food security, poverty reduction, and broader development. A recurring debate in the development literature is the relative emphasis to place on the roles of small-scale farms versus large-scale farms in fostering agricultural growth and economic development. In the 1960s, T.W. Schultz's landmark study, *Transforming Traditional Agriculture* (1964), convincingly argued the case for the efficiency of small-scale family operated farms and their responsiveness to new markets and technologies. This, together with the success of the Green Revolution in the 1970s, placed small-scale farm productivity at the center of the development agenda. Other work also showed that broad-based gains in productivity of small-scale farmers favored better development outcomes in terms of overall economic growth, employment generation, and poverty reduction (Mellor, 1976). The much greater success of Asian countries in building on the Green Revolution to transform their economies and reduce poverty relative to Latin America with its highly unequal agrarian structure, further re-enforced this development model.

Recent reviews (Lipton, 2009; World Bank, 2007) have re-affirmed the potential of smallholder agriculture in a number of respects. In particular, growth in smallholder agriculture has been shown to have a disproportionately higher impact on poverty reduction than growth in other sectors (Loayza and Raddatz, 2010; Christiaensen et al., 2011). Unequal land ownership in agriculture may have broader and longer run costs; in the USA during the late 19th century high inequality in land ownership at county level reduced investments in public goods such as schools, due to effects on local tax schedules (Vollrath, 2009).

However, disillusion with the limited success of smallholder-based efforts to improve productivity in sub-Saharan Africa (Collier and Dercon, 2009) and the apparent success of Brazil in establishing a vibrant agricultural sector based on much larger farms have led some countries to view the development of large-scale mechanized farming as the path to modernization of the sector. Such concerns are reinforced by recent evidence that, in India, farms are too small and under-mechanized and that consolidation of land holdings could result in significant increases in productivity (Foster and Rosenzweig, 2010). The emphasis on large farms has been reinforced by the apparent export competitiveness of 'megafarms' in Latin America and Eastern Europe and a move by institutional investors into agriculture, in part in response to the 2008 global food crisis.

At the same time, experience with establishment of large farms in the course of history has been largely negative. Reference to greater efficiency of 'modern' large farms applying 'scientific' methods was often just a pretext to acquired large amounts of land without putting them into productive use. Instead a monopoly on land was combined with other policy distortions to deprive local populations of opportunities and drive down wages (Binswanger et al., 1995), with far-reaching and long-lasting negative effects (Baland and Robinson, 2008; Conning and Robinson, 2007; Nugent and Robinson, 2002). The irregularities and corruption associated with many contemporaneous land transfers have led some observers to view these as a new 'land grab' (Zoomers, 2010). Concerns center around the potential of such farms to generate employment, provide market access to small producers, and whether public policy can or should regulate such transfers to contribute to broader development goals.

Against this backdrop, this paper has three objectives. First, we review recent evidence on the establishment and evolution of large farms across regions. This illustrates that such units often emerged in response to policy biases or market failures related to availability of infrastructure, technology, and property rights. The environmental, social, and productivity impact was strongly affected by these factors, highlighting the importance of well-defined property rights and a clear, transparent, and enforceable regulatory framework, provision of public goods, and undistorted factor prices. If, as was often the case, these conditions were absent, strategies based on large farms were associated with significant social and environmental risks, often leading to negative outcomes that were not conducive to longer-term development.

Second, a discussion of key determinants of the way the agricultural sector is organized highlights that, while large operations have historically had a dominant role in plantation crops, agricultural production, in contrast to marketing or processing, is not generally characterized by significant economies of scale. Larger units have advantages in accessing credit or lumpy inputs but the ability of family farms to overcome these through collective action, together with owner-operators' superior incentives imply that, in contrast to other industries, farming is still overwhelmingly dominated by family-owned businesses. A key reason for the size of family farms to increase over time is rising wages in the nonagricultural economy and the desire to equalize returns to labor across sectors. Three recent developments may affect these relationships, namely (i) new technology that makes it easier to standardize and/or monitor large farm operations; (ii) increased consumer demand for social and environmental standards and certification even for traditional low value commodities; and (iii) a desire to expand cultivation into previously uncultivated areas where, in the absence of in-migration, labor is scarce.

Third we recognize that in some circumstances, the superior access to capital, technology and markets offered by large farms may have a role in developing land-abundant regions. We identify areas related to the regulatory and policy framework, property rights, and the ability to transfer resources to more efficient producers that will need to be addressed if large farms are to successfully contribute to overall development.

14.2 Evidence on the rise of large farms in land-abundant regions

While there is little evidence of significant recent changes in agrarian structure in land scarce countries (Lipton, 2009), many land-abundant countries are characterized by rising investment in large-scale farming based on a nonfamily corporate model, a trend that can but need not be accompanied by growing concentration of land ownership (Deininger et al., 2011; UNCTAD, 2009). Table 14.1 provides characteristics of a sample of very large farming operations in land-abundant countries or regions within countries.[1]

The largest operations, all of them in developing or transition countries, share some characteristics. With operational units that often exceed

Table 14.1 Examples of very large corporate farms in developing and transition countries

Company	**Main country (s) of operation**	**Commodities**	**Crop area**	**Comment**
Sime Darby	Malaysia, Indonesia	Oil palm	600,000 ha +	Planned investment of $1+ billion in 220,000 ha plantation in Liberia
Cosan	Brazil	Sugarcane-ethanol	300,000 ha own & 300,000 contract growers	Shell Oil joint venture to double production with $12 bn investment
El Shaikh Mustafa El Amin Co	Sudan	Grains	250,000 ha	
El Tejar	Argentina, Brazil and Paraguay	Grains, oilseeds	≈1,000,000 ha	Expanding to Colombia
Ivolga	Russia and Kazakhstan	Grains, oilseeds	≈1,000,000 ha	
Fibria	Brazil	Fast growth Eucalyptus	500,000 ha	Merger of Aracruz and JVC

Source: Review of company websites and interviews.

10,000 ha, they are bigger than the largest farms in comparable land-abundant regions in developed countries. These units are often horizontally integrated into corporations controlling hundreds of thousands of hectares with the largest now approaching a million ha of good cropland and sales above $1 billion annually. Vertical integration with processing, marketing, and export logistics is common and business models depart substantially from that of family farming characteristic of developed countries, often separating ownership, management and labor. At the same time, there are big inter-regional differences. Historical evidence on establishment and evolution of large farms across regions can help illustrate the diversity of conditions.

14.2.1 Latin America

Following the liberalization of markets and trade in the 1980s, relatively land-abundant countries in Latin America, including Argentina, Brazil, Paraguay and Uruguay, capitalized on growing global demand to increase their position in world markets for several major products such as soybean, sugar, and meat in processes involving massive land expansion. Most widely known is forest clearing for extensive livestock ranching and establishing land rights in the Amazon basin where, in less than two decades (1990–2006), the cattle population more than doubled and pasture expanded by 24 million ha (Pacheco and Poccard Chapuis, 2009). Unclear boundaries of public land, weak enforcement of environmental regulations, and legislation that required land clearing in order to establish property rights contributed to a rapid expansion of cultivated area by both small and large-scale farms. Even if small farmers were the first to expand the frontier, farm sizes concentrated rapidly thereafter. As most of this land, often of very poor quality, was not put to productive use, impacts were often negative.

A second process was the expansion of soybeans and other crops in the *cerrado* (savannah) region of Brazil by using varieties, soil amendments and conservation tillage developed through heavy public investment in research and development that allowed cultivation of soils that were previously considered unsuitable for agriculture. This was a major technological success that dramatically increased production and exports. Impacts on rural poverty, however, were below potential as capital subsidies and labor laws encouraged highly mechanized cultivation rather than more labor intensive production that could have had higher employment and poverty-impacts (Rezende, 2005; World Bank, 2009a). Currently, the median farm size in the Cerrado is more than 1,000 ha and many companies operate more than 100,000 ha of cropland in this region. The apparent efficiency of farms up to 10,000–20,000 ha has been attributed to preferential access to services such as credit and extension (Helfand and Levine, 2004).

Finally, in Southern Brazil, production of sugarcane, often for ethanol, is expanding rapidly, under a more mixed regime. About half of production is from medium farmers with an average of about 50 ha. Much of the rest is produced in vertically integrated operations with mills on land they manage and operate. While average operated size per mill is some 13,000 ha, some very large operators farm over 300,000 hectares. With a strong institutional environment in southern Brazil, significant economic and social impacts have been generated from the industry relative to the extensive grazing that it replaced (Martinelli et al., 2011).

Argentina presents a somewhat different picture. There, farm management companies, *pools de siembra,* have emerged that own neither land nor machinery but rent in land and contract machine operators. This business model emerged during Argentina's financial crisis, when having access to outside capital provided a significant advantage. With clear property rights allowing easy contracting, several companies farm more than 100,000 ha, most of it rented. The largest companies, many traded publicly, operate across several countries in the region. Access to highly qualified agronomists who undergo continued training and are organized hierarchically allows adoption of near-industrial methods of quality control and production at low cost. Competitive land lease markets, with contracts renewed annually, imply that at least part of any efficiency savings of Argentine's large operators are passed on to landowners, who often receive lease payments above what they may have been able to earn by self-cultivation. While land ownership has remained relatively unchanged, agricultural production has become more concentrated; the 30 largest companies control some 2.4 million ha (Manciana et al., 2009).

Finally, positive experiences with investment in large-scale farming have been recorded in Peru's Pacific region. There auctions of some 235,500 ha of public land in a very transparent process with strong technical vetting brought in almost $50 million in investment over the past 15 years, underpinning the country's emergence as a major high-value agro-exporter of horticultural produce and generating large numbers of jobs (Hernandez, 2010).

14.2.2 Eastern Europe and Central Asia

Since 1990, Eastern Europe and Central Asia has undergone far-reaching transition from the former Soviet system of collective and state farms to new agrarian structures. In areas of low population density where collectives were divided into small plots allocated to members, the plots were quickly rented back by companies with access to finance and machinery. These companies were often created from former collective farms whose former managers could easily identify land owners and consolidate land parcels and shares. Services, institutions, and logistics were also geared to large-scale production. In land-abundant Russia, Ukraine and Kazakhstan, large farms were better able to deal with daunting financing, infrastructure, and technology constraints of the transition than smaller operators. The share of area under corporate farms 10 years after the transition was 60 per cent in Kazakhstan and 45 per cent in Russia (Swinnen, 2009). In Russia, the 30 largest holdings farm 6.7 million ha or 5.5 per cent of cultivated area and in Ukraine, the largest 80 control 5.1 million ha or 15 per cent of cultivated area (Byerlee, Lissitsa and Savanti, 2012). Most of these companies are home grown, although they may rely on investment and technology transfer from abroad with several now publicly traded in European stock exchanges. An influx of outside capital has helped to replace some of the sector's largely obsolete capital stock, creating spillovers in terms of employment and wage growth (Petrick, 2012).

Much of the land is leased but land rents relative to land of comparable quality in other parts of the world are very low. Competitive markets for land rental have yet to emerge as imperfections in financial markets as well as those for inputs and output often make owner-cultivation difficult. Land owners' weak bargaining power reduces rental rates and few of the potential benefits from large-scale cultivation are transmitted to them.

14.2.3 Southeast Asia

The perennial crop sector in Southeast Asia illustrates the plantation model of large-scale farming. Malaysia and Indonesia produce nearly 90 per cent of the world's palm oil, production of which has expanded rapidly in response to growing global demand for edible oils and strong government support. Given the processing requirements, large-scale production close to the processing unit, often complemented by outgrower schemes, is the norm, with the sourcing area for a typical palm oil mill averaging around 10,000 ha. In many cases, companies have integrated operational units horizontally to form some very large firms. Eight of the world's 25 largest agricultural production–based companies identified in the 2009 *World Investment Report* have major interests in oil palm (UNCTAD, 2009). There has also been a strong trend toward consolidation in the industry through mergers and by vertical integration with refining oil and manufacturing of palm oil and palm kernel oil products. Several large oil palm companies now control plantations of 200,000–800,000 ha of oil palm.

Oil palm has had a mixed development record. On the one side it has been a major source of employment and poverty reduction. In contrast to annual crops, oil palm is highly labor intensive and the industry is estimated to have created an estimated 1.7 to 3 million jobs. Smallholders participate usually in association with plantations and their share of area has quickly grown to reach 40 per cent in Indonesia. However, more than half of the expansion of oil palm was at the expense of natural forests (Koh and Wilcove, 2008). Concerns abound about oil palm expansion as a contributor to loss of biodiversity, greenhouse gas emissions, and social conflict due to a failure to recognize local land rights, opaque and poorly understood contractual agreements and limited benefit-sharing with local communities (World Bank, 2009b).

Rubber provides an interesting contrast. Large rubber plantations often opened areas by establishing processing facilities, markets, and roads and importing needed labor. After processing and infrastructure was established, production almost entirely shifted from large plantations to 2–3 ha farms with smallholders now making up 80 per cent of world rubber production (Hayami, 2010). Rubber's high labor intensity, emergence of production systems adapted to smallholders' capital constraints, and more flexible processing requirements than those for oil palm all facilitated this transition.

14.2.4 Sub-Saharan Africa

In Africa after independence, many countries attempted to 'modernize' their agricultural sectors through large-scale farming, providing subsidized credit, machinery, and land. These efforts almost universally failed (Eicher and Baker, 1992). One of the largest and best documented cases was mechanized large-scale sorghum and sesame production in Sudan that was supported by the World Bank in the 1960s and then scaled up by financiers from the Gulf following the 1970s oil price spike, in an attempt to transform the country into a regional breadbasket. Schemes with very favorable access to land and subsidized credit for machinery attracted civil servants and businessmen who mostly hired managers for farms of over 1,000 ha, with some over 100,000 ha. While some 5.5 million ha were converted to arable land according to official statistics, estimates put the area informally encroached upon at up to 11 million ha (Government of Sudan, 2009). Encroachment on traditional users' land rights led to serious conflict. Partly due to the ensuing tenure insecurity, investment was low and most mechanized farms rely on low-level technology. Yields are only 0.5 t/ha and have been stagnant or declining (Figure 14.1) relative to 4 t/ha in comparable agro-ecological environment in Australia.

These problems were not unique to Sudan. Efforts to introduce mechanized rainfed wheat in Tanzania on some 40,000 ha, of land that had previously been prime grazing grounds for pastoralists illustrate the challenges. After a $45 million investment, wheat production was deemed unprofitable, and production is declining (Lane and Pretty, 1991; Rogers, 2004). Nigeria's large-scale mechanized irrigated wheat schemes of the 1970s and 1980s have been abandoned (Andrae and Beckman, 1985).

Past success with commercial agriculture in Africa was mostly limited to traditional export crops such as cotton, cocoa, and coffee produced by smallholders, and more recently horticultural exports, by both small and large farms. Large-scale production of plantation crops often with outgrowers, such as sugarcane in Southern Africa and oil palm in West Africa also had some success. Although smallholder-based growth remains critical to achieve poverty reduction in Africa (World Bank, 2007) there is increasing recognition of the need to overcome serious

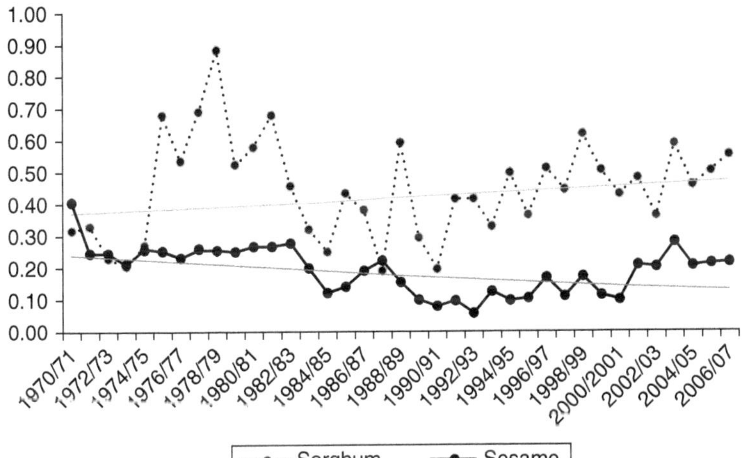

Figure 14.1 Yields on semi-mechanized farms, Sudan, 1970–2007 (t/ha)

Source: Government of Sudan 2009.

Note: Yields are for rainfed production.

Table 14.2 Extent of large land acquisitions in selected African countries, 2004–2009

Country	No. of investment projects	Total area (1,000 ha)	Median size (ha)	Share of domestic investors in total area
Ethiopia	406	1,190	700	49
Liberia	17	1,602	59,374	7
Mozambique	405	2,670	2,225	53
Sudan	132	3,965	7,980	78

Source: Deininger et al. (2011).

market imperfections if smallholders are to play this role (Hazell et al., 2010). In the wake of the demise of parastatals, institutional arrangements for effective service provision to smallholders have not yet been addressed adequately (Dorward et al., 2009).

Recent land acquisitions in Africa attracted large amounts of media attention because they were quantitatively large; in fact, compared to an annual rate of area expansion of cultivated area of some 1.8 million ha in the 1961–2007 period, demand in 2009 alone amounted to some 39.7 million hectares (Deininger et al., 2011). Data from six countries where reliable information could be gathered highlight that the size of lands transferred recently is significantly above what was observed in the past. Total transfers in 2004–2009, in millions of ha (Table 14.2) amounted to 4.0 ha in Sudan, 2.7 in Mozambique, 1.2 in Ethiopia and 1.6 in Liberia (mainly renegotiation of existing agreements).

At the same time, case studies by Deininger et al. (2011) identified key risks from (i) weak land governance and an associated failure to recognize, protect, or -if voluntary transfer can be agreed upon- properly compensate local communities' land rights; (ii) lack of capacity to process and manage large-scale investments, through inclusive and participatory consultations that result in clear and enforceable agreements; (iii) investor proposals that were non-viable technically, or inconsistent with local visions and national plans for development, in some cases leading investors to encroach on local lands to make ends meet economically; and (iv) resource conflict with negative distributional and gender effects.

In most cases, expected job creation and net investment were either not recorded or were very low. Often, progress with implementation was well behind schedule. As a result, local people have often suffered asset losses but received few or none of the promised benefits, implying that -even if expected positive effects materialize at some point in the future, poor locals may have ended up subsidizing rich foreign investors.

At the same time, case studies document that well-executed investments can provide benefits. These accrue through four main channels, namely (i) social infrastructure, often supported by community development funds using land compensation; (ii) employment and jobs; (iii) access to markets and technology for local producers; and (iv) local or national tax revenue. Even if overall effects are positive, distributional issues may arise and will need to be addressed upfront to inform negotiation and contract design. For example, entrepreneurial and skilled people could gain from jobs creation through an investment while vulnerable groups or women lose access to livelihoods without being compensated.

14.3 Why agricultural production in dominated by owner-operated farms

In most countries, both rich and poor, agriculture is dominated by owner-operated family units that combine ownership of the main means of production with management. Indeed, at a global scale, agriculture is one of few industries based overwhelming based on a family firm model; that is, farms are owner operated and rely largely on family labor (Lipton, 2009).

A key reason is that agricultural production has few technical (dis) economies of scale, implying that a range of production forms can coexist. Even though farming accounts for 22 per cent of the global agricultural value chain, it makes up a mere 0.2 per cent of equity market capitalization (Brookfield Agricultural Group, 2010). As of October 2009, there were only seven publicly listed farming companies worldwide, three in Brazil and Argentina and four in Ukraine and Russia. By contrast, agricultural processing, input industries, and sometimes output markets are characterized by significant economies of scale largely related to fixed costs (e.g., R&D, large processing units) which has often given rise to concentration in these industries (World Bank, 2007).

There are three reasons for the endurance of the family farm model even in rich countries (Allen and Lueck, 1998; Binswanger and Deininger, 1997; Deininger, 2003). First, as residual claimants to profit, family workers will be more likely to work hard than wage workers who require costly supervision in spatially dispersed production. Owner operators also have an intimate knowledge of local soil and climate, often accumulated over generations, that gives them an advantage in tailoring management to local conditions and the flexibility to quickly adjust management decisions to site, seasonal and market conditions. Finally, family farms have considerable flexibility to adjust labor supply to the seasonality and annual variability of production since family labor can more easily be reallocated to other tasks on and off the farm.

A well-known and important exception to the superior performance of owner-operated units of production over those relying on wage labor is in plantation crops, where economies of scale in processing and the need for close coordination of production and processing can make plantations more efficient. The need for quick processing of some harvest products to avoid deterioration, often within 24–48 hours, requires tight adherence to delivery and harvesting schedules and transmits economies of scale in processing to the production stage (Binswanger and Rosenzweig, 1986). For this reason, sugar and palm oil mills usually run their own plantations to ensure a base load for processing. The scale of these has increased significantly; new sugarcane mills in Brazil for example, may capture produce from up to 100,000 ha versus 20,000 ha two decades ago. Concentrating production also lowers transport costs from the field to the processing point. Spatial concentration of production in large estates owned by mills in Brazil may reduce total costs by some 20 per cent, compared to dispersed smallholder models (as practiced in Kenya) by lowering transport costs to the mill.

Finally, plantations that specialize in perennial crops have developed highly structured 'industrial type' production processes that facilitate labor supervision and management efficiency. A focus on a single crop with relatively low seasonality of operations provides year round employment and allows managers and workers to develop specialized skills. The modern tropical plantation is akin to highly specialized stall-fed livestock operations in industrial countries which, for the same reasons, have moved away from family farm to nonfamily corporate farming.[2]

In most industrialized countries, a key factor contributing to growing farm sizes has been rising wages in the nonagricultural sector that led farm operators to seek ways to attain incomes comparable to what they can obtain in other sectors of the economy (Eastwood et al., 2010). Normally this implies substitution of capital for labor and an increase of farm size over time in line with wage rates. As Figure 14.2 illustrates, both variables moved together closely in the United States for most of the 20th century, suggesting that the desire to obtain a comparable nonagricultural income was the main factor driving changes in the average size of operational holdings (Gardner, 2002). Still even large farms in the US

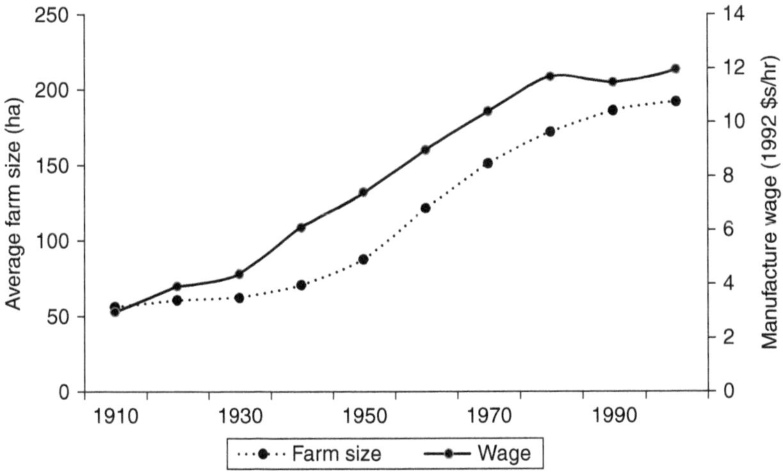

Figure 14.2 Evolution of United States farm size and non-farm manufacturing wage
Source: Based on Gardner (2002).

are mostly owner-operated rather than company-owned and arable crop farms rarely exceed 5000 ha.

Further, the capital requirements of farm operations typically increase with economic development, with higher levels of technology, and investment in land and other improvements, as well as investment in labor-saving machines. Although small agricultural operations have advantages in acquiring labor and local knowledge, they in many cases have difficulty acquiring capital. The high transaction costs of providing formal credit in rural markets mean that the unit costs of borrowing and lending decline with loan size and bias lending against small farmers. Raising interest rates on small loans does not overcome this problem, as it will lead to adverse selection (Stiglitz and Weiss, 1981). Unless ways are found to provide small farmers with access to finance (through, for example, credit cooperatives), their inability to obtain financing may outweigh any supervision cost advantages they have over larger farms (Chavas, 2001).

14.4 Factors favoring recent establishment of super-farms

In addition to secular shifts of labor out of the agricultural sector, three main factors that have recently contributed to increased farm size are (i) new technology that makes it easier to supervise labor or occupy it continuously; (ii) the limited availability of labor in frontier areas, possibly exacerbated by high capital requirements of land clearance and infrastructure construction; and (iii) greater emphasis on integrated supply chains and certification of produce.

Recent innovations in crop breeding, tillage, and information technology may make labor supervision easier and reduce diseconomies of scale of very large operations. Pest-resistant and herbicide-tolerant varieties facilitated broad adoption of zero tillage and, by reducing the number of steps in the production process and the labor intensity of cultivation, allowed management of larger areas. The ability to have machinery operations guided by GPS technology rather than driver's skills makes close supervision of labor less relevant while information technology can generate data to help better supervise labor and manage large areas. The scope for substituting crop and pest models and remotely sensed information on field conditions for personal observation also reduces the advantage of local knowledge and experience in tactical farm decisions while climate change reduces the value of traditional knowledge. Private operators in Argentina and Ukraine assert that, with modern technology, a good manager can effectively supervise operational units of 10,000 to 15,000 ha for grain and oilseeds.

With changes in technology and markets, the ability to acquire and process information also gives advantages to managers with high levels of formal schooling and technical education -the 'value of the ability to deal with disequilibria' (Schultz, 1975). This is particularly important for new crops and frontier areas where managers skilled in modern methods may enjoy advantages. Unit costs of acquiring and processing information also decline with farm size (Collier and Dercon, 2009; Feder and Slade, 1985). Large farms that employ highly trained managers may enjoy an efficiency advantage under conditions of rapidly changing markets and technologies, and in opening new areas to agriculture.

Expansion of certification, introduced as buyers in high income countries demand certification of social and environmental sustainability, into 'bulk commodities' can also provide advantages to large operations. Industry-led organizations, such as the Roundtable on Sustainable Palm Oil or Responsible Soy, the Better Sugar Initiative, and EU biofuels standards, have all been put in place in the past decade to develop certification standards and procedures. The high fixed costs of gaining certification and the need to preserve product identity through the supply chain provide advantages to large operating units in integrated supply chains. While the added cost of certifying smallholders can often be justified in high-value products, it poses challenges for bulk commodities such as palm oil. Standards may favor large operations in other ways as well; for example, environmental standards that prohibit burning of sugarcane prior to harvesting to reduce carbon emissions essentially rule out manual harvesting, disadvantaging smallholders and reducing labor requirements by half.

Beyond these factors, large companies' ability to integrate operational units horizontally or vertically in marketing and processing can provide additional advantages in a number of respects.

If markets are not working well, large firms can improve coordination with processors or shippers, and reduce transactions costs and risks through vertical integration. For example, integration of with livestock production with grain and oilseed production in Russia and Ukraine reflects efforts by large livestock operations to assure feed supplies. Vertical integration also allows companies to fill gaps in public services. In Brazil or Ukraine, a number of large companies constructed their own port terminals for export, shielding them from the limitations imposed by public facilities. This is consistent with studies in Russia that fail to find any inherent economies of size in farm production but clear advantages of large farms in terms of lower transactions costs and higher product prices (Svetlov and Hoekmann, 2009), suggesting that the ability to overcome market imperfections is a key driver toward large farms in Russia (Koester, 2007).

The ability of vertically or horizontally integrated firms to access foreign capital markets, possibly by issuing equity, can provide large agricultural firms with additional advantages, especially where local financial markets do not operate well. In some cases, Argentinean companies that obtain loans abroad pay only half of the rate that local banks demanded from farmers, if they could get credit at all. Such advantages, which are particularly relevant where significant start up costs, such as soil amendments, irrigation, and establishment of perennial crops, are required to make land arable but do not return a positive cash flow for several years, can well affect industry structure in the long term.

Large firms, even if they are not vertically integrated, can also leverage their superior bargaining power' as markets for agricultural inputs and outputs are often highly concentrated. In Argentina, large companies with more bargaining power are reported to be able to reduce input prices and increase output prices by 10–20 per cent (Manciana et al., 2009). Likewise, spatial covariance of risk implies that, even in developed countries, markets for agricultural insurance are often incomplete. Diversification of operations across large geographical areas can allow large companies to self-insure against weather risks, thereby overcoming these difficulties.

14.5 Conclusions and policy implications

Expected increases in the demand for agricultural products, whether as food, feed or inputs into other industries such as biofuels has led to an increase in the number and size of large farms and new business models involving a mix of large and smaller operations are evolving. This trend is notable in Latin America and Eastern Europe, for perennials in Southeast Asia, and recently in sub-Saharan Africa. In addition to factors that have long underpinned the expansion of large operations such as the economies of scale in plantation crops, policy distortions, and large farms' superior ability to deal with imperfections in markets for finance and insurance, four factors are likely to affect future evolution of agrarian structures, namely (i) technical change that makes it easier to standardize supervision of the production process for bulk commodities; (ii) the ability of large operations to benefit from horizontal and vertical integration and exercise market power, especially in situations where there provision of public goods such as infrastructure and technology is deficient; (iii) standards and associated requirements for certification and traceability that favor large operations; and (iv) inelastic labor supply, together with high capital requirements for expanding cultivation into suitable but hitherto uncultivated areas.

A strong historical bias against export agriculture combined with high agricultural potential in many areas with low population density imply that the challenge is particularly large for Africa where governments hope to enlist the private sector to overcome long-standing bottlenecks in availability of infrastructure and technology and to link rural areas to global markets for output and finance. While there has been a huge volume of announced investments, they have largely failed to live up to expectations. In the past, gaps in the policy and regulatory framework have often implied that area expansion led to land concentration and a 'resource curse' rather than sustainable broad-based growth. This suggests that, if such investment is to provide economic and social benefits, a proper public sector role is to set policy, provide complementary public goods, and assist local people in screening investments and investors. Three priority areas for attention are (i) property rights to and proper valuation of land; (ii) labor market impacts and technical as well as economic viability; and (iii) the ability to flexibly reallocate land in case an investment fails.

Property rights to land: In many cases, traditional notions of land being 'owned' by the state or by traditional authorities led to it being transferred for free or well below its opportunity cost. This results in a range of speculative or economically non-viable deals going forward, often with negative environmental or social consequences as investors struggle to make a profit on land that once made important contributions to local livelihoods. Recognition of existing property rights, proper land valuation and taxation, and ensuring that decisions on land transfers are taken with the consent of local people can help improve economic and social outcomes. In areas with high potential and good market access where pressure is likely to be high, systematic registration of property rights, possibly at community level, together with establishment of transparent and accountable mechanisms for decision-making are needed. Some countries, e.g. Mexico which registered more than 100 million hectares in less than a decade, had considerable success with this and many African countries have put in place legislation allowing similarly rapid registration of group rights.

Employment, social, and environmental effects: Except for some perennials, large farms' ability to productively employ labor is often very limited, much below that of smallholder agriculture. Combining the advantage of large farms, in terms of access to markets, infrastructure, and technology, with the local knowledge, flexibility, and superior incentives of smallholders through appropriately structured partnerships such as outgrower schemes could have considerable employment and social benefits. Realizing such partnerships requires transparency and access to information to strengthen local communities' bargaining power and their ability to ensure that contractual arrangements, once entered, are actually complied with. Establishing minimum standards, improving transparency, and allowing independent third-party verification will thus be important to avoid negative consequences. While much can be done by the private sector, creation of the necessary preconditions is an important role of the public sector.

Flexible arrangements for land transfer: Even in well-established industries, the share of newly formed firms surviving for more than 5 years is often low. In the environment discussed here, lack of proven technology, weak institutions, and high levels of market and price risk may lead to even higher numbers of firms exiting the industry or in need for restructuring. In many African countries, land that had been given to investors cannot be transferred easily. A policy framework that implies high opportunity cost of holding land (e.g. because rental fees or land taxes are collected effectively) and provides mechanisms for allow more efficient operators to gain access to land through decentralized processes will reduce the danger of large amounts of potentially very productive land being locked up in speculative holdings.

While our review suggests that operational farm sizes may be more flexible than believed in the past, so that a wide range of farms sizes could be competitive in a global setting, available empirical evidence is limited and suffers from a number of methodological shortcomings. There is thus need for more in-depth study of productivity-, welfare-, social, and environmental impacts of large farms relative to smaller ones and the impact of policies on the evolution of the farm size structure. To the extent that many new players now view land acquisition as a promising strategy, such research will be important to not only improve understanding of this phenomenon but also to guide the formulation of appropriate policies that can help countries support development of an efficient, equitable and competitive agricultural sector.

Notes

This article is excerpted and updated from Klaus Deininger and Derek Byerlee, 'The rise of large farms in land-abundant countries: Do they have a future?' *World Development*, 40, 701–14, 2012.

1. Land abundance is defined in terms of area suitable for cultivation that is not currently under cultivation. We find little evidence of a shift toward large-scale farming in land scarce countries. However, some countries such as Indonesia are characterized by land scarcity (Java) and land abundance (outer islands).
2. In developing countries, a modern day equivalent to the plantation crop is fresh horticulture for export. Not only is the produce highly perishable, but the harvest must be closely coordinated with shipping schedules (usually air). In addition, export markets have very stringent quality requirements and demand backward traceability of output to the farm level.

References

Allen, D. and Lueck, D. (1998) 'The Nature of the Farm', *Journal of Law and Economics*, 41(2), 343–86.

Andrae, G. and Beckman, B. (1985) *The Wheat Trap: Bread and Underdevelopment in Nigeria* (London and Uppsala: Scandinavian Institute for African Studies and Zed Books).

Baland, J.M. and Robinson, J.A. (2008) 'Land and Power: Theory and Evidence from Chile', *American Economic Review*, 98(5), 1737–65.

Binswanger, H.P. and Deininger, K. (1997) 'Explaining Agricultural and Agrarian Policies in Developing Countries', *Journal of Economic Literature*, 35(4), 1958–2005.

Binswanger, H.P., Deininger, K. and Feder, G. (1995) 'Power, Distortions, Revolt and Reform in Agricultural Land Relations', *Handbook of Development Economics*, 3B, 2659–772.

Binswanger, H.P. and Rosenzweig, M.R. (1986) 'Behavioural and Material Determinants of Production Relations in Agriculture', *Journal of Development Studies*, 22(3), 503–39.

Brookfield Agriculture Group (2010) *Farmland Investment Thesis: Why Brazilian Farmland Will Outperform* (New York: Brookfield Asset Management Inc).

Byerlee, D., Lissitsa, A. and Savanti, P. (2012) 'Corporate Models of Broadacre Crop Farming: International Experience from Argentina and Ukraine', *Farm Policy Institute Journal*, 9(2), 13–25.

Chavas, J.P. (2001) 'Structural Change in Agricultural Production: Production Economics, Technology, and Policy', in B. Gardner and G.C. Rausser (eds), *Handbook of Agricultural Economics* (North Holland: Elsevier).

Christiaensen, L., Demery, L. and Kuhl, J. (2011) 'The (evolving) Role of Agriculture in Poverty Reduction – An Empirical Perspective', *Journal of Development Economics*, 96(2), 239–54.

Collier, P. and Dercon, S. (2009) 'African Agriculture in 50 years: Smallholders in a Rapidly Changing World', Paper presented at the expert meeting on how to feed the world in 2050. Rome: Food and Agriculture Organization of the United Nations.

Conning, J.H. and Robinson, J.A. (2007) 'Property Rights and the Political Organization of Agriculture', *Journal of Development Economics*, 82(2), 416–47.

Deininger, K. (2003) *Land Policies for Growth and Poverty Reduction: A World Bank Policy Research Report* (Oxford and New York: World Bank and Oxford University Press).

Deininger, K., Byerlee, D., Lindsay, J., Norton, A., Selod, H. and Stickler, M. (2011) *Rising Global Interest in Farmland: Can It Yield Sustainable and Equitable Benefits?* (Washington, D.C.: World Bank).

Dorward, A., Kydd, J., Poulton, C. and Bezemer, D. (2009) 'Coordination Risk and Cost Impacts on Economic Development in Poor Rural Areas', *Journal of Development Studies*, 45(7), 1093–112.

Eastwood, R., Lipton, M. and Newell, A. (2010) 'Farm Size', in P.L. Pingali and R.E. Evenson (eds), *Handbook of Agricultural Economics* (North Holland: Elsevier).

Eicher, C.K. and Baker, D.C. (1992) 'Research on Agricultural Development in Sub-Saharan Africa: A Critical Survey', in L. Martin (ed.), *A Survey of Agricultural Economics Literature; Vol IV Agriculture in Economic Development 1940s–1990s* (Minneapolis, MN: University of Minnesota Press).

Feder, G. and Slade, R. (1985) 'The Role of Public Policy in the Diffusion of Improved Agricultural Technology', *American Journal of Agricultural Economics*, 67(2), 423–8.

Foster, A. and Rosenzweig, M.R. (2010) 'Barriers to Farm Profitability in India: Mechanization, Scale, and Credit Markets', University of Pennsylvania Working Paper, Philadelphia.

Gardner, B.L. (2002) *US Agriculture in the 20th Century. How It Flourished and What It Cost* (Cambridge, MA: Harvard University Press).

Government of Sudan (2009) *Study on the Sustainable Development of Semi-mechanized Rainfed Farming* (Khartoum: Ministry of Agriculture and Forestry).

Hayami, Y. (2010) 'Plantation agriculture', in P.L. Pingali and R.E. Evenson (eds), *Handbook of Agricultural Economics* (North Holland: Elsevier).

Hazell, P., Poulton, C., Wiggins, S. and Dorward, A. (2010) 'The Future of Small Farms: Trajectories and Policy Priorities', *World Development,* 38(10), 1349–61.

Helfand, S.M. and Levine, E.S. (2004) 'Farm Size and the Determinants of Productive Efficiency in the Brazilian Center-West', *Agricultural Economics,* 31(2–3), 241–9.

Hernandez, M. (2010) 'Establishing a Framework for Transferring Public Land: Peru's Experience', Paper presented at the Annual Bank Conference on Land Policy and Administration, 26 and 27 April 2010, Washington D.C.

Koester, U. (2007) 'Super-large Farms: The Importance of Institutions', Paper presented at the 102nd Seminar of the European Association of Agricultural Economists, 17 and 18 May 2007, Moscow.

Koh, L.P. and Wilcove, D.S. (2008) 'Is Oil Palm Agriculture Really Destroying Tropical Biodiversity', *Conservation Letters,* 1(1), 60–4.

Lane, C. and Pretty, J.N. (1991) 'Displaced Pastoralists and Transferred Wheat Technology in Tanzania', *IIED Gatekeeper Series* No. 20. London: International Institute for Environment and Development.

Lipton, M. (2009) *Land Reform in Developing Countries: Property Rights and Property Wrongs* (New York: Routledge).

Loayza, N.V. and Raddatz, C. (2010) 'The Composition of Growth Matters for Poverty Alleviation', *Journal of Development Economics,* 93(1), 137–51.

Manciana, E., Trucco, M. and Pineiro, M. (2009) 'Large Scale Acquisition of Land Rights for Agricultural or Natural Resource-based Use: Argentina. Buenos Aires', Draft paper prepared for the World Bank.

Martinelli, L.A., Garrett, R., Ferraz, S. and Naylor, R. (2011) 'Sugar and Ethanol Production as a Rural Development Strategy in Brazil: Evidence from the State of São Paulo', *Agricultural Systems,* 104(5), 419–28.

Mellor, J.W. (1976) *The New Economics of Growth: A Strategy for India and the Developing World* (Ithaca, NY: Cornell University Press).

Nugent, J.B. and Robinson, J.A. (2002) 'Are Endowments Fate?' Center for Economic and Policy Research Working Paper 3206. London.

Pacheco, P. and Poccard Chapuis, R. (2009) 'Cattle Ranching Development in the Brazilian Amazon: Emerging Trends from Increasing Integration with Markets', Bogor, Indonesia: Center for International Forestry Research.

Petrick, M., Wandel, J. and Karsten, K. (2012) *Economic and Social Impacts of Recent Agro-investment in Kazakhstan's Grain Region* (IAMO, Halle, Germany).

Rezende, G.C.D. (2005) 'Politicas trabalhista e fundiaria e seus efeitos adversos sobre o emprego agricoloa, a etrutura agraria e o desenvolvimento territorial rural no Brasil', Texto para discussao No. 1108. Rio de Janeiro: Instituto de Pesquisa Economica Aplicada (IPEA).

Rogers, P.J. (2004) 'Saskatoon on the Savanna: Discursive Dependency, Canadian-guided Agricultural Development and the Hanang Wheat Complex', Paper presented at the 45 annual international studies association conference, Montreal, Quebec.

Schultz, T.W. (1964) *Transforming Traditional Agriculture* (New Haven: Yale University Press).

Schultz, T.W. (1975) 'The Value of the Ability to Deal with Disequilibria', *Journal of Economic Literature,* 13(3), 827–46.

Stiglitz, J.E. and Weiss, A. (1981) 'Credit Rationing in Markets with Imperfect Information', *American Economic Review,* 71(3), 393–410.

Svetlov, N. and Hoekmann, B. (2009) 'Optimal Farm Size in Russian Agriculture', Paper presented at the Conference of the International Association of Agricultural Economists, Beijing 16–23 August 2009, Beijing, China.

Swinnen, J.F.M. (2009) 'Reforms, Globalization, and Endogenous Agricultural Structures', *Agricultural Economics,* 40(6), 719–32.

UNCTAD (2009) *World Investment Report 2009: Transnational Corporations, Agricultural Production, and Development* (New York and Geneva: United Nations).

Vollrath, D. (2009) 'The Dual Economy in Long-run Development', *Journal of Economic Growth,* 14(4), 287–312.

World Bank (2007) *Agriculture for Development: World Development Report 2008* (Washington, D.C.: World Bank).

World Bank (2009a) *Awakening Africa's Sleeping Giant: Prospects for Competitive Commercial Agriculture in the Guinea Savannah Zone and Beyond* (Washington DC: The World Bank).

World Bank (2009b) *Environmental, Economic and Social Impacts of Oil Palm in Indonesia: A Synthesis of Opportunities and Challenges* (Jakarta: World Bank, Indonesia Country Office).

Zoomers, A. (2010) 'Globalisation and the Foreignisation of Space: Seven Processes Driving the Current Global Land Grab', *Journal of Peasant Studies,* 37(2), 429–47.

15

Using the Land Governance Assessment Framework to Help Secure Rural Land Rights: Framework and Experience Thus Far

Klaus Deininger and Thea Hilhorst

15.1 Background and motivation

Relatively stagnant or low productivity of land use in many areas, soaring global demand for land as a source of food, fuel, and fiber or as a source of environmental amenities, and demands for structural transformation to transfer labor out of agriculture and provide space for urban development –all these factors imply that land governance has emerged as a key determinant of sustainable growth and poverty reduction.
It will be critical in particular to

(i) increase incentives for land-related investment and resource conservation;
(ii) provide a basis for low-cost operation of land markets and the associated development of financial markets based on the ability of using land as collateral; and
(iii) empower asset holders, in particular women, in the long-term.

In the past, efforts to improve governance of land and natural resources have often been frustrated by

(i) the technical complexity and context specific nature of land issues;

(ii) the fact that responsibility for handling land is distributed among many public institutions that are often ill-coordinated; and
(iii) the high stakes involved, and the scope for resistance to change by stakeholders benefiting from the status quo.

All this has often resulted in large amounts of resources being spent on studies that were not followed by action or by narrow interventions that failed to bring sustained improvement. In fact, a large body of literature suggests that land-related programs have in many cases been high risk, difficult to scale up, and unsustainable.

Policy pronouncements at global (Food and Agricultural Organization of the UN, 2012) and regional level (African Union, 2009) recognize this. They acknowledge that avoiding similar disappointment requires a country-driven process to generate consensus on the status of land governance among a diverse set of stakeholders (private sector, government, civil society, academia), to translate this into actionable priority policy recommendations, and to regularly follow up on progress towards improved land governance. Yet they provide little guidance on how to structure such a process in practice.

This chapter describes initial experience from country-level application of the Land Governance Assessment Framework (LGAF), a tool that uses existing information to systematically compare a country's land governance with global good practice in a structured, broad-based and participatory process. The outcome is validated publicly and translated into priority policy recommendations that can feed into country strategies and the design and evaluation of innovative pilots to develop scalable approaches to improving land governance, plus a process for country-level monitoring that builds on the process achieved.

We first describe the substantive areas covered and modalities of implementation before reviewing results from their application in a number of countries, to argue that assessing a country's land governance against a global benchmark and using a multi-stakeholder approach to not only provide continuity in the longer term but also to create a constituency for continued reform can help to deal with this in a way that combines action with learning, and generates additional information and knowledge over time.

15.2 The LGAF: substance and implementation modalities

To make sector-specific indicators of land governance policy relevant and use them as a diagnostic tool to assess a country's situation and, on the basis of the identified shortcomings, come up with a set of policy recommendations or areas for future research, a methodology and process are needed. This section describes the substantive framework to guide such an assessment and the methodology to come up with a consensus ranking that is sufficiently robust to be presented to policymakers. It then reviews experience with implementation thus far and sets out a number of lessons and potential next steps.

15.2.1 Substantive areas and indicators

Based on global experience, five key areas of good land governance have been identified, namely

(i) a legal, institutional and policy framework that recognizes existing rights, enforces them at low cost, and allows users to exercise them in line with their aspirations and in a way that serves the benefit of society as a whole;
(ii) arrangements for land use planning and taxation conducive to the avoidance of negative externalities and supporting effective decentralization;
(iii) clear identification of state land and its management in a way that cost-effectively provides public goods; use of expropriation as a last resort only, to establish public infrastructure with quick payment of fair compensation and effective mechanisms for appeal; and mechanisms for divestiture of state lands that are transparent and maximize public revenue;
(iv) public provision of land information in a way that is broadly accessible, comprehensive, reliable, current and cost-effective in the long run; and
(v) accessible mechanisms to authoritatively resolve dispute and manage conflict with clearly defined mandates, and low cost of operation.

In addition, modules on large-scale land acquisitions, forestry and urban land tenure regularization are available for countries where these issues are important.

To summarize information in a structured way that is understandable by policymakers and can be compared across countries, we chose to build on the methodology used by the Public Expenditure and Financial Accountability assessment tool (PEFA).[1] The five thematic areas introduced above serve as the basis for 21 land governance indicators (LGIs). Each of the LGIs is then broken down into between two and six 'dimensions' for which, at least in principle, objective empirical information can be obtained. While it is important to avoid implicit value judgments or a one-size-fits-all approach, global good practice and extensive interaction with land professionals, refined through pilot country case studies from around the globe, has been used to establish a list of pre-coded statements that can be used to rank each of the about 80 dimensions. A description of the dimensions, but not the ranking framework, is given in Table 15.1.

While the general framework to identify comparable indicators is adopted from the PEFA, there are key differences. First, to ensure that the nuances of local legislation and practice are adequately captured, the main responsibility for the conduct of the exercise is not with outside experts who visit the country for a short period but with a country coordinator who is also a local expert in law or land administration.[2] Second, dimensions to be ranked are grouped into sets of eight to ten. Expert panels of three to five members with experience in the relevant topic are then formed to come up with consensus rankings for indicators in their area of expertise, drawing on background information provided by the country coordinator as well as on experience and informal interviews. To illustrate this, Table 15.2 provides two examples of ranking dimensions based either on quantitative information (in broad ranges) or qualitative assessment.[3] Finally, rather than being compressed into a relatively short time period, the entire exercise is conducted over a three to five month period so as to allow sufficient time for deliberation and consensus building.

15.2.2 Implementation modalities

Figure 15.1 illustrates the different steps involved in the diagnostic phase of the LGAF, which can be grouped into inception, assembly of background documentation, rankings by expert panels to produce a draft report, public validation and policy maker workshops to obtain a final report with specific policy recommendations and follow-up activities.[4]

Inception phase: To prepare the ground for a substantively meaningful and inclusive exercise, the inception phase includes three sets of activities, namely

(i) a review and if necessary an adaptation of the LGAF implementation manual to identify any areas where customization to country conditions may be needed;

Table 15.1 LGAF dimensions ordered by thematic areas

THEMATIC AREA 1. LEGAL AND INSTITUTIONAL FRAMEWORK		
LGI-1. Recognition of a continuum of rights: **The law recognizes a range of rights held by individuals as well as groups (including secondary rights, as well as rights held by minorities and women)**		
1	i	Existing legal framework recognizes rights held by most of the rural population, either through customary or statutory tenure regimes.
	ii	Existing legal framework recognizes rights held by most of the urban population, either through customary or statutory tenure regimes.
	iii	The tenure of most groups in rural areas is formally recognized, and clear regulations exist regarding groups' internal organization and legal representation
	iv	Group tenure in informal urban areas is formally recognized and clear regulations exist regarding the internal organization and legal representation of groups.
	v	The law provides opportunities for those holding land under customary, group or collective tenure to fully or partially individualize land ownership/use. Procedures for doing so are affordable, clearly specified, safeguarded, and followed in practice.
LGI-2. Enforcement of rights: **The rights recognized by law are enforced (including secondary rights as well as rights by minorities and women)**		
2	i	Most communal lands have boundaries demarcated and surveyed/mapped and communal rights registered.
	ii	Most individual properties in rural areas are formally registered.
	iii	Most individual properties in urban areas are formally registered.
	iv	A high percentage of land registered to physical persons is registered in the name of women, either individually or jointly.
	v	Common property under condominiums is recognized, and there are clear provisions in the law to establish arrangements for the management and maintenance of this common property.
	vi	Loss of rights as a result of land use change outside the expropriation process, compensation in cash or in kind is paid such that these people have comparable assets and can continue to maintain prior social and economic status.

***LGI-3. Mechanisms for recognition of rights:* The formal definition and assignment of rights, and the process of recording of rights, accord with actual practice or, where it does not, provides affordable avenues for establishing such consistency in a non-discriminatory manner**

3	i	Non-documentary forms of evidence are used alone to obtain full recognition of claims to property when other forms of evidence are not available.
	ii	Legislation exists to formally recognize long-term, unchallenged possession, and this applies to both public and private land, although different rules may apply.
	iii	The costs for first-time sporadic registration for a typical urban property is low compared to the property value.
	iv	There are no informal fees that need to be paid to effect first registration.
	v	The requirements for formalizing housing in urban areas are clear, straightforward and affordable, and are implemented consistently in a transparent manner.
	vi	There is a clear, practical process for the formal recognition of possession, and this process is implemented effectively, consistently and transparently.

***LGI-4. Restrictions on rights*: Land rights are not conditional on adherence to unrealistic standards.**

4	i	There are a series of regulations regarding urban land use, ownership and transferability that are for the most part justified on the basis of overall public interest, and that are enforced.
	ii	There are a series of regulations regarding rural land use, ownership and transferability that are for the most part justified on the basis of overall public interest, and that are enforced.

***LGI-5. Clarity of mandates and practice:* Institutional mandates concerning the regulation and management of the land sector are clearly defined, duplication of responsibilities is avoided and information is shared as needed.**

5	i	There is a clear separation in the roles of policy formulation, implementation of policy through land management and administration and the arbitration of any disputes that may arise as a result of implementation of policy.
	ii	The mandated responsibilities exercised by the authorities dealing with land administration issues are clearly defined and non-overlapping with those of other land sector agencies.
	iii	Assignment of land-related responsibilities between the different levels of government is clear and non-overlapping.
	iv	Information related to rights in land is available to other institutions that need this information at reasonable cost and is readily accessible, largely due to the fact that land information is maintained in a uniform way.

Continued

Table 15.1 Continued

THEMATIC AREA 1. LEGAL AND INSTITUTIONAL FRAMEWORK		
LGI-6. Equity and non-discrimination in the decision-making process: **Policies are formulated through a legitimate decision-making process that draws on inputs from all concerned. The legal framework is non-discriminatory, and institutions to enforce property rights are equally accessible to all**		
6	i	A comprehensive policy exists or can be inferred by the existing legislation. Land policy decisions that affect sections of the community are based on consultation with those affected, and their feedback on the resulting policy is sought and incorporated in the resulting policy.
	ii	Land policies incorporate equity objectives that are regularly and meaningfully monitored, and their impact on equity issues is compared to that of other policy instruments.
	iii	Implementation of land policy is costed, and the expected benefits identified and compared to cost, and there are sufficient budget, resources and institutional capacity for implementation.
	iv	Land institutions report on land policy implementation in a regular, meaningful and comprehensive way, with reports being publicly accessible.
THEMATIC AREA 2. LAND USE PLANNING, MANAGEMENT, AND TAXATION		
LGI-7. Transparency of land use restrictions: **Changes in land use and management regulations are made in a transparent fashion, and provide significant benefits for society in general rather than just for specific groups.**		
7	i	In urban areas, public input is sought in preparing and amending changes in land use plans, and the public responses are explicitly referenced in the report prepared by the public body responsible for preparing the new public plans. This report is publicly accessible.
	ii	In rural areas, public input is sought in preparing and amending land use plans, and the public responses are explicitly referenced in the report prepared by the public body responsible for preparing the new public plans. This report is publicly accessible.
	iii	Mechanisms to allow the public to capture significant share of the gains from changing land use are regularly used and applied transparently based on clear regulation.
	iv	Most land that has had a change in land use assignment in the past three years has changed to the destined use.

***LGI-8. Efficiency in the land use planning process:* Land use plans and regulations are justified, effectively implemented, do not drive large parts of the population into informality, and are able to cope with population growth.**

8	i	In the largest city in the country, urban development is controlled effectively by a hierarchy of regional/detailed land use plans that are kept up to date.
	ii	In the four major cities, urban development is controlled effectively by a hierarchy of regional/detailed land use plans that are kept up to date.
	iii	In the largest city in the country, the urban planning process/authority is able to cope with the increasing demand for serviced units/land, as evidenced by the fact that almost all new dwellings are formal.
	iv	Existing requirements for residential plot sizes are met in most plots.
	v	The share of land set aside for specific use that is used for a non-specified purpose in contravention of existing regulations is low.

***LGI-9. Speed and predictability of enforcement of restricted land uses:* Development permits are granted promptly and predictably.**

9	i	Requirements to obtain a building permit are technically justified, affordable and clearly disseminated.
	ii	All applications for building permits receive a decision within a short period of time.

***LGI-10. Transparency of valuations:* Valuations for tax purposes are based on clear principles, applied uniformly, updated regularly, and publicly accessible**

10	i	The assessment of land/property values for tax purposes is based on market prices with minimal differences between recorded values and market prices across different uses and types of users, and valuation rolls are regularly updated.
	ii	There is a policy that valuation rolls be publicly accessible, and this policy is effective for all properties that are considered for taxation.

***LGI-11. Collection efficiency:* Resources from land and property taxes are collected, and the yield from land taxes exceeds the cost of collection**

11	i	There are limited exemptions to the payment of land/property taxes, and the exemptions that exist are clearly based on equity or efficiency grounds and applied in a transparent and consistent manner.
	ii	Most property holders liable for land/property tax are listed on the tax roll.
	iii	Most assessed property taxes are collected.
	iv	The amount of property taxes collected exceeds the cost of staff in charge of collection by a factor of more than 5.

Continued

Table 15.1 Continued

THEMATIC AREA 3. MANAGEMENT OF PUBLIC LAND		
LGI-12. Identification of public land and clear management: **Public land ownership is justified, inventoried, under clear management responsibilities, and relevant information is publicly accessible**		
12	i	Public land ownership is justified by the provision of public goods at the appropriate level of government, and such land is managed in a transparent and effective way.
	ii	The majority of public land is clearly identified on the ground or on maps.
	iii	The management responsibility for different types of public land is unambiguously assigned.
	iv	There are adequate budgets and human resources to ensure responsible management of public lands.
	v	All the information in the public land inventory is accessible to the public.
	vi	Key information for land concessions is recorded and publicly accessible.
LGI-13. Justification and time-efficiency of expropriation processes: **The state expropriates land only for overall public interest, and this is done efficiently**		
13	i	A minimal amount of land expropriated in the past three years is used for private purposes.
	ii	The majority of land that has been expropriated in the past three years has been transferred to its destined use.
LGI-14. Transparency and fairness of expropriation procedures: **Expropriation procedures are clear and transparent, and compensation in kind or at market values is paid fairly and expeditiously**		
14	i	Where property is expropriated, fair compensation, in kind or in cash, is paid so that the displaced households have comparable assets and can continue to maintain prior social and economic status.
	ii	Fair compensation, in kind or in cash, is paid to all those with rights in expropriated land, regardless of the registration status.
	iii	Most expropriated land owners receive compensation within one year.
	iv	Independent avenues to lodge a complaint against expropriation exist and are easily accessible.
	v	A first instance decision has been reached for the majority of complaints about expropriation lodged during the last three years.

***LGI-15. Transparent process and economic benefit:* Transfer of public land to private use follows a clear, transparent and competitive process, and payments are collected and audited.**

15	i	Most public land disposed of in the past three years is through sale or lease through public auction or open tender process.
	ii	A majority of the total agreed payments are collected from private parties on the lease of public lands.
	iii	All types of public land are generally divested at market prices in a transparent process irrespective of the investor's status (e.g. domestic or foreign).

THEMATIC AREA 4. PUBLIC PROVISION OF LAND INFORMATION

***LGI-16. Completeness:* The land registry provides information on different private tenure categories in a way that is geographically complete and searchable by parcel as well as by right holder and can be obtained expeditiously by all interested parties**

16	i	Most records for privately held land registered in the registry are readily identifiable in maps in the registry or cadastre.
	ii	Relevant private encumbrances are recorded consistently and in a reliable fashion, and can be verified at low cost by any interested party.
	iii	Relevant public restrictions or charges are recorded consistently and in a reliable fashion, and can be verified at a low cost by any interested party.
	iv	The records in the registry can be searched by both right holder name and parcel.
	v	Copies or extracts of documents recording rights in property can be obtained by anyone who pays the necessary formal fee, if any.
	vi	Copies or extracts of documents recording rights in property can generally be obtained within 1 day of request.

***LGI-17. Reliability:* Registry information is updated, sufficient to make meaningful inferences on ownership**

17	i	There are meaningful published service standards, and the registry actively monitors its performance against these standards.
	ii	Most ownership information in the registry/cadastre is up to date.

***LGI-18. Cost-effectiveness and sustainability:* Land administration services are provided in a cost-effective manner.**

18	i	The cost for registering a property transfer is minimal compared to the property value.
	ii	The total fees collected by the registry exceed the total registry operating costs.
	iii	There is significant investment in capital in the system to record rights in land so that the system is sustainable but still accessible by the poor.

Continued

Table 15.1 Continued

THEMATIC AREA 4. PUBLIC PROVISION OF LAND INFORMATION		
LGI-19. Transparency: **Fees are determined and collected in a transparent manner**		
19	i	A clear schedule of fees for different services is publicly accessible and receipts are issued for all transactions.
	ii	Mechanisms to detect and deal with illegal staff behavior exist in all registry offices, and all cases are promptly dealt with.
THEMATIC AREA 5. DISPUTE RESOLUTION AND CONFLICT MANAGEMENT		
LGI-20. Assignment of responsibility: **Responsibility for conflict management at different levels is clearly assigned in line with actual practice, relevant bodies are competent in applicable legal matters, and decisions can be appealed against.**		
20	i	Institutions for providing a first instance of conflict resolution are accessible at the local level in the majority of communities.
	ii	There is an informal or community-based system that resolves disputes in an equitable manner, and decisions made by this system have some recognition in the formal judicial or administrative dispute resolution system.
	iii	There are no parallel avenues for conflict resolution or, if parallel avenues exist, responsibilities are clearly assigned and widely known, and explicit rules for shifting from one to the other are in place to minimize the scope for forum shopping.
	iv	A process and mechanism exist to appeal rulings on land cases at reasonable cost, with disputes resolved in a timely manner.
LGI-21. Low level of pending conflict: **The share of land affected by pending conflicts is low and decreasing**		
21	i	Land disputes in the formal court system are low compared to the total number of court cases.
	ii	A decision in a land-related conflict is reached in the first instance court within 1 year in the majority of cases.
	iii	Long-standing land conflicts are a small proportion of the total pending land dispute court cases.

Table 15.2 Illustration of ranking framework for two dimensions

LGI-16, Dim. I	Assessment
Mapping/charting of registry records is complete.	**A** – More than 90% of records for privately held land in the registry are readily identifiable in maps held by the registry or the cadastre. **B** – Between 70% and 90% of records for privately held land in the registry are readily identifiable in maps held by the registry or the cadastre. **C** – Between 50% and 70% of records for privately held land in the registry are readily identifiable in maps held by the registry or the cadastre. **D** – Less than 50% of records for privately held land in the registry are readily identifiable in maps held by the registry or the cadastre.
Comments *Analysis & options for improvement:* *Data source/reliability:*	
LGI-7 Dimension iii	**Assessment**
The public captures benefits arising from changes in permitted land use.	**A** – Mechanisms that allow the public to capture a significant share of the gains from changing land use are regularly used and applied transparently based on clear regulation. **B** – Mechanisms that allow the public to capture a significant share of the gains from changing land use are applied transparently but not always used. **C** – Mechanisms that allow the public to capture a significant share of the gains from changing land use are rarely used and applied in a discretionary manner. **D** – Mechanisms that allow the public to capture a significant share of the gains from changing land use are not used or not applied transparently.
***Comments for** LGI-2 (i)* *Analysis & options for improvement:* *Data source/reliability:*	

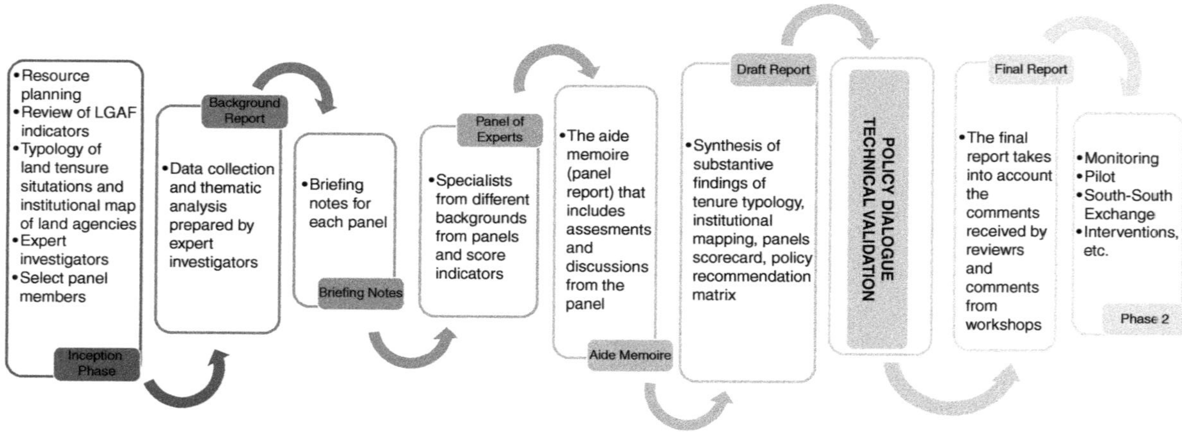

Figure 15.1 Specific steps in LGAF implementation

(ii) identification of the team, in particular expert investigators and panel members from a wide range of sectors as well as formulation of a time schedule; and
(iii) if not done earlier, formal communication with relevant authorities to ensure their formal buy-in as evidence by appointment of a person to liaise with relevant ministries and departments, and an agreement to make specific data available.

From a substantive point of view, this phase also is used to establish a tenure typology that describes key types of tenure in the country, quantifies the area and population under each type, and identifies key gaps and overlaps for each of them. Similarly, a map of institutions in the sector identifies functions performed by these at different levels, to identify gaps and overlaps and an indication of staffing and budgets.

Assembly of background documentation: The country coordinator is responsible for compilation of relevant background studies to be made available to those who actually rank indicators in expert panels. To provide a common basis of information that is indispensable as a basis of consensus on rankings or priority actions, three sets written output are needed. These are prepared by a country coordinator, with support from a government liaison to provide access to administrative data (for example on the extent of female rights; collection of taxes; adherence to rules in case of expropriation; transparency of public land dispositions; and the nature, area, and age of disputes) as well as expert investigators who prepare background reports in the four areas of land tenure, land use policy, public land management and the land registry. In each of these, relevant material from existing studies and 'grey' literature is synthesized in a background report by specialists in the relevant areas, normally subcontracted by the country coordinator. Once reports are reviewed and validated, information is then summarized in panel briefing notes.

Expert panels: Rankings for each of the dimensions are assigned by panels of key stakeholders such as lawyers, academics, members of business chambers, banks, NGO representatives, government officials, land professionals and others (such as builders requiring permits) who interact with land institutions and thus are able to assess performance in the sector. This is done in eight work sessions of about one day per topic, organized by the coordinator.[5] Each dimension is discussed in detail, to arrive at a consensus ranking and agreed policy priorities. Based on their experience, panel members should be able to identify both good and deficient performance, and the underlying reasons. Cases of good performance can hold lessons for other countries. Recommendations on how to deal with unsatisfactory performance may be identified directly or give rise to the need for more detailed study, allowing derivation of recommendations that can be prioritized. Discussions are summarized in minutes and the record of these discussions is reviewed and agreed upon by panelists. The material from panel minutes is then synthesized in a draft country report.

Validation and policy workshop: Once approved by panel members, the country report is reviewed by international peer reviewers to provide input. The results are incorporated, and the report is presented to a public national workshop to validate the results and to prioritize policy conclusions and the associated monitoring indicators. These are then presented to key policymakers during a policy workshop that is organized shortly after validation of the policy conclusions. A key goal is to formulate a policy matrix identifying a limited set of clear priorities or areas where further information needs to be collected, with a time frame (short- to medium- or long-term), responsibilities and indicators for tracking progress. These recommendations emerge from the panels, are sharpened during the technical validation workshop, and discussed with policymakers during the policy dialogue. While the initial assessment does not provide a magic solution to the range of land governance challenges, the priority setting of policy recommendation and timeline helps to sequence reforms and link them to critical policy outcomes, thereby allowing land to be put higher on the policy agenda and to create a constituency for reform by involving many stakeholders.

Monitoring: To the extent that it is locally driven, the diagnostic application of the LGAF is not intended as a one-off intervention but as the establishment of a local constituency and platform that can regularly assess progress in improving land governance and provide technical advice on actions needed in this respect. While much of the input into such follow-up will be qualitative (for example, whether certain changes with respect to policy or institutions have been undertaken), quantitative data to provide the basis for greater nuance in terms of specific indicators and variation across regions can be obtained by including land modules with key questions in national household surveys, establishing mechanisms to better capture, organize and review data generated by routine administrative processes (such as coverage with maps or routine information on land transactions, prices, or land-related conflicts), and interpreting statistics used by the private sector.

15.3 Experience in applying the LGAF

15.3.1 Implementation status

Table 15.3 summarizes progress in implementing LGAFs across regions. The exercise has been completed in eleven countries; seven have background material completed and are in the process of conducting or validating panels, and nine are (at the time of writing) in the inception phase. Much of the initial emphasis has been on Africa, where eight countries have completed the process and nine have started, being at various stages of implementation.

The LGAF is built on four key assumptions. First, legal provisions may differ significantly from what is actually implemented on the ground due to lack of clarity (or conflicting legal provision), failure to pass the regulations needed to implement existing laws, or weak implementation capacity. This implies that any analysis will have to go beyond legal statements to assess what is faced by the users of land administration systems. Second, in many countries land sector issues have been extensively analyzed at the technical level, but the information generated is not well known or disseminated; a dialogue using existing information rather than extensive new analysis is thus possible, and can in fact help identify priority areas for in-depth study based on overall assessment of land governance. Third, while the cross-cutting nature of land issues is recognized in principle, the lack of dialogue and data sharing between

Table 15.3 Evidence of stakeholder participation in LGAFs conducted thus far

	Africa	Eastern Europe	Latin America	Asia
Inception	Liberia, Sudan, Uganda, South Sudan	Moldova	Colombia, Honduras	India (AP, KA, OR, GJ, WB, BI), Bangladesh, Indonesia (Kalimantan)
Panel preparation	Gambia, Senegal, Mauritania, Mali, Cameroon			Philippines, Vietnam
Report preparation	DRC, Rwanda		Brazil (Para, Piaul)	
Monitoring & expansion	Madagascar, Malawi, Nigeria, South Africa, Ghana	Ukraine, Georgia	Peru	

land institutions often impedes progress and realization of synergies. Finally, as land governance and institutions are context-specific, the involvement of local experts is critical for actionable recommendations. At the same time, the challenges to be addressed are similar across countries, so that implementing a standardized assessment tool such as the LGAF is feasible and offers opportunities for the sharing of experience and learning from good practice.

15.3.2 Substantive insights

Table 15.4 provides rankings of key dimensions in eight recently completed LGAFs (Georgia, Ghana, Nigeria, South Africa, Brazil, Madagascar, Malawi, and the Democratic Republic of Congo (DRC)) to illustrate level insights emerging from a cross-country comparison of rankings. Dimensions where some countries do well while others rank badly are obvious candidates for experience sharing and knowledge transfer. Dimensions that rank low across many countries constitute constraints, whose removal may require a global effort to develop either methodologies or awareness and political momentum. Based on Table 15.4, the mapping of communal rights; urban planning; openness of public land transactions; and the speed of resolving land conflicts appear to belong in this category. Finally, while aggregation of rankings across dimensions to construct a 'land governance index' at country level is difficult to defend methodologically,[6] scanning rankings at country level points towards marked differences in the maturity of land institutions. While sustained improvement is very unlikely to happen quickly, institutional reforms to establish independent institutions and properly structure partnerships with the private sector have allowed considerable progress in cases such as Georgia's.

Although laws recognize local and community rights in principle, a 'rights recognition gap' often limits the ability to effectively enforce these. One reason is the limited mapping or registration of such claims, which makes it difficult to identify them on the ground, often compounded by complex and costly procedures for formalization. With rising implicit land values, traditional leaders in many countries have started to map boundaries of land under their own jurisdiction, often in ways that fail to follow due process and end up disempowering women or the poor, as in Ghana. Evidence from a number of countries suggests that even if females enjoy equal land rights by law, land may be registered in the name of men only and thus implicitly discriminate

Table 15.4 Summary of rankings for key dimensions in existing LGAFs

1. LEGAL & INSTITUTIONAL FRAMEWK			GE	GH	NG	SA	BR	MG	MW	DRC
Recognition of a continuum of rights										
1	i	Land tenure rights recognition (rural)	A	A	A	B	A	A	B	
1	ii	Land tenure rights recognition (urban)	A	A	A	B	B	C	C	A
1	iii	Rural group rights recognition	D	A	C	B	C	B	C	C
1	iv	Urban informal group rights recognition		B	C	C	C	D	C	B
1	v	Opportunities for individualization	D	B	C	C	D	A	C	D
Enforcement of Rights										
2	i	Mapping/registration of communal land	D	D	D	D	D	D	D	D
2	ii	Registration of individual rural land	A	D	D	A	A	D	D	D
2	iii	Registration of individual urban land	A	D	D	A	A		C	D
2	iv	Formal recognition of women's rights	C	D	D	A	A	C	C	
2	v	Condominium regime.	C	C	B	A	C	A	C	A
2	vi	Compensation due to land use changes	D	C	B	B	D	C	C	D
Mechanisms for Recognition										
3	i	Non-doc. evidence to recognize rights	B	C	C	C	C	C	B	B
3	ii	Recognition of long-term possession	C	C	D	C	A	A	B	B
3	iii	Formal fees for 1st time registration low	C	C	D	D	C	D	B	
3	iv	No high informal fees for 1st time reg.	C	D	C	B	A	D	B	
3	v	Housing formalization feasible & affordable	B	C	C	C	A	D	B	C
2. LAND USE PLANNING AND TAXATION										
7	i	Urban planning based on public input	C	B	C	B	C	B	D	D
7	ii	Rural planning based on public input	C	D	D	B	D	B	D	C
7	iii	Public capture of changes in land use	B	C	C	B	C	D	D	C
7	iv	Speed of land use change	C	A	D	A	C	B	A	B

Continued

Table15.4 Continued

2. LAND USE PLANNING AND TAXATION			GE	GH	NG	SA	BR	MG	MW	DRC
Efficiency of Land Use Planning										
8	i	Planned dev. process: largest city	C	C	D	A	D	B	A	B
8	ii	Planned dev. process: 4 next cities	C	C	D	A	D	C	C	D
8	iii	Planning copes with urban growth	C	C	C	C	D	C	C	D
8	iv	Plot size adherence	B	C	C	A	D	D	D	B
8	v	Plans for other uses in line with reality	A	D	D		B	B	C	C
Speed and Predictability										
9	i	Res. building permits affordable/transp.	A	C	C	B	C	C	C	C
9	ii	Time to get building permit	A	C	C	A	C	C		A
Transparency of Valuation										
10	i	Clear process of property valuation	D	C	D	A	C	C	B	C
10	ii	Public availability of valuation rolls	A	C	C	A	C	B	A	B
Tax Collection Efficiency										
11	i	Property tax exemptions justified	A	C	B	A	A	C	A	B
11	ii	Completeness of tax roll	A	D	D	A	A	C	A	C
11	iii	Assessed property taxes are collected	A	C	C	B	B	C	D	C
11	iv	Taxes higher than cost of collection	C	C	D	A		B	A	C
3. MANAGEMENT OF PUBLIC LAND										
Identification and management of public land										
12	i	Pub. ownership justified	A	B	C	B	B	B	B	B
12	ii	Complete recording of public land	C	C	C	A	A	C	B	A
12	iii	Management resp. for public land	A	B	C	C	B	B	C	B
12	iv	Institutions resourced properly	A	C	D	C	C	D	C	C
12	v	Public land inventory w. public access	B	C	C	A	A	D	C	C
12	vi	Key info on land concessions is public.	A	B	B	C	A	C	C	C

Incidence of Expropriation										
13	i	Exprop. land transferred to privates	A	A	C	A		B	A	A
13	ii	Speed of use of expropriated land	A	D	C	A	A	A	A	A
Transparency of Procedures										
14	i	Comp. for exprop of ownership	A	B	C	C	A	C	B	C
14	ii	Comp. for exprop of other rights	A	B	C	C	D	C	C	C
14	iii	Promptness of compensation	A	C	D	B	A	C	C	D
14	iv	Independent & accessible appeal	A	B	D	B	A	B	A	D
14	v	Appeal is time-bounded	A	C	C	D	D	B	C	D
Transparent Processes for Divestiture										
15	i	Openness of public land transactions	A	D	D	D	D	A	D	D
15	ii	Collection of payments for public leases	A	D	C	C	A	C	D	D
15	iii	Modalities of lease/sale of public land	A	D	B	C	D	D	B	D
4. PUBLIC PROV. OF LAND INFORMATION										
Completeness of Registry Information										
16	i	Mapping of registry records	C	B	D	A	A	D	B	D
16	ii	Relevant private encumbrances	A	A	A	A	B	C	A	A
16	iii	Relevant public restrictions	A	C	C	C	A	C	C	A
16	iv	Searchability of the registry	A	C	A	A	A	C	A	D
16	v	Accessibility of registry records	A	A	B	A	A	A	B	A
16	vi	Timely response to requests	A	A	C	A	B	D	B	C
Reliability of Registry Records										
17	i	Registry focus on client satisfaction	A	B	D	C	B	D	B	D
17	ii	Cadastral/registry info up-to-date	D	B	D	A	D	C	C	C
Cost Effectiveness and Sustainability										
18	i	Cost to register transfer	A	C	D	C	A	D	D	B
18	ii	Fin. sustainability of registry	A	D	D	A	A	B	D	A
18	iii	Capital investment	A	C	D	A	D	C	D	C

Continued

Table15.4 Continued

4. PUBLIC PROV. OF LAND INFORMATION			GE	GH	NG	SA	BR	MG	MW	DRC
Transparency										
19	i	Fee schedule public	A	C	C	A	A	B	B	A
19	ii	Informal payments discouraged	A	D	D	A	A	C	D	D
5. CONFLICT RESOLUTION										
Responsibility for Conflict Resolution										
20	i	Access of conflict resolution	A	B	B	B	B	A	B	B
20	ii	Informal dispute resolution recognized	B	A	A	C	A	C	C	A
20	iii	Forum shopping	A	B	B	C	D	B	C	B
20	iv	Possibility of appeals	B	C	C	D	C	C	C	C
Low Level of Pending Conflicts										
21	i	Conf. res. in formal system	A	C	B				B	C
21	ii	Speed of formal resolution	A	D	D	D	D	D	D	D
21	iii	No. of long-standing conflicts	A	D	D	D	D	C	C	D
LARGE SCALE ACQUISITION										
Large scale land acquisition										
LS	1	Direct and transparent negotiations	A	B	C	D				C
LS	2	Sufficient information required	B	C	C	D				D
LS	3	Information is public	B	D	C	C				A
LS	4	Benefit/risk sharing in contracts	A	B	C	D				D
LS	5	Effective approval process	A	B	D	C				A
LS	6	Social reqs defined & implemented	B	B	C	C				C
LS	7	Env'l reqs clearly defined, implemented	B	C	D	C				D
LS	8	Thorough public review of proposals	A	D	C	C				D
LS	9	Compliance with safeguards checked	B	D	D	C				C
LS	10	Avenues to lodge complaints	B	D	D	C				D

against females. Unless such biases are addressed, formalization may not enhance economic development.

Especially in situations with rapid population growth, planning legislation and the plans derived from it are often outdated and bear little resemblance to reality. Planning, which is often top-down and lacks public input, then follows development rather than the reverse, and service delivery for the expanding urban centers becomes costly or impossible. Weak property valuation and limited ability to improve tax collection, due to differences in the transparency of valuation, completeness of the tax roll, and the extent to which taxes will actually accrue to local governments may limit the public's ability to capture benefits from land use changes. Weak protection of land rights in the urban periphery, including low or non-payment of compensation for expropriation, may also encourage over-expansion of cities, with negative implications.

The acquisition of land through eminent domain often involves very limited compensation (for which only formally registered but not customary land may be eligible) that may not be paid for a long time, and with limited scope for appeal. Many countries also require customary land to be expropriated before any transfer to private investors is possible. While the purported intention is to protect potentially ill-informed customary land holders against unscrupulous interests, the record of state institutions in this respect has often been poor and many country examples point towards better ways (minimum standards, publicity of contracts, independent review panels) to achieve this objective. In many contexts, physical identification of state land on the ground is near impossible and often such land – especially if it was acquired long time ago – is heavily encroached upon. Good experience with divestiture of such land in transparent auctions to contribute to public resources exists in a number of countries.

Providing comprehensive and current information affordably is a core function of land administration institutions, and is a necessary, though by no means sufficient, condition for other benefits to materialize. Yet in many instances institutions are not self-financing, and are unable to retain the user fees they collect; they depend instead on handouts, reducing the incentive to invest and innovate to sustainably improve service quality. Even where they work well, land institutions may serve only a tiny minority due to limited coverage, an issue that is most pronounced in South Africa. Institutional sustainability may be further jeopardized by unrealistic limits on the subdivision of transfer fees/duties of up to 10 percent of property values or more, possibly due to limited entry to registration professions. These create strong disincentives for registration, and may eventually render unsustainable even great advances in first-time adjudication.

Rising demand for land all over the world creates opportunities to draw in private investment to integrate smallholders into value chains and use land that may be either unutilized or underutilized for economic development. The results from the large-scale land acquisition module show that many countries are ill-prepared for this, as they lack essential preconditions, including ways to

(i) identify available land by balancing agro-ecological potential and infrastructure access;
(ii) market available land in ways that attract capable investors (for instance, by providing infrastructure or risk capital) while at the same time maximizing social returns;
(iii) cost-effectively document existing land rights before any investment starts;
(iv) provide assistance to local land holders in contract negotiations and monitoring;
(v) monitor and ensure adherence to environmental and social norms;
(vi) allow public access to information on contract details, economic and social outcomes, and technical details, to allow rapid replication of success and learning from failure;
(vii) quickly resolve disputes in a way that is acceptable to all parties; and
(vii) allow for the transfer of assets from non-performing ventures to more productive uses in ways that do not undermine local welfare.

With such gaps, responsible investors may well consider it too risky to commit resources.

One key benefit from applying the LGAF has been the establishment of a stakeholder group at national level that not only includes most or all relevant public and private sector institutions but also has acquired an understanding of the overall framework for land governance and thus can champion a policy dialogue on these issues. For example in Nigeria, while the inappropriate nature of legislation was (and still is) well recognized, there was no body to move the debate forward. A key recommendation from the LGAF process was to re-establish a Presidential Technical Committee for Land Reform to pilot and evaluate approaches to solving the country's tenure issues, coordinate policy reform between the Ministries concerned, and follow up with individual states (who have considerable latitude in terms of land policy). In Malawi, LGAF results provided the impetus for tabling a Land Bill that had been languishing in Parliament for more than five years and resulted in establishment of a task force cutting across different ministries. In the DRC, the process helped to inform a national road map for land tenure reform that will be fed into pilot schemes to harmonize data on concessions between ministries, secure tenure in urban and rural settings, and explore options to resolve conflict in the country's eastern part. In Georgia, which has been identified in the World Bank's 'Doing Business' survey as a top reformer of property registration, the LGAF identified gaps in terms high transaction costs of land transfers, treatment of community and forest land, and efforts to attract investors that are now being addressed through a project supported by the Bank.

15.4 Challenges ahead

While experience highlights the usefulness of the LGAF to provide a technical assessment of a country's land governance, identify priority policy issues to address, and set in motion a dialogue that can help include land issues more prominently in national development strategies, it is a starting point rather than an end in itself. Three follow-up activities are particularly prominent:

Experience sharing: One of the key benefits of a structured technical assessment of land governance across countries is that it helps to quickly identify any potential for the transfer of knowledge and experience. With technology reducing the cost of addressing many land issues, this implies vast scope to document and share good practice. This extends to states or provinces which often formulate and implement land policies in federal countries. In fact, there may be considerable scope for subnational assessments not only at state or province level but also for cities or municipalities with high fiscal or legislative autonomy.

Monitoring: The fact that land institutions are not required to regularly report publicly on progress against targets weakens accountability and often creates difficulty in including land issues within national strategies or regional efforts. In such a context, the LGAF process can help to

(i) set legitimate targets for monitoring,
(ii) institutionalize follow-up by continuing to draw on the stakeholder groups involved in the initial assessment; and

(iii) identify sources of information -via regular censuses and household or sector-specific surveys in combination with administrative data (for example on registered transactions) to regularly assess progress.

Piloting: While significant resources will eventually be required to sustainably address the shortcomings identified, the most immediate need is often for well-designed and carefully evaluated pilots in key areas (regularization, conflict resolution, planning regulations, options for urban expansion, transparency of land transfers, and access to data on them) and to develop and document ways to deal with critical constraints in a way that can be quickly scaled up.

Notes

1. PEFA is a broad partnership, started in 2001, aiming to support integrated and harmonized approaches to assessment and reform in the field of public expenditure, procurement and financial accountability. It aims to strengthen recipient and donor ability to (i) assess the condition of country public expenditure, procurement and financial accountability systems, and (ii) develop a practical sequence of reform and capacity-building actions, in a manner that: encourages country ownership; reduces the transaction costs to countries; enhances donor harmonization; allows monitoring of progress of country public finance management performance over time; better addresses developmental and fiduciary concerns; and leads to improved impact of reforms. See www.pefa.org for details.
2. In the countries covered thus far, country coordinators have been associated with think tanks, civil society, universities and independent firms.
3. There is no intention to aggregate across indicators to come up with an 'overall' score of land governance at the country level, as this would be difficult to justify methodologically and almost meaningless in practice. At the same time, the fact that assessments are carried out for the same indicators provides an opportunity to identify best practice in a structured manner and transfer it across countries.
4. The manual as well as information on country-level LGAFs is available at http://go.worldbank.org/AYREZ423W0.
5. There are eight panels: on (i) land tenure; (ii) institutional arrangements; (iii) urban land use, planning and development; (iv) rural land use and policy; (v) land valuation and taxation; (vi) public land management; (vii) public provision of land information; and (viii) dispute resolution, plus any panels on additional topics (e.g. large-scale land acquisition).
6. In light of the diverse nature of dimensions, simply aggregating indicators across qualitative and quantitative dimensions is difficult to defend, and a more limited set of quantitative indicators, clearly linked to the diagnostic assessment, seems preferable. Efforts to do so are under way, building on insights from completed LGAFs.

References

African Union (2009) 'Land Policy in Africa: A Framework to Strengthen Land Rights, Enhance Productivity and Secure Livelihoods', Addis Ababa: African Union and Economic Commission for Africa.

Food and Agricultural Organization of the UN (2012) 'Voluntary Guidelines on the Responsible Governance of Tenure of Land, Fisheries and Forests in the Context of National Food Security', Rome: FAO.

16
Conclusions

Stein T. Holden, Keijiro Otsuka and Klaus Deininger

16.1 Scope of the study

Rural poverty remains widespread and persistent in South Asia and Sub-Saharan Africa (SSA) and this is the case in both land-abundant and land-scarce countries. The unequal distribution of land ownership and cultivation rights constitutes a fundamental characteristic of many poor countries, where the majority of the poor live in rural areas and depend on agriculture as a main source of income. While the land distributions in China, northern Vietnam, and Ethiopia are egalitarian due to past land reform, many farmers are poor as they have been allocated only tiny plots of land with weak individual land rights, which may have suppressed their incentives to invest in land and to transfer land to other more productive farmers. The rural poor have limited access not only to land but also to off-farm income sources, as they are generally uneducated and do not possess skills needed in non-farm jobs (Otsuka et al., 2009).

The historical context matters for current land tenure systems, which have been shaped by colonial policies and land tenure reforms in the past. Our study examined land tenure reforms and their impacts in countries in SSA and Asia with highly diverse historical contexts within a unified analytical framework. We grouped the study countries into the four categories:

(a) countries in Asia (India and Nepal) that have very skewed land distributions with widespread landlessness and severe poverty, and where Land to the Tiller policies have been implemented that aimed to strengthen tenants' land rights;
(b) countries in SSA with a colonial history (Malawi and South Africa) that resulted in skewed land distribution and near landlessness, and

where Market-assisted Land Redistributions have been implemented to redistribute land to the poor;

(c) former socialist countries (China, Ethiopia, and Vietnam) that went through broad-scale radical land reforms that resulted in land distributions that were egalitarian but with weak and insecure tenure rights, even though these countries have recently undertaken reforms that have strengthened individual tenure security and transfer rights to land; and

(d) a country (Uganda) with a colonial history, with a mixture of freehold, leasehold and customary tenure rights, that is attempting to establish unified and strengthened individual land rights.

Furthermore, we have assessed a number of forest land tenure reforms. These reforms include

(a) devolution of forest tenure management from state to communities (India, Kenya, and Nepal), and

(b) individualization of forest land tenure (China) and farmland tenure (Ethiopia) aiming to strengthen individual incentives to plant and manage trees and forest land.

First of all, we hypothesized that tenure insecurity, which is caused by private as well as state actions, negatively affects the various types of rights, and this in turn affects investment, production efficiency and welfare in a society. Second, we hypothesized that tenure reforms that have (whether intentionally or unintentionally) reduced the tenure security of landowners have resulted in inefficient land use and have not contributed to poverty reduction. Indeed, the inverse correlation is often observed between farm size and crop yield per unit of land, because large landowners, who would otherwise rent out at least a part of their land, cultivate large tracts of land extensively, whereas land-poor farmers cultivate small patches of land intensively with the use of family labor. Third, we hypothesized that tenure reforms that have enhanced tenure security of land owners have enhanced production efficiency, investment incentives and sustainability, as well as land transfers and land access for the poor.

Since the majority of the rural poor are landless agricultural workers, tenants or marginal and small farmers[1] who do not have favorable access to land, an obvious way to eradicate or reduce rural poverty is to redistribute land from large landowners to the landless or near-landless households in countries with unegalitarian land distribution. An alternative is to regulate land rent at a low level in favor of poor tenants. In fact, such policies, known as the Land to the Tiller programs and land tenancy reforms have already been implemented in Asia (Otsuka, 2010). In some countries in SSA, such as South Africa and Malawi, large estates were dissolved and the land was redistributed to smaller farmers with limited rights to transfer land. The question is whether such policies are in fact effective in achieving the intended goal of eradicating rural poverty. Another question is whether such policies are conducive to the efficient use of usable land, which has been becoming scarcer over time due to rapid population growth on limited land resources.

Under the Land to the Tiller program, land rented out to a tenant may be confiscated and transferred to the tenant; under such conditions, the landowner does not possess secure ownership rights on agricultural land. Or if the land is owned collectively under a system with limited individual rights, the current cultivator, who possesses the land use right and temporarily leases out a part of the cultivated land, may lose the use rights on the leased parcel; in other words, that cultivator's land use rights are insecure. The critical question is if such a landowner or cultivator is willing to rent out their land to land-poor households.

If tenants' rights are strongly protected under the tenancy reform laws, landowners may not be able to terminate the tenancy contract regardless of the performance of a tenant. Under such a condition, will the tenant have any incentives to work hard and to observe the contractual agreements with the landowner on the maintenance and improvement of the landed properties? If the tenant shirks and misbehaves, the landowner is unlikely to rent out the land. If a large landowner does not want to rent out the land to land-poor tenants, who, then, will cultivate that land? Possibly the landowner will undertake large-scale own cultivation, employing a large number of agricultural workers, or he or she will go for more extensive or mechanized farming. But whether such arrangements are efficient and equitable is a major question.

Similar issues arise for the management of forests. If the community does not own the forestland, or if its forestland ownership rights are insecure, there is no guarantee that trees planted, when matured, will be harvested by the community or those community members who have planted and looked after them. Then, does the community have incentives to protect and take care of forests? In practice, forest is often owned by the government but seldom protected or managed by it, resulting in *de facto* open access deforestation. As a result, forest tenure reforms have been introduced to transfer the use rights of forestland to the community in many countries. Community management may be more conducive to efficient or effective management of forests than government management, partly because the incentives to manage forests are stronger and partly because the transaction costs of organizing collective action are lower (Otsuka and Place, 2001). An alternative to community forest management is private ownership and management, which is being introduced in China. Under what conditions private management is more desirable than community management from the social point of view is a critical question.

The series of questions raised above illustrate not only the complexity of land tenure issues, or issues of land property rights, but also the central importance of this issue in identifying policies to promote the efficient, equitable and sustainable management of land. Policymakers in Asia have rarely asked questions about whether the land tenure reforms implemented in the past have achieved their intended goals. In addition, policymakers in SSA generally do not know what the consequences of land tenure reforms in Asia have been. We believe that this is highly undesirable, because SSA now faces land issues similar to those faced by Asia a few decades earlier, as continued population explosion has led to increasing scarcity of land in SSA (Holden et al., 2008).[2] There is a huge scope for Africans to learn from the Asian experience, and vice versa. It is our hope that SSA will learn from Asian experience, so not repeat the mistakes committed by many Asian countries, while Asia should reconsider its past land tenure reforms.

It must be clearly understood that transfer of land ownership rights and regulation of land rent are not easy tasks, because the landowners who risk making a loss as a result of the reform make every effort to evade the implementation of the land tenure reforms or to change them in a direction to maximize their own benefits ('élite capture'). Classic examples from Land to the Tiller reforms are to distribute the land ownership to a large number of relatives by changing the names of registered owners so that each landowner appears to own a tiny amount of land, to evict tenants with a claim to self-cultivate, or to rotate tenants from season to season in order to confuse the issue of which tillers the land is supposed to be transferred to. If such perverse conduct by the landowners cannot be avoided, then the land tenure reforms can result in even greater inequity and inefficiency than before. The issues are far from trivial in view of the widespread rural poverty and stagnant agricultural productivity in poor agrarian economies in South Asia and SSA, and this study has attempted to fill our knowledge gaps in these areas.

16.2 Major findings

Part I of the book dealt with tenure reform approaches that have been applied in countries with unegalitarian land distribution associated with landlessness and severe poverty because of limited alternative livelihood opportunities. Part II dealt with countries that through radical land reforms have managed to achieve much more egalitarian land distribution, but at the cost of weak tenure rights and high levels of tenure insecurity; attempts to remedy these problems have been made by introducing new tenure reforms that strengthen tenure security and individual land rights. Part III assessed alternative property rights regimes for forestland where state appropriation of such land and exclusion of the local people often has resulted in *de facto* open access deforestation and forest degradation. Also dealt with was the impact of strengthening the land rights of farmland on incentives to plant and grow trees on the edges of farm fields or in small farm woodlots. Decentralization of such land rights to communities and individual households are among the more recent approaches, and we attempted to assess the results in a variety of contexts. Part IV was initially concerned with the recent sharp rise in commercial demand by foreign companies for land in land-abundant countries, and the establishment of large farms even in land-scarce countries in SSA. In particular, we wanted to explore whether large farms are viable, whether they threaten the tenure security of smallholder farmers, and whether they provide any lessons for the future of land tenure reforms in Asia and SSA. Secondly, based on the findings in this book, this concluding chapter also attempts to outline equitable and efficient land tenure reform policies, which are also conducive to the sustainable management of land and natural resources.

16.2.1 Major findings from Part I

The basic hypothesis we examined in Part I was that land redistribution reforms such as the Land to the Tiller program have actually resulted in insecure ownership rights to land, leading in turn to inefficient allocation of land by restricting tenancy transactions. More specifically, we examined the following hypothesis:

> **Hypothesis 1:** With unequal land distribution and insecure ownership rights, the inverse correlation between farm size and productivity arises and becomes stronger to the extent that land tenancy transactions are restricted.

In Chapter 2 on Nepal, where the Land to the Tiller program has been implemented, it is observed that many landowners refrain from leasing out their land because of the fear of losing part of it, if it is rented out to tenants for more than a few years. In fact, Hypothesis 1 is clearly supported by the statistical analysis which implies that the Land to the Tiller program leads not only to inefficiency of land use but also to inequity, as the most land-poor farmers cannot easily lease in additional land. As a result, the inverse relationship between farm size and crop yields is observed because the land-poor low-caste households, because of their limited access to land and off-farm employment, have to concentrate their labor on tiny farms. In Chapter 4, the case of land ownership reforms in South Africa is analyzed, in which large estates managed by white farmers were dissolved and the land redistributed to black farmers who used to be agricultural workers or engaged in non-farm jobs and so are inexperienced in farm management. Due to the preconception that large mechanized farms are efficient, the government encourages the operation of large farms, even though many black farmers prefer smaller-scale farming. As a result, a whole range of new farms, from small to large, have been established. Although the data availability is limited, the analysis in this chapter indicated that the inverse correlation between farm size and land productivity has emerged in South Africa, rendering support for Hypothesis 1. In Malawi (Chapter 5), some large estates were dissolved and farms of two hectares have been sold to a large number of land-poor farmers coming from other, more land-scarce, areas. Although tenancy and land sales were prohibited in the settlement areas, farm size has been fixed at two hectares per farm household, so that we hardly expected to observe a sharp inverse correlation between farm size and productivity.[3] In Uganda (Chapter 8), we observed an inverse relationship in all the tenure systems, even after more market-friendly reforms had been introduced – but the relationship was less negative in the freehold tenure system than in the customary and mailo tenure systems, where land markets are still less developed.

If tenancy rights are strengthened at the price of landowner rights, not only are land rental and sales markets suppressed but also the tenants' incentives to work hard and invest in land are lost, particularly under the share tenancy arrangement. Thus, we examined the following hypothesis as well:

> **Hypothesis 2:** If land ownership rights are weak, land market transactions, whether renting or purchase, will be suppressed. Likewise, if tenancy rights are strengthened in a *de jure* sense, landowners will

attempt to undermine these, and tenants are more likely to be evicted, and less likely to have their contracts renewed, and they will become less willing to work hard and invest in land improvements.

Land to the Tiller policies as an approach to land redistribution from the land-rich to the land-poor is the case in point where landowners' *de jure* property rights were weakened while tenants' *de jure* property rights were strengthened. A consequence of this policy was that landowners no longer wanted to offer sharecropping contracts where renewal of the contract used to be conditional on the performance of the tenant. In other words, landowners could no longer use the threat of eviction as a mechanism to enhance their tenants' work efforts, because the automatic renewal of contracts implied that the tenant could claim strong land use rights. Likewise, it became too risky for landowners to retain their best and most productive tenants. So the policy turned out to be counterproductive, and made tenants *de facto* less tenure secure. Allocative inefficiency and inefficient sharecropping contracts, characterized as Marshallian inefficiency, are therefore likely to arise under circumstances with ownership insecurity, limited monitoring and enforcement capacity of landowners, and this strengthened tenants' land use rights.

In Asia, share tenancy, in which output is shared between landowner and tenant at the ratio of 50:50 or sometimes 33:67 (the latter for the tenant), is common. Since marginal revenue for the tenant arising from additional effort or additional investment is a portion of marginal product of labor or marginal return to investment, a tenant's work and investment incentives tend be thwarted. In order to reduce or mitigate the moral hazard, a landowner usually chooses trustworthy share tenants, and terminates the contract if the tenant's conducts are unsatisfactory (for example, Otsuka, 2010; Holden et al., 2008). In West Bengal (Chapter 3), tenancy rights are strongly protected, and the output share for the tenant has increased due to the tenancy law reform.[4] It is found that owner-cum-share tenants invest more and work harder on their own plots than on tenanted plots, which supports the second part of Hypothesis 2.

Whether share tenants always shirk significantly or shirk particularly when a landowner's rights are weakened is debated. Actually, the undersupply of work effort is found in Nepal (Chapter 2), where high-caste landowners sharecrop out their land to other high-caste tenants because they are afraid of losing leased-out land to the low-caste tenants that are more likely to claim the land rights. In Ethiopia, where rights of share tenants are not particularly protected, significant Marshallian inefficiency is found for landowners with weak land rights, such as female landowners that have not received land certificates and/or who have sharecropped out their land to less efficient in-law tenants (Ghebru and Holden, 2012).[5] Although sweeping conclusions on the efficiency of share tenancy cannot be made easily, it seems fair to conclude that it is not as inefficient as generally thought, because of the selection of dependable or trustworthy tenants by landlords as well as the potential threat of termination of contract for those tenants who shirk in the absence of protection of tenancy rights (Otsuka et al., 1992; Holden et al., 2008).

16.2.2 Major findings from Part II

Part II is concerned with the impacts of reforms to strengthen tenure security of owners and/or enhance their transfer rights in form of rentals and possibly sales. If land ownership rights are strengthened, landowners are willing to rent out or sell land to land-poor households in countries with unegalitarian land distribution, though it is likely that those who purchase the land may be wealthy in non-land resources. In Part II we examined the following hypothesis:

> **Hypothesis 3:** With enhanced ownership rights to land, land markets become more active and land is allocated to more efficient producers.

Although land ownership rights fundamentally rest with the government or 'the people', individual land rights have been strengthened in Ethiopia (Chapter 6) and in Vietnam (Chapter 7). It has been shown that land certification in Ethiopia has stimulated investment in soil conservation and tree planting (see also Chapter 13), land productivity (Holden et al., 2009; Deininger et al., 2008, 2011), and land rental activity (Holden et al., 2011; Deininger et al., 2011). While the selling and mortgaging of land remains illegal in Ethiopia, in Vietnam with a similar radical land reform history to that of Ethiopia, even the right to sell land has been approved, making the individual land rights closer to *de facto* perfect private property rights.[6] In Uganda, too (Chapter 8), land ownership rights, including the rights to sell and rent out, have been strengthened, particularly in areas under the freehold tenure system. In all these three countries in common, land market transactions have been activated. In Ethiopia, where there are cultural restrictions preventing women from using oxen to help cultivate the land, female landowners are more actively engaged in renting out land after their tenure security and rental rights have been strengthened through land certification; productivity on rented land has also been enhanced over time. In Uganda, where individual land rights are strongest under the freehold system, land sales markets are particularly active. These results clearly support Hypothesis 3.

Furthermore, in Vietnam and Uganda not only tenants but also purchasers of land are generally found to be land-poor households.[7] Thus, despite the common fear that only wealthy, and usually landed, farmers can afford to purchase land, it is actually the relatively land-poor households who have purchased land. Thus, land market transactions in general seem both efficient and equitable, at least in these two countries.

16.2.3 Major findings from Part III

Secure land rights are also important for forest management, as they determine who reaps the benefits of investing in the protection and management of trees and forests. Part III is concerned with the impacts of forest tenure reforms on both the efficiency of forest management and the equity of distribution of forest resources. In the countries which are covered by this study in Chapters 9 to 13, that is, Nepal, India, China, Kenya, and Ethiopia, forestland was owned or managed by the government; however, serious deforestation and degradation of forest conditions have taken place in these countries, which induced forest tenure reforms ranging from the devolution of management rights of forests to the community (in Nepal, India and China, and in Kenya to some extent) or to individual households (in China). Also promoted is the planting of trees on individual farmland in Ethiopia and Kenya, where land rights are secure or strengthened. We tested the following hypothesis in Part III:

> **Hypothesis 4:** Deforestation is followed by reforestation or planting of trees on individual farmland, if use rights of forestland are granted to the community or individuals, or if individual rights on individual farmland are strengthened.

In general, Hypothesis 4 is supported. In the Inner Tarai region of Nepal (Chapter 9), when forest was owned and 'managed' by the government higher population density resulted in more severe deforestation and forest degradation because of the higher demand for forest products and land for farming. After forest use rights were handed over to the community, however, higher population density led to more intensive management of community forests, which is expected to lead to reforestation. In China where degraded but higher potential forestland was allocated to individual farmers (Chapter 10), forest tenure security was strengthened, particularly in areas where forestland certificates were distributed, and improved tenure security stimulated investments in forestland. In Kenya, where community forests are vigilantly protected (Chapter 12), farmers began growing trees on farms. In this country, whether and to what extent community forests are rehabilitated and forest resources can be exploited sustainably remains to be seen. In Ethiopia (Chapter 13), where community forests were degraded severely under the collective management regime, farmers became active in planting trees on private farms, particularly on those with land rights certificates.

Individualization of forestland tenure, which occurred in China, was unique, as the more usual forest tenure reform is to transfer forestland use rights to the community, as has occurred in Nepal, India, and Kenya. According to the China study, however, valuable forest plots, characterized by closer location to roads, with flatter slopes, and the availability of irrigation, are more likely to be converted to individually managed plots. This is consistent with the finding of Kijima et al. (2000) where the individualization of forestland tenure took place in post-war Japan, as community-managed copse forests were converted to valuable timber forests, which require stronger work incentives to manage trees. Further enquiry is needed to identify conditions under which community management functions better than individual management and vice versa.

In addition, taking advantage of the availability of household data, the India study in Chapter 10 enquires whether and to what extent community management is detrimental to the welfare of the poor households. It is found that while community management reduces over-exploitation of firewood by restricting labor time for firewood collection, the reduction in firewood collection is significantly higher for poorer households. Therefore, it seems that there is a tradeoff between efficiency and equity of forest management.

16.2.4 Major findings from Part IV

Since the food crisis in 2008, there has been a sharp increase in the demand for farmland by foreign firms in SSA. These foreign firms attempt to manage large mechanized farms, even in land-scarce countries (Chapter 14). Large mechanized farms may be efficient in land-abundant and labor-scarce high-income economies, partly because land and machineries are cheap relative to labor, and partly because machinery can be substituted for labor (Otsuka, 2013). Since farm operations are highly mechanized, monitoring of hired labor is not a major constraint on the operation of such large farms. There is, however, no evidence that such large foreign farms are efficient in SSA, where labor is cheap but machinery is relatively expensive (Chapter 14). According to Pingali et al. (1987), a mechanized farming system is unlikely to be profitable even in land-abundant countries in SSA, because the mechanized system is more labor-intensive than the extensive farming systems currently adopted. In all likelihood, therefore, large mechanized farms are not efficiently managed in SSA. Then, the next question is why mechanized large farms managed by foreign firms have been recently established in SSA, including areas where land is relatively scarce and labor is cheap.

In many countries in SSA, most of the land is not formally registered and allocated to individual cultivators in accordance with informal customary tenure rules. Such land is often formalized as the property of the state. With increased demand from outside investors, the way in which such land is handed out has become one of the most egregious forms of bad governance, outright corruption (for example, bribery of government officials to obtain public land at a fraction of market value), squandering of public wealth, eviction of local populations living on the land, and often resulting in local resentment and long-term conflict (Chapter 15). Avoiding such outcomes will require developing clear, transparent, and socially acceptable processes based on recognition of existing occupancy rights and negotiation with current land users; publicizing contract terms (including payments to be received at different levels); and conducting regular and independent audits.

Recent international initiatives to improve land governance in Africa include the establishment of Voluntary Guidelines on Tenure Governance, initiated by FAO (2012); the Land Governance Assessment Framework discussed in Chapter 15, the Land Policy Initiative of the UN Economic Commission for Africa that includes the development of a Strategic Plan and Roadmap for the period 2012–2016 (UNECA, 2012), and the Declaration on Land Issues and Challenges in Africa by the African Union (African Union, 2009).

Effective management of public land is impossible, because more often than not there is no inventory of such land. Lack of a public land inventory creates opportunities for well-connected individuals to capture state assets through squatting, often with negative environmental impacts. Wide implementation of land expropriation raises the risk of public officials using their powers in ways that promote private rather than public interests and that can encourage rent seeking and political meddling. Expropriation procedures should thus be clear and transparent, with fair compensation in kind or cash at market values made available expeditiously. The key principle is that land transfers to private parties should be based on users' voluntary and informed agreement and should provide them with a fair proportion of the proceeds. Independent valuation of land assets should thus, where possible, be the norm when market systems for valuation have been established. The basic problem is, however, that such systems do not exist in most of the land-abundant areas where land has now been handed over to investors. Those whose land rights are affected will need access to mechanisms for appeal that can provide authoritative rulings quickly and in an independent and objective way. Maintaining a minimum given standard of living for those who are negatively affected should be a key compensation objective. Expansion of a low-cost broad-scale and participatory land registration and certification scheme, such as that implemented in the highlands of Ethiopia, is an approach that should be tested in areas under increasing pressure and where local land rights are still informal and highly insecure.

16.3 Towards equitable and efficient land tenure reforms

A fundamental characteristic of agricultural production in low-income countries is the absence of scale economies because of the difficulty in supervising workers in spatially dispersed agricultural fields. Yet mechanization to replace labor is unprofitable in most cases, due to the low cost of labor. Because of the high monitoring costs, agricultural labor markets do not work well except at very simple tasks, such as weeding and harvesting, which are amenable to easy supervision (Hayami and Otsuka, 1993).[8] Thus historically, large farms have not been formed by private initiatives. In fact, the *haciendas* and *latifundia* in Latin America, and the estates in eastern and southern Africa, which employ a large number of agricultural wage workers, were created by colonial governments. We may therefore question the land use efficiency implications of the rapid expansion of a number of large farms corresponding to the rapidly rising demand for land since the food crisis of 2008, even in land-abundant countries in SSA. In many other areas in developing countries, small-scale family farms are dominant.[9] The small farms have advantage over large farms because of the use of family labor, in contrast to large farms which have to rely on hired labor, or mechanization, or much more extensive land use. Thus, large farms often tend to lease out part of their land to tenants. Otherwise or even then, the inverse correlation between farm size and productivity tends to emerge because of the inefficiency of large farms (Chapters 2, 4, 8; Larson et al., 2012).[10]

We would like to argue that respecting the land tenure rights of small farms and the use rights of forestland is the most critical step towards the efficient, equitable and sustainable management of both farmland and forestland in land-scarce countries. In contrast, the past land tenure reforms, particularly the Land to the Tiller programs implemented in South Asia, as well as the state management of forests, led to inefficiency and inequity, importantly because of the lack of recognition that land rights and tenure security play a key role in the allocation and management of farmland and forestland. In conclusion, we would like to argue that a basis for efficient and equitable land tenure reforms rests in the establishment of secure land rights, be it individual or communal. The secure ownership rights of farmland will facilitate efficient and equitable transaction of land rights through land rental and land sales markets, and induce proper investments in land improvement. Similarly, the secure long-term use rights of forestland will promote efficient and sustainable management of forest resources by restricting their over-exploitation and facilitating silvicultural operations.

We do not imply, however, that grossly unequal land ownership distribution can be mitigated significantly by voluntary land market transactions. Credit market imperfections preclude efficient and equitable land transactions between land-rich and land-poor households. Thus, we do not deny the importance of redistributive land reform: we argue, however, that such reform must be implemented without creating major inefficiency and inequity. For this reason, we advocate the spirit of the Market-assisted Land Redistribution reform, because in contrast to the Land to the Tiller approach, this organizes the voluntary sales of underutilized land by large landowners to smallholders; therefore, it should be less susceptible to undermining by the large landowners. However, there are many challenges, especially political economy ones, faced by such redistribution programs. Example of issues we have to resolve include the identification of the appropriate farm size, organizational model, appropriate new sellers and owners, and appropriate institutional structures with complementary social services to establish sustainable livelihoods. The costs are likely to be very high, implying the possibility of facing severe funding constraints.

In order to support Market-assisted Land Redistribution, we would like to advocate; (1) progressive land tax, (2) establishment of a land bank, and (3) improvement of land administration systems. Due to low land tax, many households own land just for social status or emergency relief rather than for farming. Imposing a progressive land tax would induce land sales by large and inefficient landowners. Such an effect would be strengthened by the inverse correlation between farm size and productivity. Redistribution of land through land rental and sales markets rather than administration processes with inadequate compensation could be a more peaceful approach to achieve socially equitable and efficient land distribution (Hayami et al., 1990). There is evidence that land rental markets in particular can help resource poor households to access land, but also that in some African countries, land sales markets have in the past contributed to more equitable land distribution (Holden et al., 2008). It is, however, not possible to achieve truly equitable and efficient land allocation through land sales markets unless the government provides support for credit for those who wish to purchase land.

The introduction of land banks, which provide loans for land-poor households to buy land, could be an important supplementary institution; instead of paying 50 percent of the value of output as land rent to the landlord, the tenant can pay it to the bank as repayments on the loans. Judging from the African experience, small farmers are likely to be major beneficiaries of land banks if established, as those farmers purchased land even in the absence of land banks. To improve land administration so as to ensure landownership security, transparent and accountable local land authority needs to be set up to establish and/or keep an updated land registry that may gradually be upgraded to a comprehensive computer-based land registry system where there is a demand and it can be afforded. In all likelihood, there is no substitute for a comprehensive support for market-based land transactions in land-scarce economies in order to achieve efficient and sustainable use of land and poverty reduction.

Notes

1. Tenants may or may not be landless, and similarly marginal and small farmers may be owner-cultivators or owner-cum-tenants.
2. Indeed, the average farm size in tropical Asia is 1.2 ha, which is not too different from the average of 1.8 ha in SSA – excluding South Africa, that is, where the average farm size exceeds 200 ha.
3. Since the number of working-age family members is not so different between farm households, the inverse relation between farm area per working-age member and crop yield is not observed, either.

4. If the landowner does not share the cost of purchased inputs, the output share for the tenant is set at 75 percent.
5. In SSA, share tenancy is common primarily in Ethiopia and Madagascar. Why this should be the case is a major conundrum.
6. 'Land rights' refers to the bundle of rights among which the right to sell is the strongest.
7. In southern Vietnam, where scale economies are arising due to heavy mechanization, however, land-owning households are major purchasers of land.
8. Labor markets also cannot function well in rain-fed areas, where busy planting and harvesting times coincide among farm households.
9. Farm size is larger in high-income economies because of the mechanization which facilitates the substitution of capital for labor.
10. Interestingly the inverse correlation was widely observed in South Asia, where land tenancy contracts are restricted by land laws, but not in Southeast Asia, where tenancy contracts are generally more active.

References

African Union (2009) *Declaration on Land Issues and Challenges in Africa*. African Union Assembly Declaration I (XIII) Rev. I. http://new.uneca.org/Portals/lpi/Documents/AU-Declaration-on-Land-Issues_ENG.pdf.

Deininger, K., Ali, D., Holden, S.T. and Zevenbergen, J. (2008) 'Rural Land Certification in Ethiopia: Process, Initial Impact, and Implications for the Other African countries', *World Development*, 36(10), 1786–812.

Deininger, K., Ali, D. and Alemu, T. (2011) 'Impacts of Land Certification on Tenure Security, Investment, and Land Market Participation: Evidence from Ethiopia', *Land Economics*, 87(2), 312–34.

Food and Agriculture Organization (2012) *Voluntary Guidelines for Governance of Tenure,* http://www.fao.org/nr/tenure/governance-of-tenure/en/

Ghebru, H. and Holden, S.T. (2012) 'Reverse Share Tenancy and Marshallian Inefficiency: Bargaining Power of Landowners under the Sharecroppers' Productivity', Paper presented at the 28th International Conference of Agricultural Economists, The Global Bio-Economy at Iguassu Falls, 18–24 August, Cataratas, Brazil.

Hayami, Y. and Otsuka, K. (1993) *The Economics of Contract Choice: An Agrarian Perspective* (Oxford: Clarendon Press).

Hayami, Y., Quisumbing, M.A. and Adriano, L.S. (1990) *Toward an Alternative Land Reform Paradigm: A Philippine Perspective* (Manila, Philippines: Ateneo de Manila University Press).

Holden, S.T., Deininger, K. and Ghebru, H. (2009) 'Impacts of Low-cost Land Certification on Investment and Productivity', *American Journal of Agricultural Economics,* 91(2), 359–73.

Holden, S.T., Deininger, K., and Ghebru, H. (2011) 'Tenure Insecurity, Gender, Low-cost Land Certification and Land Rental Market Participation', *Journal of Development Studies*, 47(1), 31–47.

Holden, S.T., Otsuka, K., and Place, F. (eds) (2008) *The Emergence of Land Markets in Africa: Assessing the Impacts on Poverty, Equity, and Efficiency* (Baltimore, MD: Resources for the Future).

Kijima Y., Sakurai, T. and Otsuka, K. (2000) 'Iriaichi: Collective vs. Individualized Management of Forests in Post-War Japan', *Economic Development and Cultural Change,* 48(4), 867–86.

Larson, D.F., Otsuka, K., Matsumoto, T. and Kilic, T. (2012) 'Can Africa's Agriculture Depend on Smallholder Farms', Background paper for *World Development Report 2013: Jobs* (Washington, D.C.: World Bank).

Otsuka, K. (2010) 'Efficiency and Equity Effects of Land Markets', in R.E. Evenson and P. Pingali (eds) *Handbook of Agricultural Economics,* Volume IV (Amsterdam: Elsevier).

Otsuka, K. (2013) 'Food Insecurity, Income Inequality, and the Changing Comparative Advantage in World Agriculture', *Agricultural Economics,* forthcoming.

Otsuka, K., Chuma, H. and Hayami, Y. (1992) 'Land and Labor Contracts in Agrarian Economies: Theories and Facts', *Journal of Economic Literature,* 30(4), 1965–2018.

Otsuka, K., Estudillo, J.P. and Sawada, Y. (eds) (2009) *Rural Poverty and Income Dynamics in Asia and Africa* (London, UK: Routledge).

Otsuka, K. and Place, F. (eds) (2001) *Land Tenure and Natural Resource Management: A Comparative Study of Agrarian Communities in Asia and Africa* (Baltimore, MD: Johns Hopkins University Press).

Pingali, P., Bigot, Y. and Binswanger, H.P. (1987) *Agricultural Mechanization and the Evolution of Farming Systems in SSA* (Baltimore, MD: Johns Hopkins University Press).

United Nations Economic Commission for Africa (2012) *Land Policy Initiative.* http://new.uneca.org/lpi/home_lpi.aspx.

Index

Lightning Source UK Ltd.
Milton Keynes UK
UKHW020627110820
367974UK00014B/430

9 781349 465866